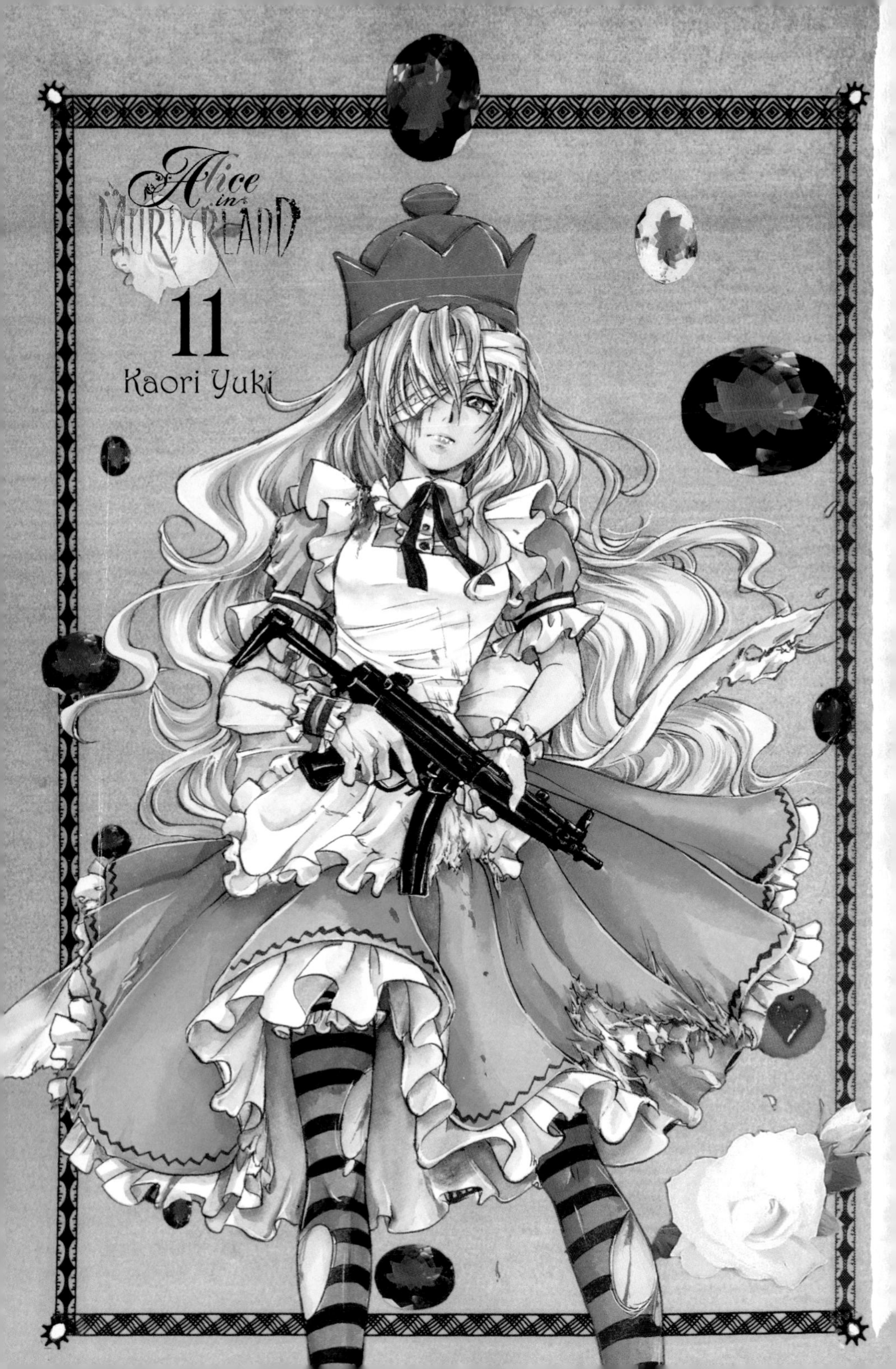
Alice in Murderland
11
Kaori Yuki

Contents

Alice in Murderland

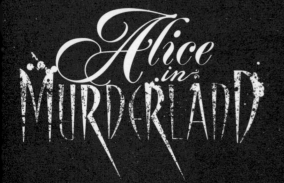

11

Kaori Yuki

Characters & Story

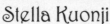

Stella Kuonji
Fourth daughter of the Kuonji family. Was taken in by the Kuonjis, along with eldest brother, Zeno. Loves Zeno.

Bloody Alice
Another personality residing within Stella that appears when she loses all reason.

Tsukito
Grandson of Kokonoe, the chief of the Black Rabbit bodyguards. The true Zeno was a personality inside of Tsukito.

Olga
Head of the Kuonji Group and matriarch of the family.

Kokonoe
Chief of the Black Rabbit bodyguards tasked with protecting the nine siblings.

The Kuonji Siblings

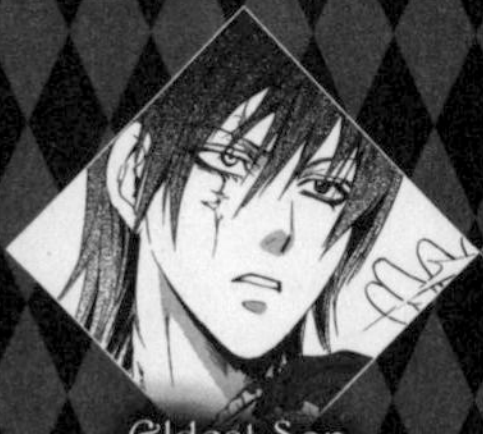

Eldest Son
Zeno
Previously thought to be Stella's beloved big brother, but actually an impostor who replaced him five years ago.

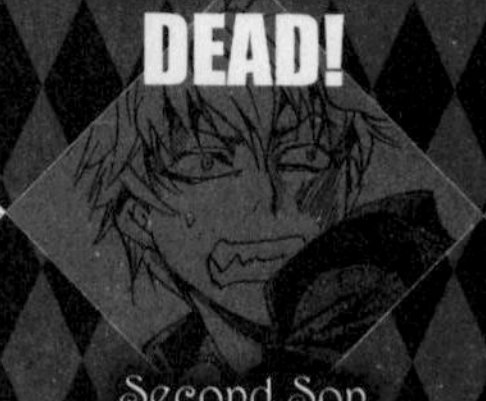
DEAD!

Second Son
Sid
The culprit behind a wave of local murders. Killed by Stella after her transformation into "Bloody Alice."

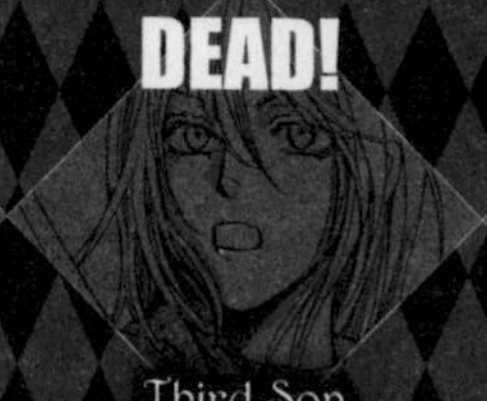
DEAD!

Third Son
Sol
Maré's older twin. Fought Stella to avenge his younger brother Maré and lost. In the end, he chose to die.

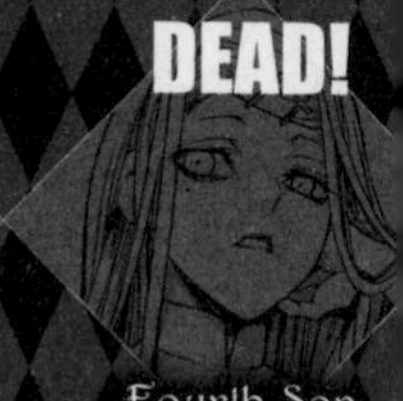
DEAD!

Fourth Son
Maré
Sol's younger twin. He and Stella had ar antagonistic relationsh and he died at the enc of their showdown.

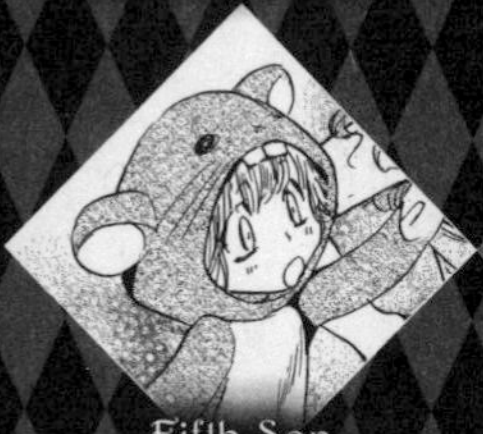

Fifth Son
Melm
The youngest of all the Kuonji siblings. Olga gave birth to him herself. Has the power to put souls into dolls.

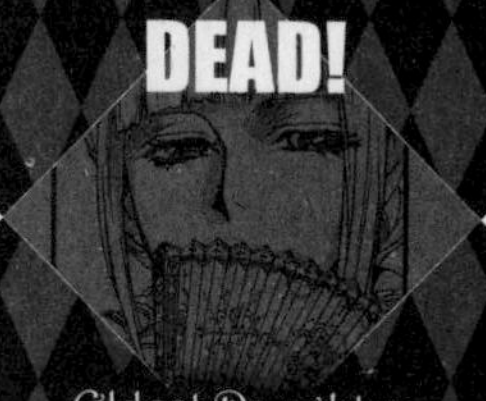
DEAD!

Eldest Daughter
Ibara
The best fighter among the siblings. She challenged Stella to a one-on-one fight, and Alice crushed her heart, killing her.

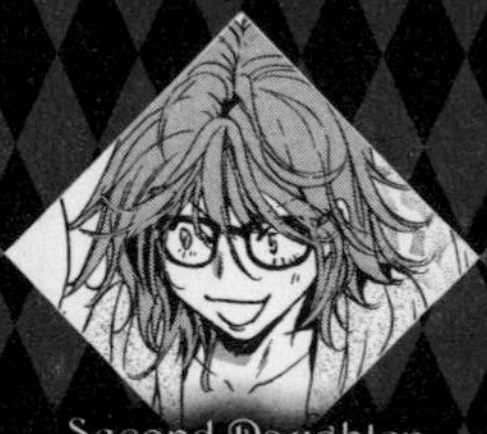

Second Daughter
Miser
Reptile *otaku*. Plotted to make her escape from the Kuonji house with her boyfriend, Io.

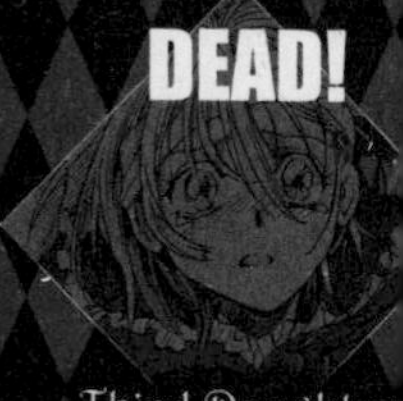
DEAD!

Third Daughter
Claire
Closest to Stella of a the siblings. Was finish off by eldest son, Zen after her showdowr with Stella.

Story

Stella, fourth daughter of the Kuonji family, world leaders of industry, finds that she must engage in a battle royale with her siblings for the sake of her eldest brother, Zeno. As a succession of challenges comes from her siblings and numerous clashes of life or death unfold, Stella fights alongside "Bloody Alice," her second battle-awakened personality. Now, with just Stella and the youngest, Melm, remaining, the final battle begins. Olga has broken a secret contract with the government that forbids her from bearing children of her own by nurturing a special larva within her womb and giving birth to a child—Melm. But as Stella fights for her life against her littlest brother, who should creep up behind her but dead big brother Sid...!? On whose head will the Kuonji crown ultimately sit?

Key Words

Secret of Elysium • A mysterious ability passed down through the Kuonji line that grants the wielder power over life and death, as well as immortality.

Bandersnatch • The true form of the members of the Kuonji family. Attempts to grow the number of people infected with its blood and steals the souls of others for family sustenance.

Murderland Rules • The nine brothers and sisters must kill one another until only one is left standing. The game must be completed within one year, by Zeno's twentieth birthday. The lone survivor will become head of the family, inheriting the Kuonji Group and all its assets.

Black Rabbits • Bodyguards who may be used by the siblings as pawns. There are special methods by which this manipulation can be accomplished.

Alice in MURDERLAND

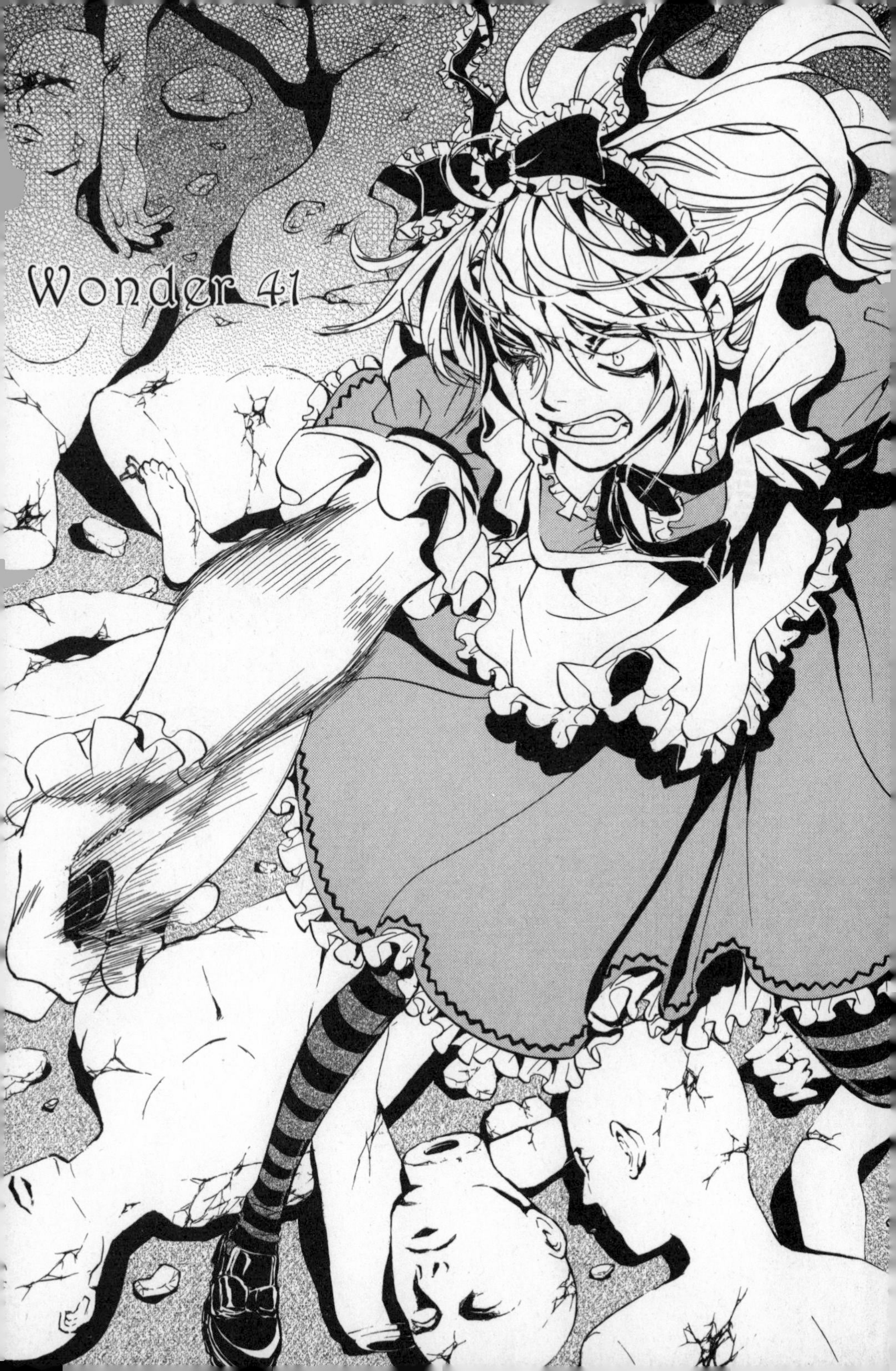
Wonder 41

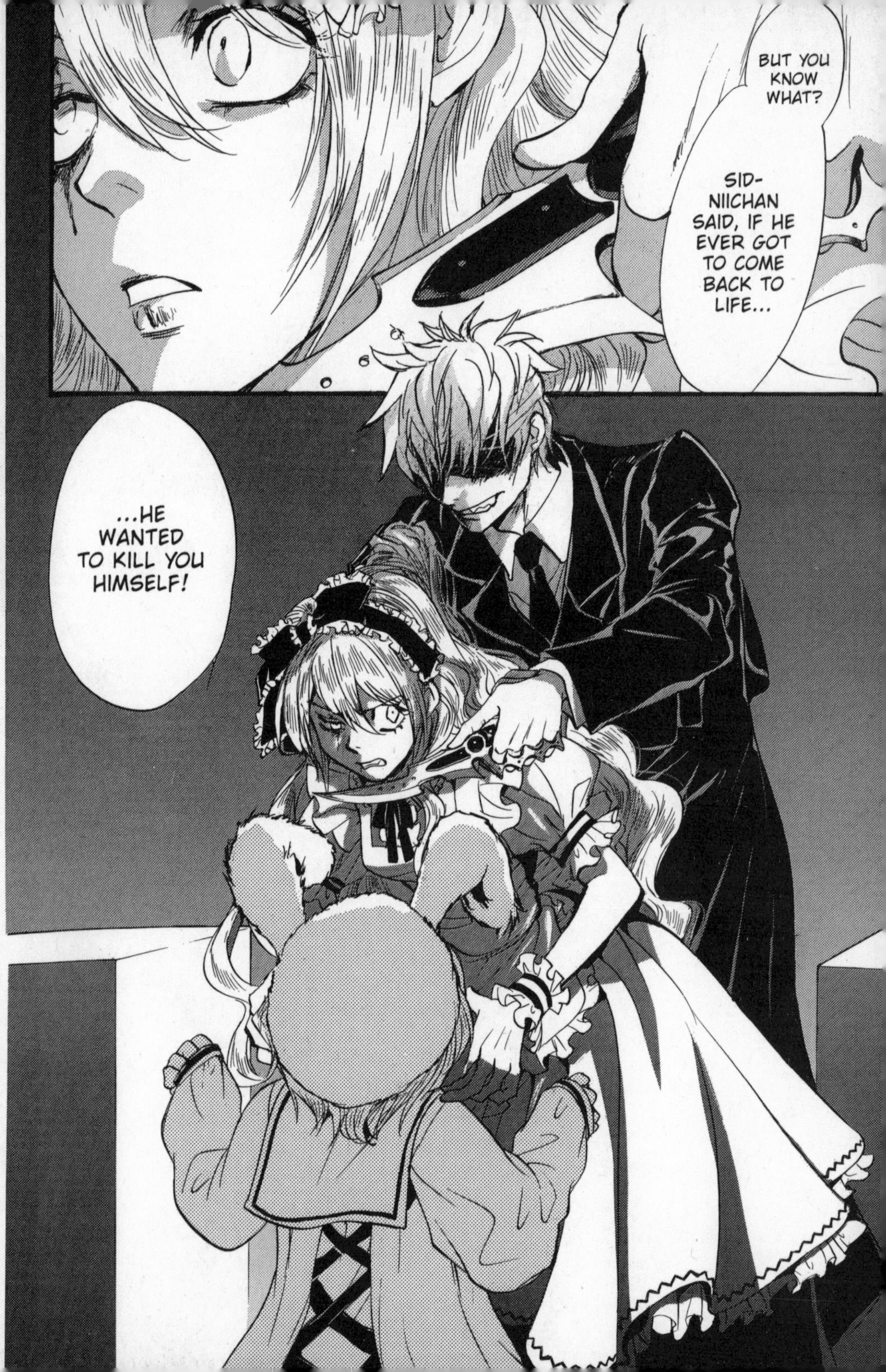
BUT YOU KNOW WHAT?
SID-NIICHAN SAID, IF HE EVER GOT TO COME BACK TO LIFE...
...HE WANTED TO KILL YOU HIMSELF!

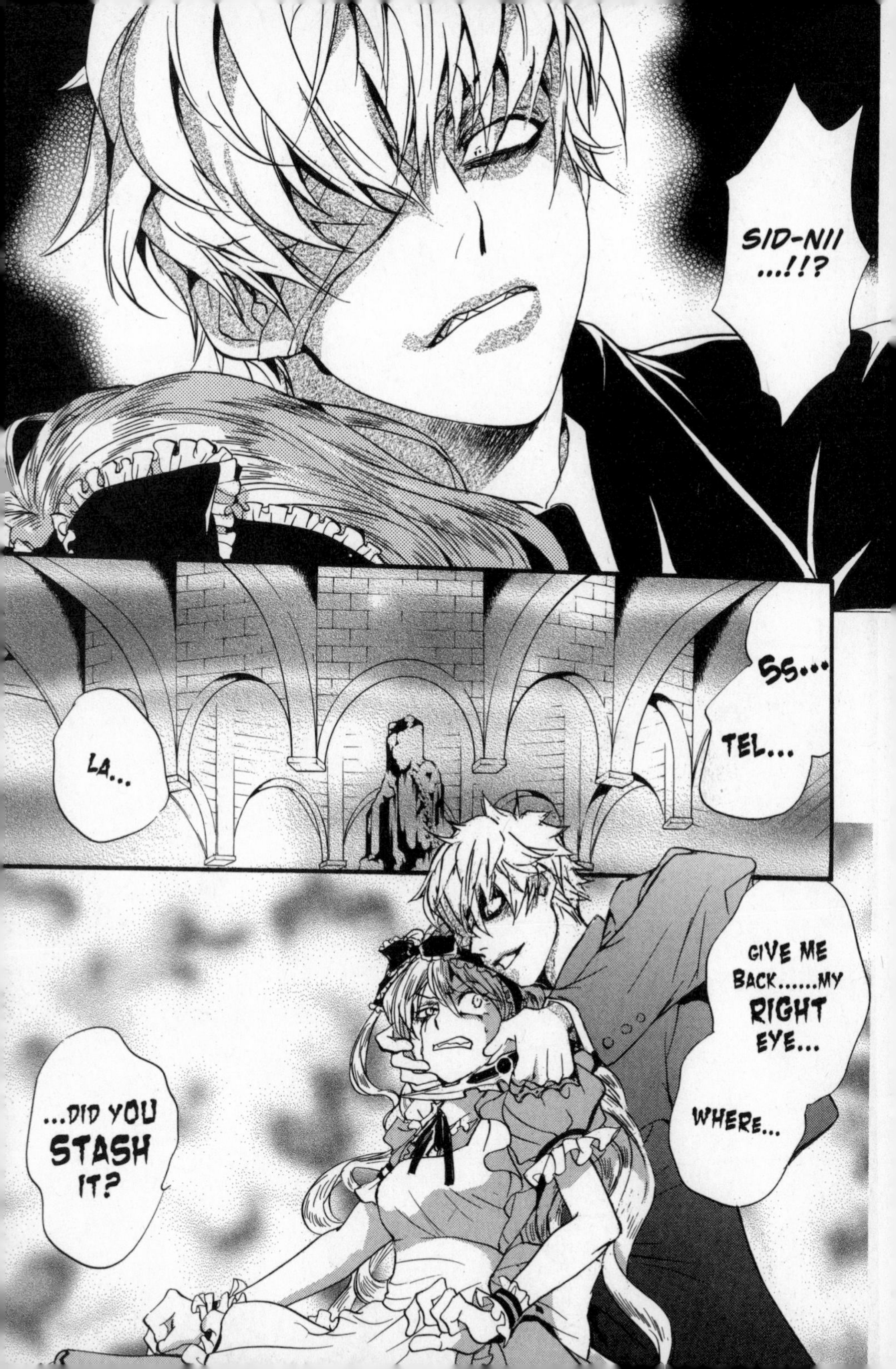
SID-NII ...!!?
SS...
TEL...
LA...
GIVE ME BACK......MY RIGHT EYE...
WHERE...
...DID YOU STASH IT?

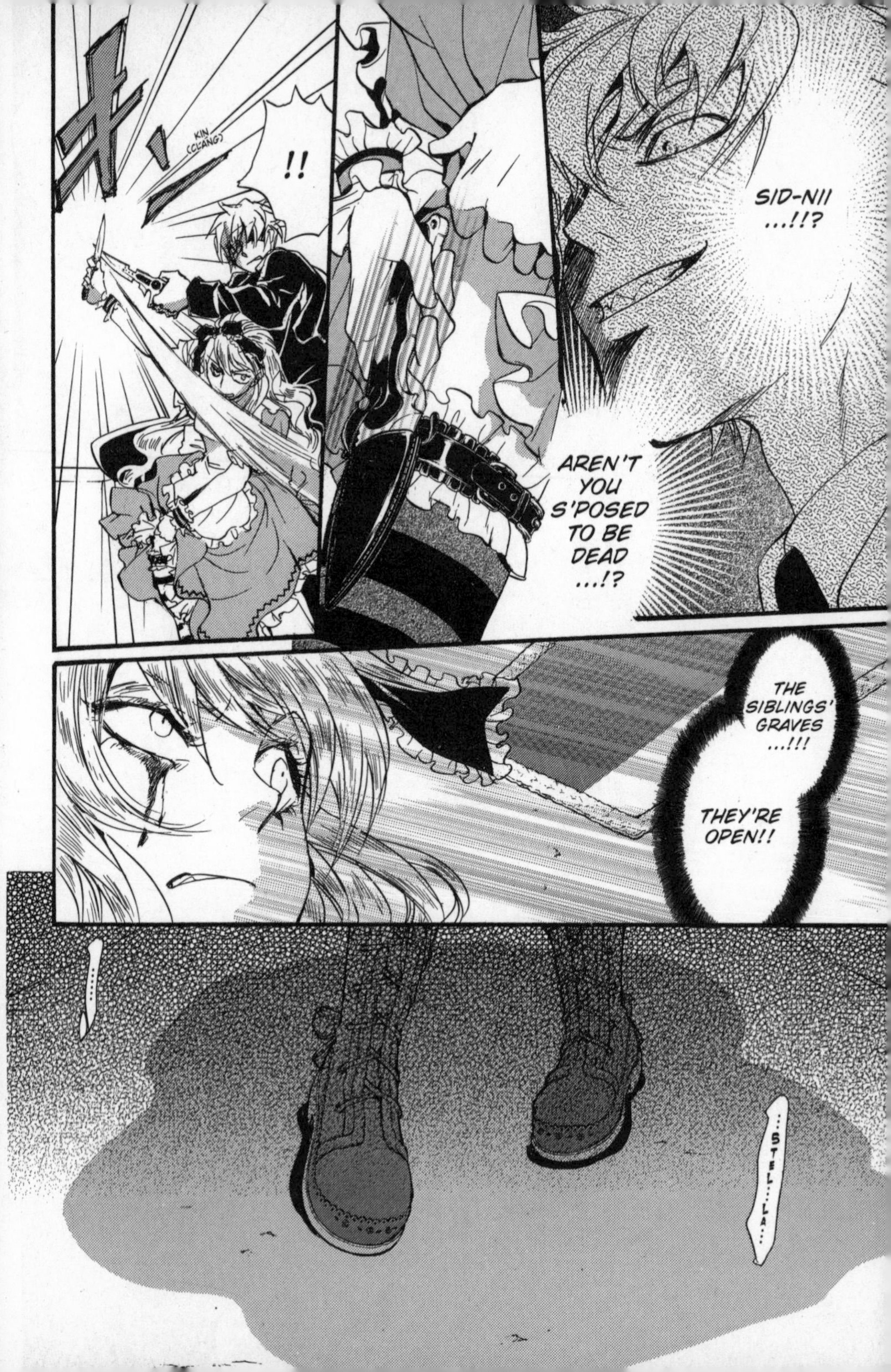
SID-NII ...!!?
AREN'T YOU S'POSED TO BE DEAD ...!?
KIN (CLANG)
!!
THE SIBLINGS' GRAVES ...!!!
THEY'RE OPEN!!
...STEL...LA...
......!

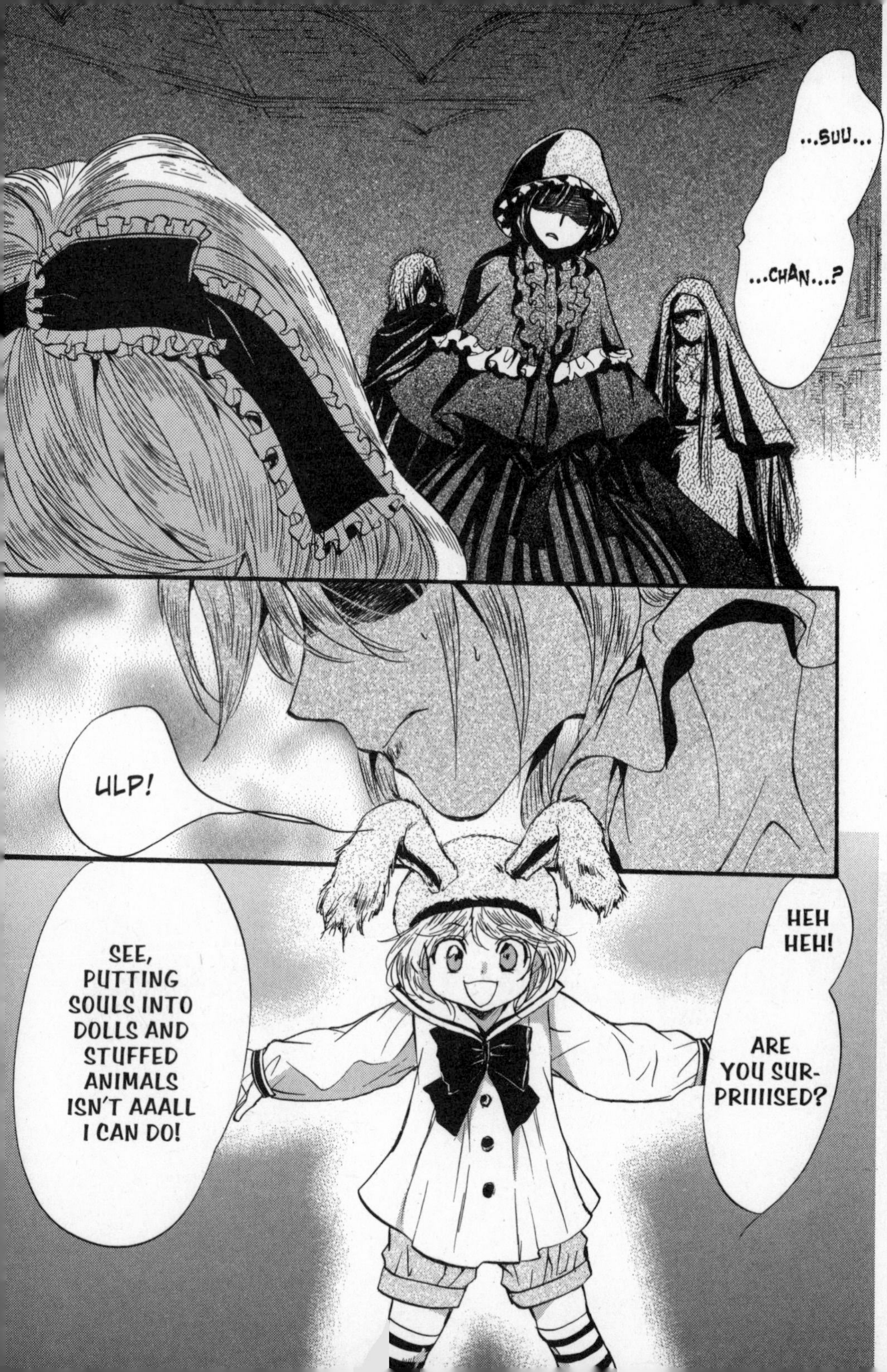
...SUU...
...CHAN...?
ULP!
HEH HEH!
ARE YOU SUR-PRIIIISED?
SEE, PUTTING SOULS INTO DOLLS AND STUFFED ANIMALS ISN'T AAALL I CAN DO!

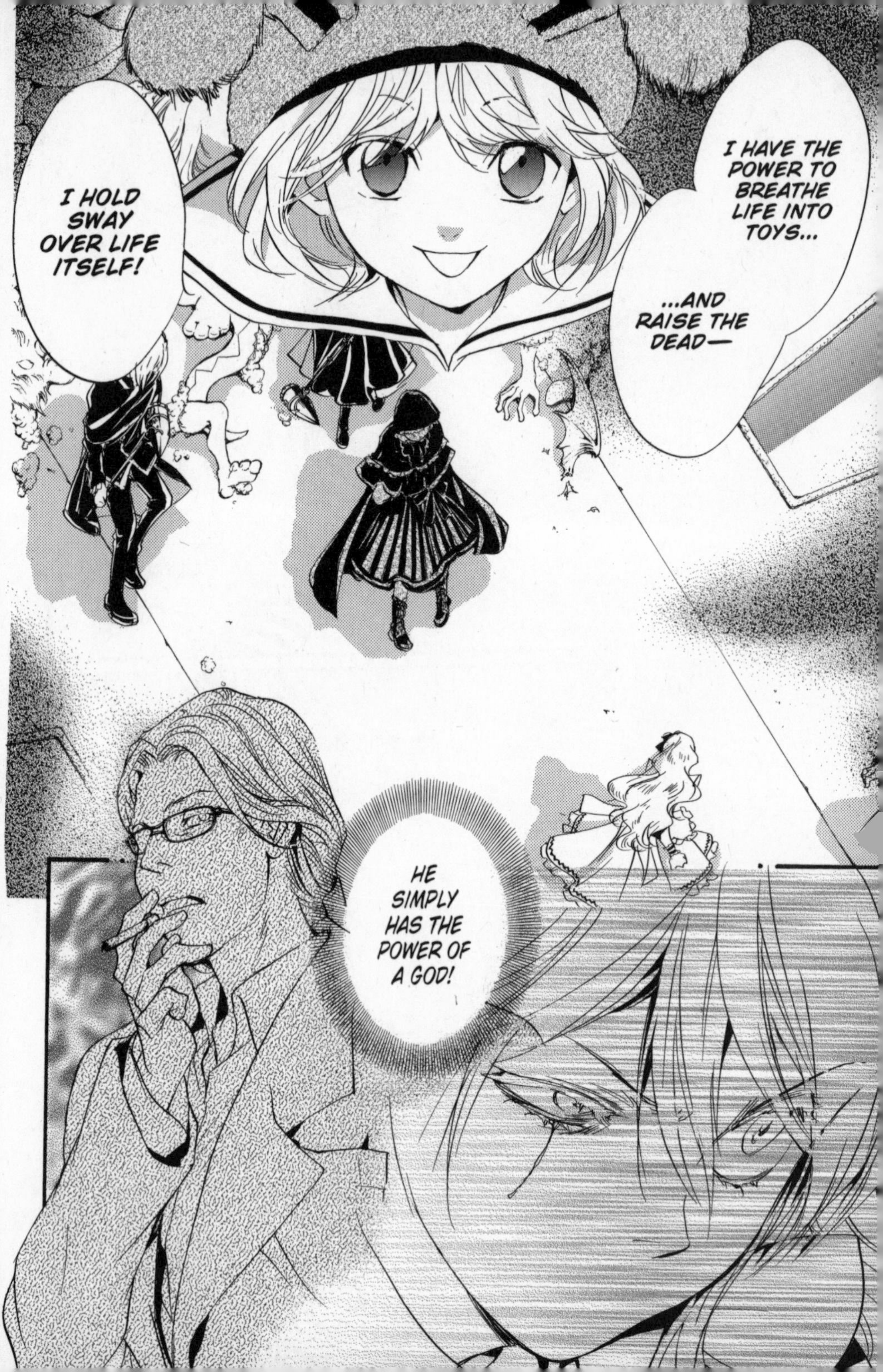
I HAVE THE POWER TO BREATHE LIFE INTO TOYS...
...AND RAISE THE DEAD—
I HOLD SWAY OVER LIFE ITSELF!
HE SIMPLY HAS THE POWER OF A GOD!

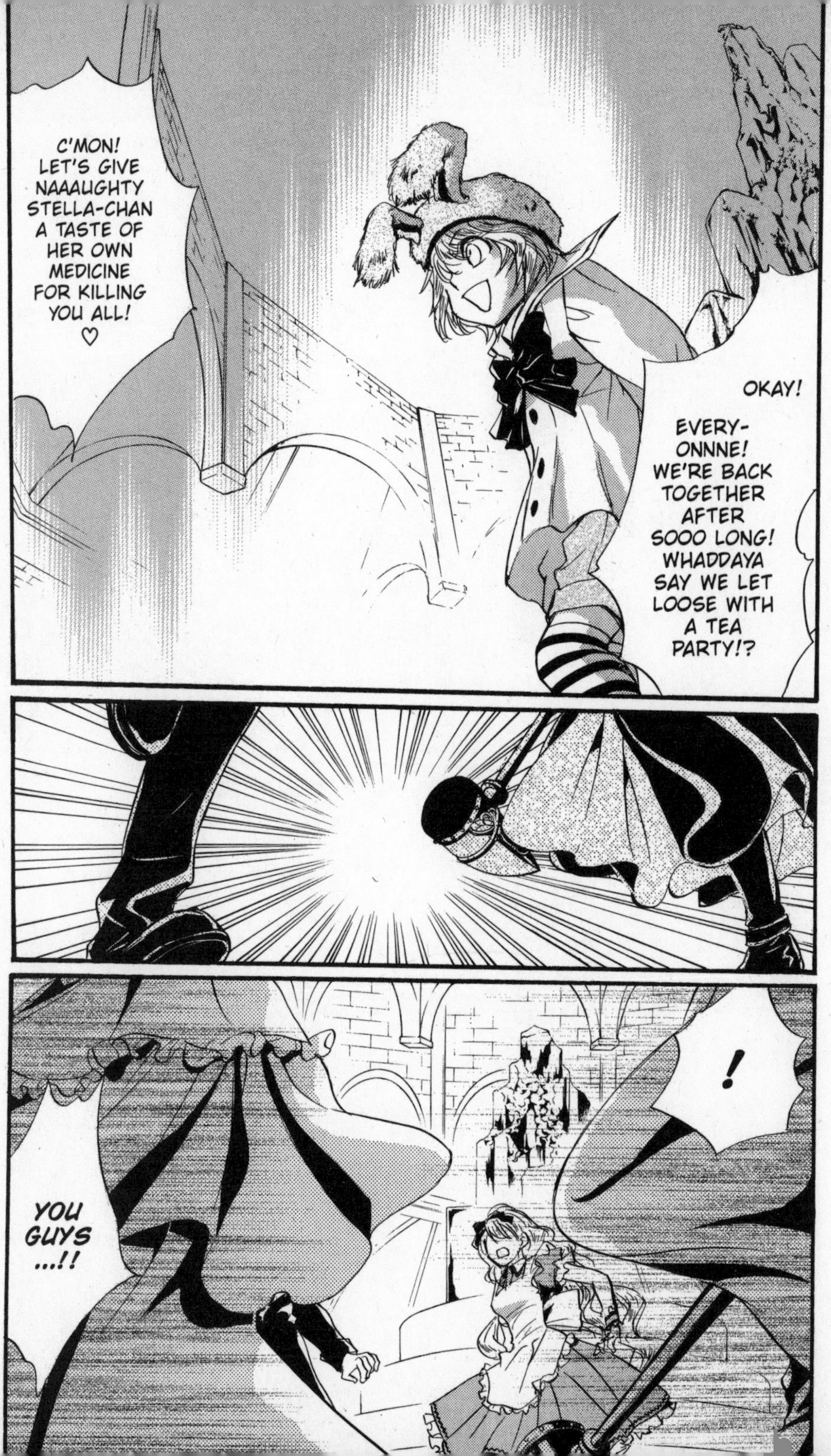
OKAY!
EVERY-ONNNE! WE'RE BACK TOGETHER AFTER SOOO LONG! WHADDAYA SAY WE LET LOOSE WITH A TEA PARTY!?
C'MON! LET'S GIVE NAAAUGHTY STELLA-CHAN A TASTE OF HER OWN MEDICINE FOR KILLING YOU ALL! ♡
!
YOU GUYS ...!!

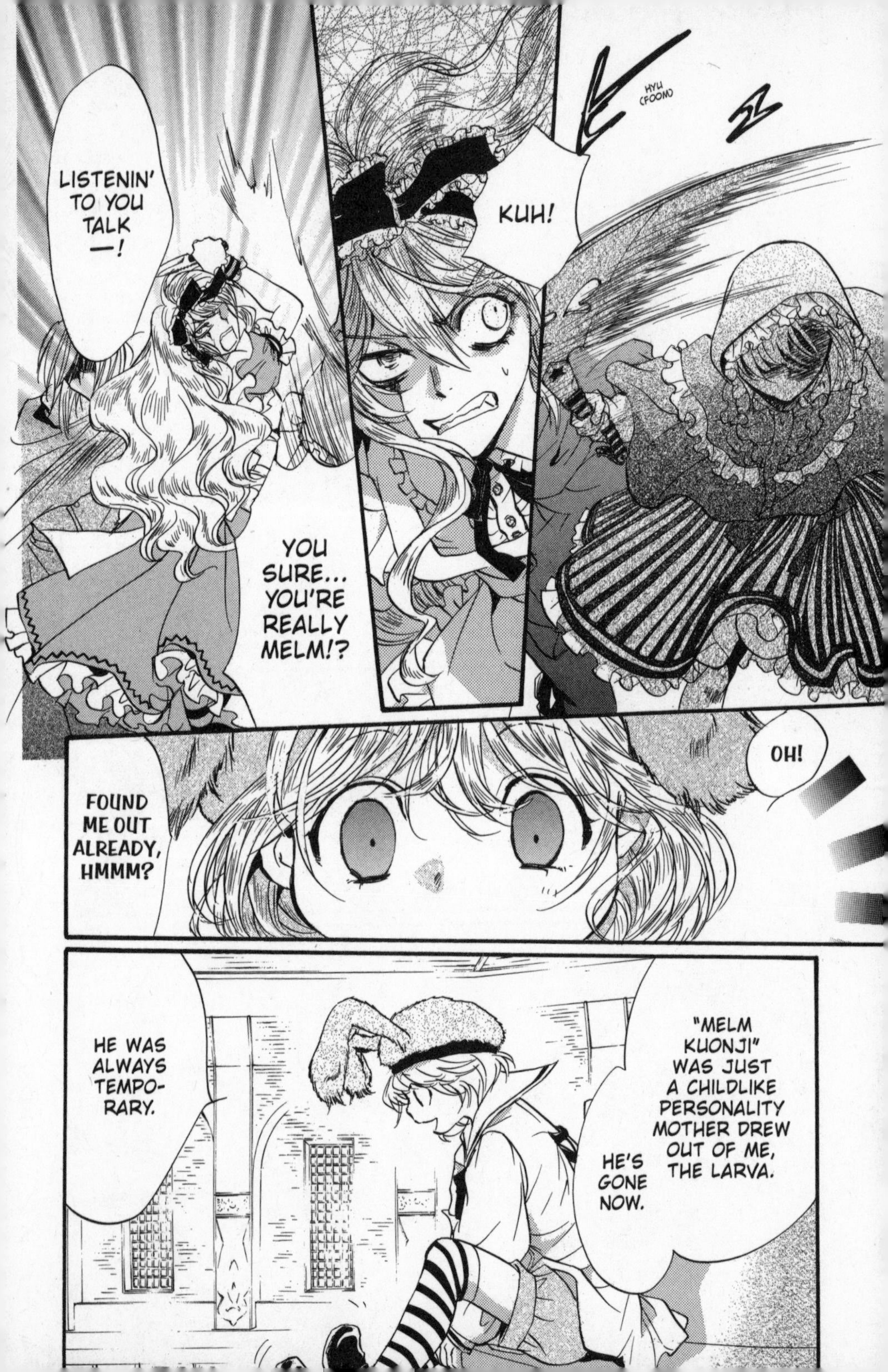

HYU (FOOM)
KUH!
YOU SURE... YOU'RE REALLY MELM!?
LISTENIN' TO YOU TALK—!
OH!
FOUND ME OUT ALREADY, HMMM?
"MELM KUONJI" WAS JUST A CHILDLIKE PERSONALITY MOTHER DREW OUT OF ME, THE LARVA.
HE'S GONE NOW.
HE WAS ALWAYS TEMPO-RARY.

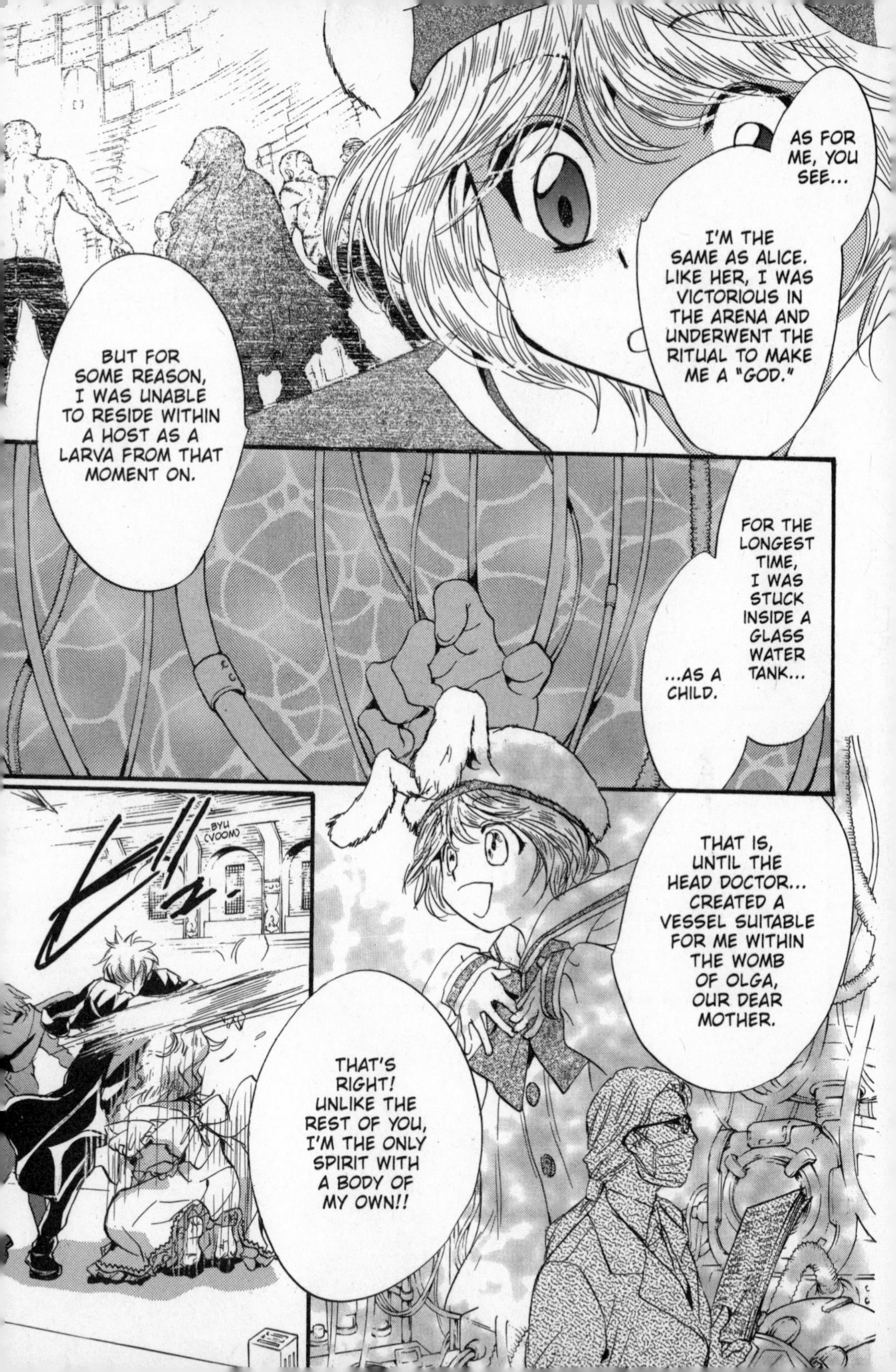
AS FOR ME, YOU SEE...
I'M THE SAME AS ALICE. LIKE HER, I WAS VICTORIOUS IN THE ARENA AND UNDERWENT THE RITUAL TO MAKE ME A "GOD."
BUT FOR SOME REASON, I WAS UNABLE TO RESIDE WITHIN A HOST AS A LARVA FROM THAT MOMENT ON.
FOR THE LONGEST TIME, I WAS STUCK INSIDE A GLASS WATER TANK...
...AS A CHILD.
THAT IS, UNTIL THE HEAD DOCTOR... CREATED A VESSEL SUITABLE FOR ME WITHIN THE WOMB OF OLGA, OUR DEAR MOTHER.
THAT'S RIGHT! UNLIKE THE REST OF YOU, I'M THE ONLY SPIRIT WITH A BODY OF MY OWN!!
BYU (VOOM)

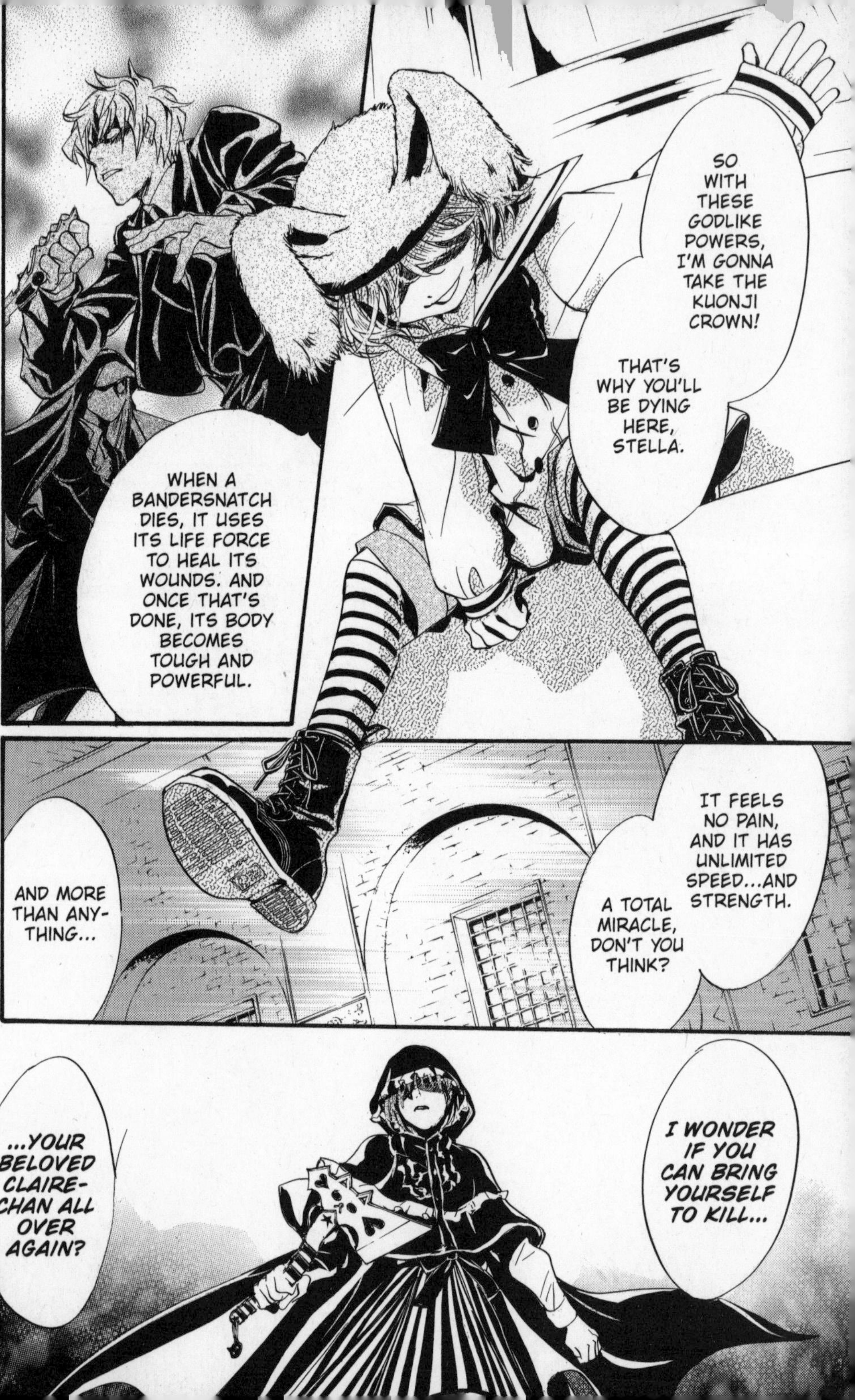
SO WITH THESE GODLIKE POWERS, I'M GONNA TAKE THE KUONJI CROWN!
THAT'S WHY YOU'LL BE DYING HERE, STELLA.
WHEN A BANDERSNATCH DIES, IT USES ITS LIFE FORCE TO HEAL ITS WOUNDS. AND ONCE THAT'S DONE, ITS BODY BECOMES TOUGH AND POWERFUL.
IT FEELS NO PAIN, AND IT HAS UNLIMITED SPEED...AND STRENGTH.
A TOTAL MIRACLE, DON'T YOU THINK?
AND MORE THAN ANY-THING...
I WONDER IF YOU CAN BRING YOURSELF TO KILL...
...YOUR BELOVED CLAIRE-CHAN ALL OVER AGAIN?

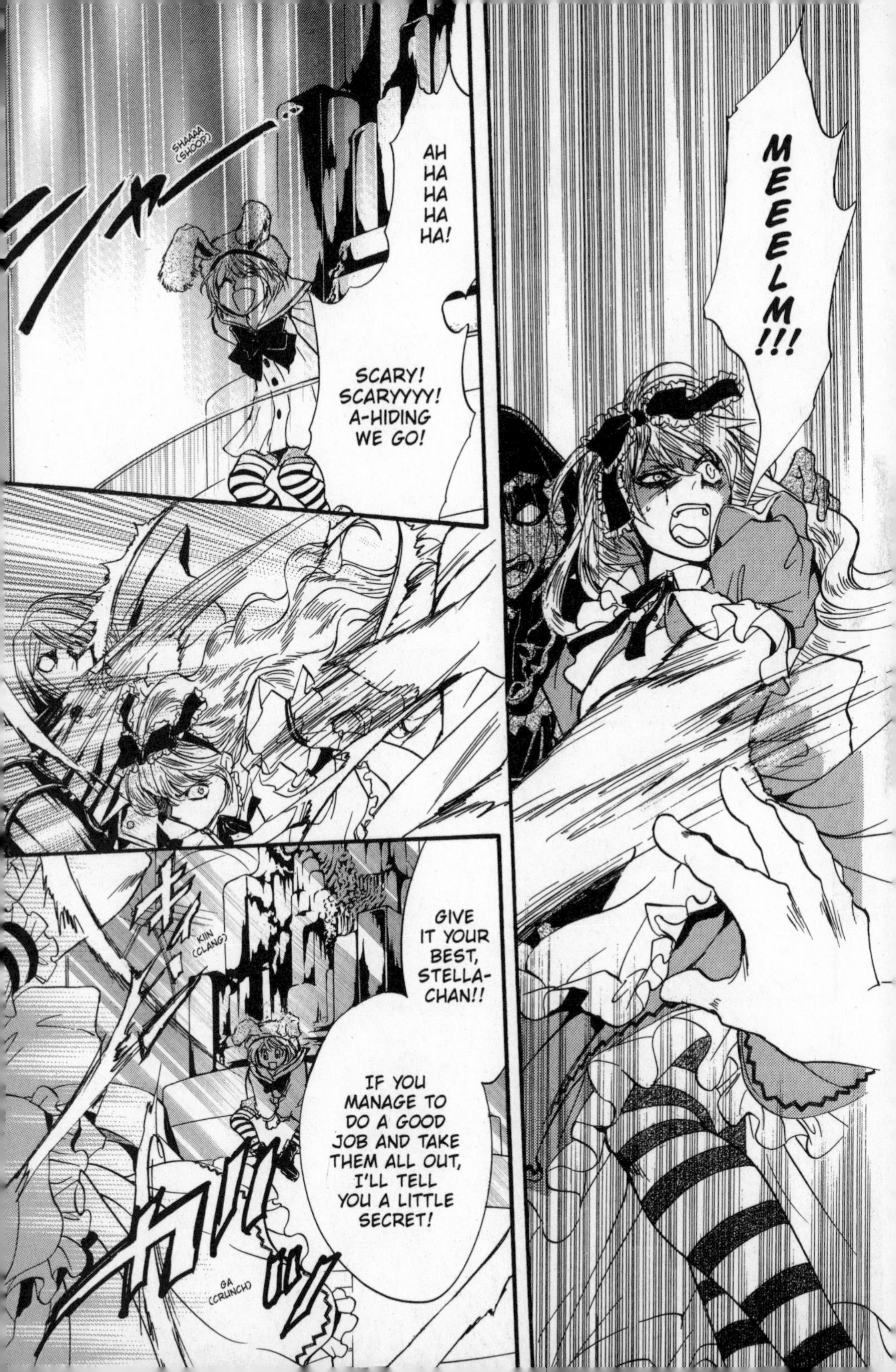
MEEEELM!!!
AH HA HA HA HA!
SHAAAA (SHOOP)
SCARY! SCARYYYY! A-HIDING WE GO!
GIVE IT YOUR BEST, STELLA-CHAN!!
KIIN (CLANG)
IF YOU MANAGE TO DO A GOOD JOB AND TAKE THEM ALL OUT, I'LL TELL YOU A LITTLE SECRET!
GA (CRUNCH)

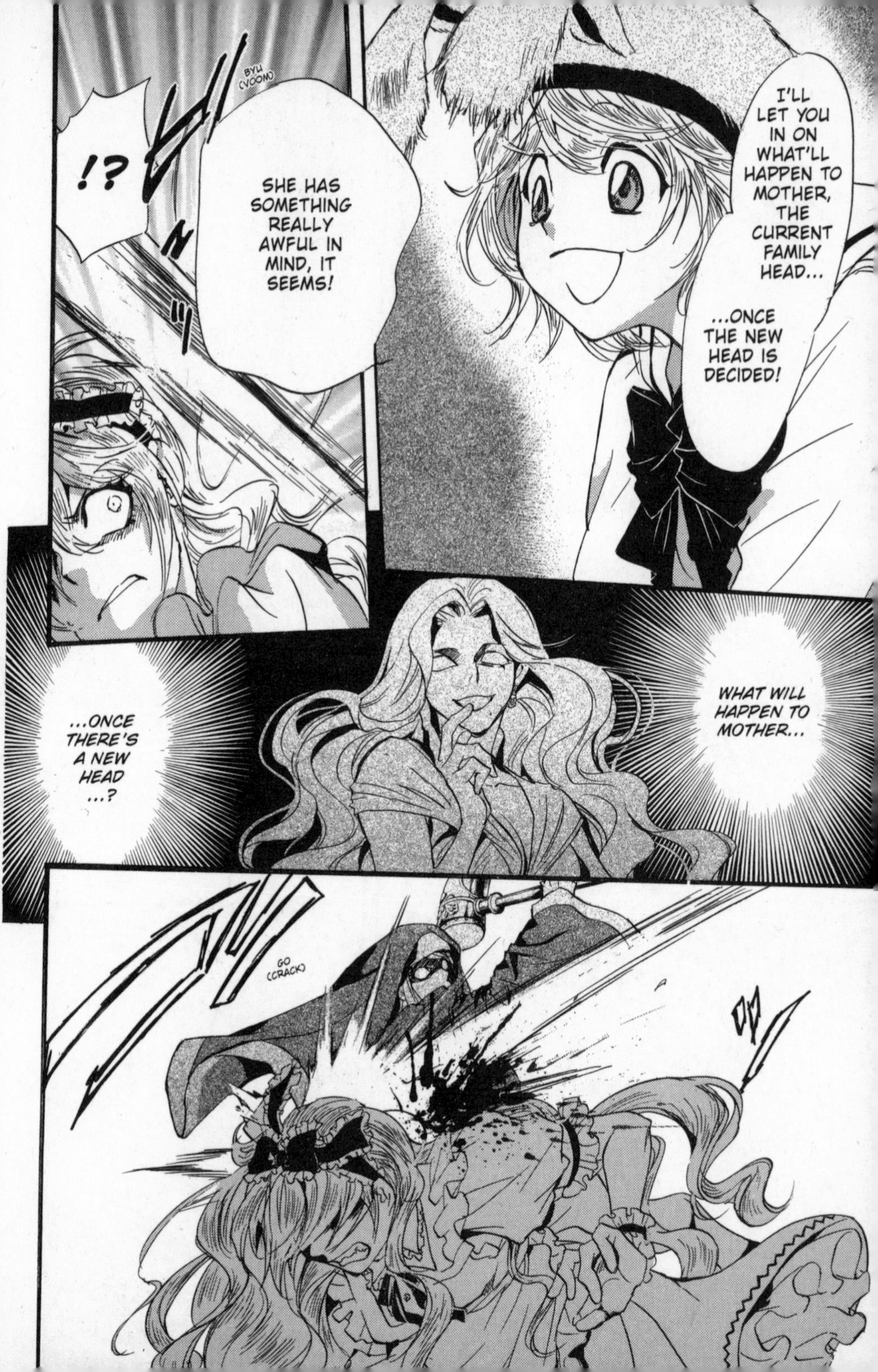
I'LL LET YOU IN ON WHAT'LL HAPPEN TO MOTHER, THE CURRENT FAMILY HEAD...
...ONCE THE NEW HEAD IS DECIDED!
BYU (VOOM)
!?
SHE HAS SOMETHING REALLY AWFUL IN MIND, IT SEEMS!
WHAT WILL HAPPEN TO MOTHER...
...ONCE THERE'S A NEW HEAD ...?
GO (CRACK)

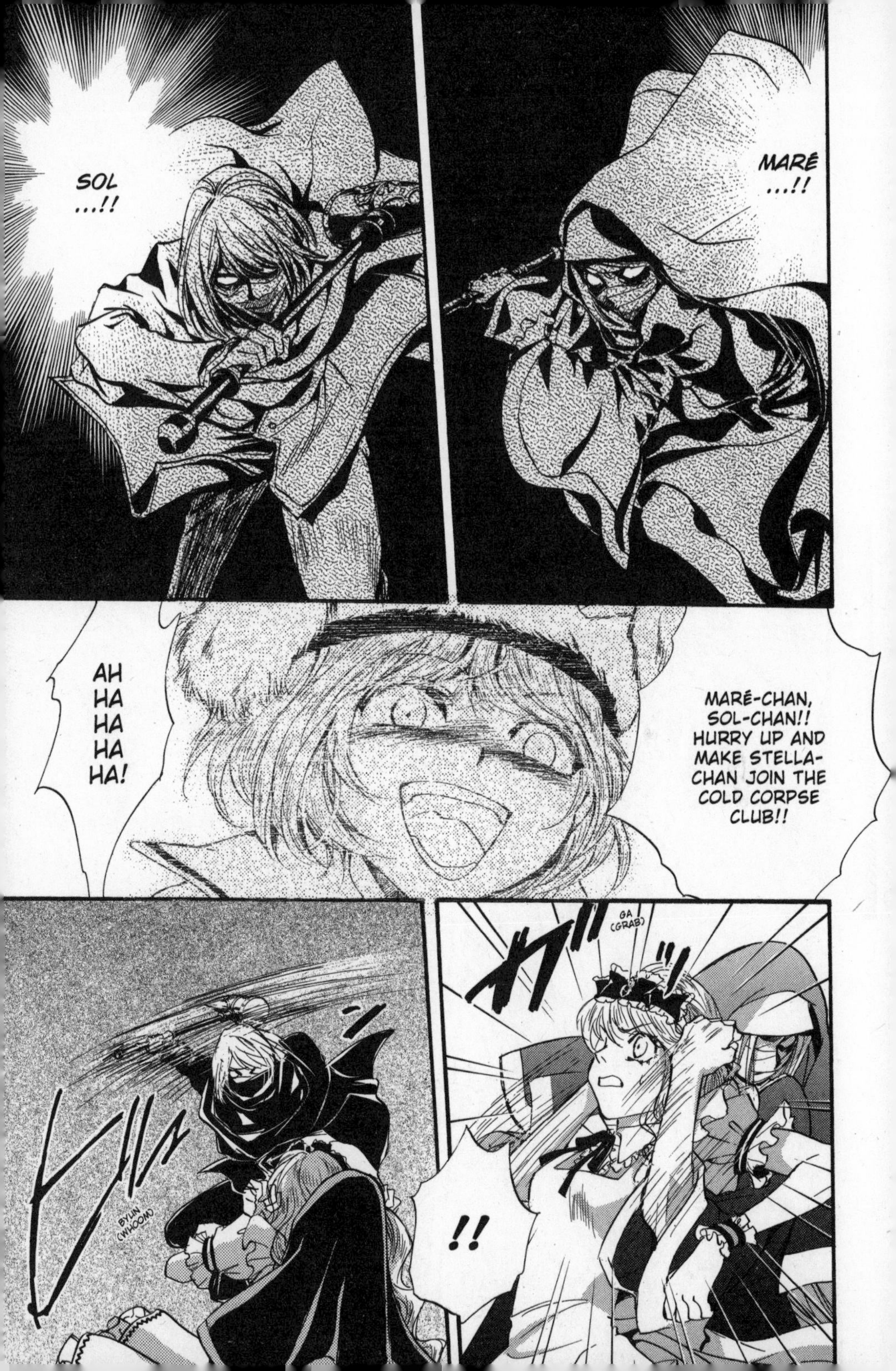
MARÉ ...!!
SOL ...!!
MARÉ-CHAN, SOL-CHAN!! HURRY UP AND MAKE STELLA-CHAN JOIN THE COLD CORPSE CLUB!!
AH HA HA HA HA HA!
GA (GRAB)
!!
BYLIN (WHOOM)

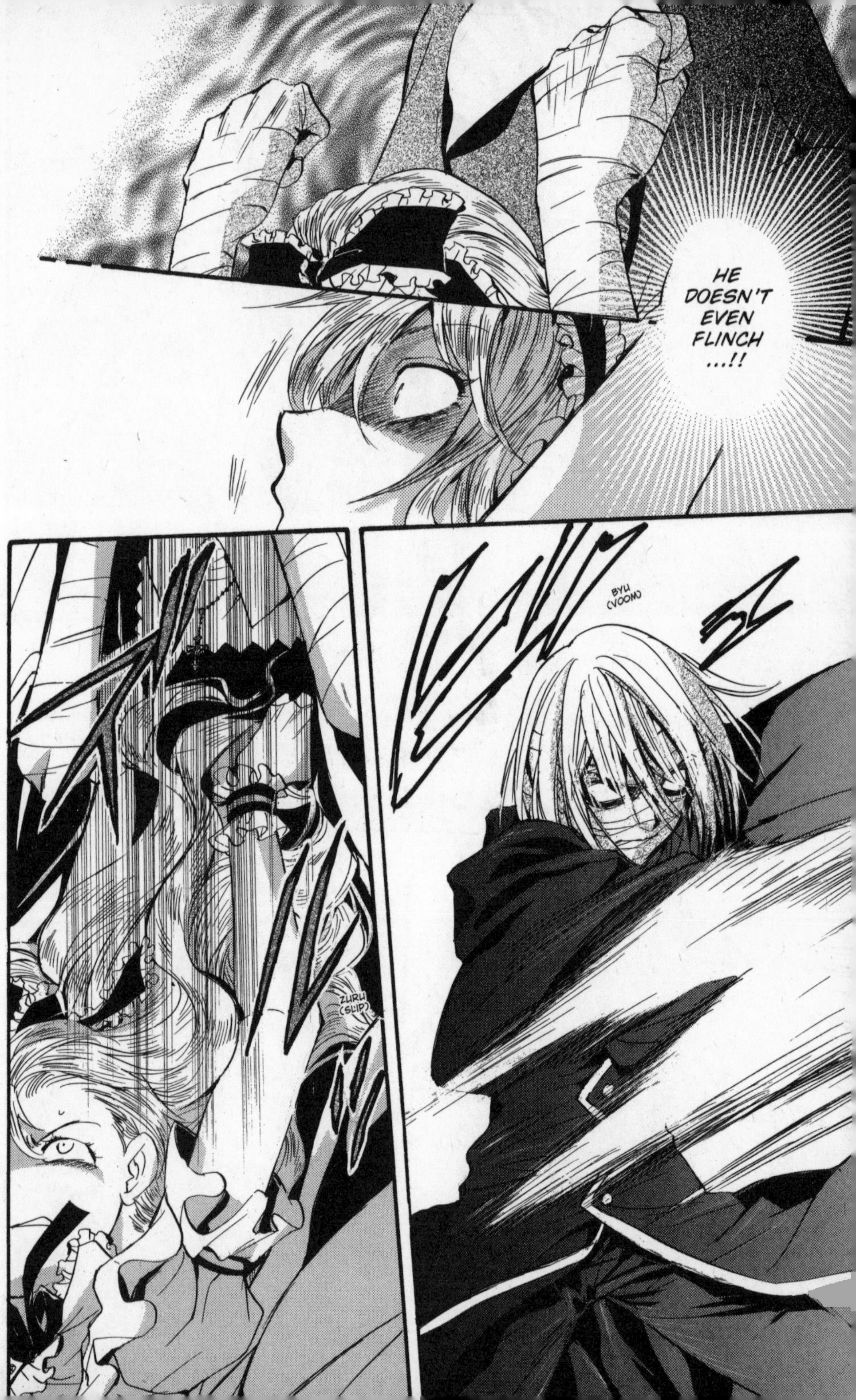
HE DOESN'T EVEN FLINCH ...!!
BYU (VOOM)
ZURU (SLIP)

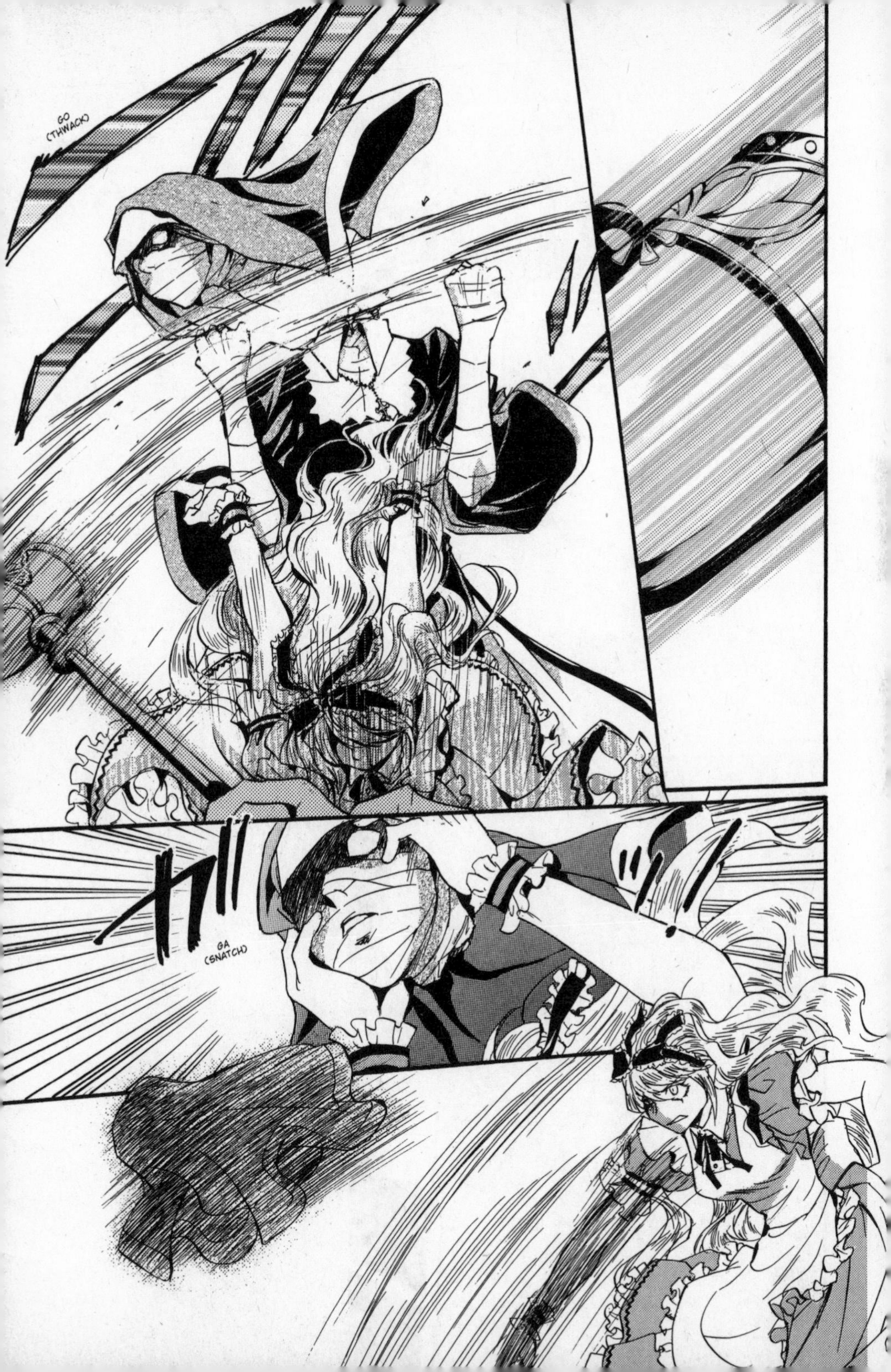
GO
(THWACK)
GA
(SNATCH)

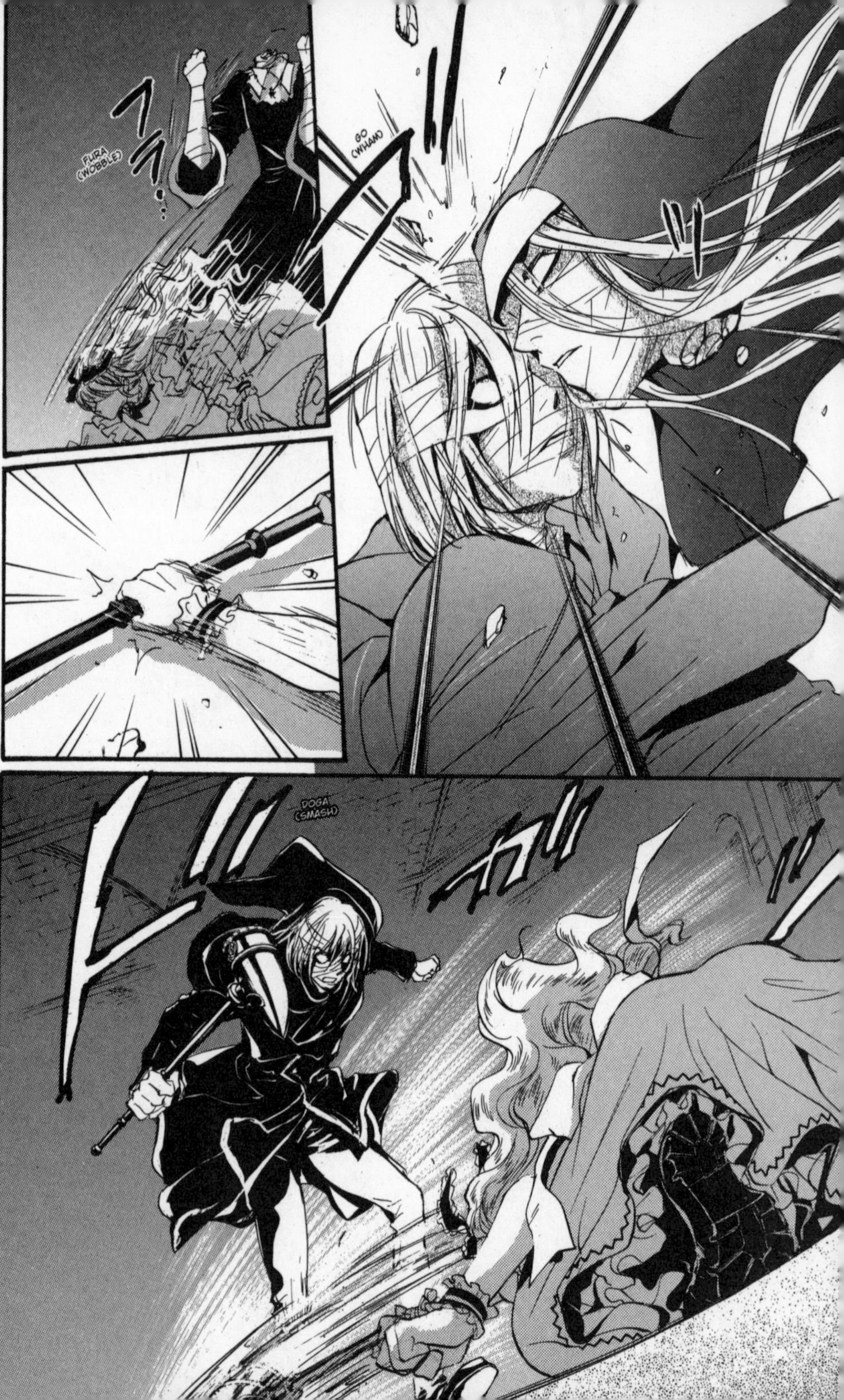
GO (WHAM)
FURA (WOBBLE)
DOGA (SMASH)

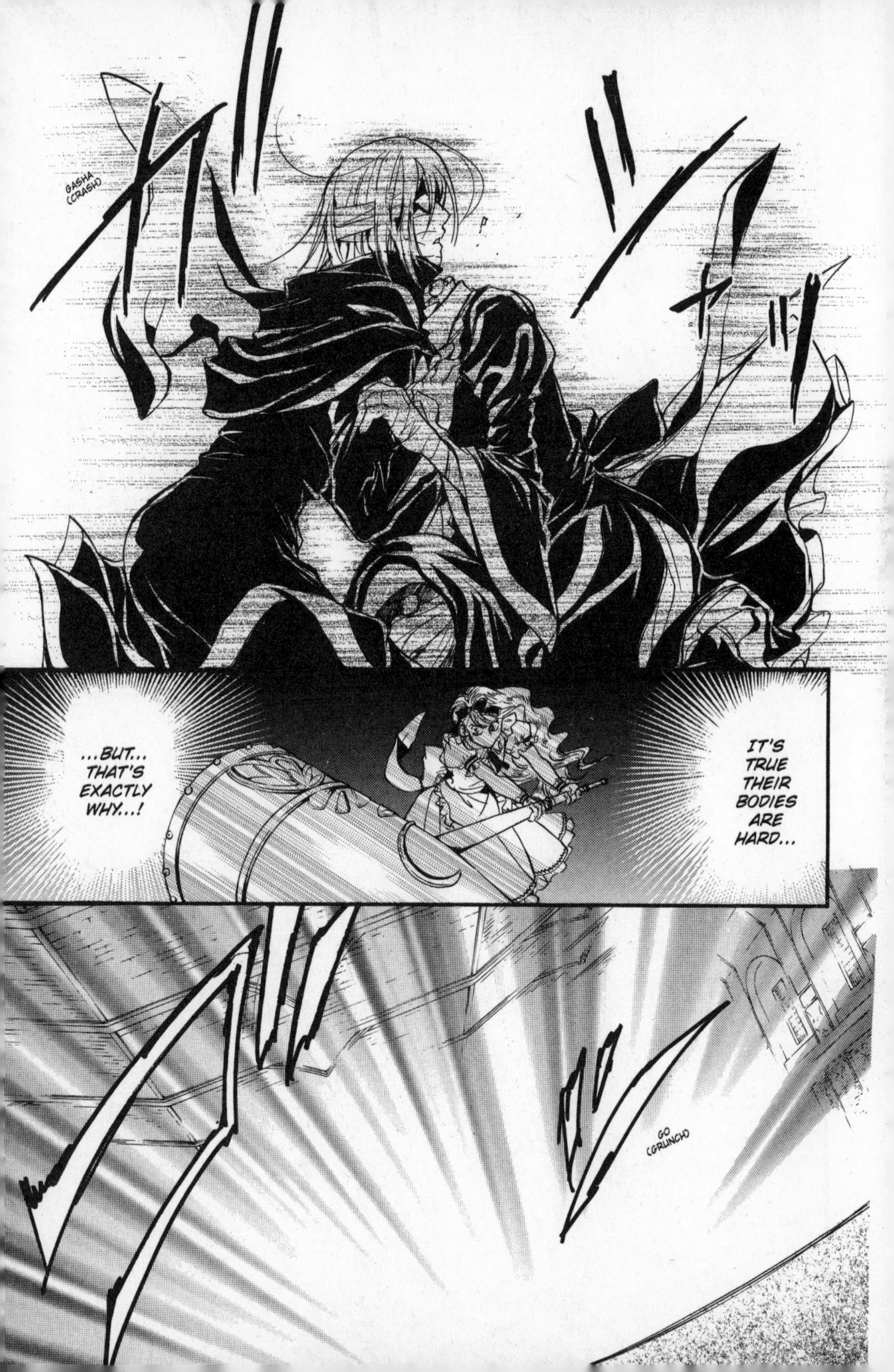
GASHA (CRASH)
IT'S TRUE THEIR BODIES ARE HARD...
...BUT... THAT'S EXACTLY WHY...!
GO (GRUNCH)

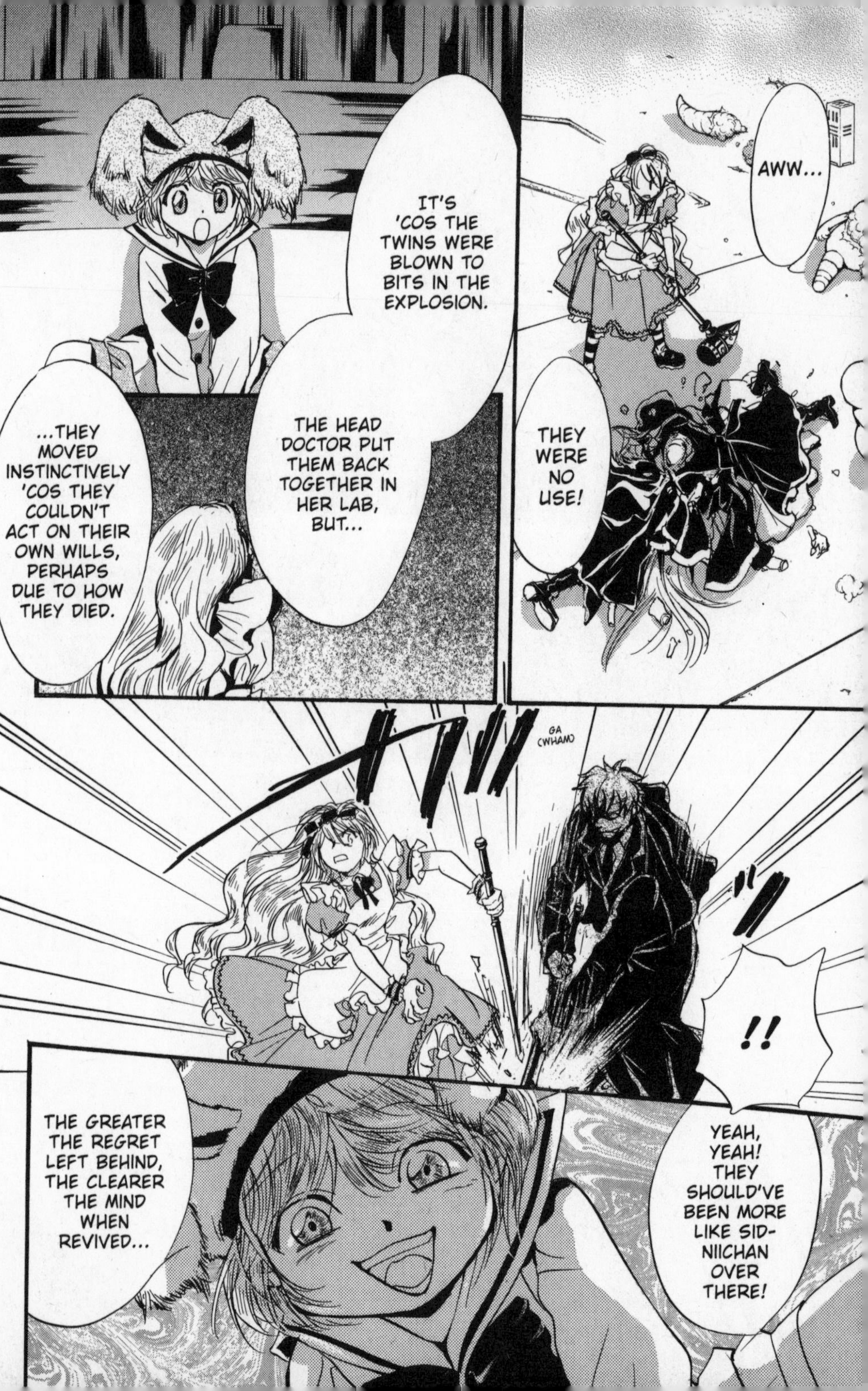
AWW...
THEY WERE NO USE!
IT'S 'COS THE TWINS WERE BLOWN TO BITS IN THE EXPLOSION.
THE HEAD DOCTOR PUT THEM BACK TOGETHER IN HER LAB, BUT...
...THEY MOVED INSTINCTIVELY 'COS THEY COULDN'T ACT ON THEIR OWN WILLS, PERHAPS DUE TO HOW THEY DIED.
GA (WHAM)
!!
YEAH, YEAH! THEY SHOULD'VE BEEN MORE LIKE SID-NIICHAN OVER THERE!
THE GREATER THE REGRET LEFT BEHIND, THE CLEARER THE MIND WHEN REVIVED...

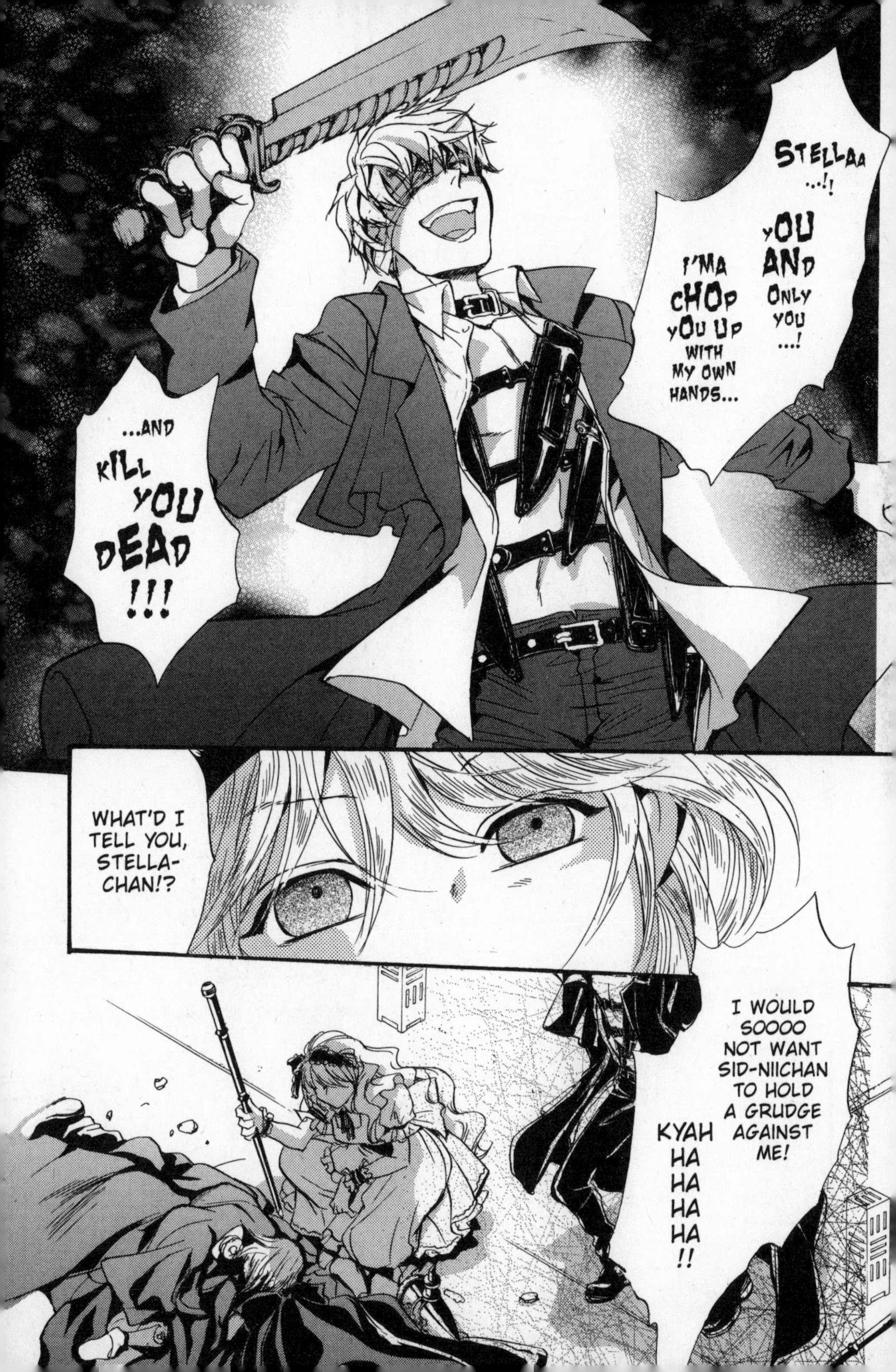
STELLAA ...!!
YOU AND ONLY YOU ...!
I'MA CHOP YOU UP WITH MY OWN HANDS...
...AND KILL YOU DEAD!!!
WHAT'D I TELL YOU, STELLA-CHAN!?
I WOULD SOOOO NOT WANT SID-NIICHAN TO HOLD A GRUDGE AGAINST ME!
KYAH HA HA HA HA!!

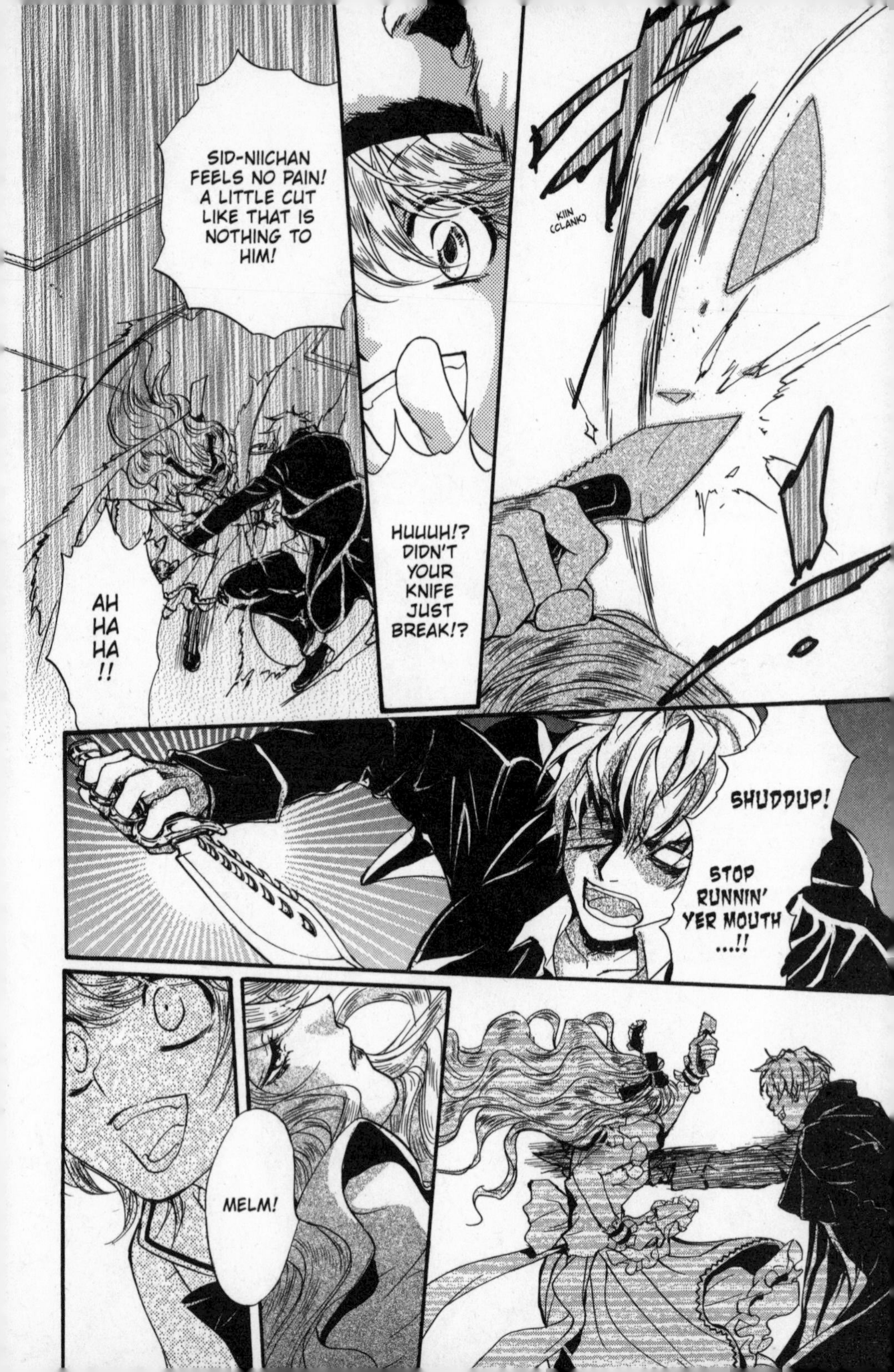
KIIN (CLANK)
HUUUH!? DIDN'T YOUR KNIFE JUST BREAK!?
SID-NIICHAN FEELS NO PAIN! A LITTLE CUT LIKE THAT IS NOTHING TO HIM!
AH HA HA!!
SHUDDUP!
STOP RUNNIN' YER MOUTH ....!!
MELM!

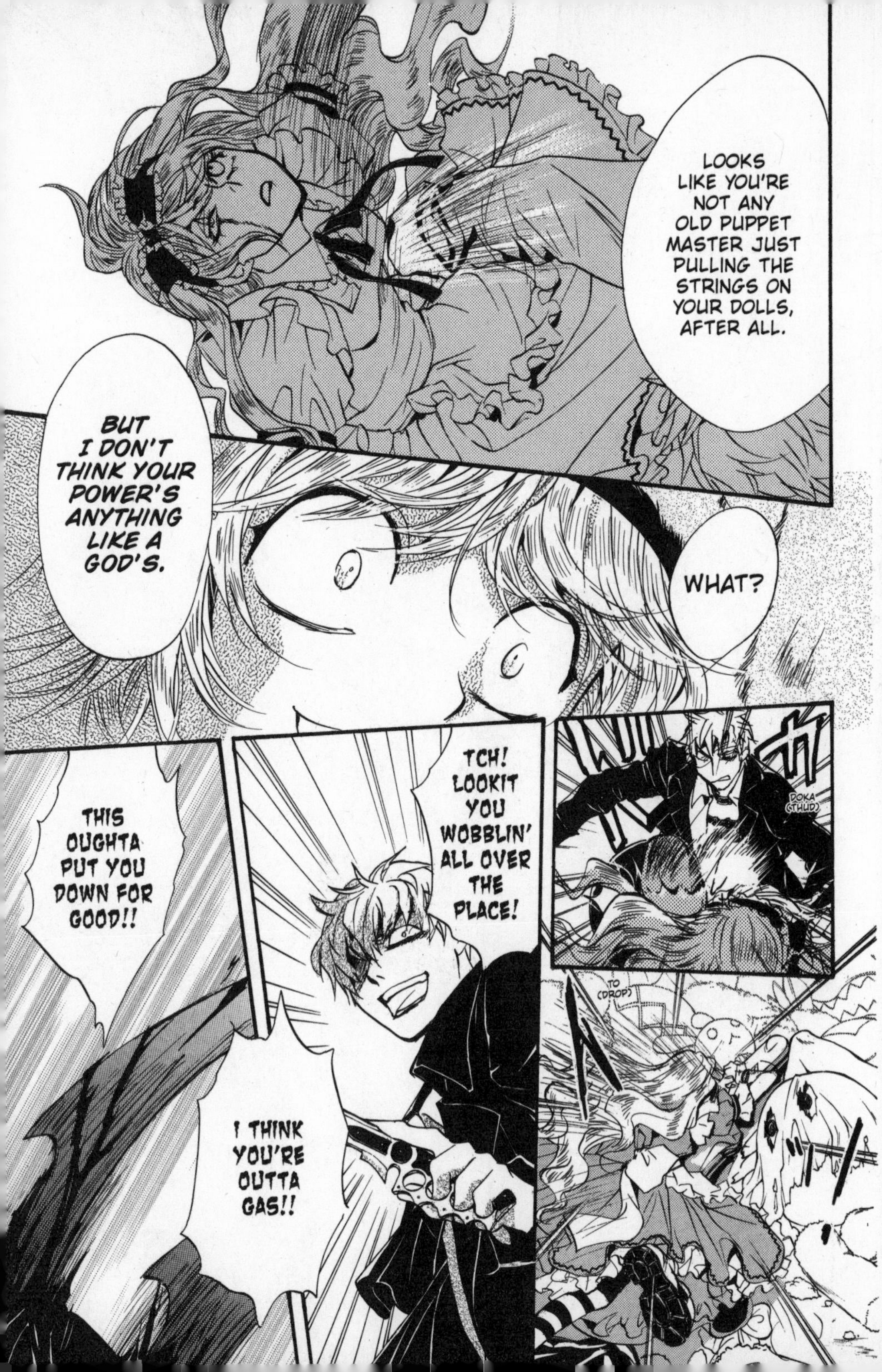
LOOKS LIKE YOU'RE NOT ANY OLD PUPPET MASTER JUST PULLING THE STRINGS ON YOUR DOLLS, AFTER ALL.
BUT I DON'T THINK YOUR POWER'S ANYTHING LIKE A GOD'S.
WHAT?
DOKA (THUD)
TO (DROP)
TCH! LOOKIT YOU WOBBLIN' ALL OVER THE PLACE!
I THINK YOU'RE OUTTA GAS!!
THIS OUGHTA PUT YOU DOWN FOR GOOD!!

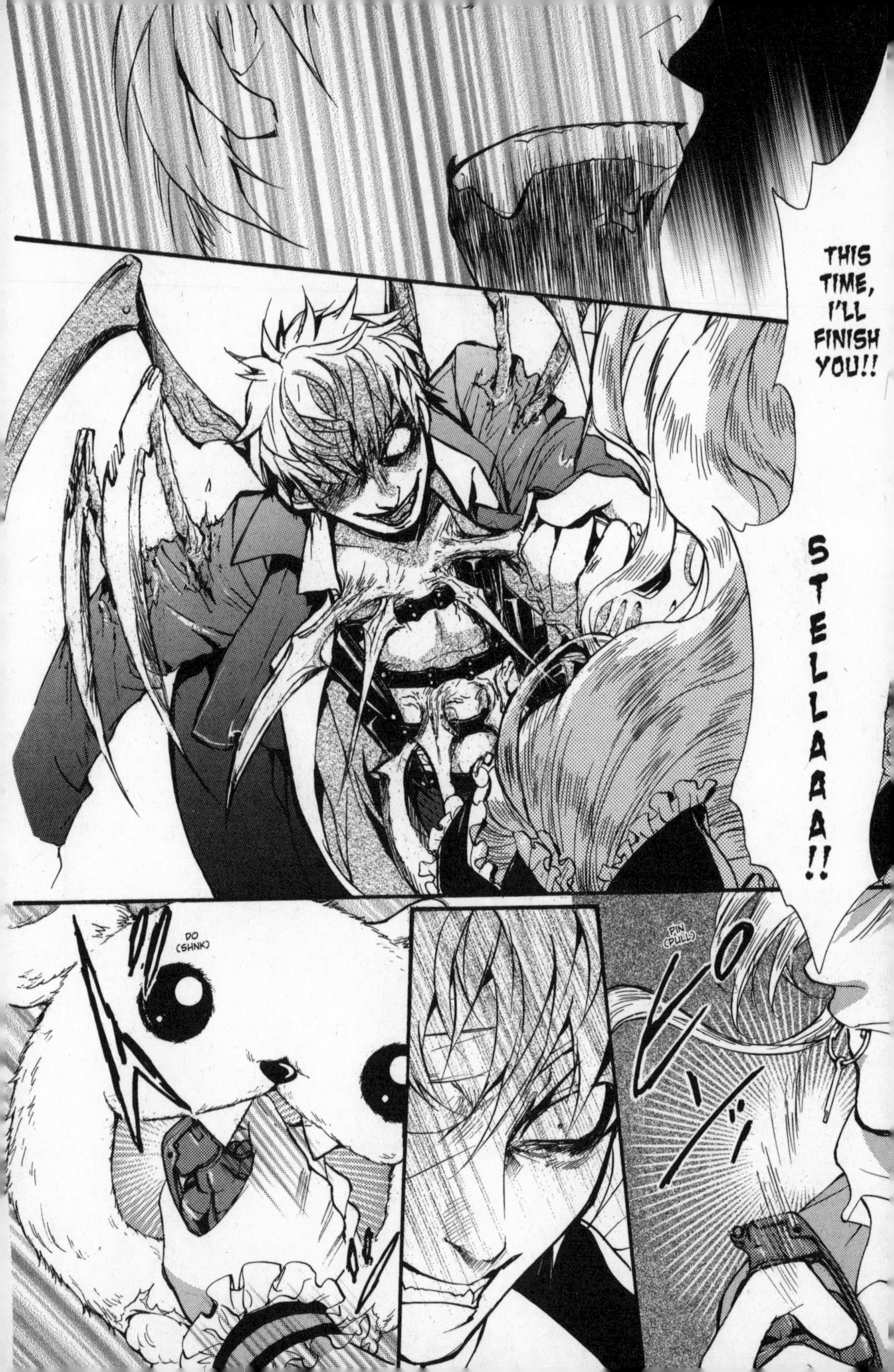
THIS TIME, I'LL FINISH YOU!!
STELLAAA!!
PIN (PULL)
DO (SHNK)

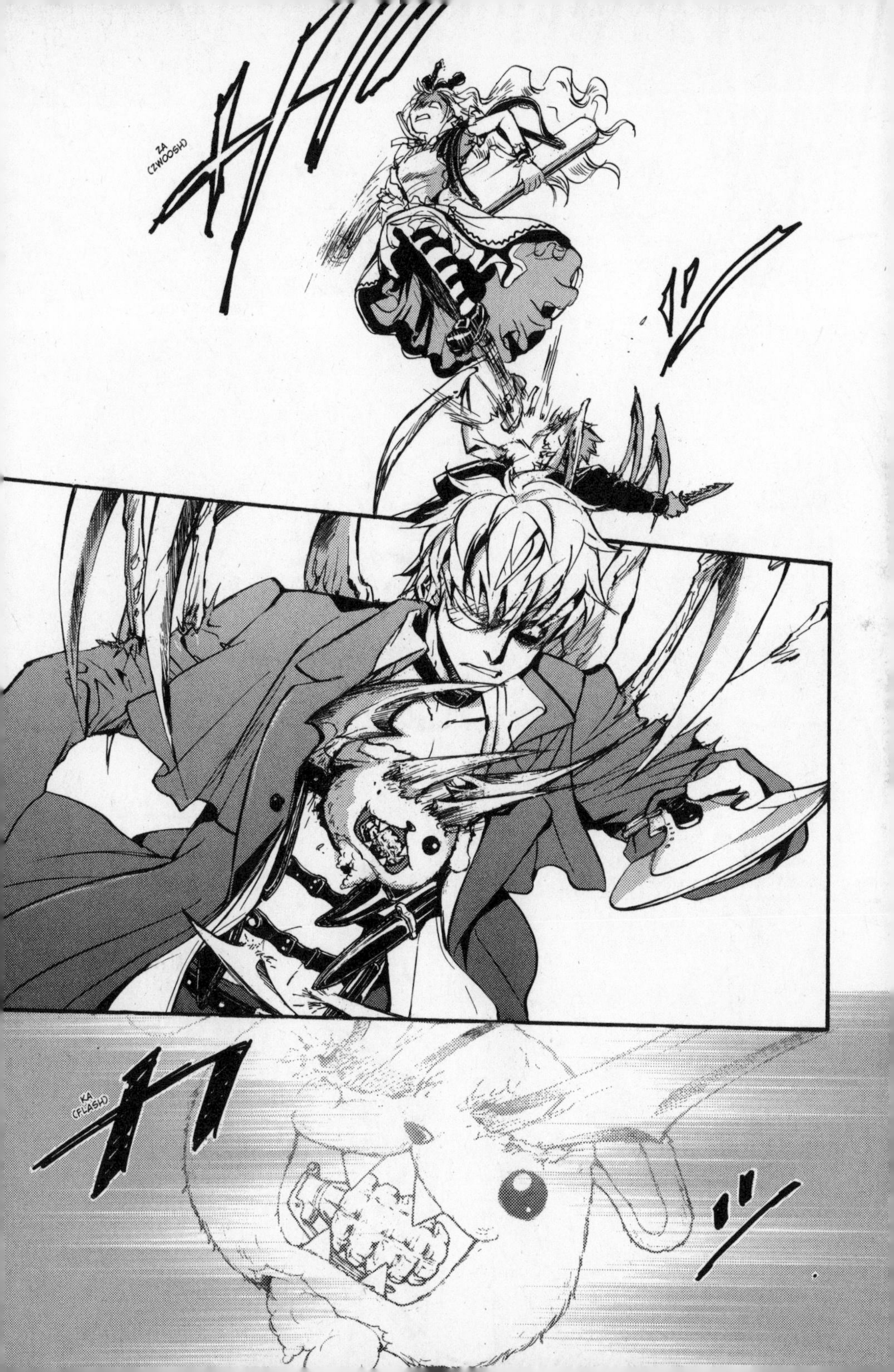
ZA
(ZWOOSH)
KA
(FLASH)

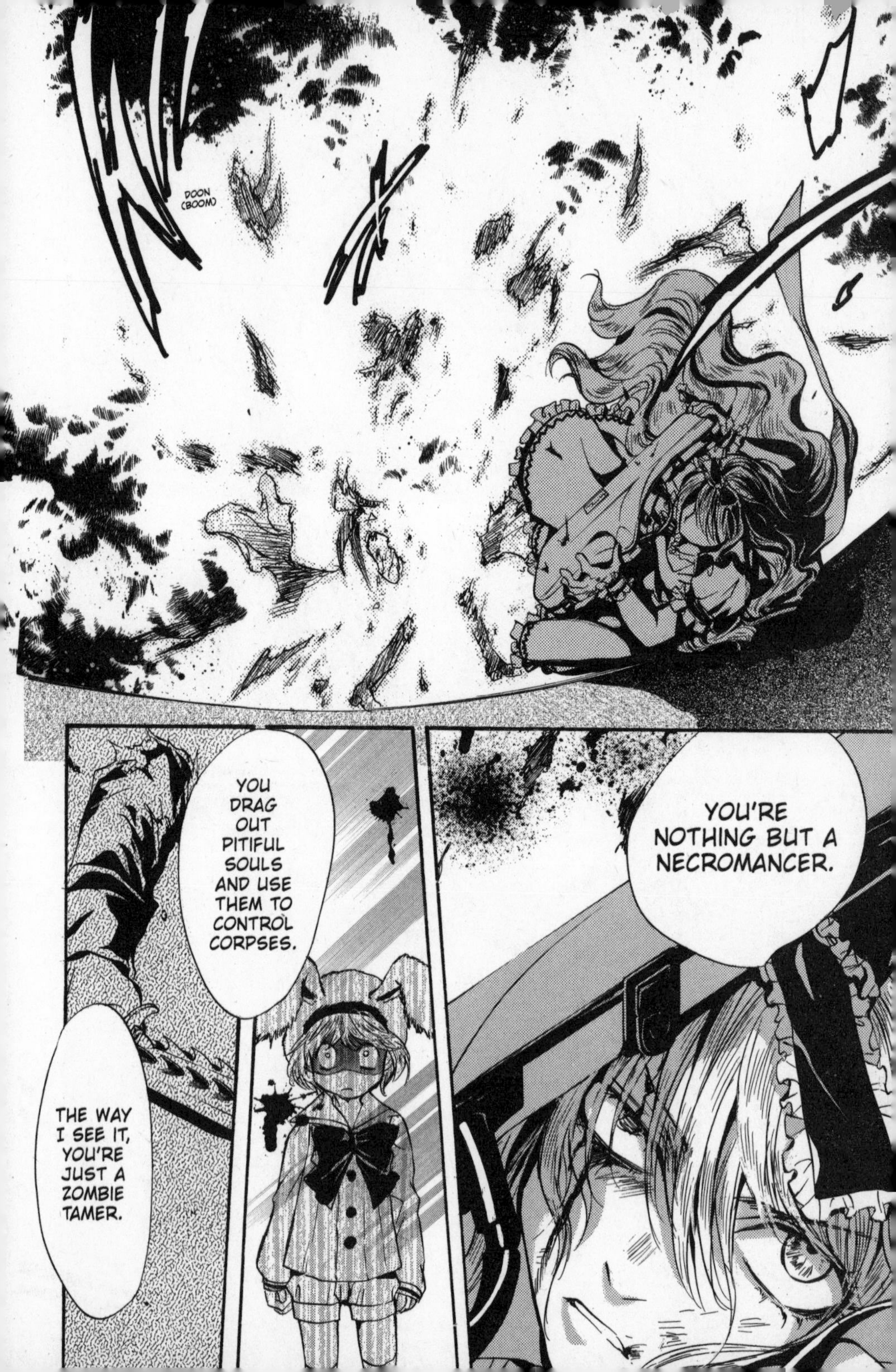
DOON (BOOM)
YOU'RE NOTHING BUT A NECROMANCER.
YOU DRAG OUT PITIFUL SOULS AND USE THEM TO CONTROL CORPSES.
THE WAY I SEE IT, YOU'RE JUST A ZOMBIE TAMER.

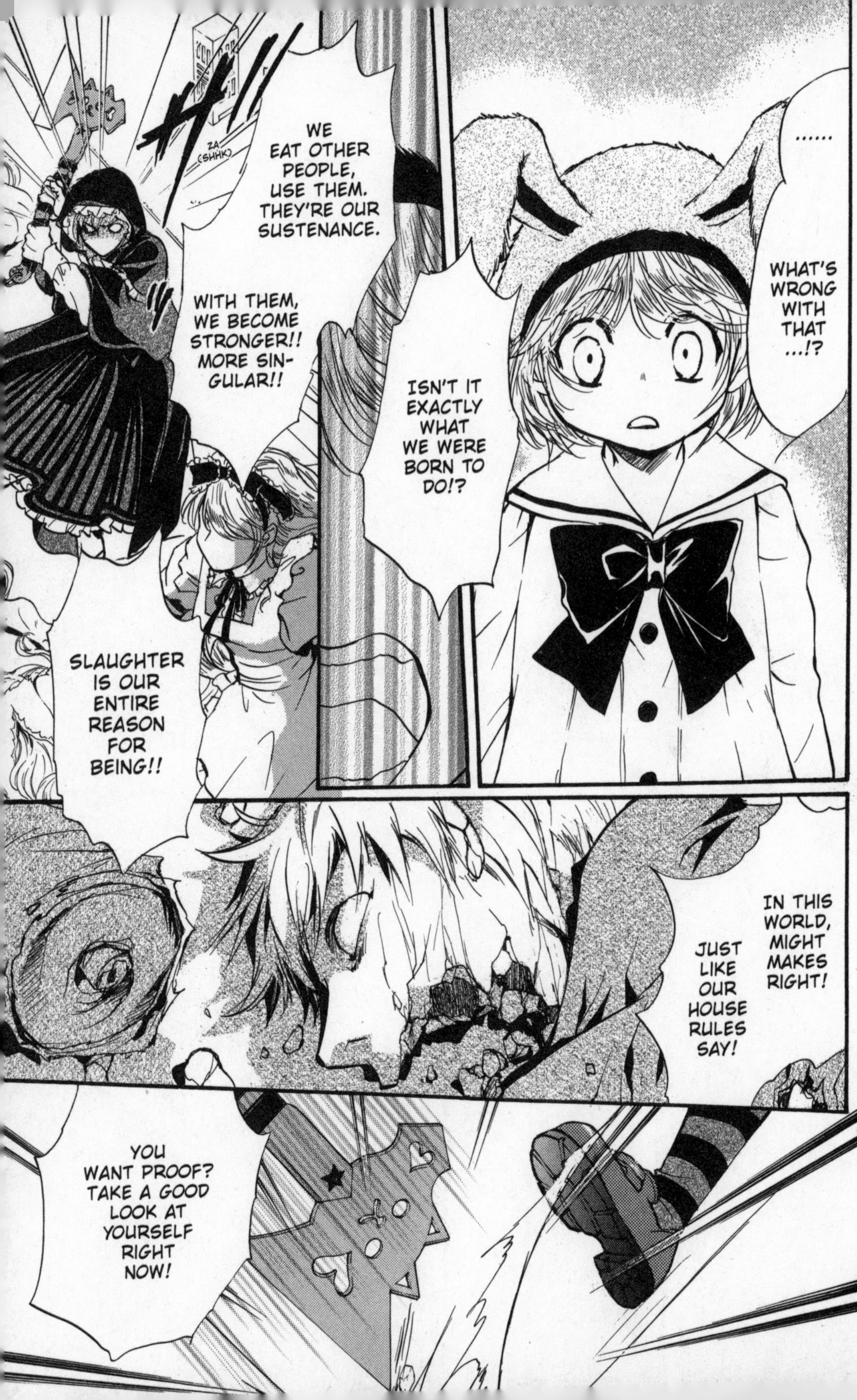
......
WHAT'S WRONG WITH THAT ...!?
ISN'T IT EXACTLY WHAT WE WERE BORN TO DO!?
WE EAT OTHER PEOPLE, USE THEM. THEY'RE OUR SUSTENANCE.
ZA (SHHK)
WITH THEM, WE BECOME STRONGER!! MORE SIN-GULAR!!
SLAUGHTER IS OUR ENTIRE REASON FOR BEING!!
IN THIS WORLD, MIGHT MAKES RIGHT!
JUST LIKE OUR HOUSE RULES SAY!
YOU WANT PROOF? TAKE A GOOD LOOK AT YOURSELF RIGHT NOW!

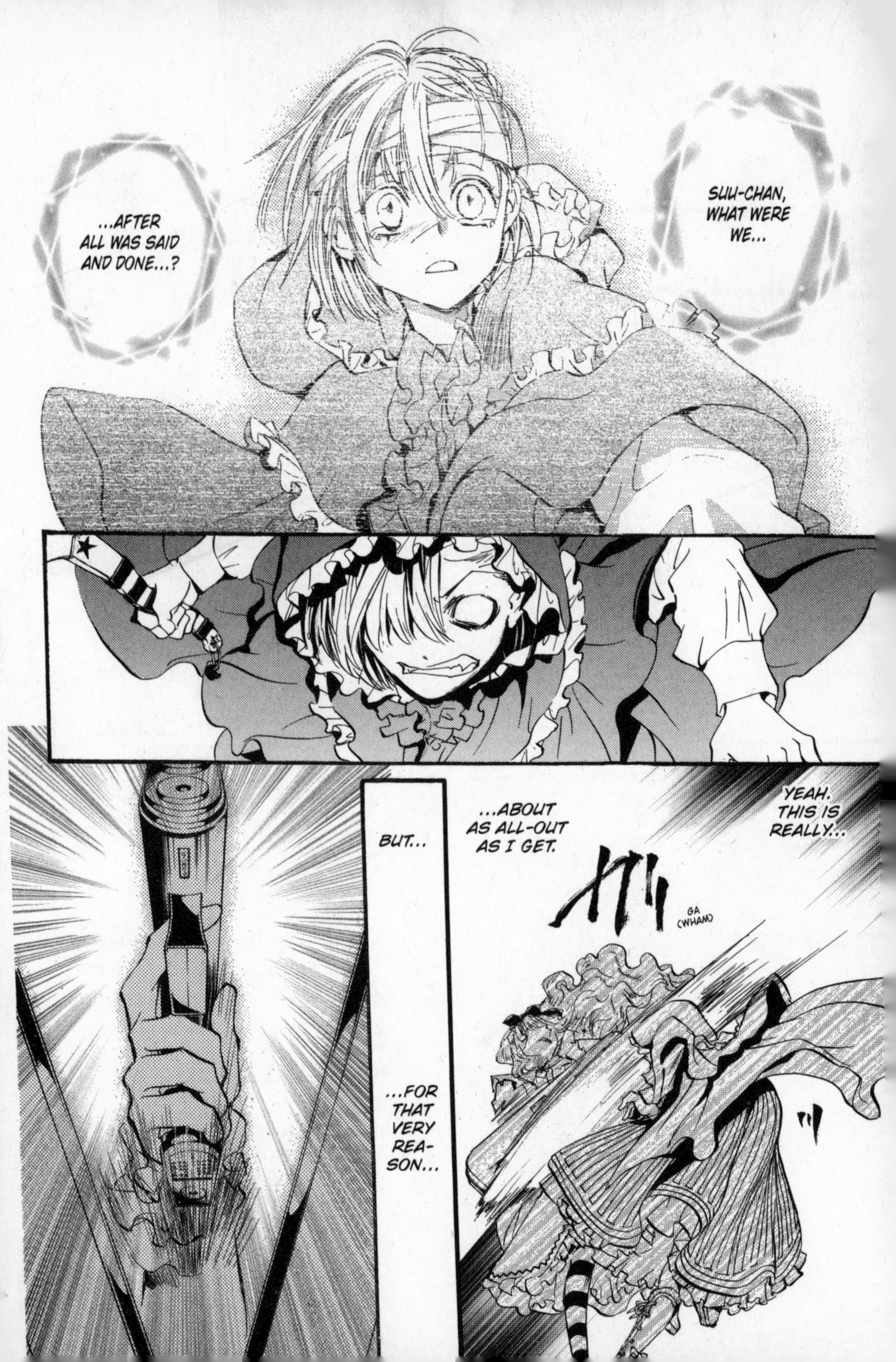
SUU-CHAN, WHAT WERE WE...
...AFTER ALL WAS SAID AND DONE...?
YEAH. THIS IS REALLY...
...ABOUT AS ALL-OUT AS I GET.
GA (WHAM)
BUT...
...FOR THAT VERY REA-SON...

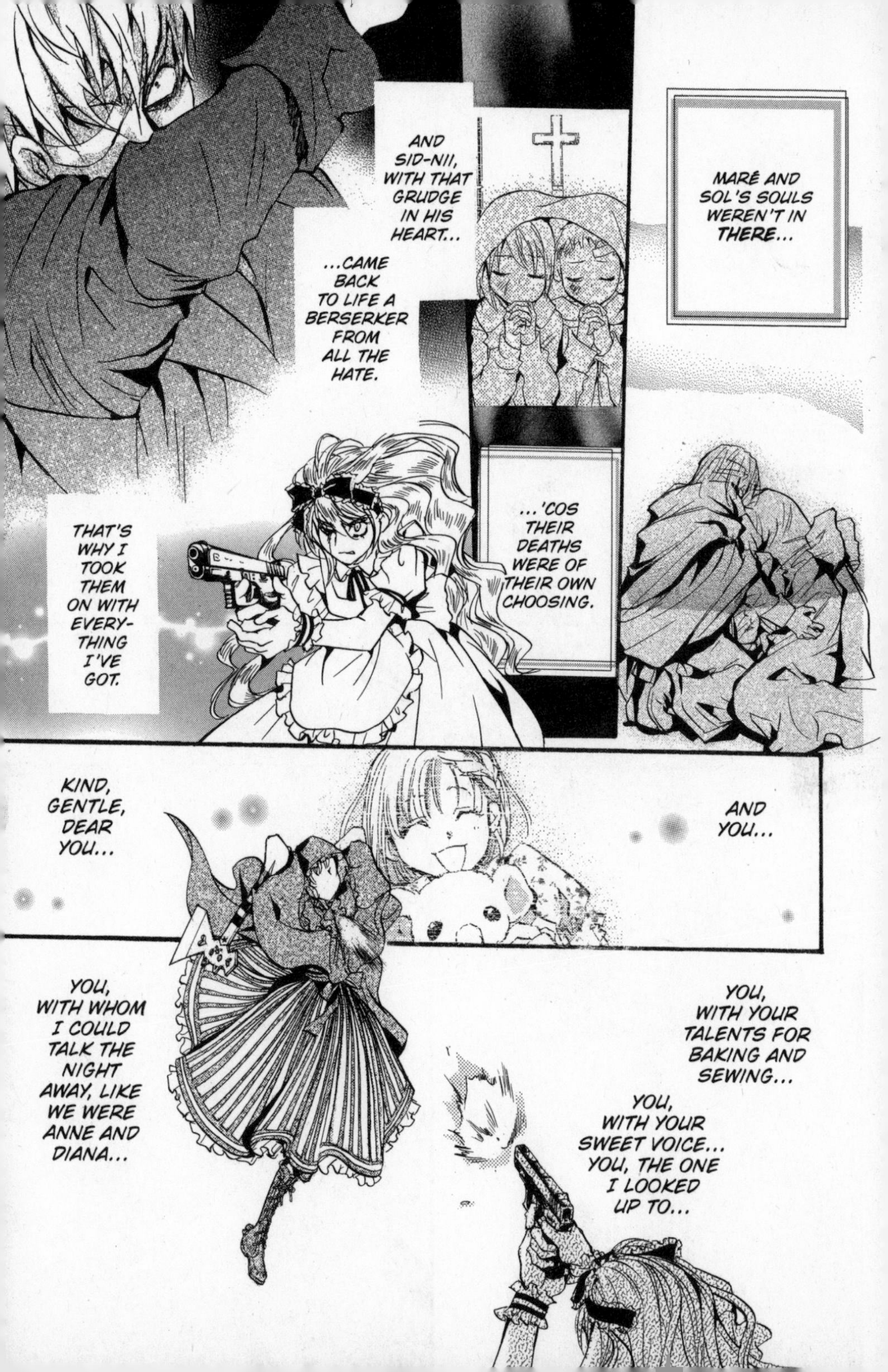
MARÉ AND SOL'S SOULS WEREN'T IN THERE...
...'COS THEIR DEATHS WERE OF THEIR OWN CHOOSING.
AND SID-NII, WITH THAT GRUDGE IN HIS HEART...
...CAME BACK TO LIFE A BERSERKER FROM ALL THE HATE.
THAT'S WHY I TOOK THEM ON WITH EVERY-THING I'VE GOT.
AND YOU...
KIND, GENTLE, DEAR YOU...
YOU, WITH YOUR TALENTS FOR BAKING AND SEWING...
YOU, WITH YOUR SWEET VOICE... YOU, THE ONE I LOOKED UP TO...
YOU, WITH WHOM I COULD TALK THE NIGHT AWAY, LIKE WE WERE ANNE AND DIANA...

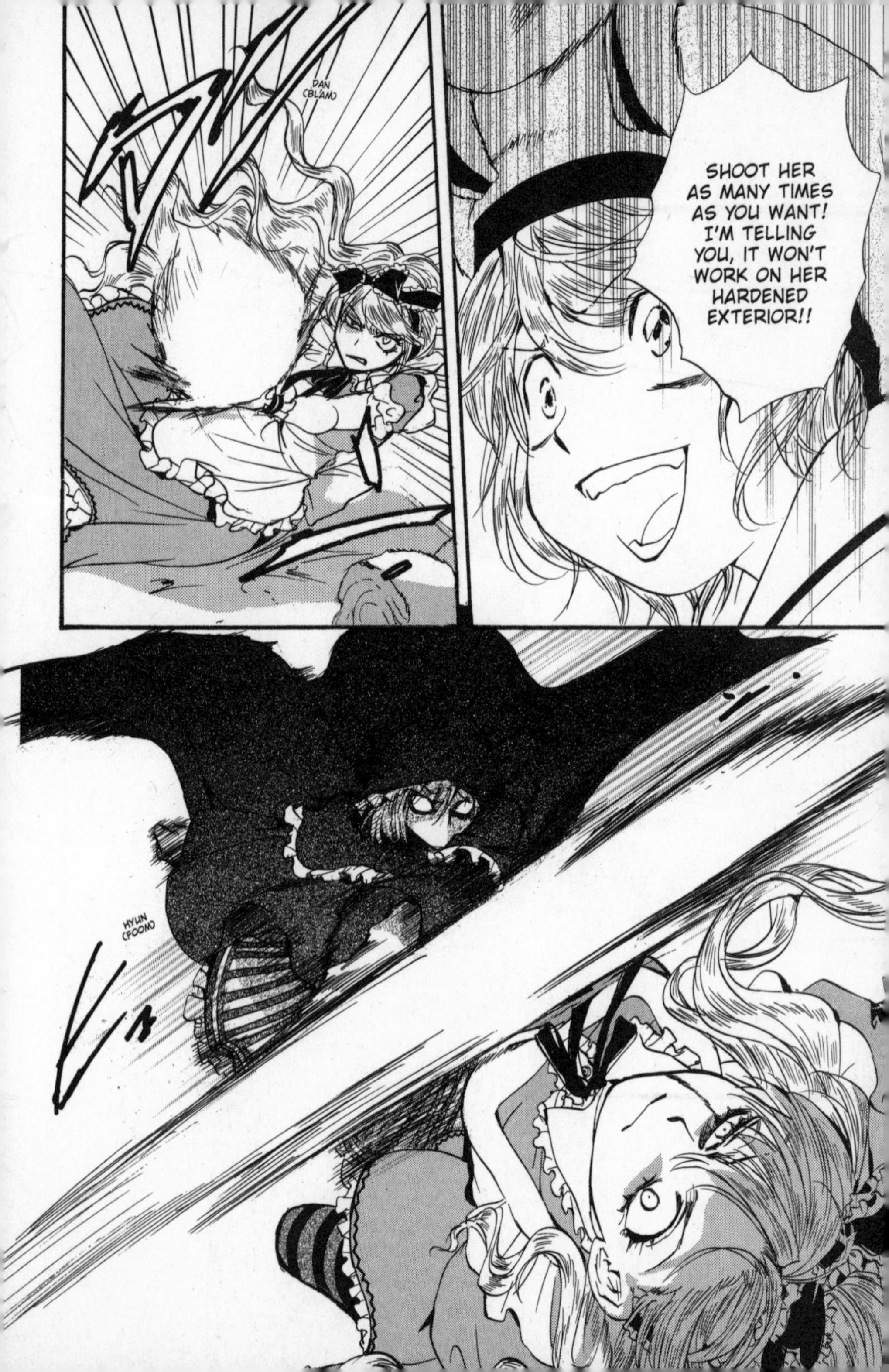
SHOOT HER AS MANY TIMES AS YOU WANT! I'M TELLING YOU, IT WON'T WORK ON HER HARDENED EXTERIOR!!
DAN (BLAM)
HYUN (FOOM)

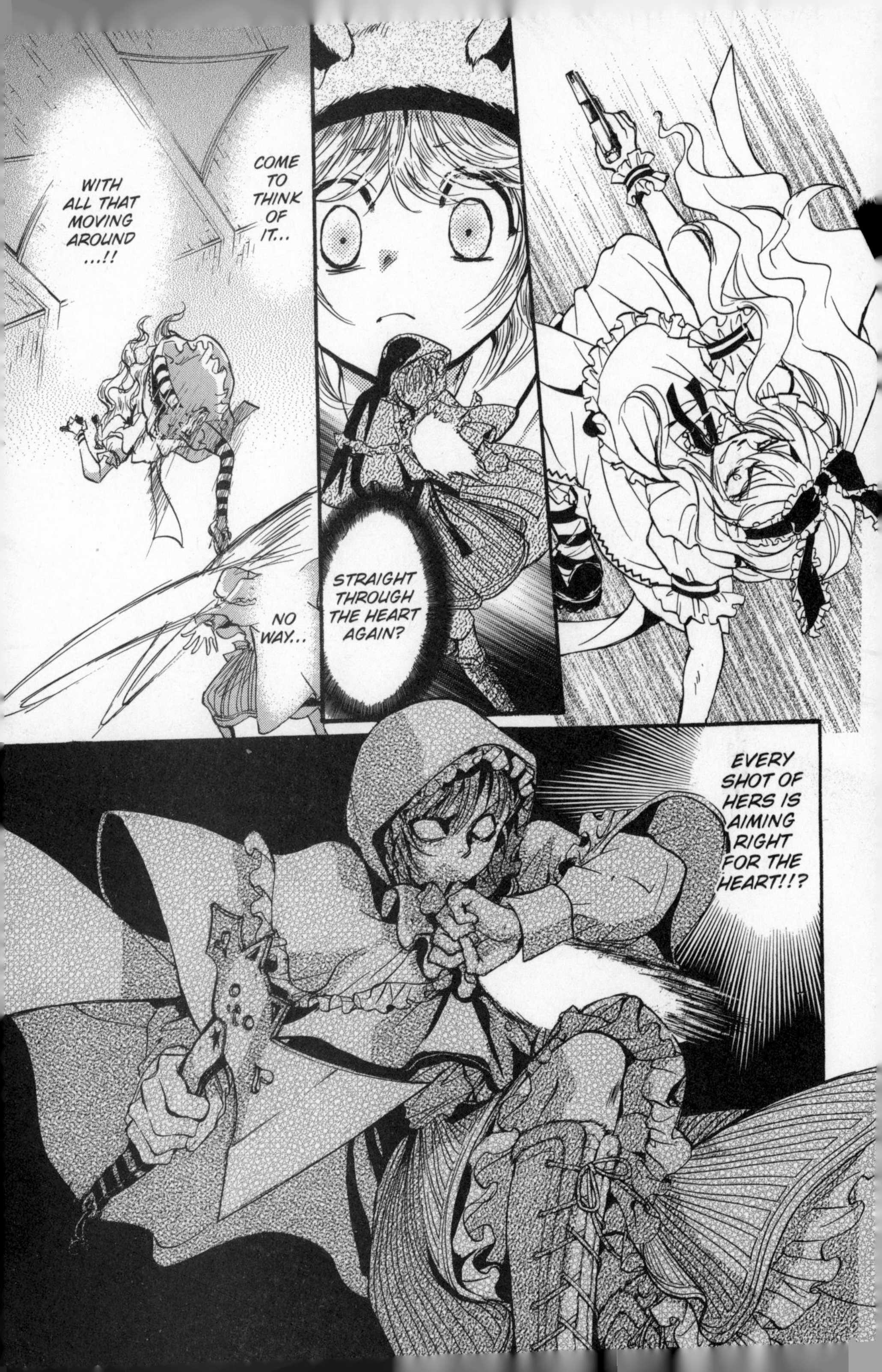
STRAIGHT THROUGH THE HEART AGAIN?
COME TO THINK OF IT...
WITH ALL THAT MOVING AROUND ...!!
NO WAY...
EVERY SHOT OF HERS IS AIMING RIGHT FOR THE HEART!!?

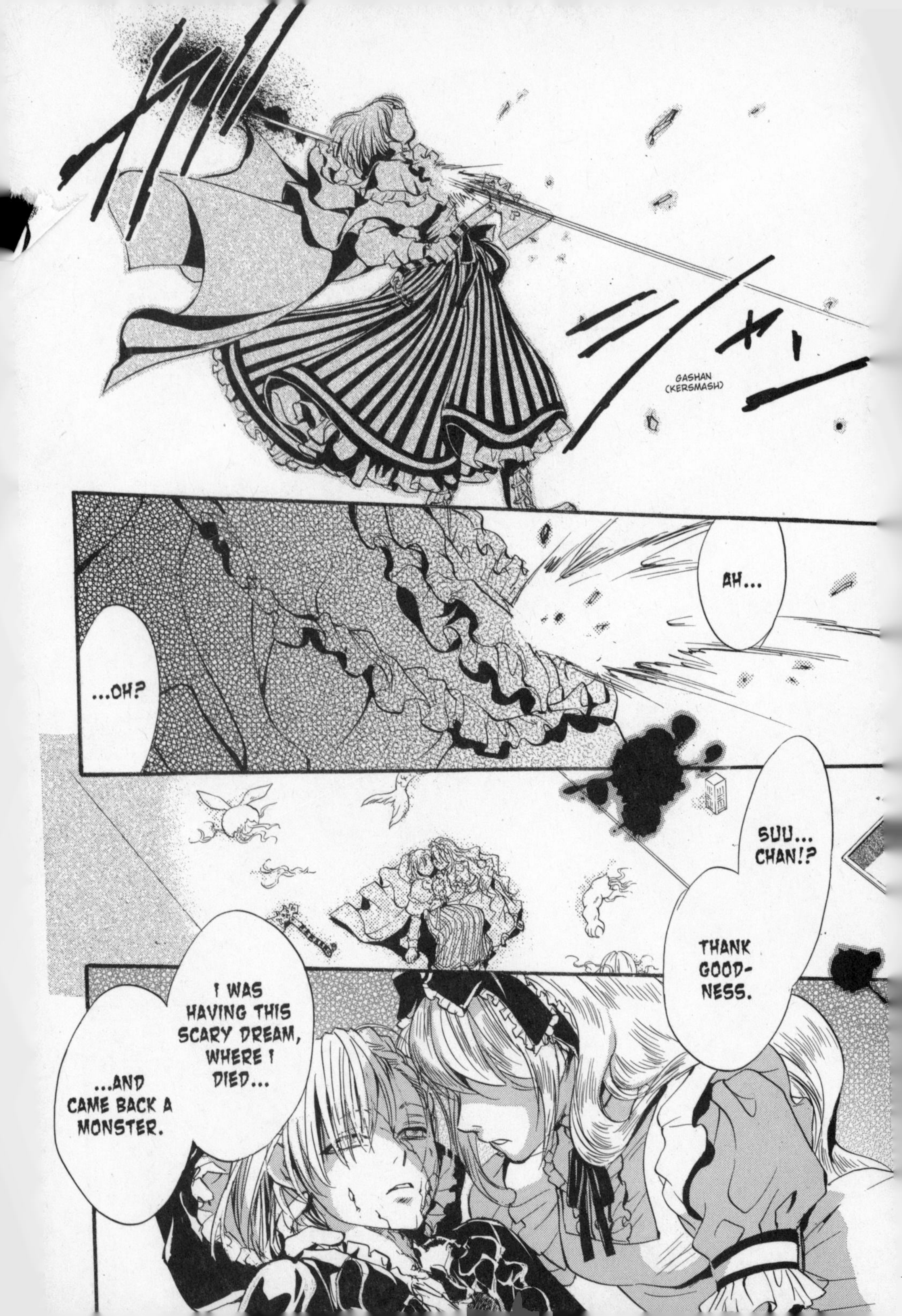
GASHAN (KERSMASH)
AH...
...OH?
SUU... CHAN!?
THANK GOODNESS.
I WAS HAVING THIS SCARY DREAM, WHERE I DIED...
...AND CAME BACK A MONSTER.

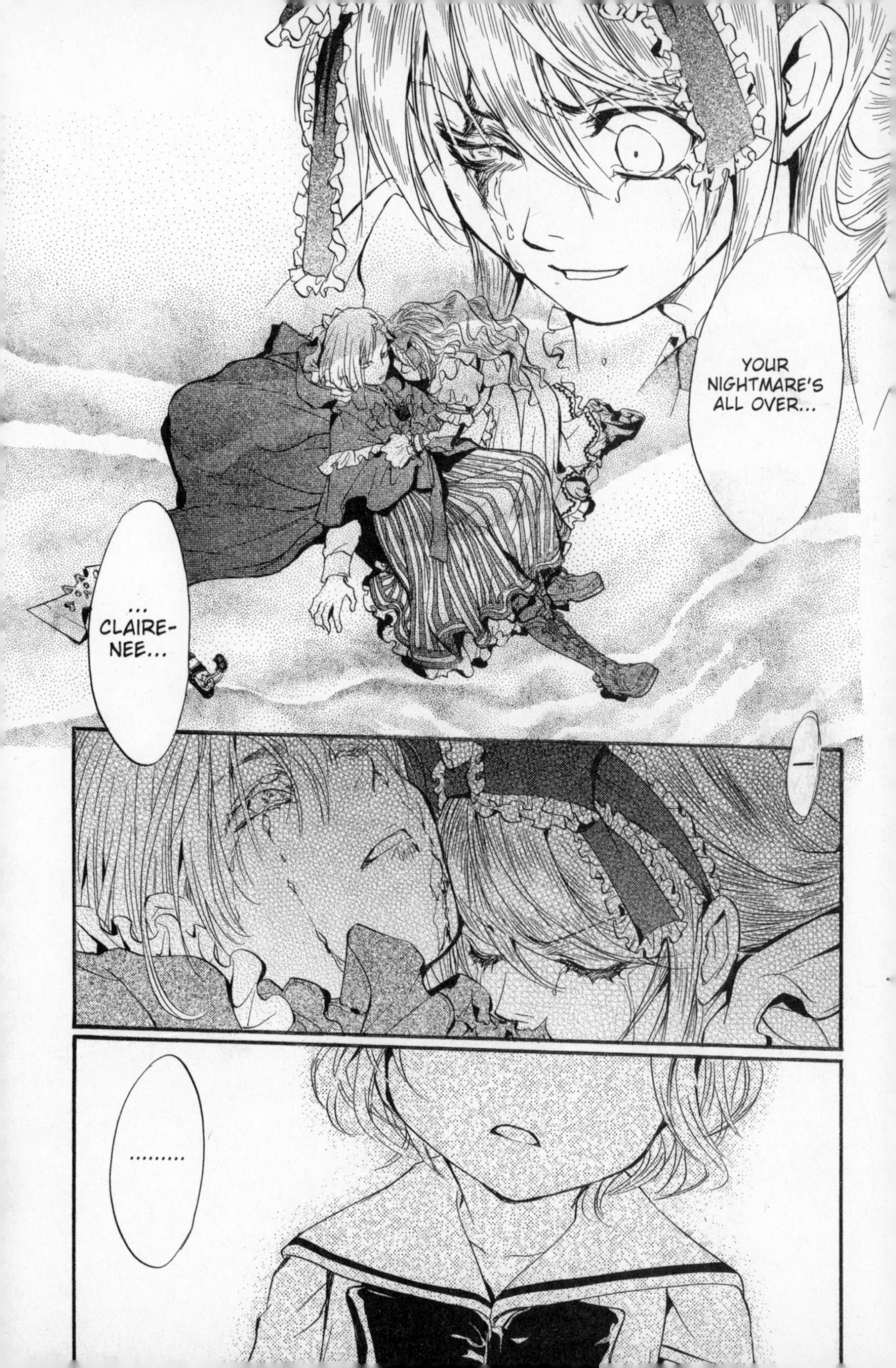
YOUR NIGHTMARE'S ALL OVER...
...CLAIRE-NEE...
—
....

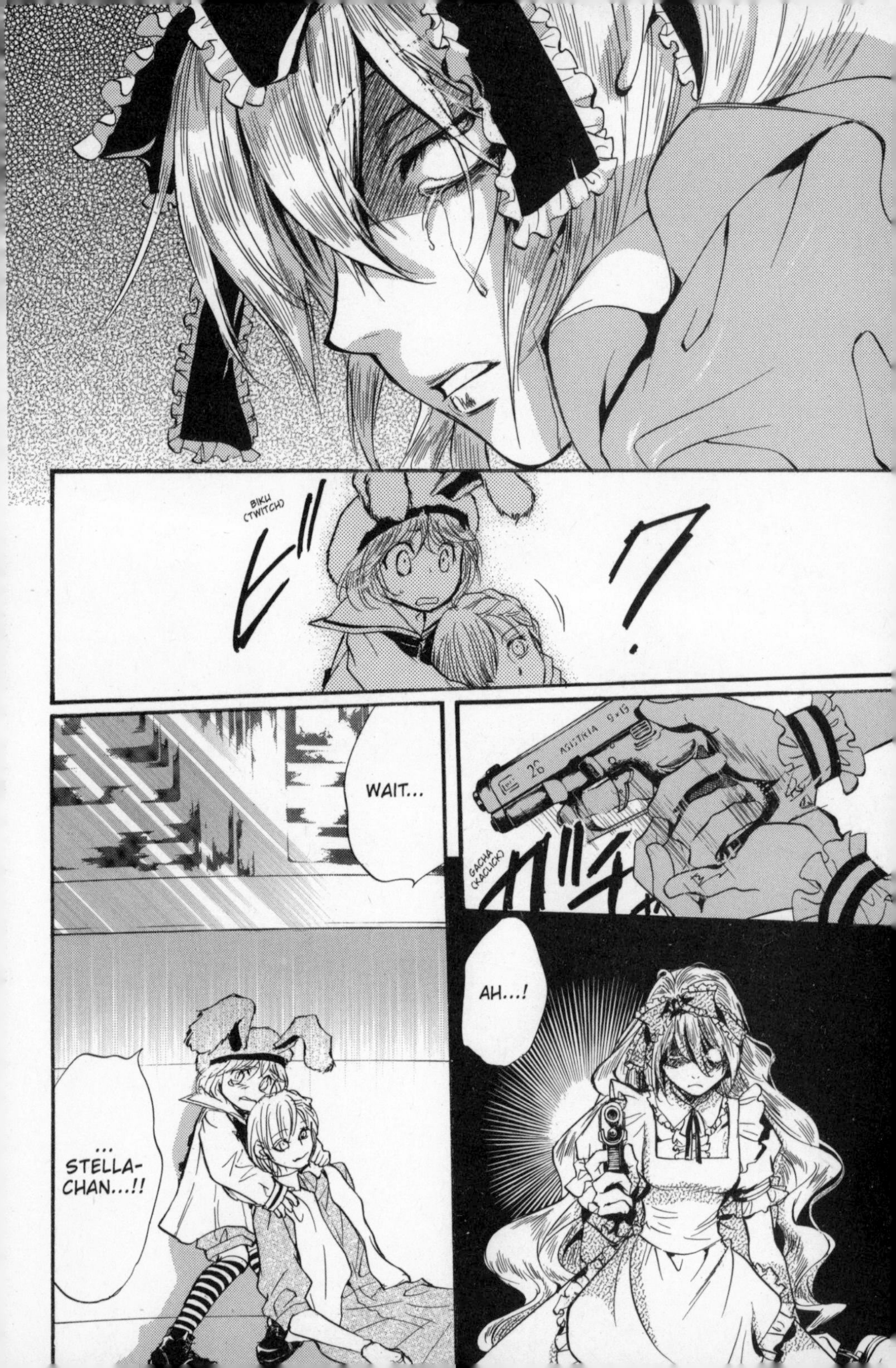
BIKU (TWITCH)
GACHA (KACLICK)
WAIT...
AH...!
... STELLA-CHAN...!!

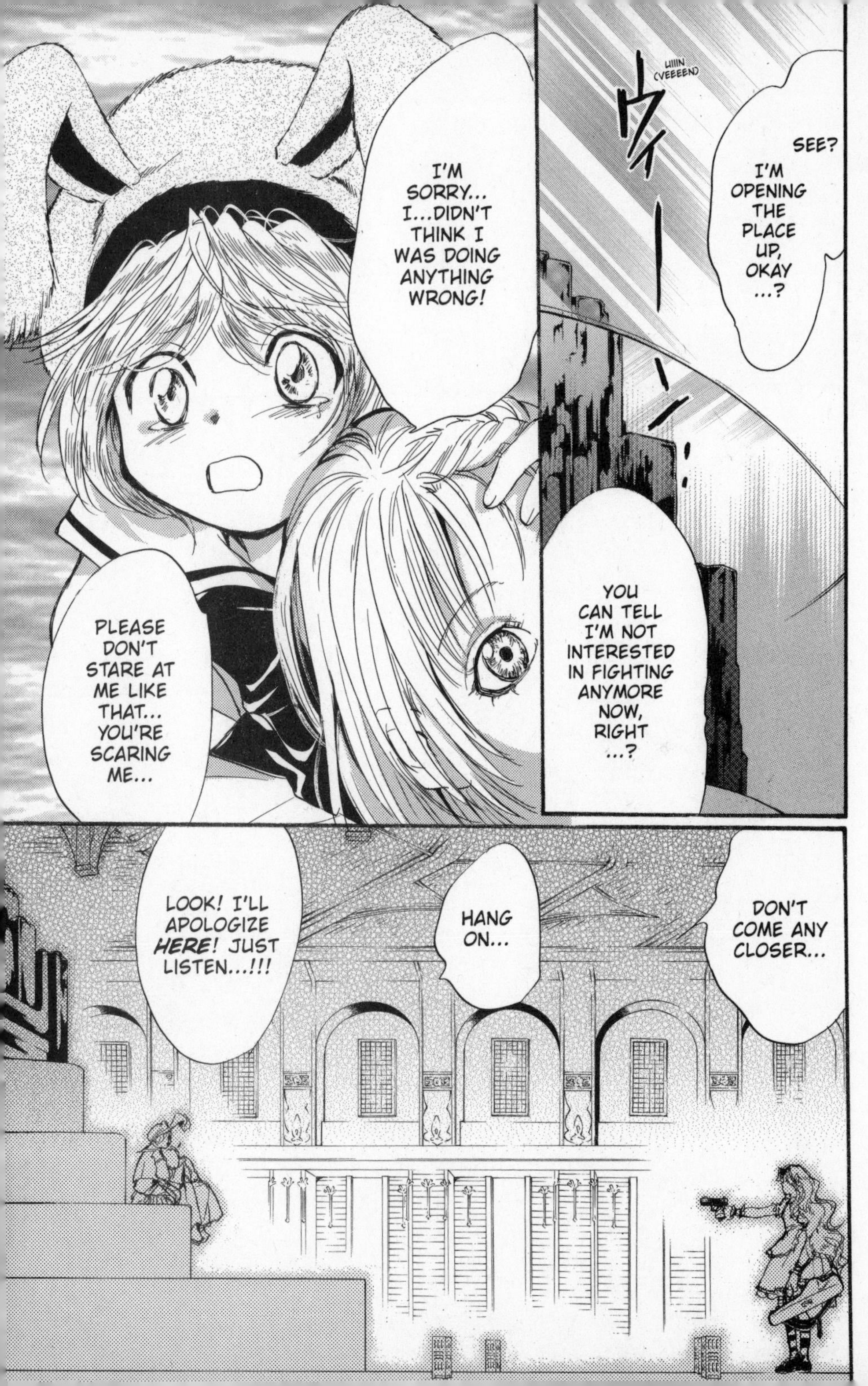
UIIIN (VEEEEND)
SEE? I'M OPENING THE PLACE UP, OKAY ...?
YOU CAN TELL I'M NOT INTERESTED IN FIGHTING ANYMORE NOW, RIGHT ...?
I'M SORRY... I...DIDN'T THINK I WAS DOING ANYTHING WRONG!
PLEASE DON'T STARE AT ME LIKE THAT... YOU'RE SCARING ME...
DON'T COME ANY CLOSER...
HANG ON...
LOOK! I'LL APOLOGIZE *HERE*! JUST LISTEN...!!!

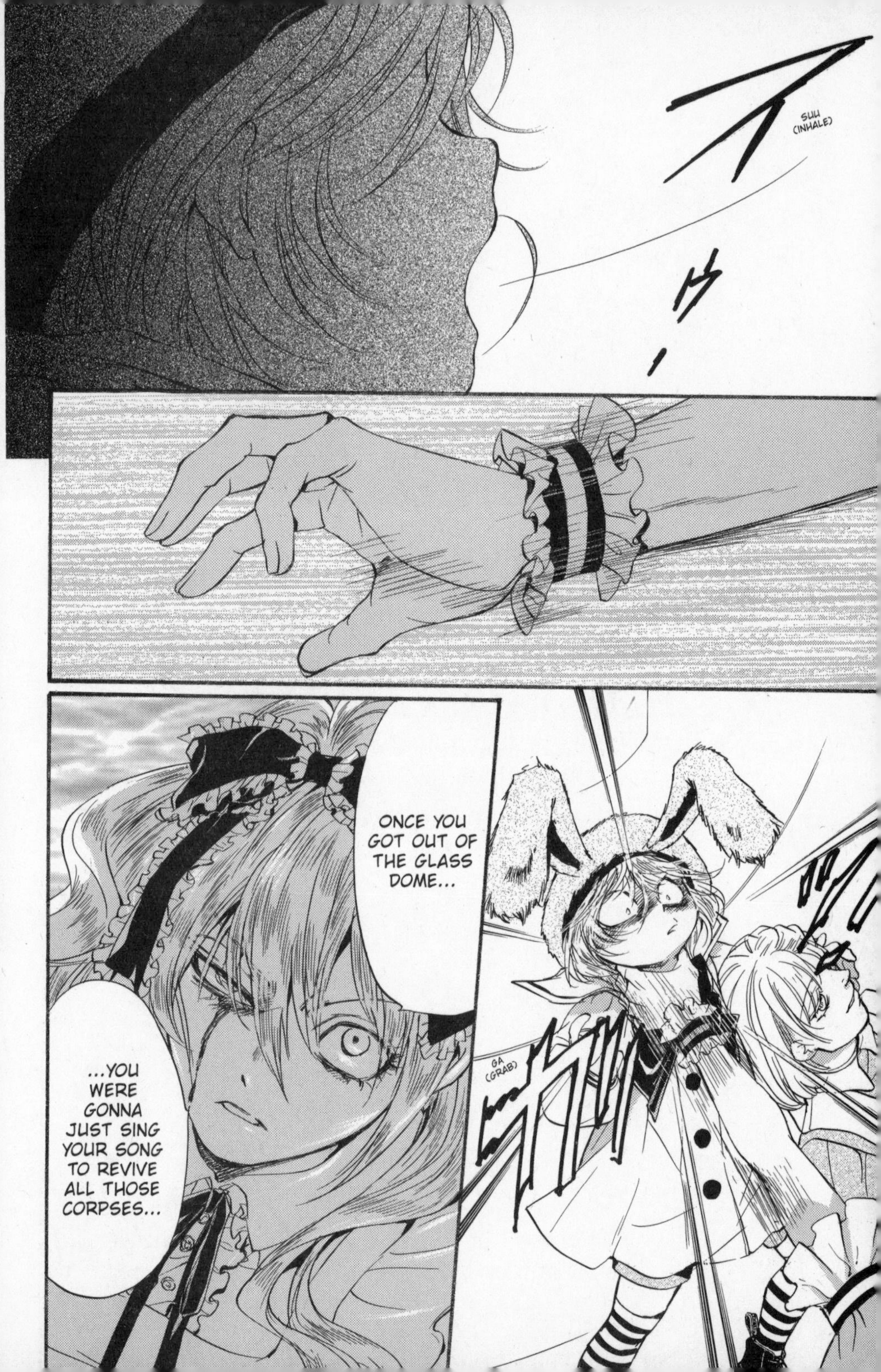
SUU (INHALE)
ONCE YOU GOT OUT OF THE GLASS DOME...
...YOU WERE GONNA JUST SING YOUR SONG TO REVIVE ALL THOSE CORPSES...
GA (GRAB)

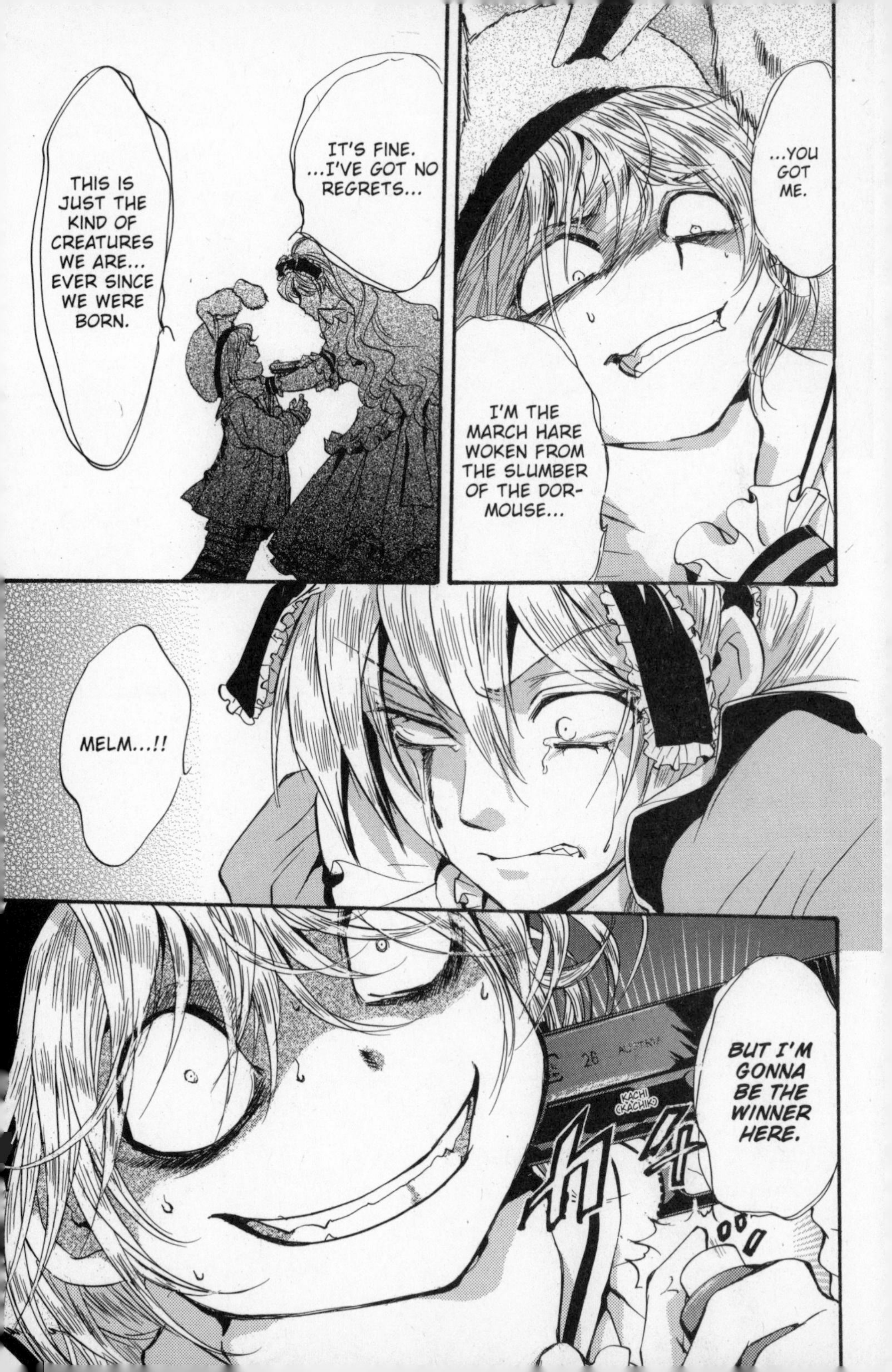
...YOU GOT ME.
I'M THE MARCH HARE WOKEN FROM THE SLUMBER OF THE DOR-MOUSE...
IT'S FINE. ...I'VE GOT NO REGRETS...
THIS IS JUST THE KIND OF CREATURES WE ARE... EVER SINCE WE WERE BORN.
MELM...!!
BUT I'M GONNA BE THE WINNER HERE.
KACHI (KACHIK)

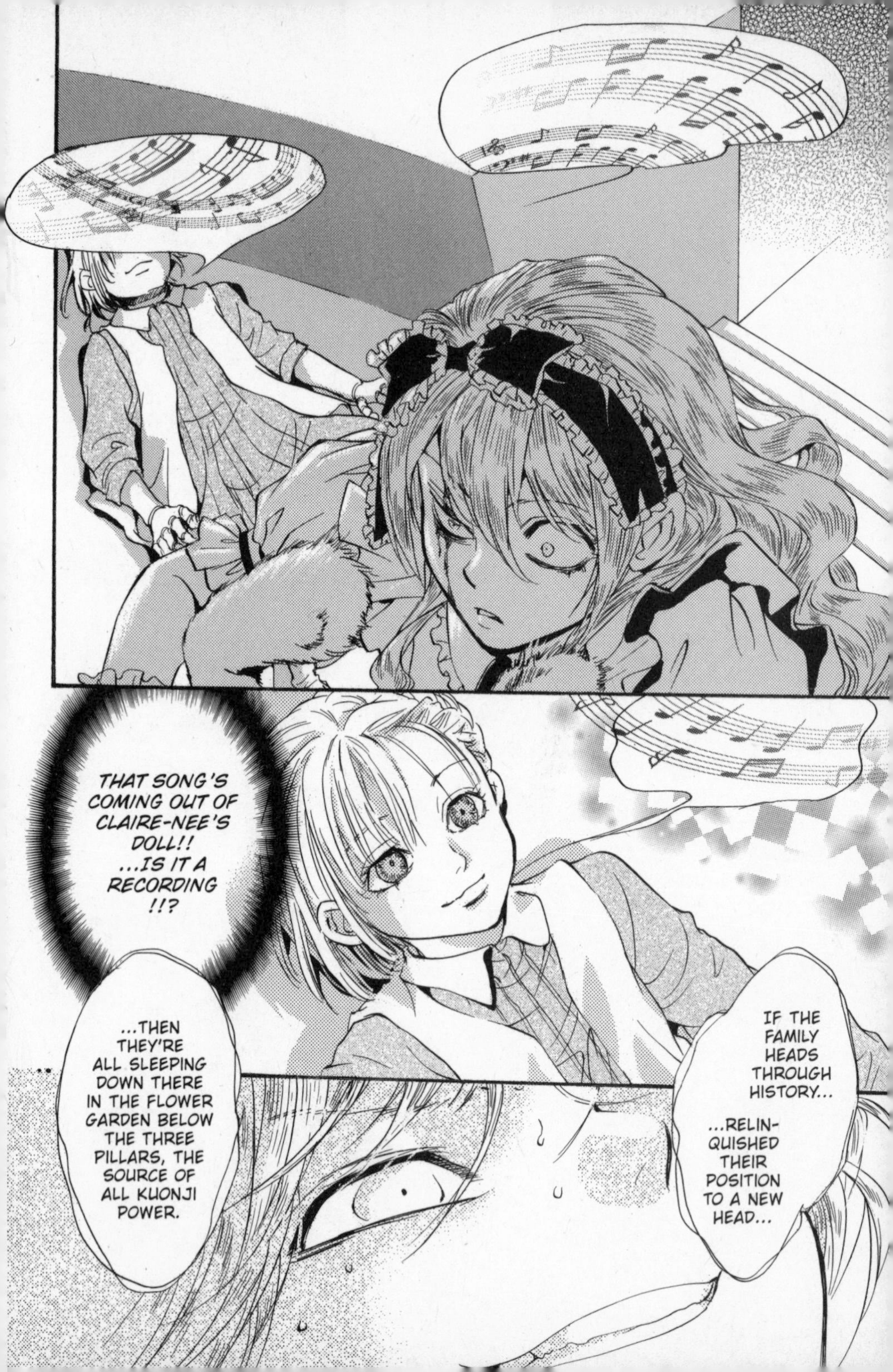
THAT SONG'S COMING OUT OF CLAIRE-NEE'S DOLL!! ...IS IT A RECORDING !!?
IF THE FAMILY HEADS THROUGH HISTORY...
...RELIN-QUISHED THEIR POSITION TO A NEW HEAD...
...THEN THEY'RE ALL SLEEPING DOWN THERE IN THE FLOWER GARDEN BELOW THE THREE PILLARS, THE SOURCE OF ALL KUONJI POWER.

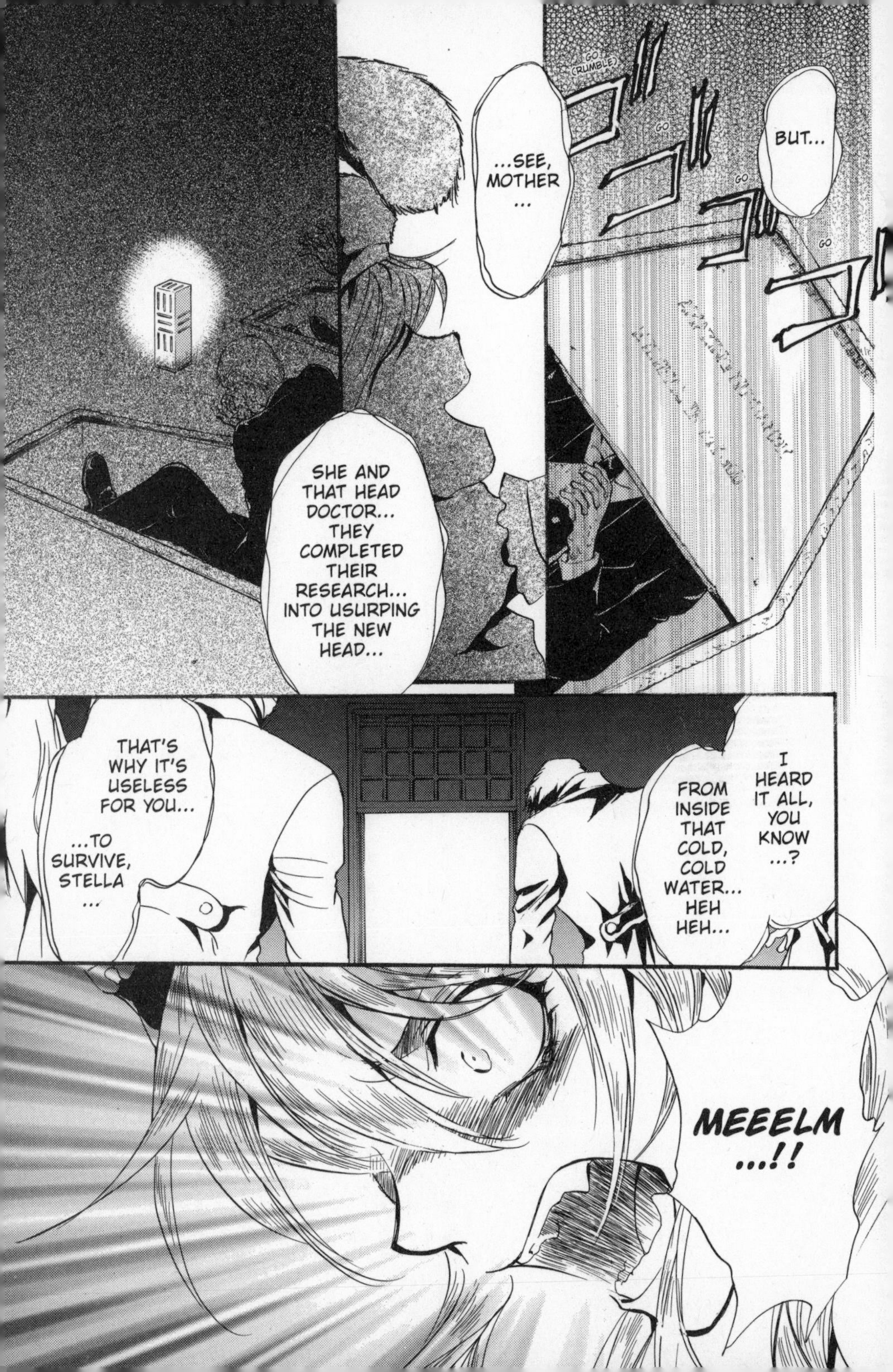
GO (RUMBLE)
GO
GO
GO
BUT...
...SEE, MOTHER ...
SHE AND THAT HEAD DOCTOR... THEY COMPLETED THEIR RESEARCH... INTO USURPING THE NEW HEAD...
I HEARD IT ALL, YOU KNOW ...?
FROM INSIDE THAT COLD, COLD WATER... HEH HEH...
THAT'S WHY IT'S USELESS FOR YOU...
...TO SURVIVE, STELLA ...
MEEELM ...!!

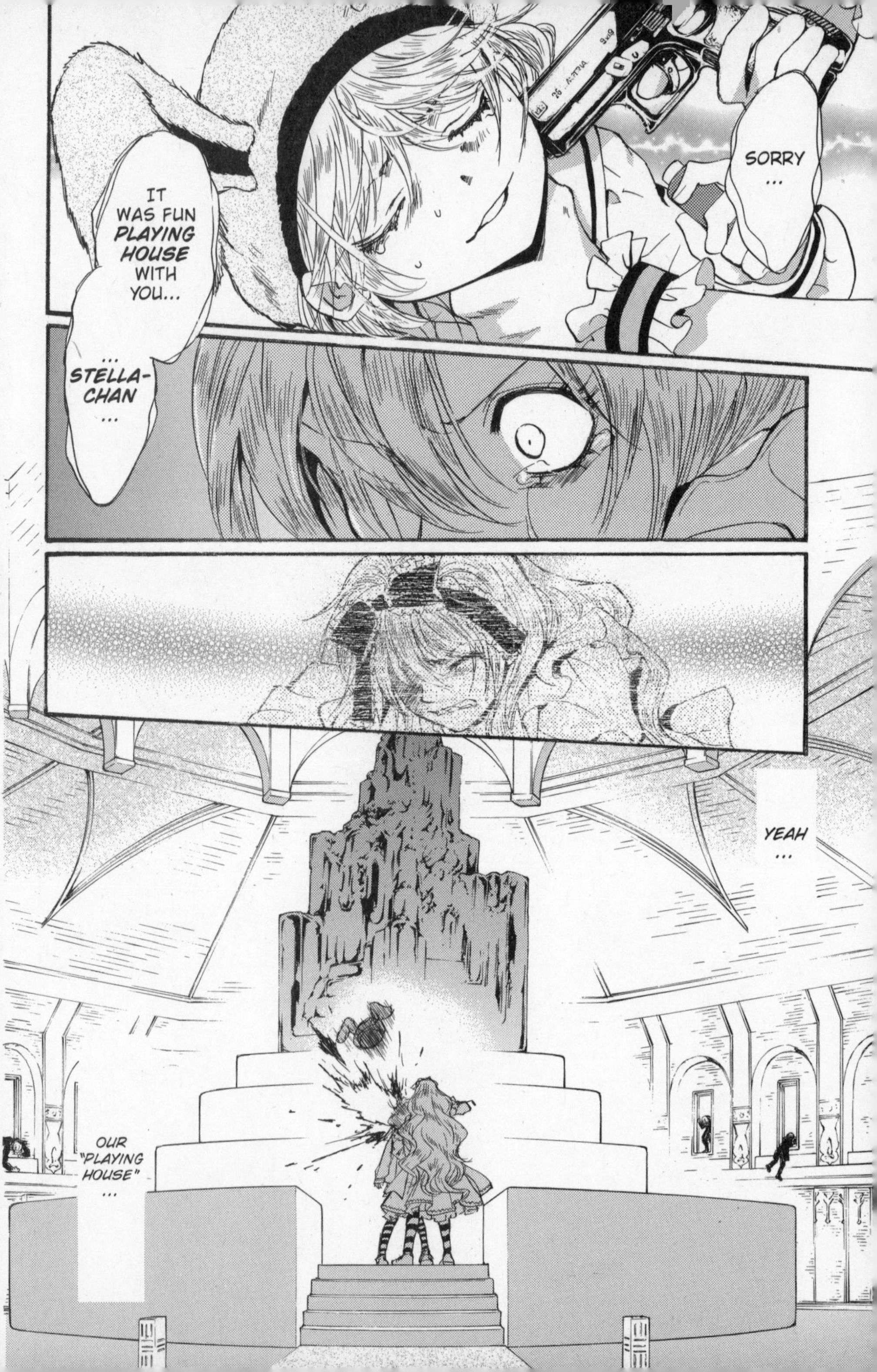
SORRY ...
IT WAS FUN PLAYING HOUSE WITH YOU...
... STELLA-CHAN ...
YEAH ...
OUR "PLAYING HOUSE" ...

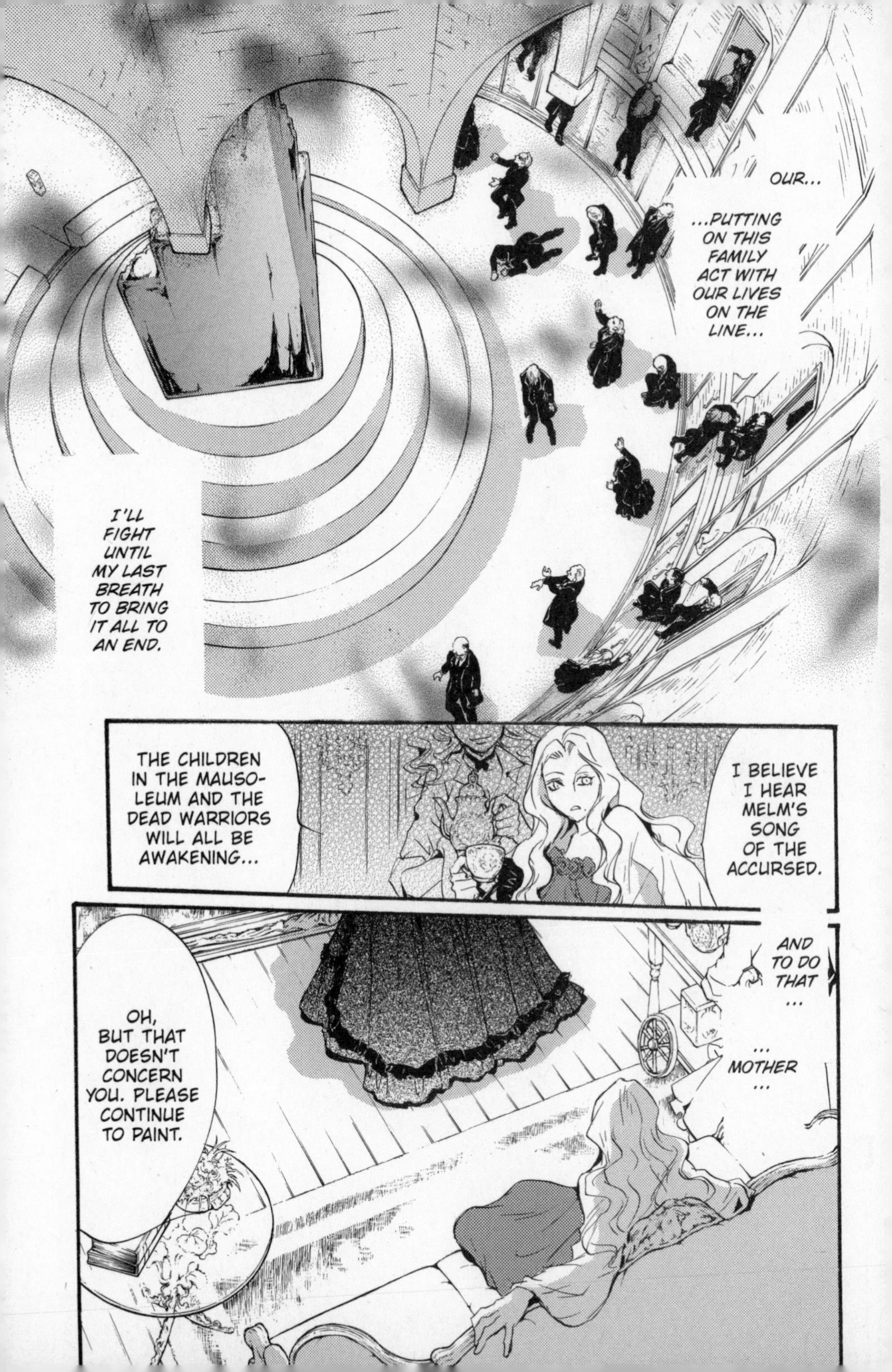
OUR...
...PUTTING ON THIS FAMILY ACT WITH OUR LIVES ON THE LINE...
I'LL FIGHT UNTIL MY LAST BREATH TO BRING IT ALL TO AN END.
I BELIEVE I HEAR MELM'S SONG OF THE ACCURSED.
THE CHILDREN IN THE MAUSO-LEUM AND THE DEAD WARRIORS WILL ALL BE AWAKENING...
AND TO DO THAT ...
... MOTHER ...
OH, BUT THAT DOESN'T CONCERN YOU. PLEASE CONTINUE TO PAINT.

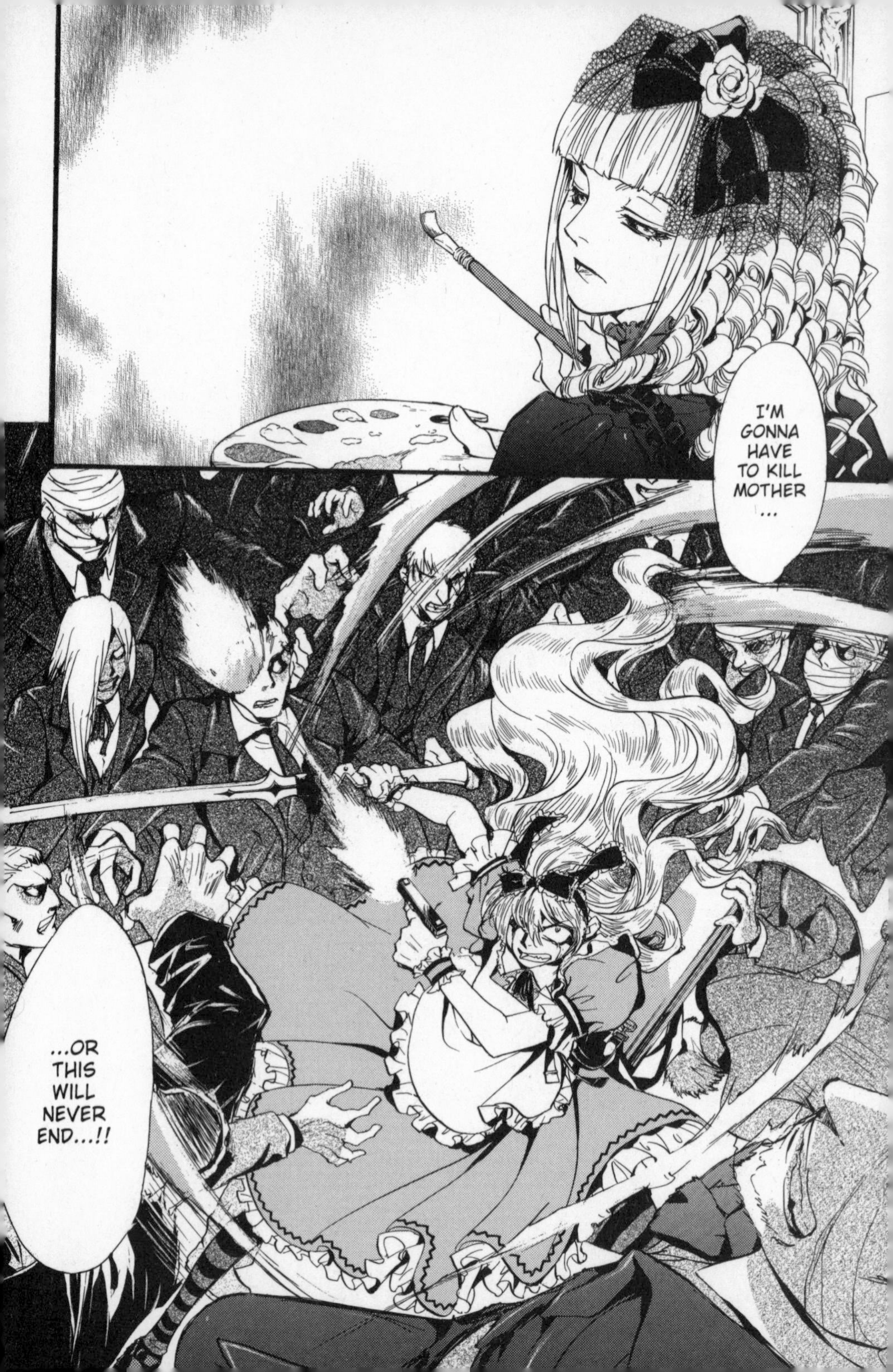
I'M GONNA HAVE TO KILL MOTHER ...
...OR THIS WILL NEVER END...!!

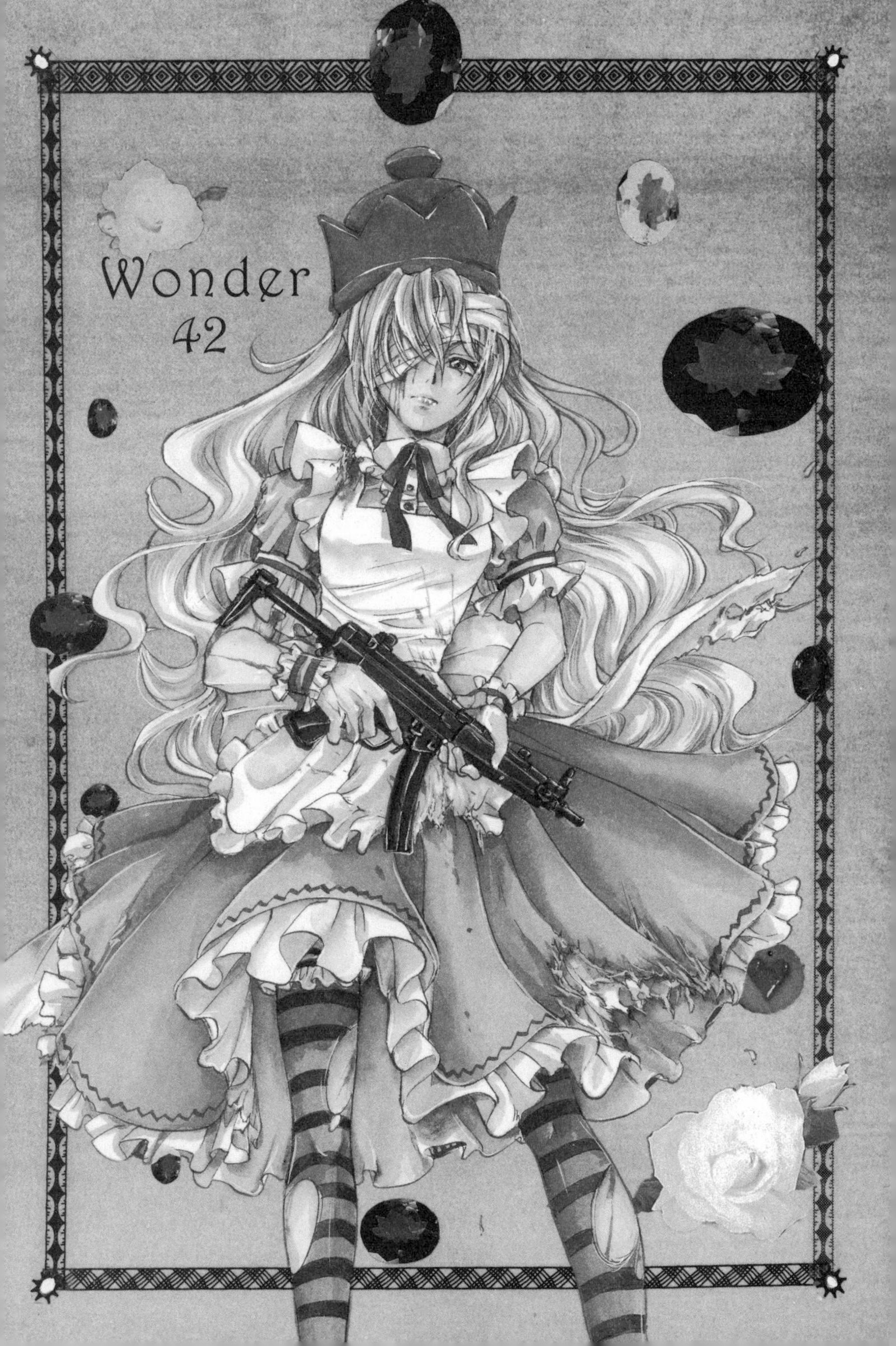
Wonder
42

Alice in MURDERLAND

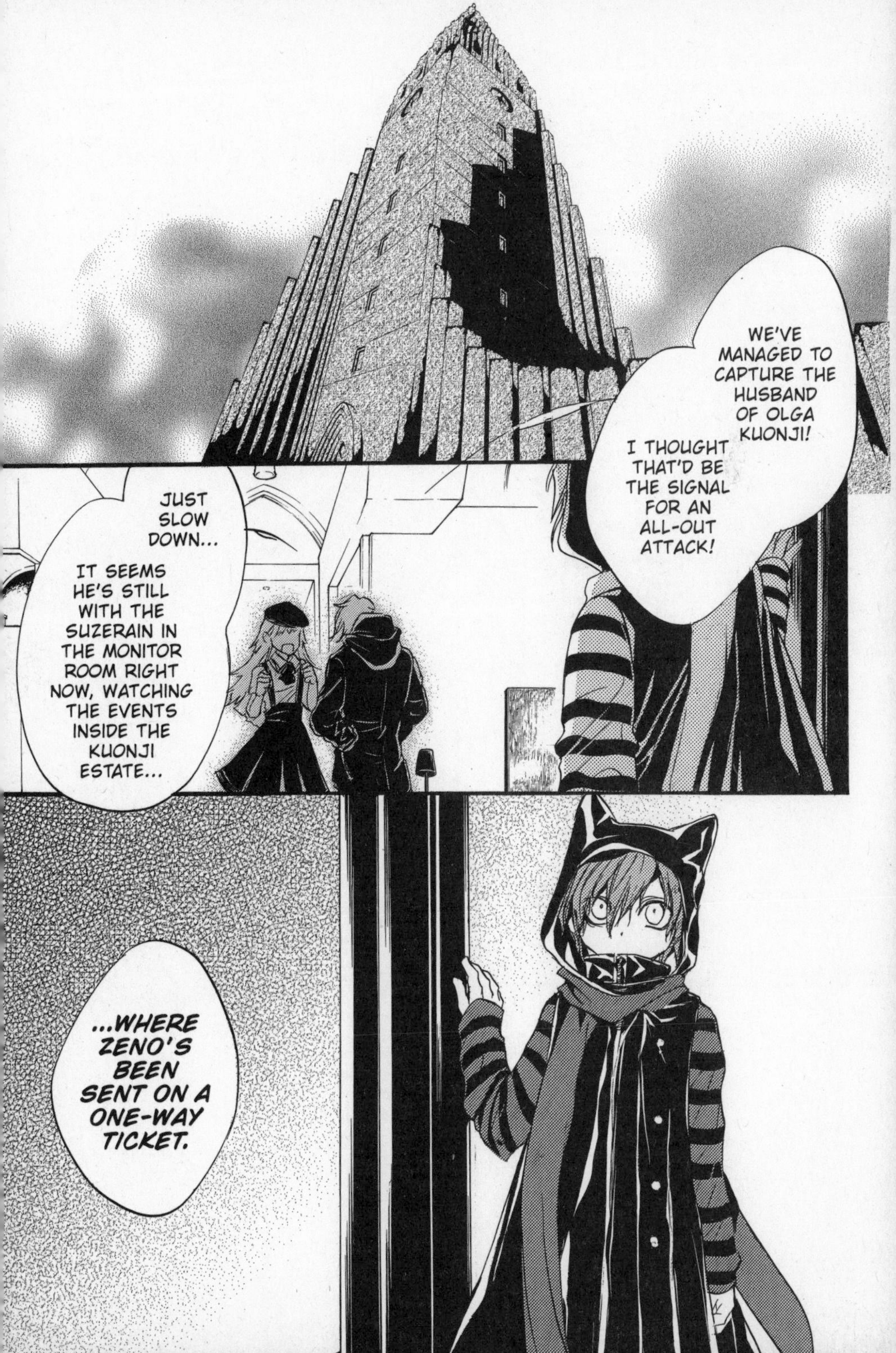
WE'VE MANAGED TO CAPTURE THE HUSBAND OF OLGA KUONJI!
I THOUGHT THAT'D BE THE SIGNAL FOR AN ALL-OUT ATTACK!
JUST SLOW DOWN...
IT SEEMS HE'S STILL WITH THE SUZERAIN IN THE MONITOR ROOM RIGHT NOW, WATCHING THE EVENTS INSIDE THE KUONJI ESTATE...
...WHERE ZENO'S BEEN SENT ON A ONE-WAY TICKET.

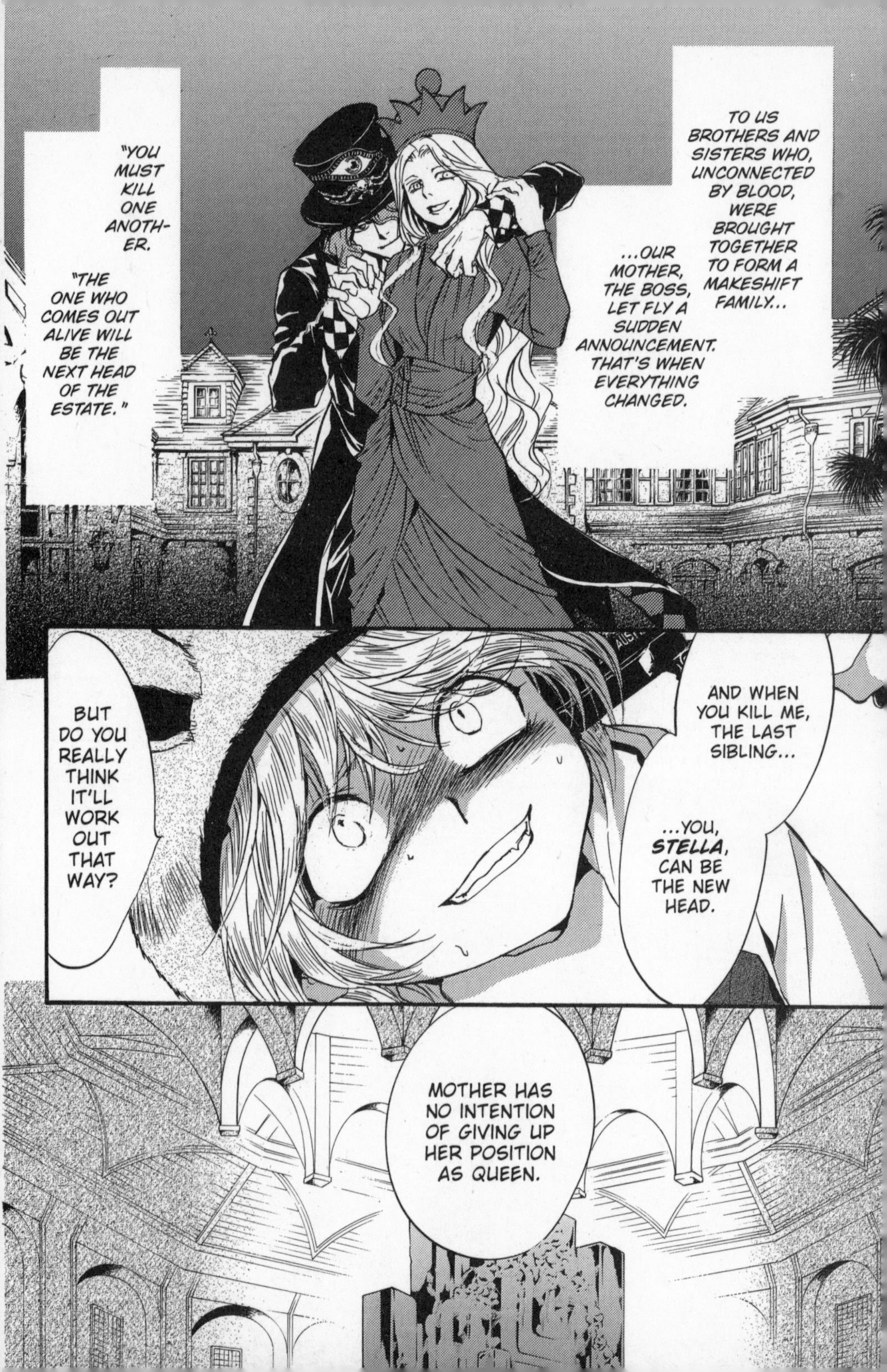
TO US BROTHERS AND SISTERS WHO, UNCONNECTED BY BLOOD, WERE BROUGHT TOGETHER TO FORM A MAKESHIFT FAMILY...
...OUR MOTHER, THE BOSS, LET FLY A SUDDEN ANNOUNCEMENT. THAT'S WHEN EVERYTHING CHANGED.
"YOU MUST KILL ONE ANOTHER.
"THE ONE WHO COMES OUT ALIVE WILL BE THE NEXT HEAD OF THE ESTATE."
AND WHEN YOU KILL ME, THE LAST SIBLING...
...YOU, **STELLA**, CAN BE THE NEW HEAD.
BUT DO YOU REALLY THINK IT'LL WORK OUT THAT WAY?
MOTHER HAS NO INTENTION OF GIVING UP HER POSITION AS QUEEN.

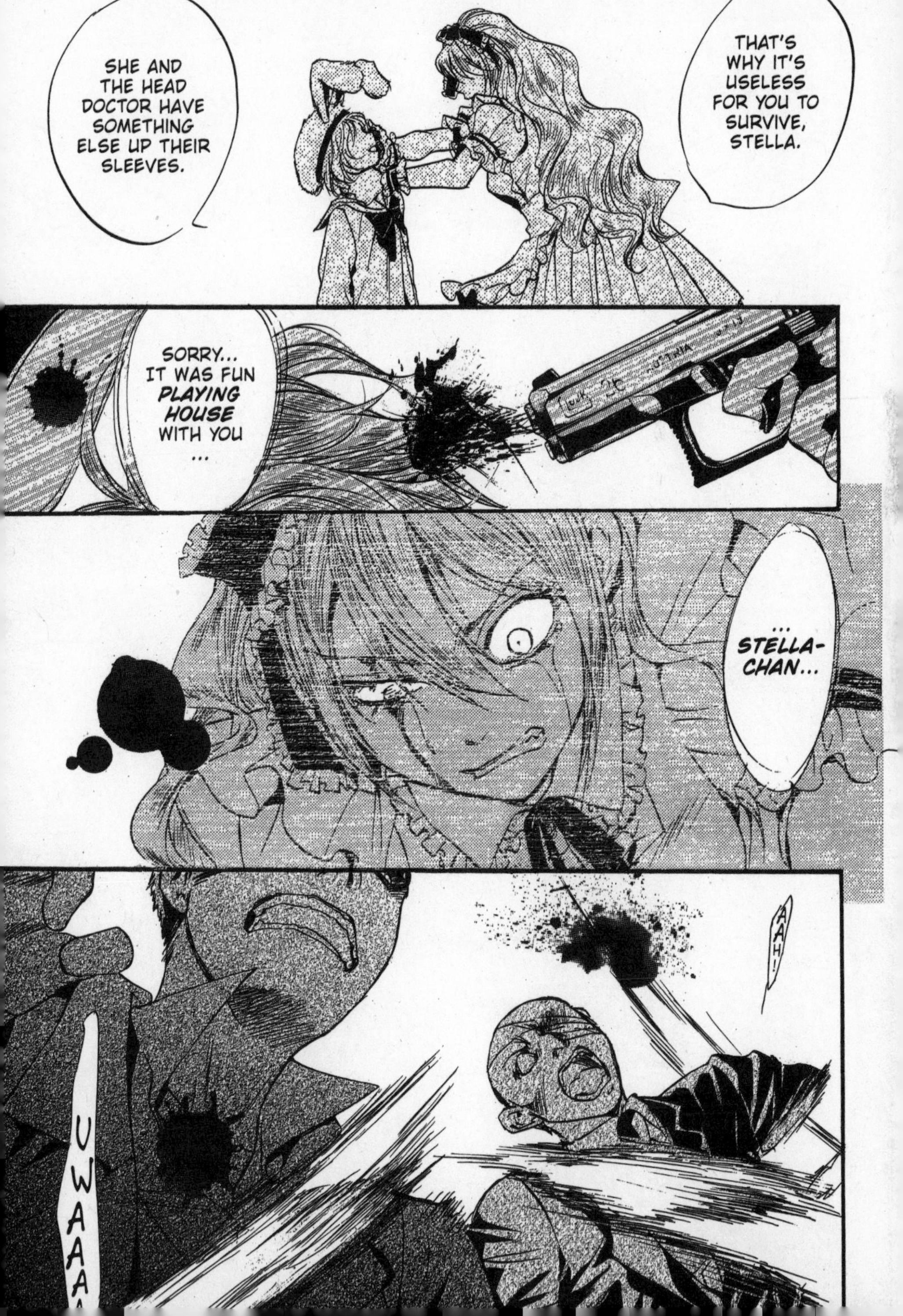
THAT'S WHY IT'S USELESS FOR YOU TO SURVIVE, STELLA.
SHE AND THE HEAD DOCTOR HAVE SOMETHING ELSE UP THEIR SLEEVES.
SORRY... IT WAS FUN *PLAYING HOUSE* WITH YOU ...
... *STELLA-CHAN...*
AAH!
UWAAAA

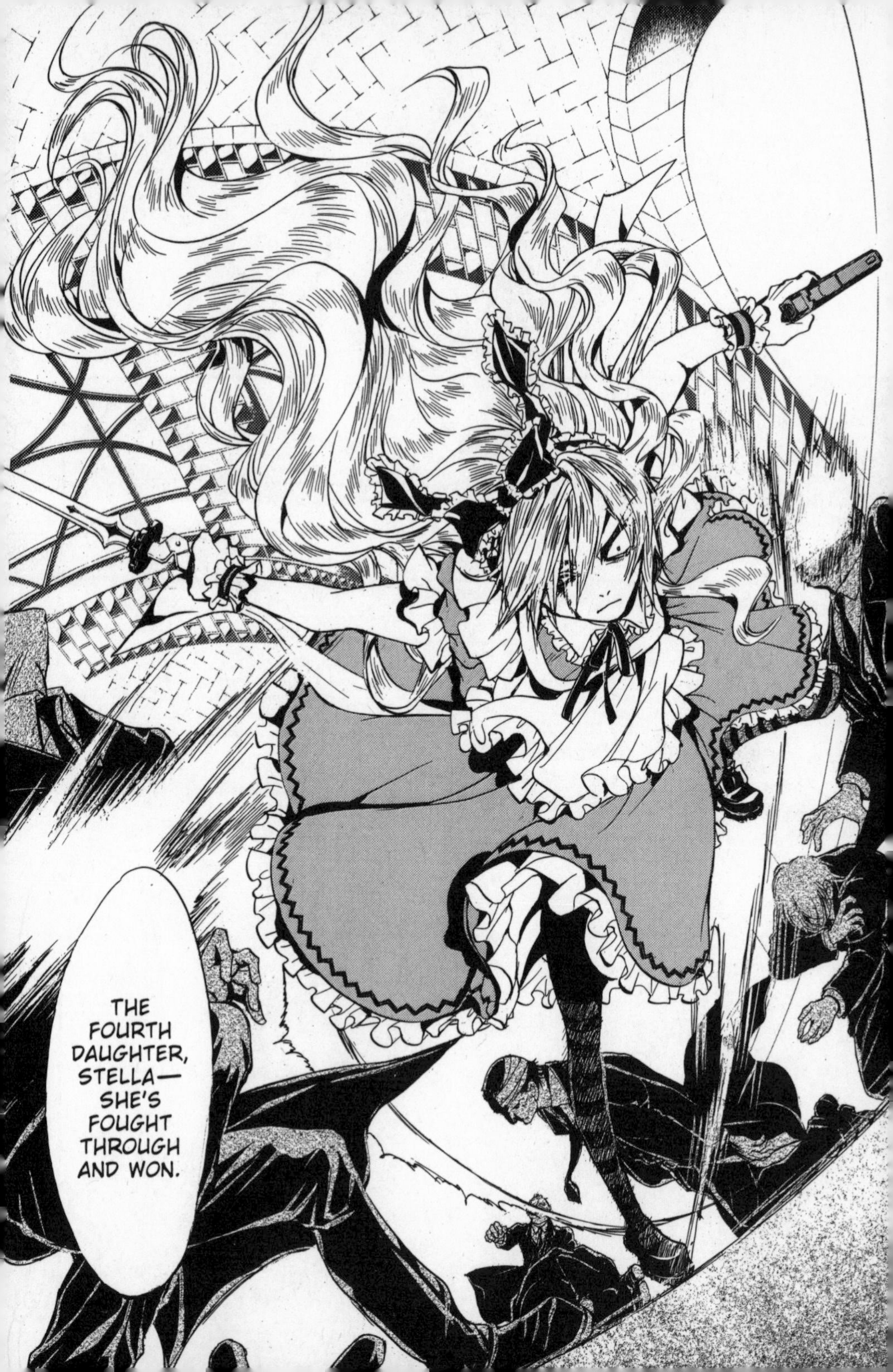
THE FOURTH DAUGHTER, STELLA— SHE'S FOUGHT THROUGH AND WON.

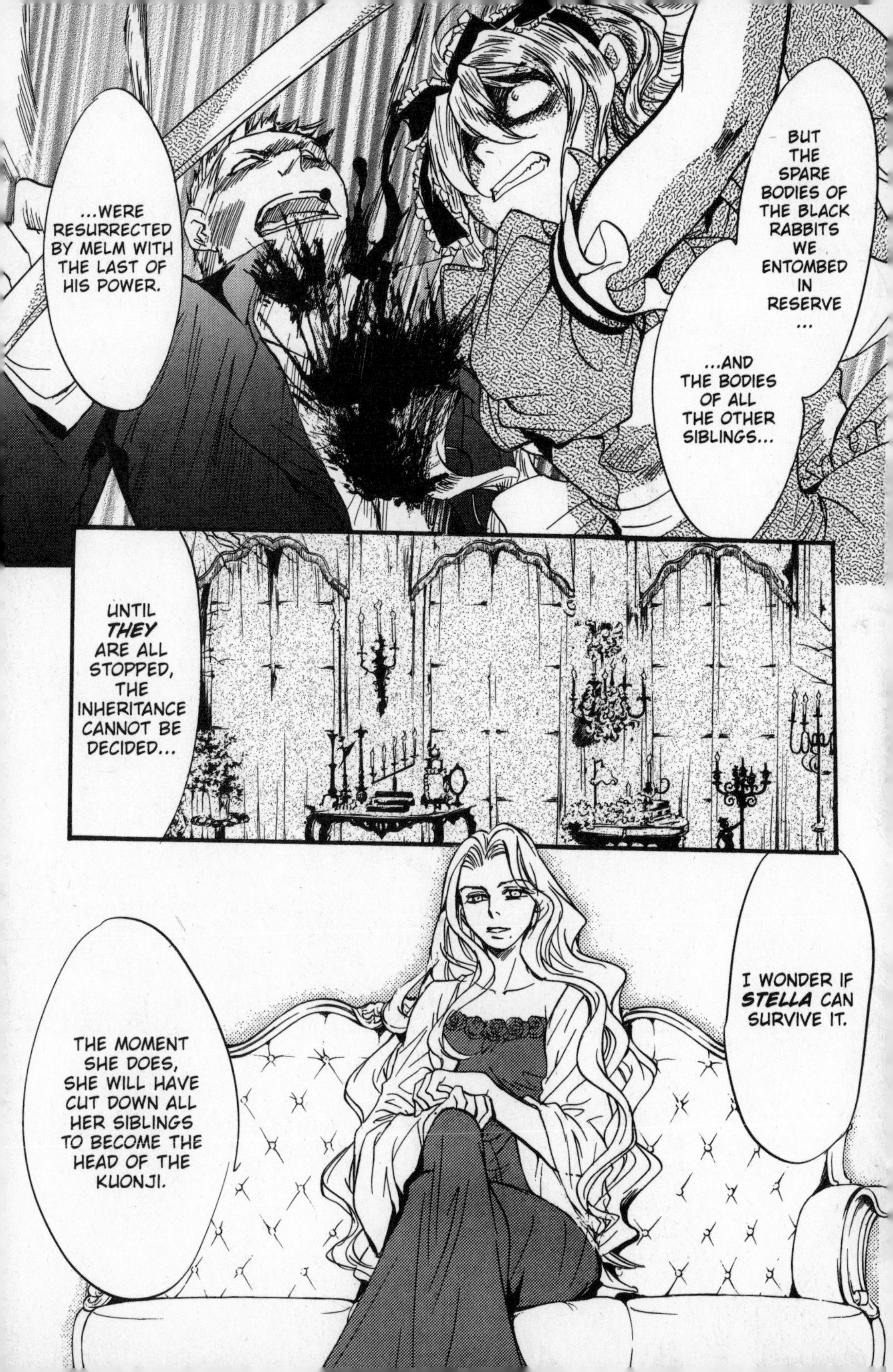
BUT THE SPARE BODIES OF THE BLACK RABBITS WE ENTOMBED IN RESERVE...
...AND THE BODIES OF ALL THE OTHER SIBLINGS...
...WERE RESURRECTED BY MELM WITH THE LAST OF HIS POWER.
UNTIL *THEY* ARE ALL STOPPED, THE INHERITANCE CANNOT BE DECIDED...
I WONDER IF *STELLA* CAN SURVIVE IT.
THE MOMENT SHE DOES, SHE WILL HAVE CUT DOWN ALL HER SIBLINGS TO BECOME THE HEAD OF THE KUONJI.

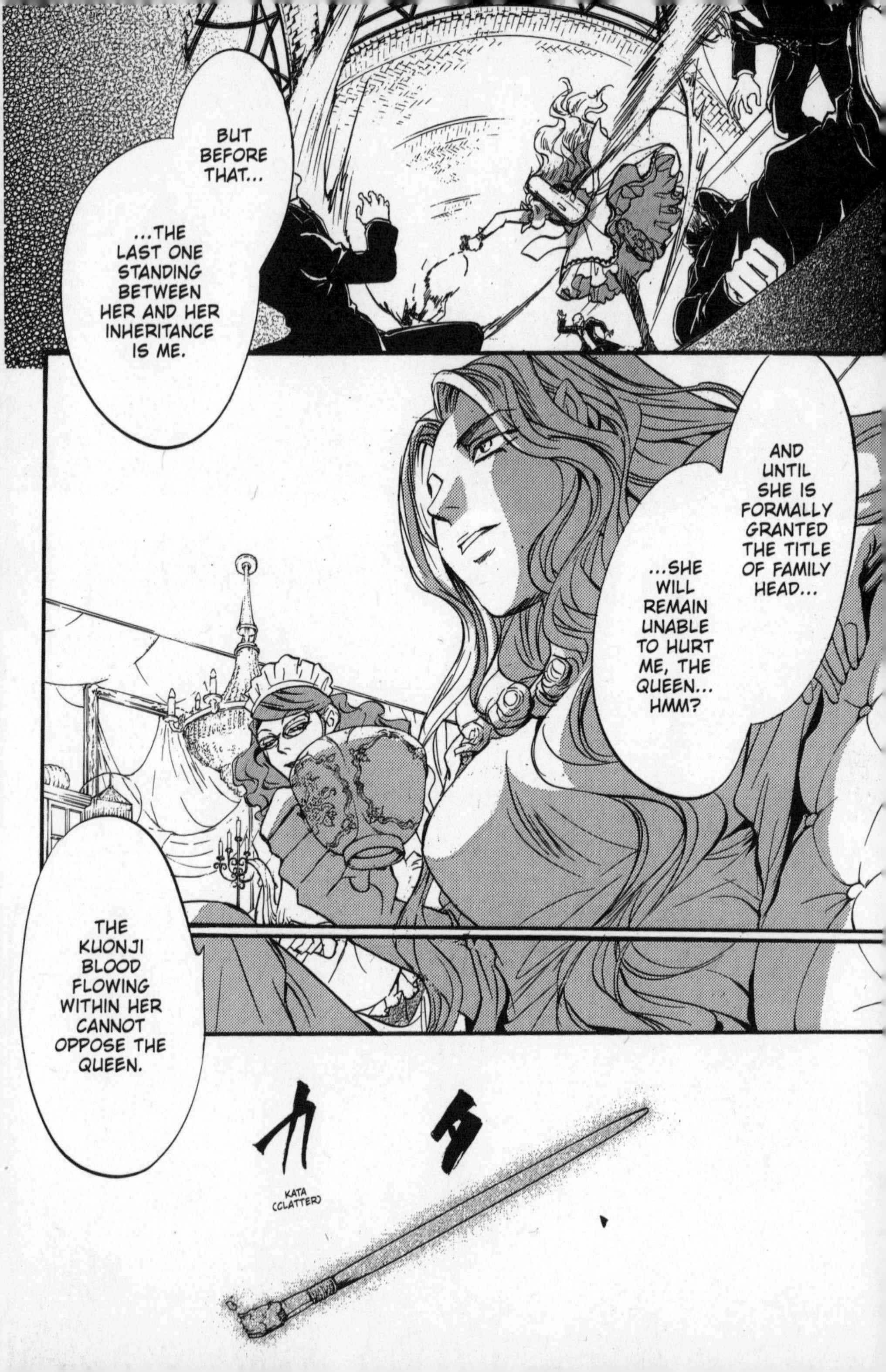
BUT BEFORE THAT...
...THE LAST ONE STANDING BETWEEN HER AND HER INHERITANCE IS ME.
AND UNTIL SHE IS FORMALLY GRANTED THE TITLE OF FAMILY HEAD...
...SHE WILL REMAIN UNABLE TO HURT ME, THE QUEEN... HMM?
THE KUONJI BLOOD FLOWING WITHIN HER CANNOT OPPOSE THE QUEEN.
カタ
KATA (CLATTER)

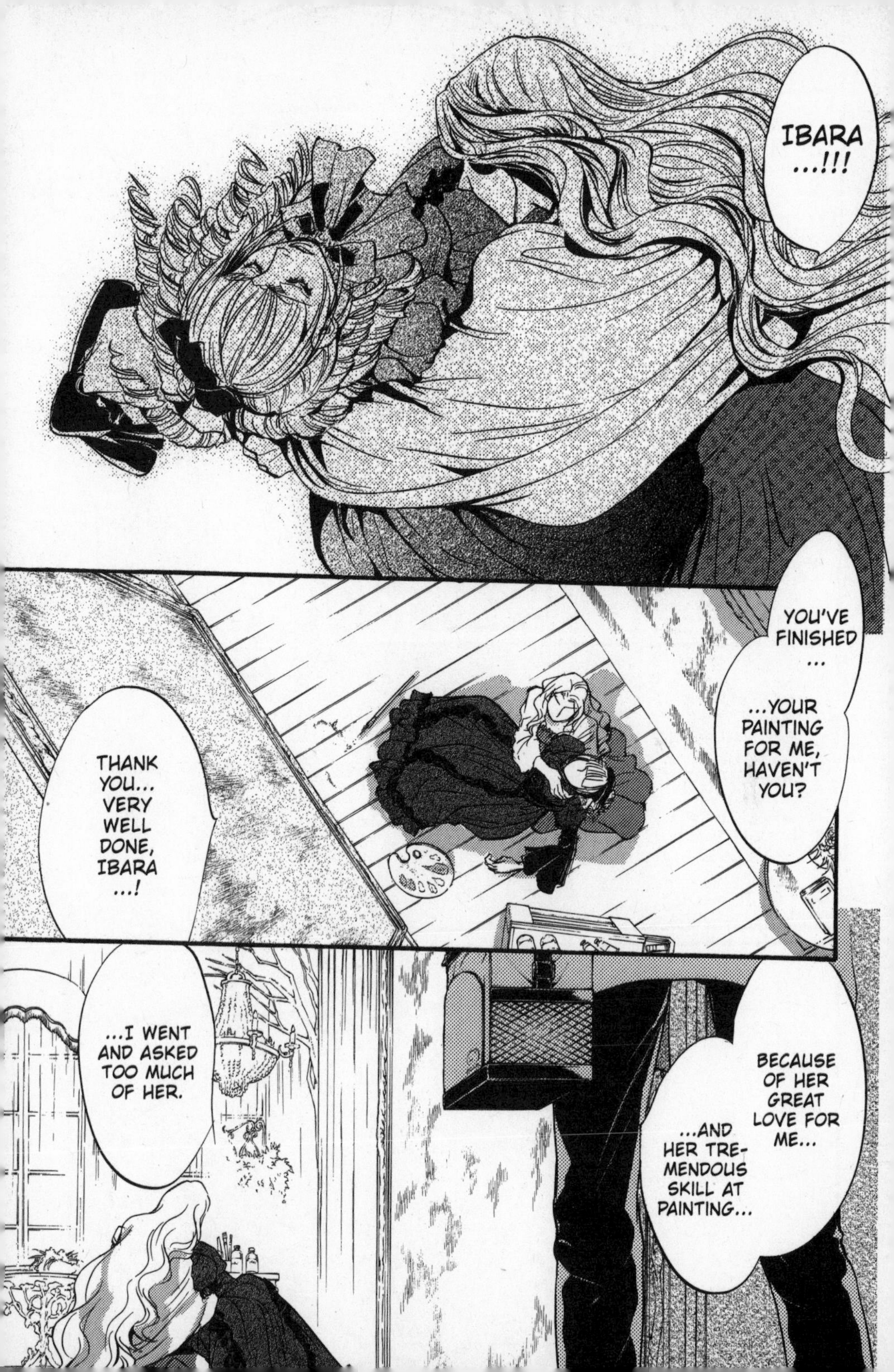
IBARA ...!!!
YOU'VE FINISHED ...
...YOUR PAINTING FOR ME, HAVEN'T YOU?
THANK YOU... VERY WELL DONE, IBARA ...!
BECAUSE OF HER GREAT LOVE FOR ME...
...AND HER TRE-MENDOUS SKILL AT PAINTING...
...I WENT AND ASKED TOO MUCH OF HER.

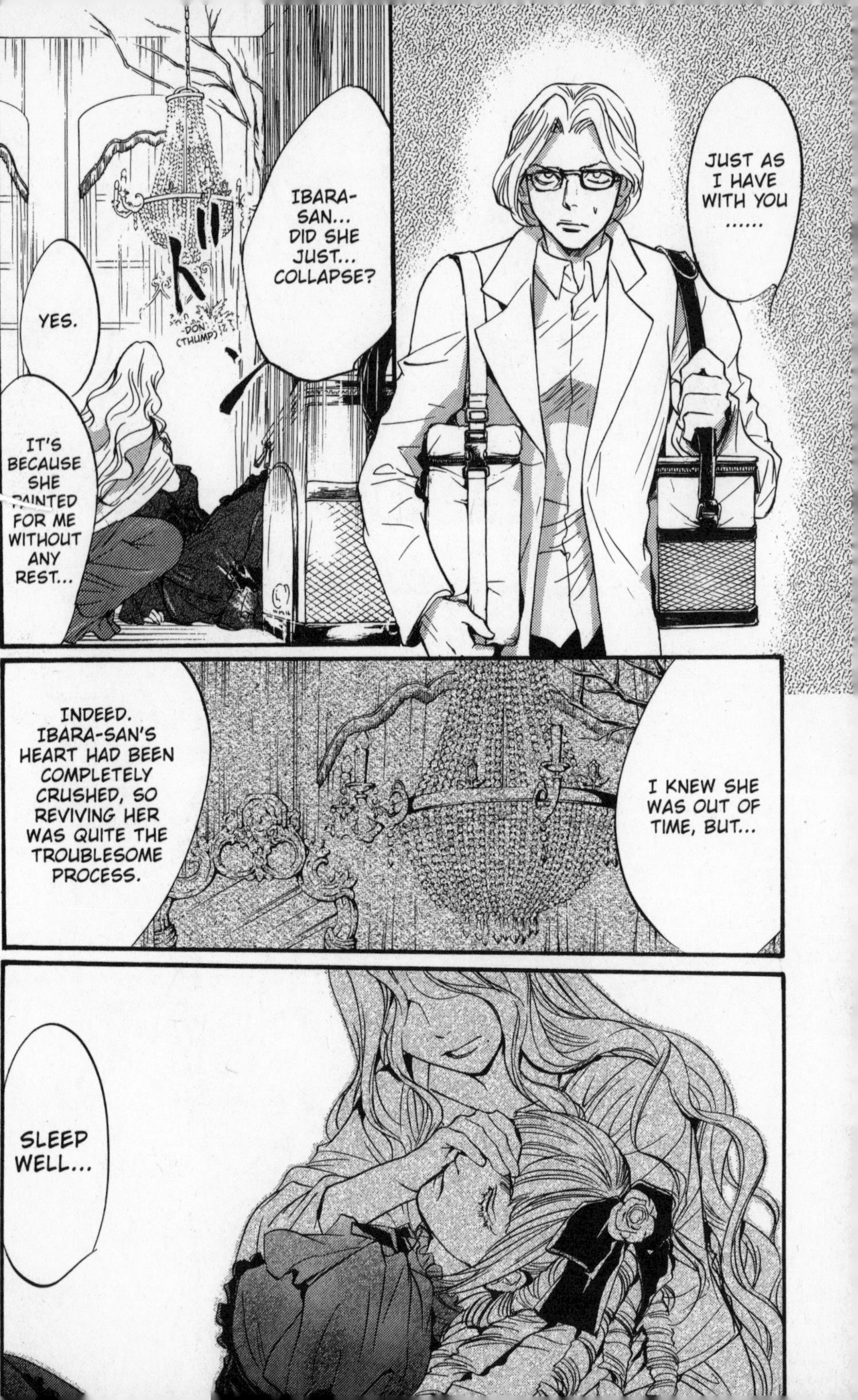
JUST AS I HAVE WITH YOU ......
IBARA-SAN... DID SHE JUST... COLLAPSE?
-DON (THUMP)
YES.
IT'S BECAUSE SHE PAINTED FOR ME WITHOUT ANY REST...
I KNEW SHE WAS OUT OF TIME, BUT...
INDEED. IBARA-SAN'S HEART HAD BEEN COMPLETELY CRUSHED, SO REVIVING HER WAS QUITE THE TROUBLESOME PROCESS.
SLEEP WELL...

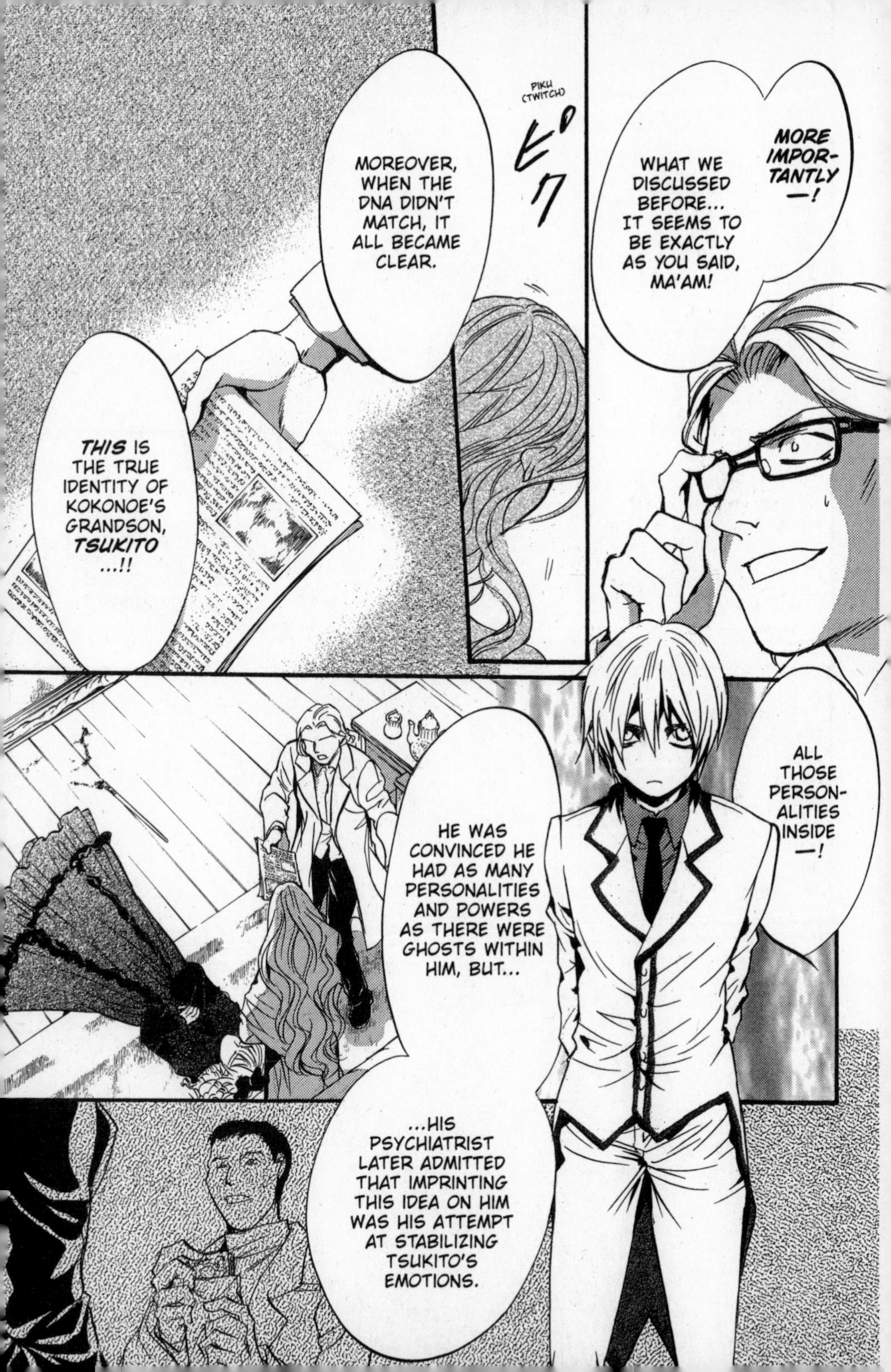
MORE IMPORTANTLY—!
WHAT WE DISCUSSED BEFORE... IT SEEMS TO BE EXACTLY AS YOU SAID, MA'AM!
ピク
PIKU (TWITCH)
MOREOVER, WHEN THE DNA DIDN'T MATCH, IT ALL BECAME CLEAR.
THIS IS THE TRUE IDENTITY OF KOKONOE'S GRANDSON, *TSUKITO*...!!
ALL THOSE PERSONALITIES INSIDE—!
HE WAS CONVINCED HE HAD AS MANY PERSONALITIES AND POWERS AS THERE WERE GHOSTS WITHIN HIM, BUT...
...HIS PSYCHIATRIST LATER ADMITTED THAT IMPRINTING THIS IDEA ON HIM WAS HIS ATTEMPT AT STABILIZING TSUKITO'S EMOTIONS.

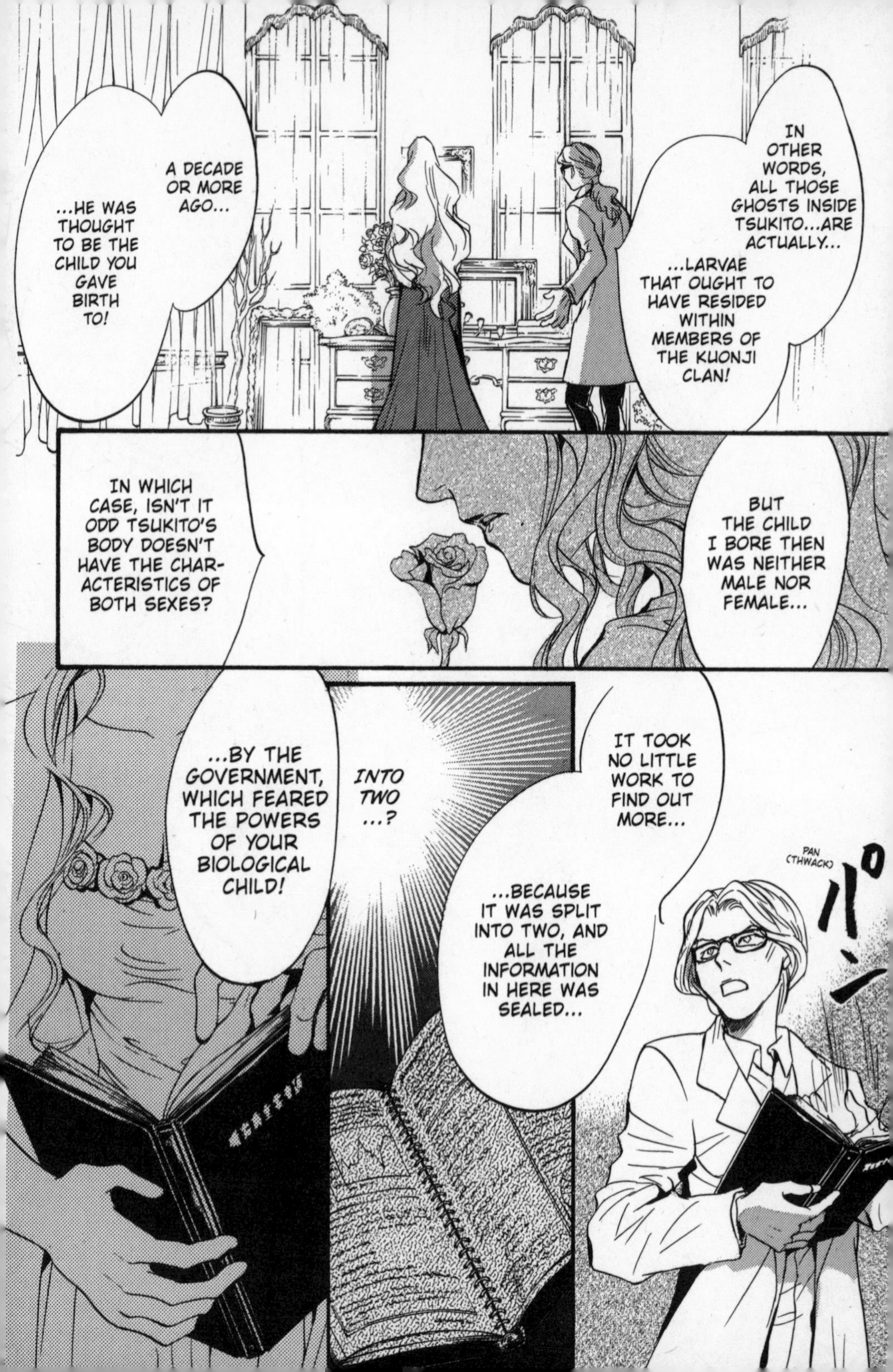
IN OTHER WORDS, ALL THOSE GHOSTS INSIDE TSUKITO...ARE ACTUALLY...
...LARVAE THAT OUGHT TO HAVE RESIDED WITHIN MEMBERS OF THE KUONJI CLAN!
A DECADE OR MORE AGO...
...HE WAS THOUGHT TO BE THE CHILD YOU GAVE BIRTH TO!
BUT THE CHILD I BORE THEN WAS NEITHER MALE NOR FEMALE...
IN WHICH CASE, ISN'T IT ODD TSUKITO'S BODY DOESN'T HAVE THE CHAR-ACTERISTICS OF BOTH SEXES?
IT TOOK NO LITTLE WORK TO FIND OUT MORE...
PAN (THWACK)
パン
...BECAUSE IT WAS SPLIT INTO TWO, AND ALL THE INFORMATION IN HERE WAS SEALED...
INTO TWO ...?
...BY THE GOVERNMENT, WHICH FEARED THE POWERS OF YOUR BIOLOGICAL CHILD!

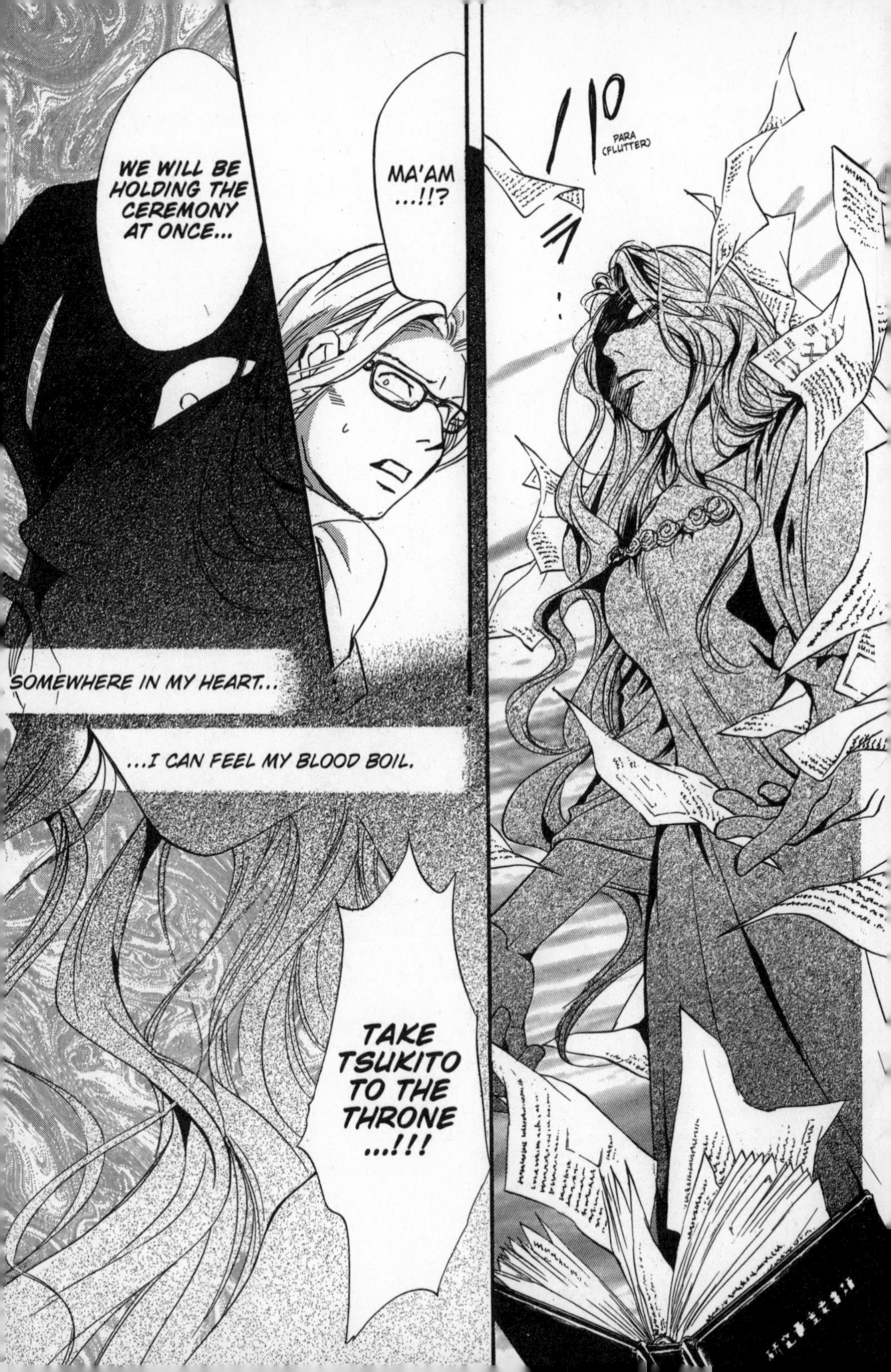
PARA (FLUTTER)
MA'AM ...!!?
WE WILL BE HOLDING THE CEREMONY AT ONCE...
SOMEWHERE IN MY HEART...
...I CAN FEEL MY BLOOD BOIL.
TAKE TSUKITO TO THE THRONE ...!!!

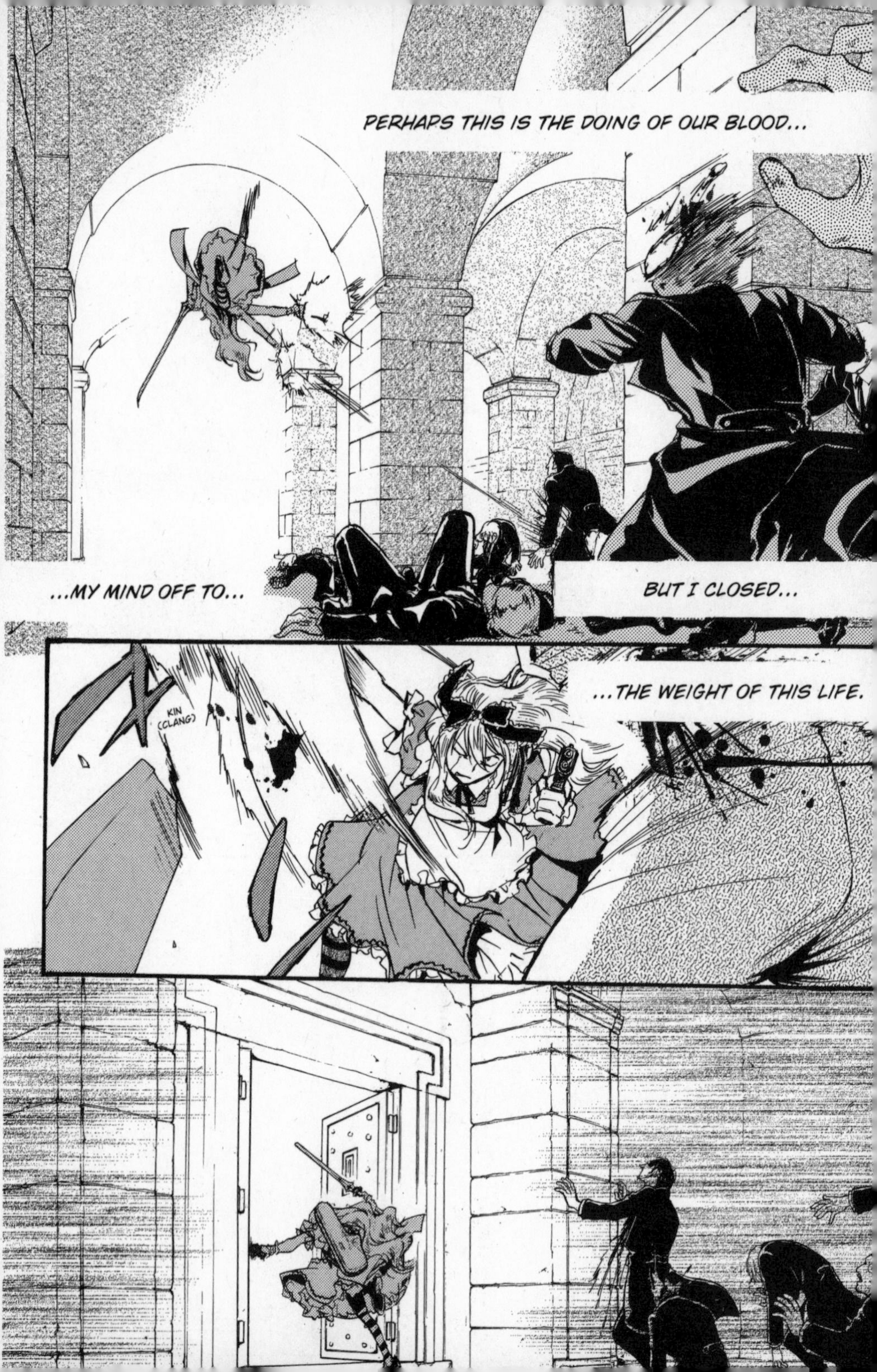
PERHAPS THIS IS THE DOING OF OUR BLOOD...
BUT I CLOSED...
...MY MIND OFF TO...
...THE WEIGHT OF THIS LIFE.
KIN (CLANG)

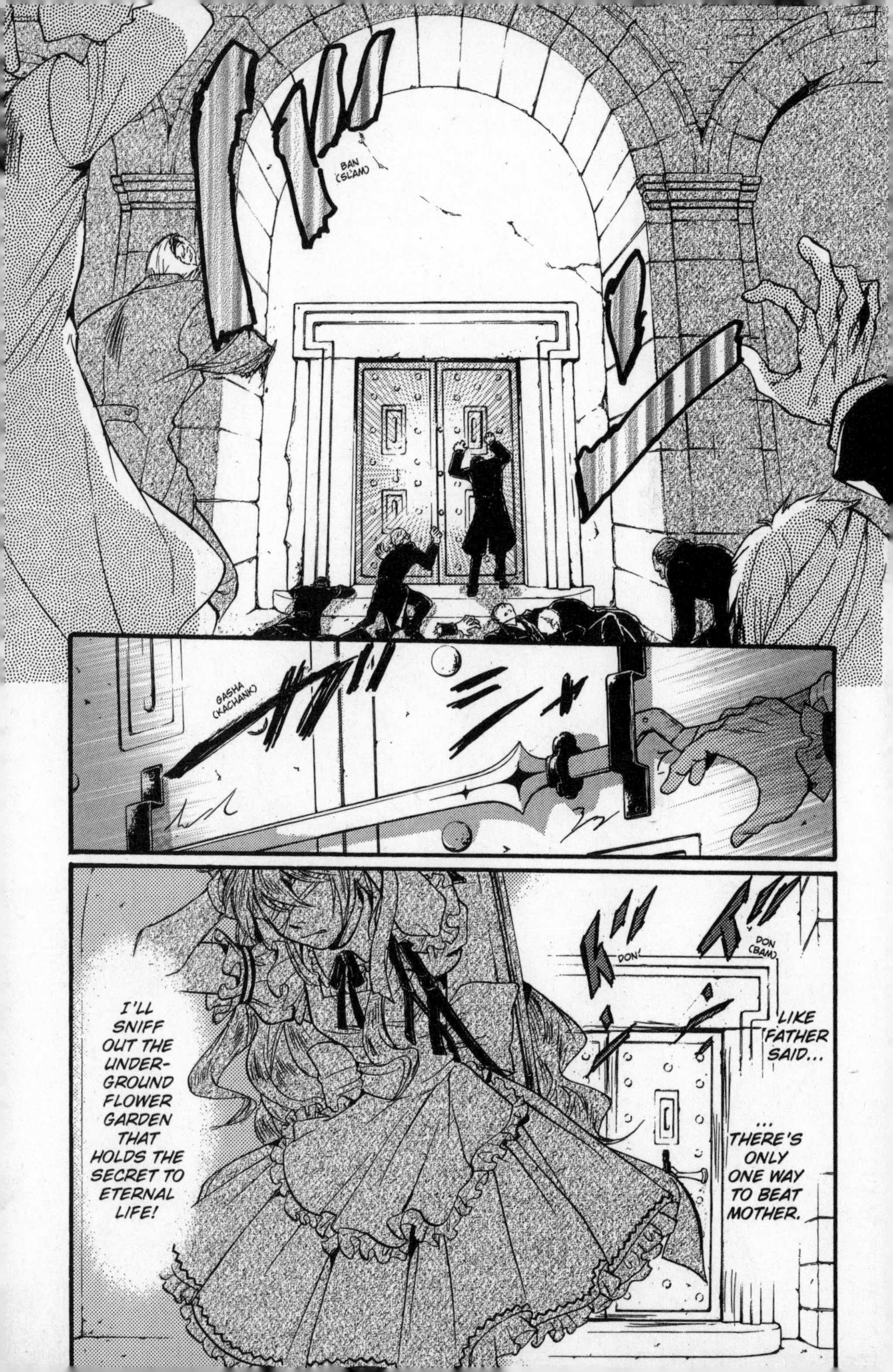
BAN (SLAM)
GASHA (KACHANK)
DON (BAM)
DON
LIKE FATHER SAID...
...THERE'S ONLY ONE WAY TO BEAT MOTHER.
I'LL SNIFF OUT THE UNDER-GROUND FLOWER GARDEN THAT HOLDS THE SECRET TO ETERNAL LIFE!

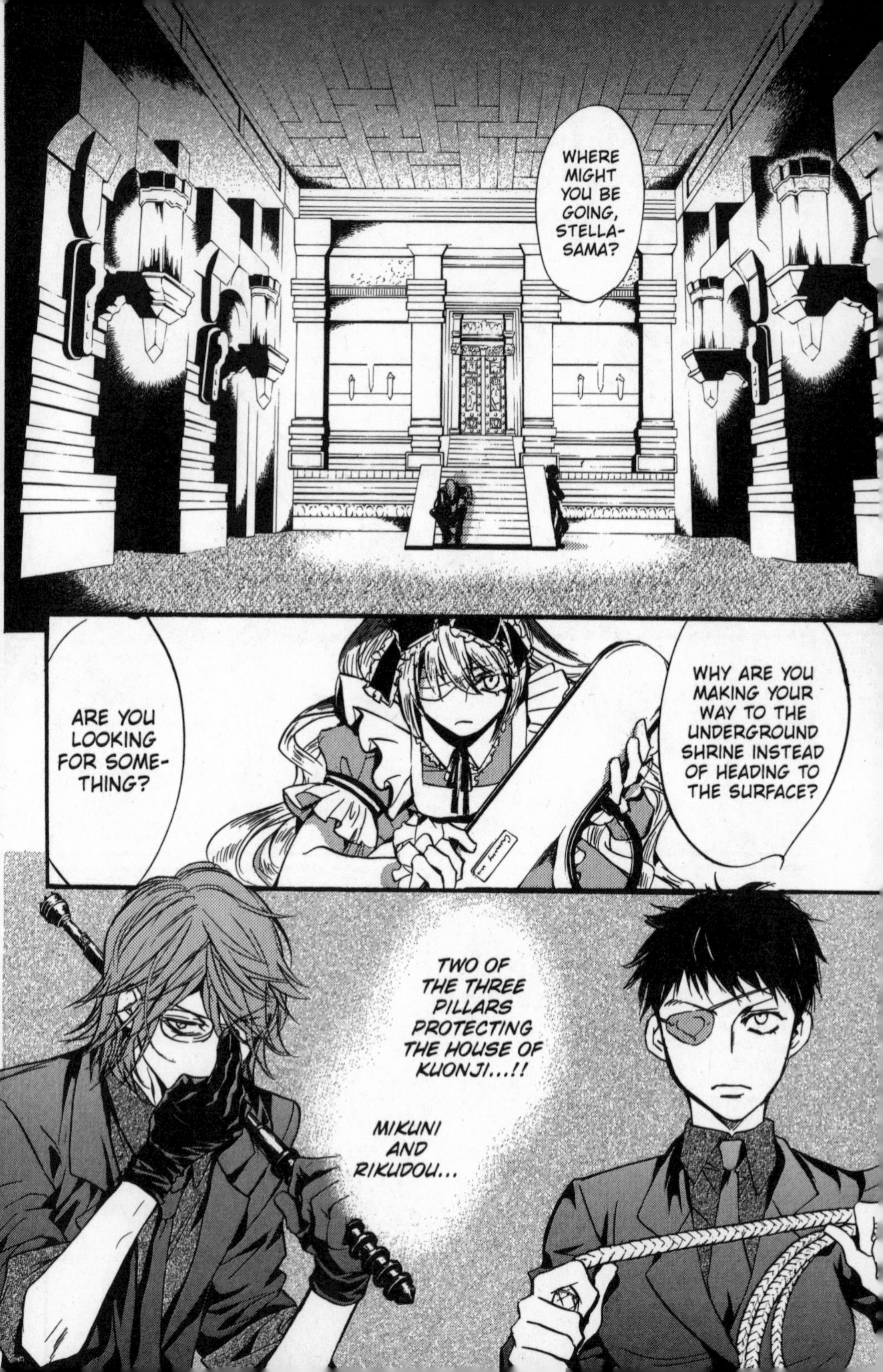
WHERE MIGHT YOU BE GOING, STELLA-SAMA?
WHY ARE YOU MAKING YOUR WAY TO THE UNDERGROUND SHRINE INSTEAD OF HEADING TO THE SURFACE?
ARE YOU LOOKING FOR SOME-THING?
TWO OF THE THREE PILLARS PROTECTING THE HOUSE OF KUONJI...!!
MIKUNI AND RIKUDOU...

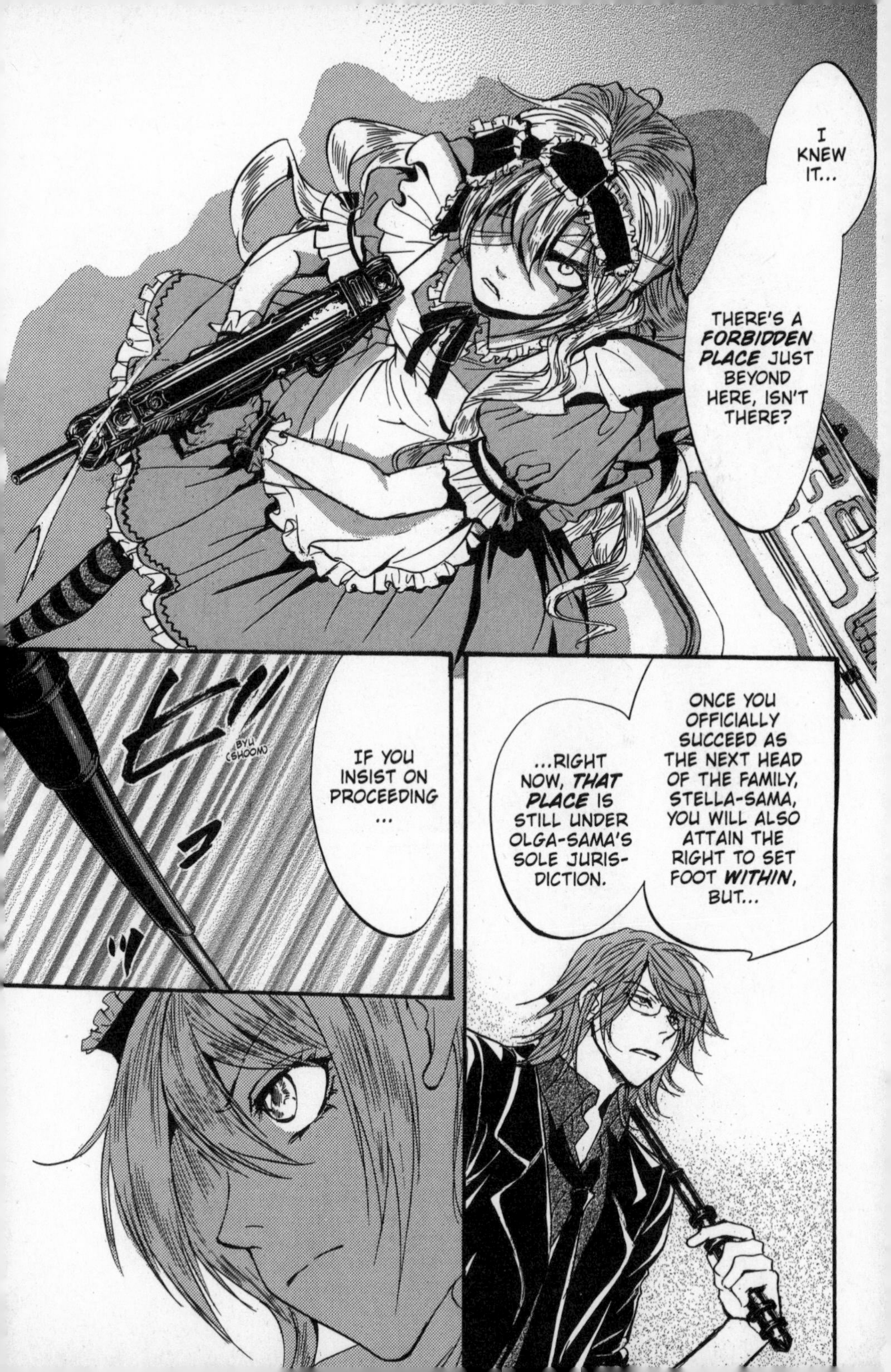
I KNEW IT...
THERE'S A *FORBIDDEN PLACE* JUST BEYOND HERE, ISN'T THERE?
ONCE YOU OFFICIALLY SUCCEED AS THE NEXT HEAD OF THE FAMILY, STELLA-SAMA, YOU WILL ALSO ATTAIN THE RIGHT TO SET FOOT *WITHIN*, BUT...
...RIGHT NOW, *THAT PLACE* IS STILL UNDER OLGA-SAMA'S SOLE JURIS-DICTION.
IF YOU INSIST ON PROCEEDING ...
BYU (SHOOM)

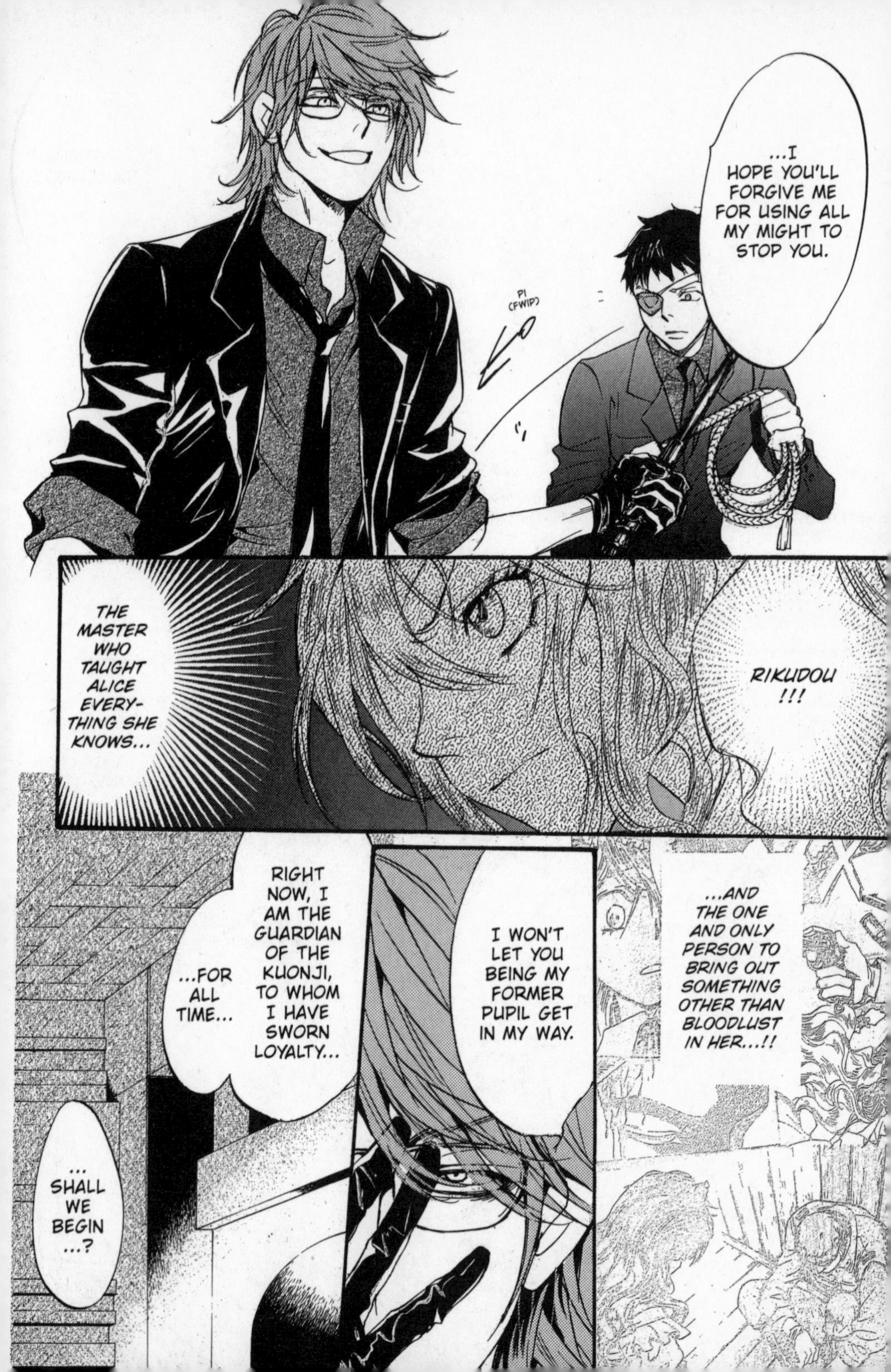
...I HOPE YOU'LL FORGIVE ME FOR USING ALL MY MIGHT TO STOP YOU.
PI (FWIP)
RIKUDOU!!!
THE MASTER WHO TAUGHT ALICE EVERY-THING SHE KNOWS...
...AND THE ONE AND ONLY PERSON TO BRING OUT SOMETHING OTHER THAN BLOODLUST IN HER...!!
I WON'T LET YOU BEING MY FORMER PUPIL GET IN MY WAY.
RIGHT NOW, I AM THE GUARDIAN OF THE KUONJI, TO WHOM I HAVE SWORN LOYALTY...
...FOR ALL TIME...
...SHALL WE BEGIN...?

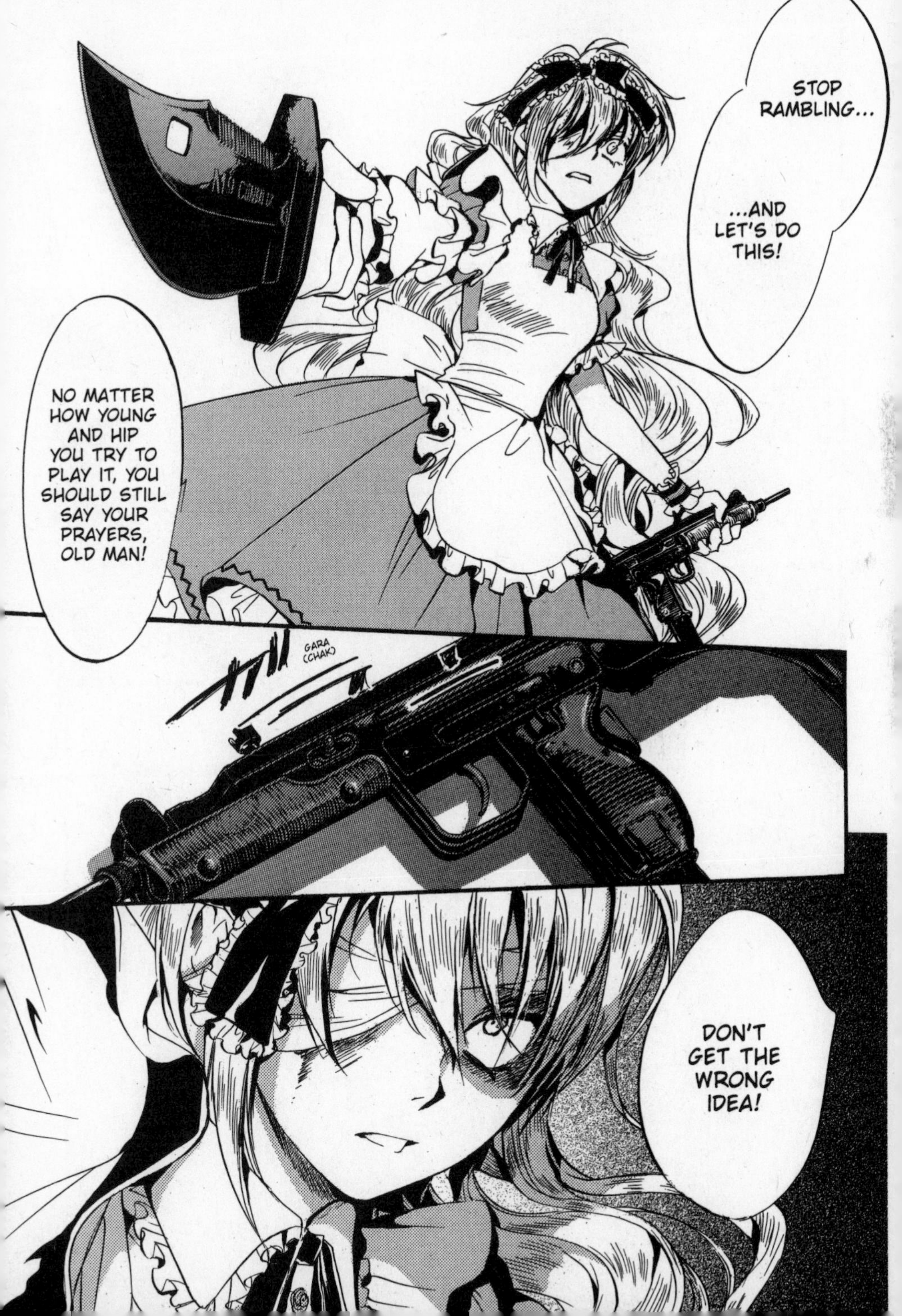
STOP RAMBLING...
...AND LET'S DO THIS!
NO MATTER HOW YOUNG AND HIP YOU TRY TO PLAY IT, YOU SHOULD STILL SAY YOUR PRAYERS, OLD MAN!
GARA (CHAK)
DON'T GET THE WRONG IDEA!

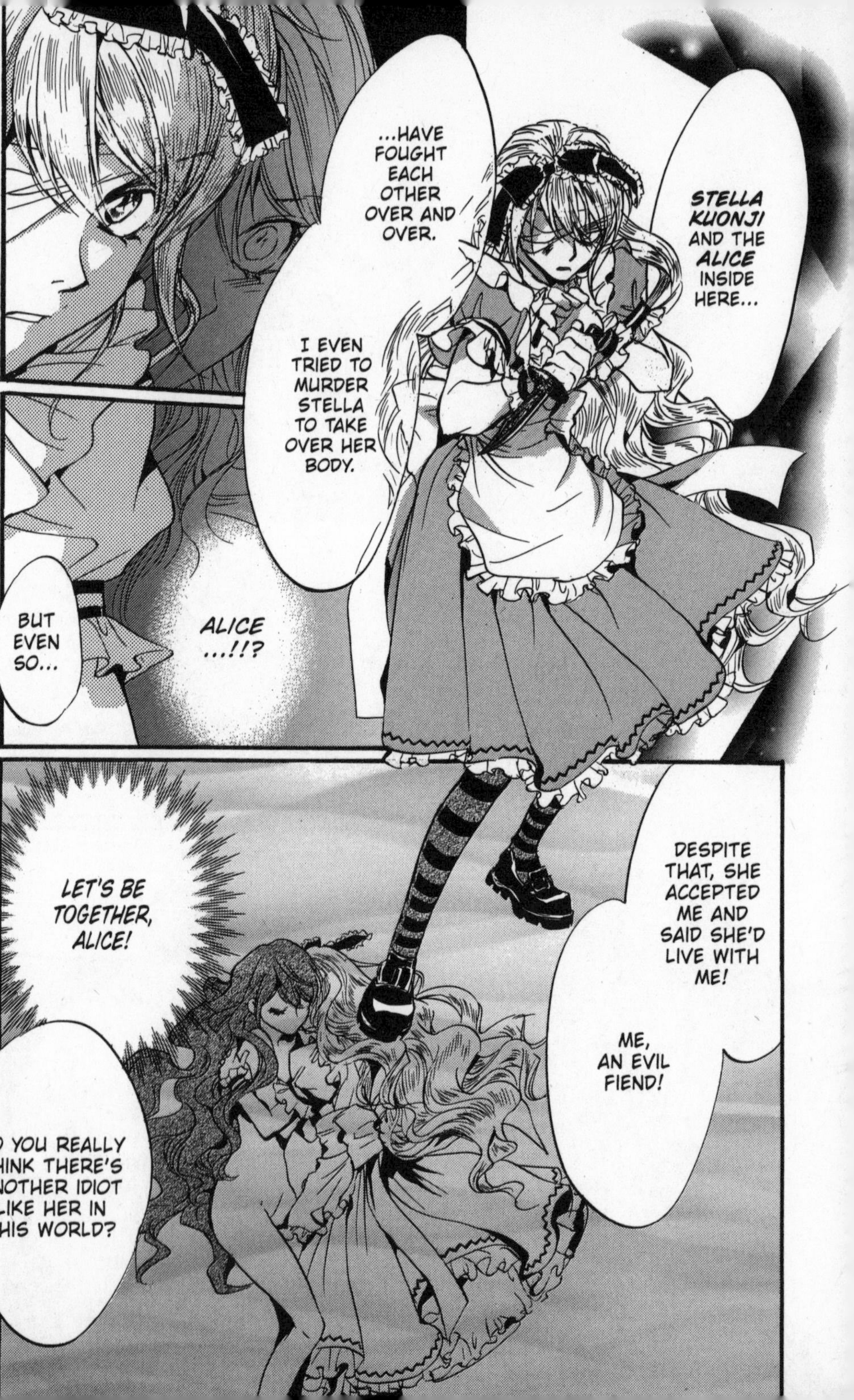
STELLA KUONJI AND THE ALICE INSIDE HERE...
...HAVE FOUGHT EACH OTHER OVER AND OVER.
I EVEN TRIED TO MURDER STELLA TO TAKE OVER HER BODY.
ALICE ...!!?
BUT EVEN SO...
DESPITE THAT, SHE ACCEPTED ME AND SAID SHE'D LIVE WITH ME!
ME, AN EVIL FIEND!
LET'S BE TOGETHER, ALICE!
DO YOU REALLY THINK THERE'S ANOTHER IDIOT LIKE HER IN THIS WORLD?

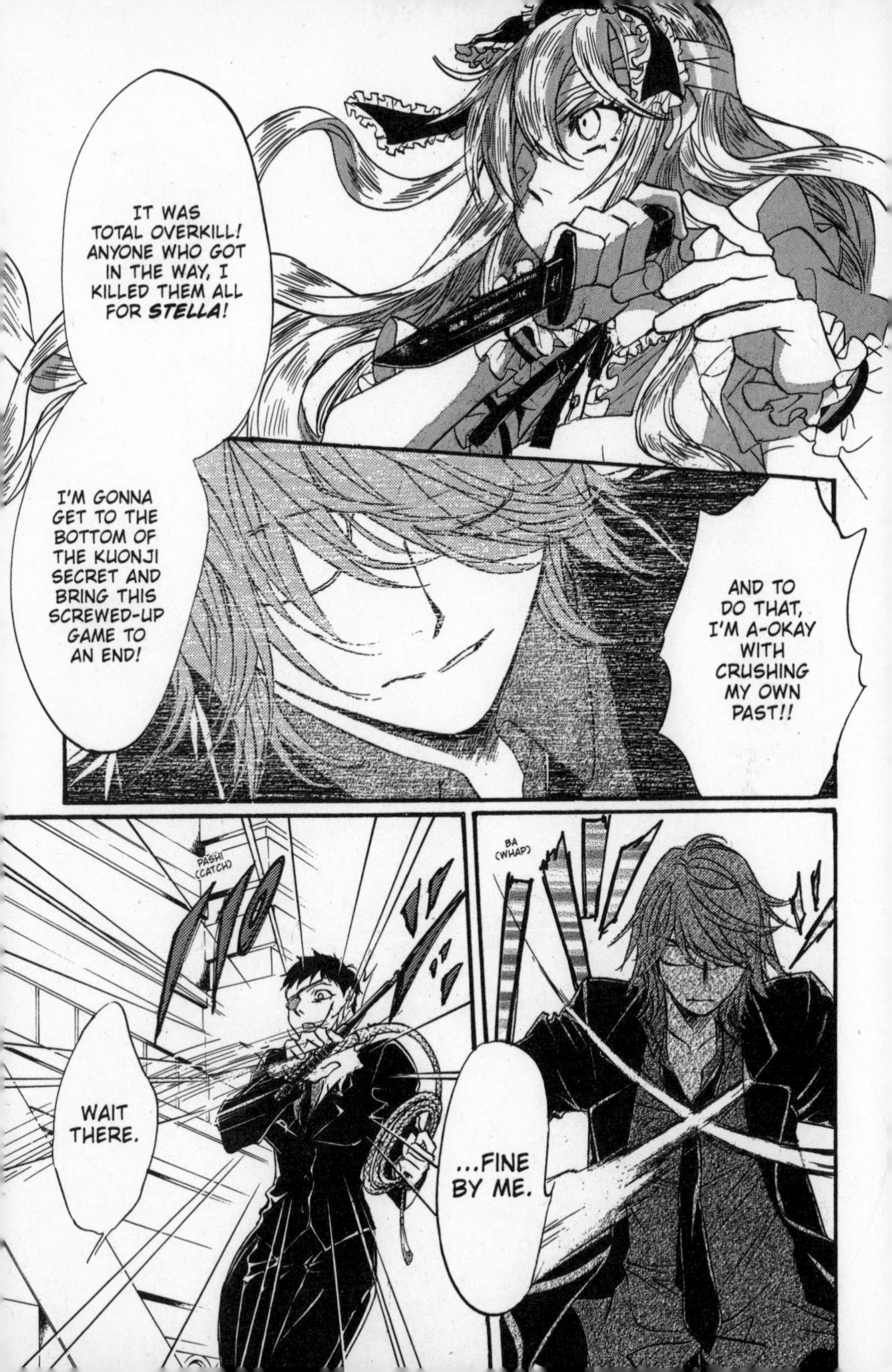
IT WAS TOTAL OVERKILL! ANYONE WHO GOT IN THE WAY, I KILLED THEM ALL FOR STELLA!
I'M GONNA GET TO THE BOTTOM OF THE KUONJI SECRET AND BRING THIS SCREWED-UP GAME TO AN END!
AND TO DO THAT, I'M A-OKAY WITH CRUSHING MY OWN PAST!!
PASHI (CATCH)
WAIT THERE.
BA (WHAP)
...FINE BY ME.

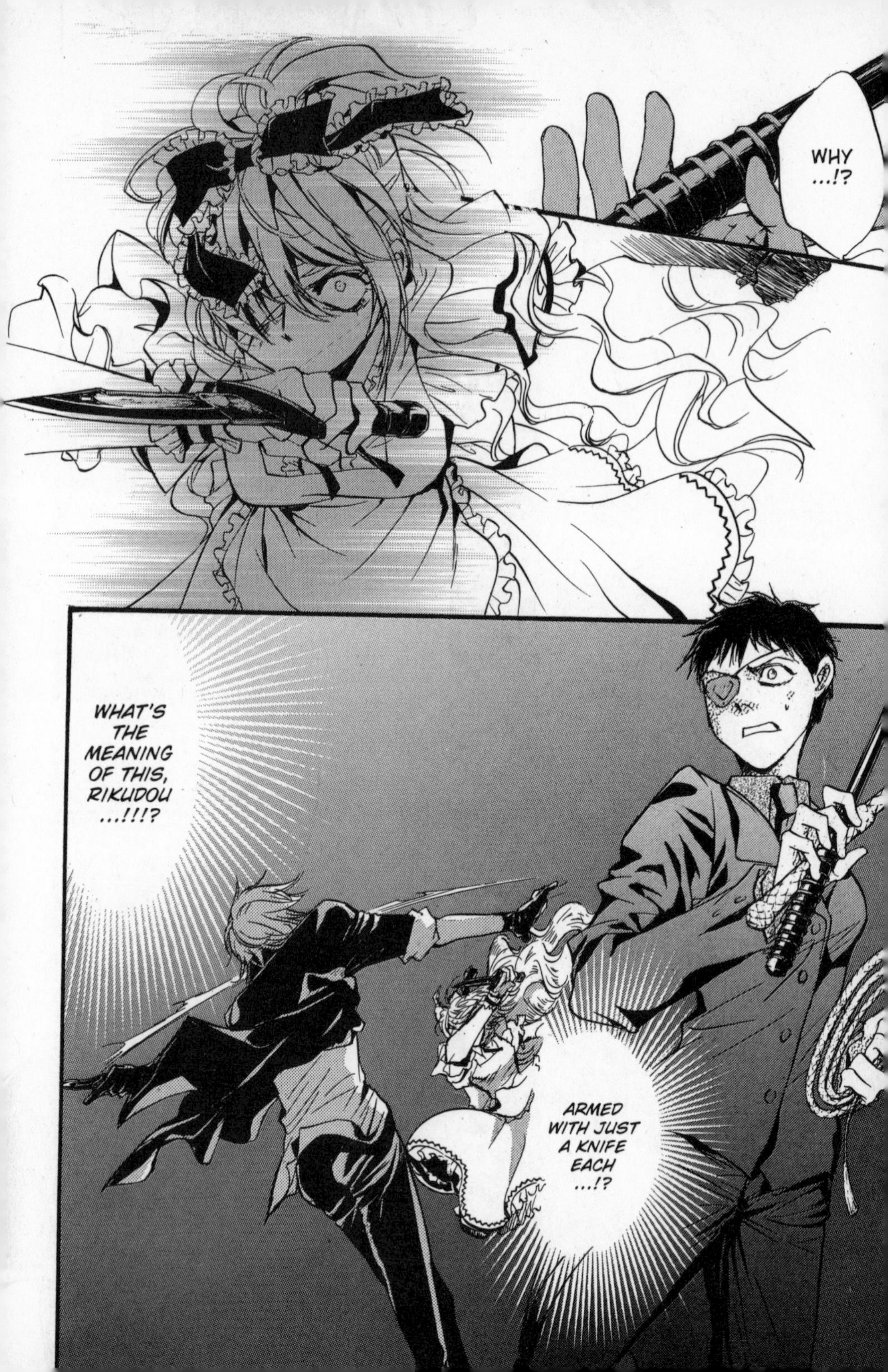
WHY ...!?
WHAT'S THE MEANING OF THIS, RIKUDOU ...!!!?
ARMED WITH JUST A KNIFE EACH ...!?

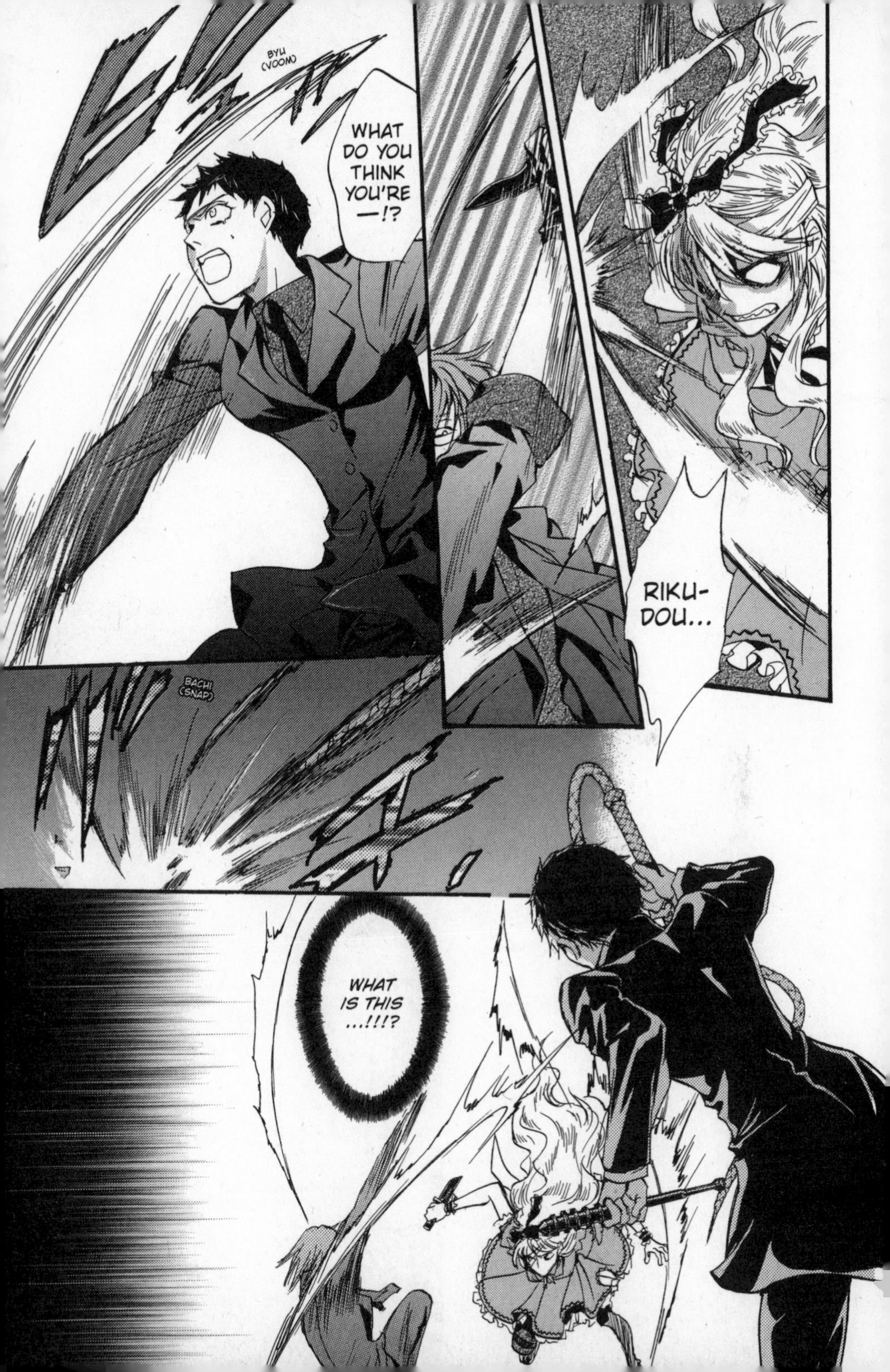
RIKU-DOU...
BYU (VOOM)
WHAT DO YOU THINK YOU'RE—!?
BACHI (SNAP)
WHAT IS THIS ...!!!?

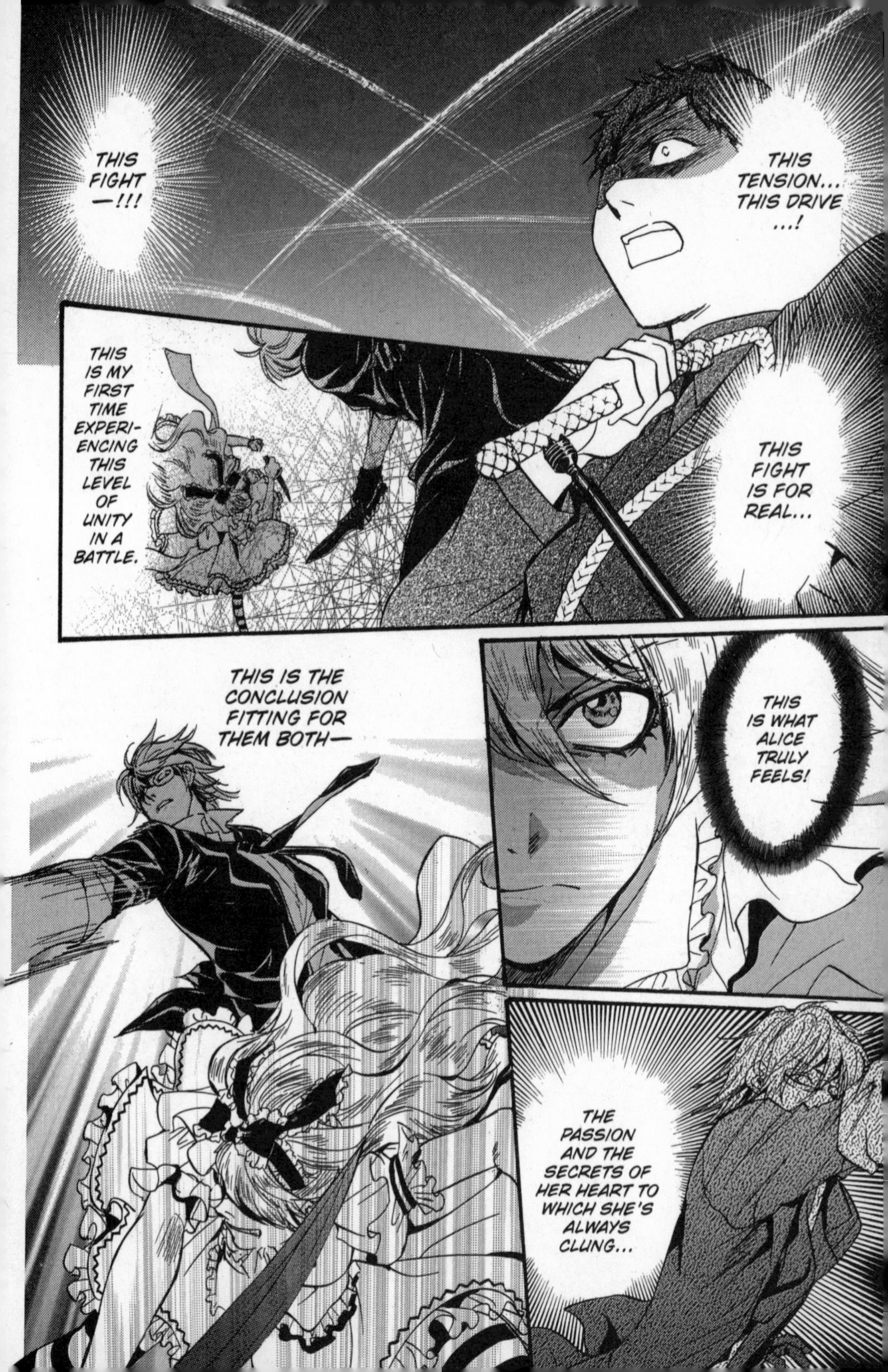
THIS TENSION... THIS DRIVE ...!
THIS FIGHT —!!!
THIS FIGHT IS FOR REAL...
THIS IS MY FIRST TIME EXPERIENCING THIS LEVEL OF UNITY IN A BATTLE.
THIS IS WHAT ALICE TRULY FEELS!
THE PASSION AND THE SECRETS OF HER HEART TO WHICH SHE'S ALWAYS CLUNG...
THIS IS THE CONCLUSION FITTING FOR THEM BOTH—

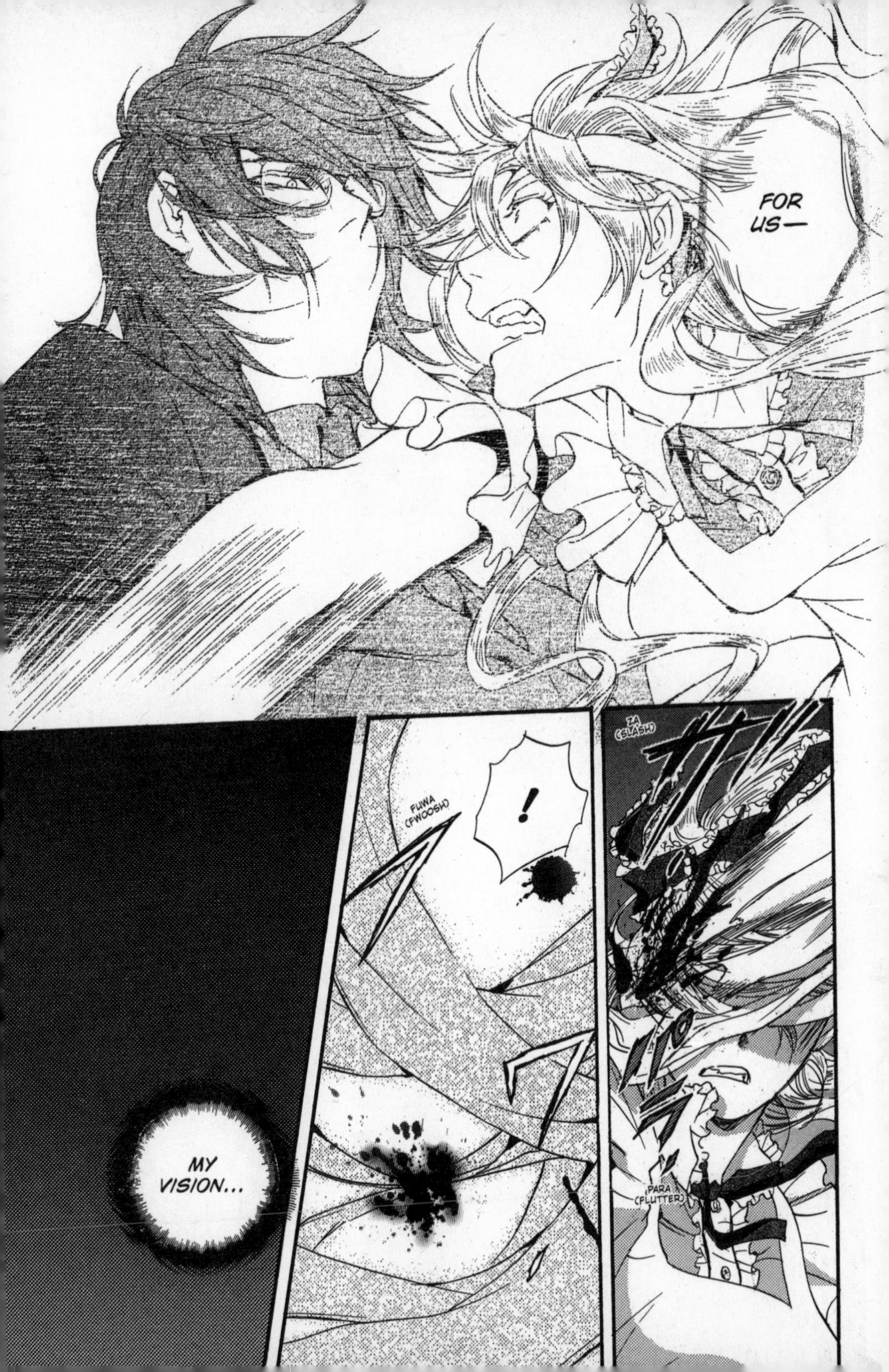
FOR US—
ZA (SLASH)
PARA (FLUTTER)
FUWA (FWOOSH)
!
MY VISION...

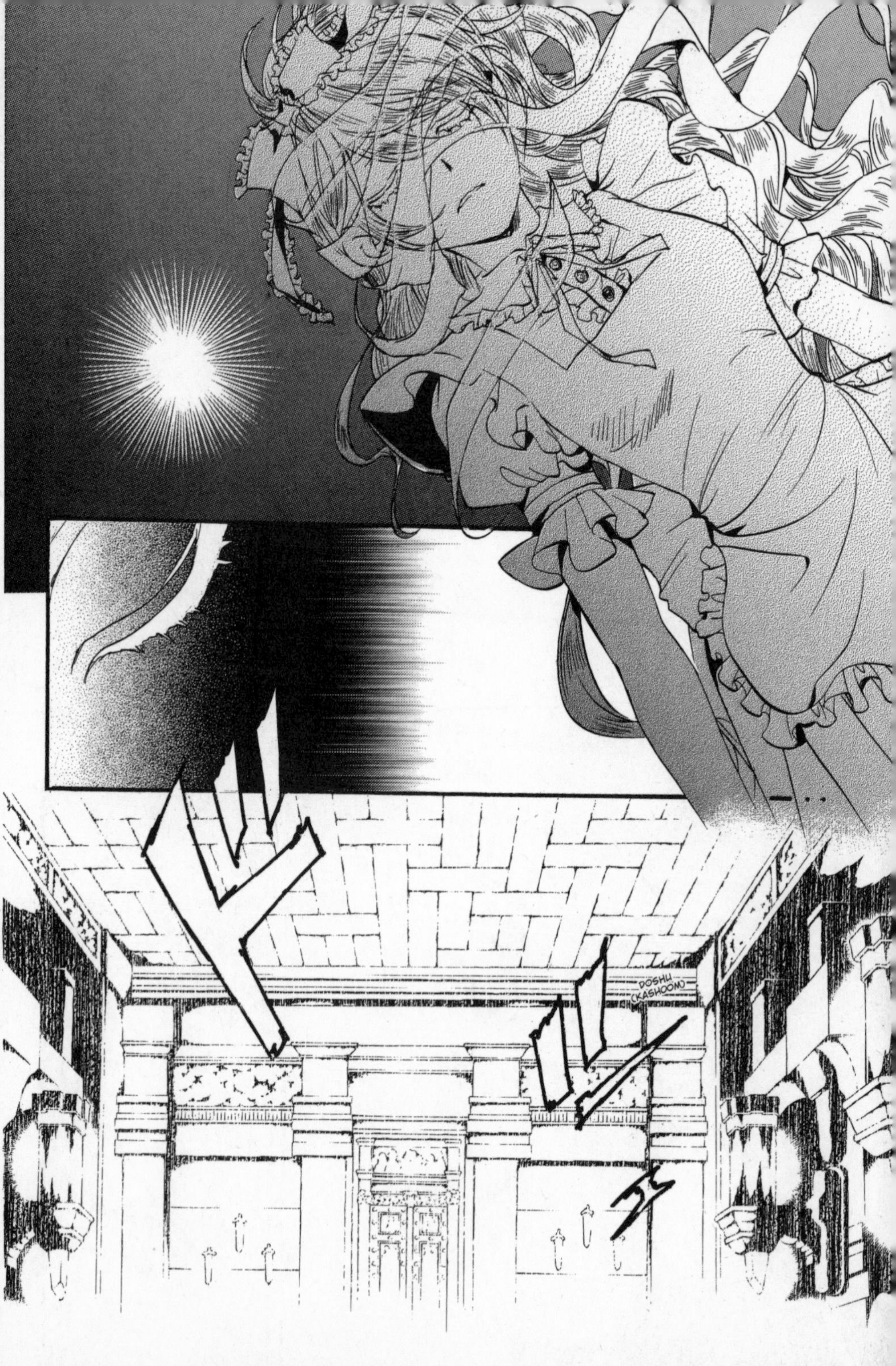
DOSHU
(KASHOON)

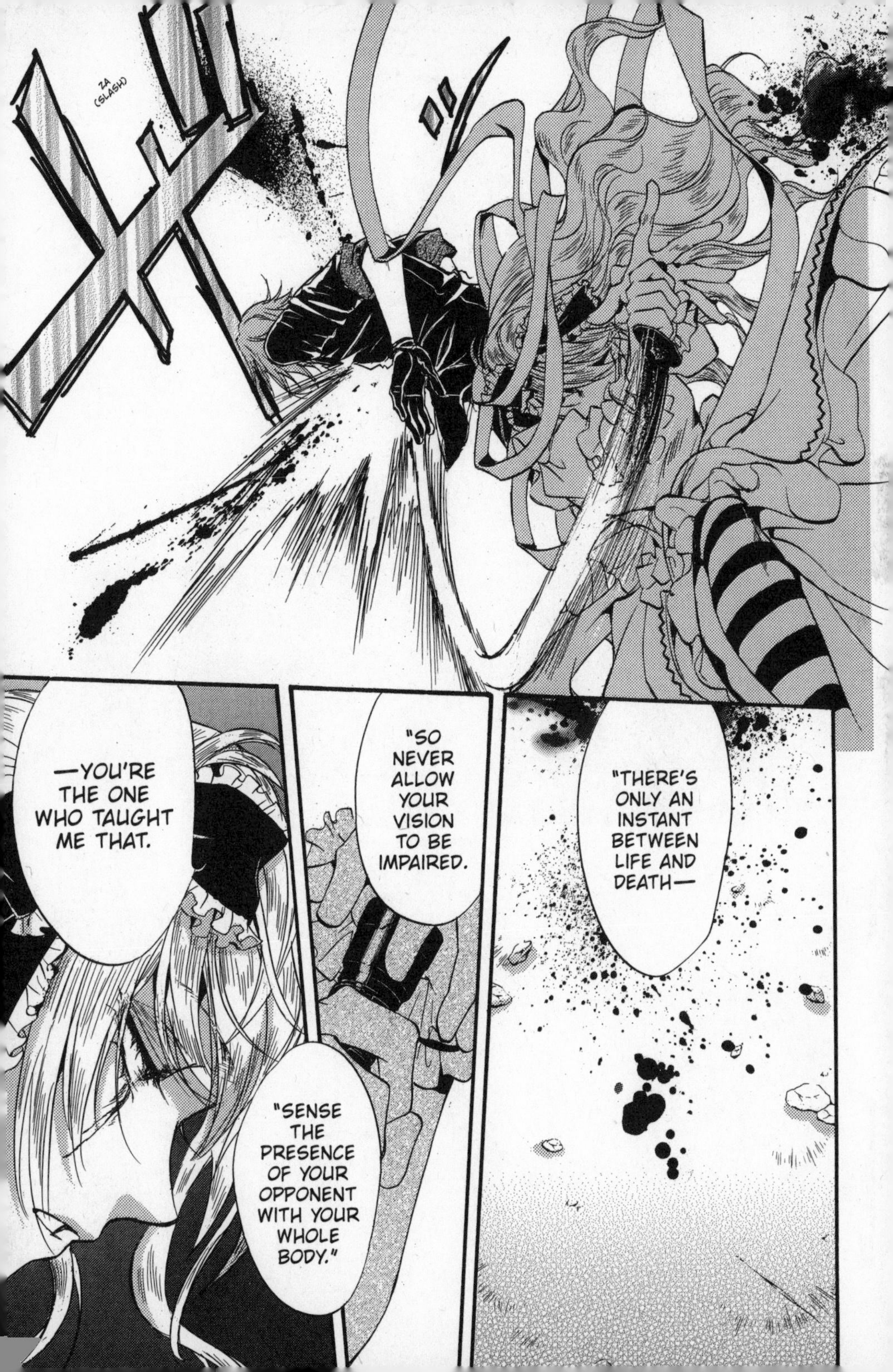
ZA (SLASH)
"THERE'S ONLY AN INSTANT BETWEEN LIFE AND DEATH—
"SO NEVER ALLOW YOUR VISION TO BE IMPAIRED.
"SENSE THE PRESENCE OF YOUR OPPONENT WITH YOUR WHOLE BODY."
—YOU'RE THE ONE WHO TAUGHT ME THAT.

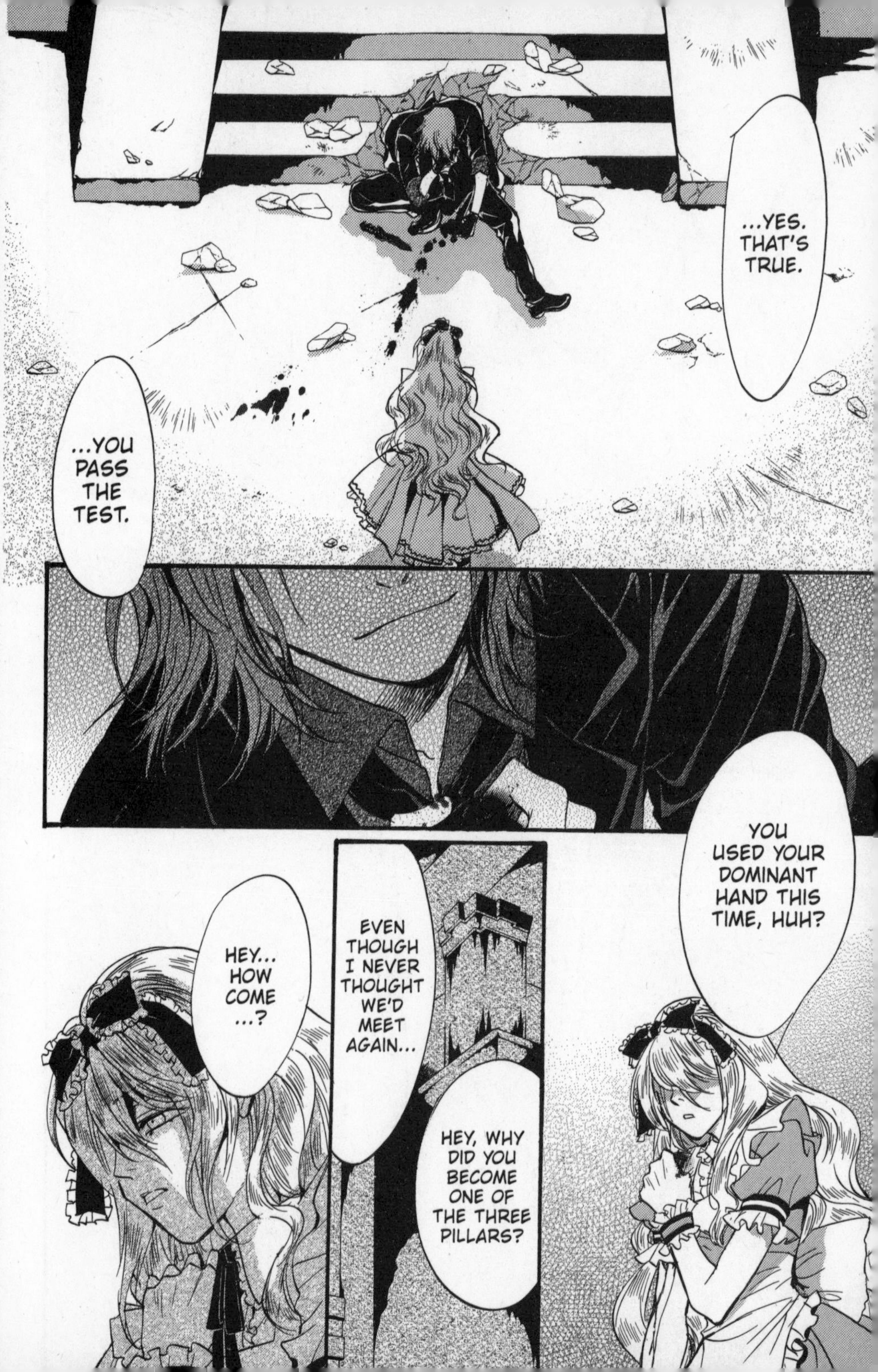
...YES. THAT'S TRUE.
...YOU PASS THE TEST.
YOU USED YOUR DOMINANT HAND THIS TIME, HUH?
EVEN THOUGH I NEVER THOUGHT WE'D MEET AGAIN...
HEY, WHY DID YOU BECOME ONE OF THE THREE PILLARS?
HEY... HOW COME ...?

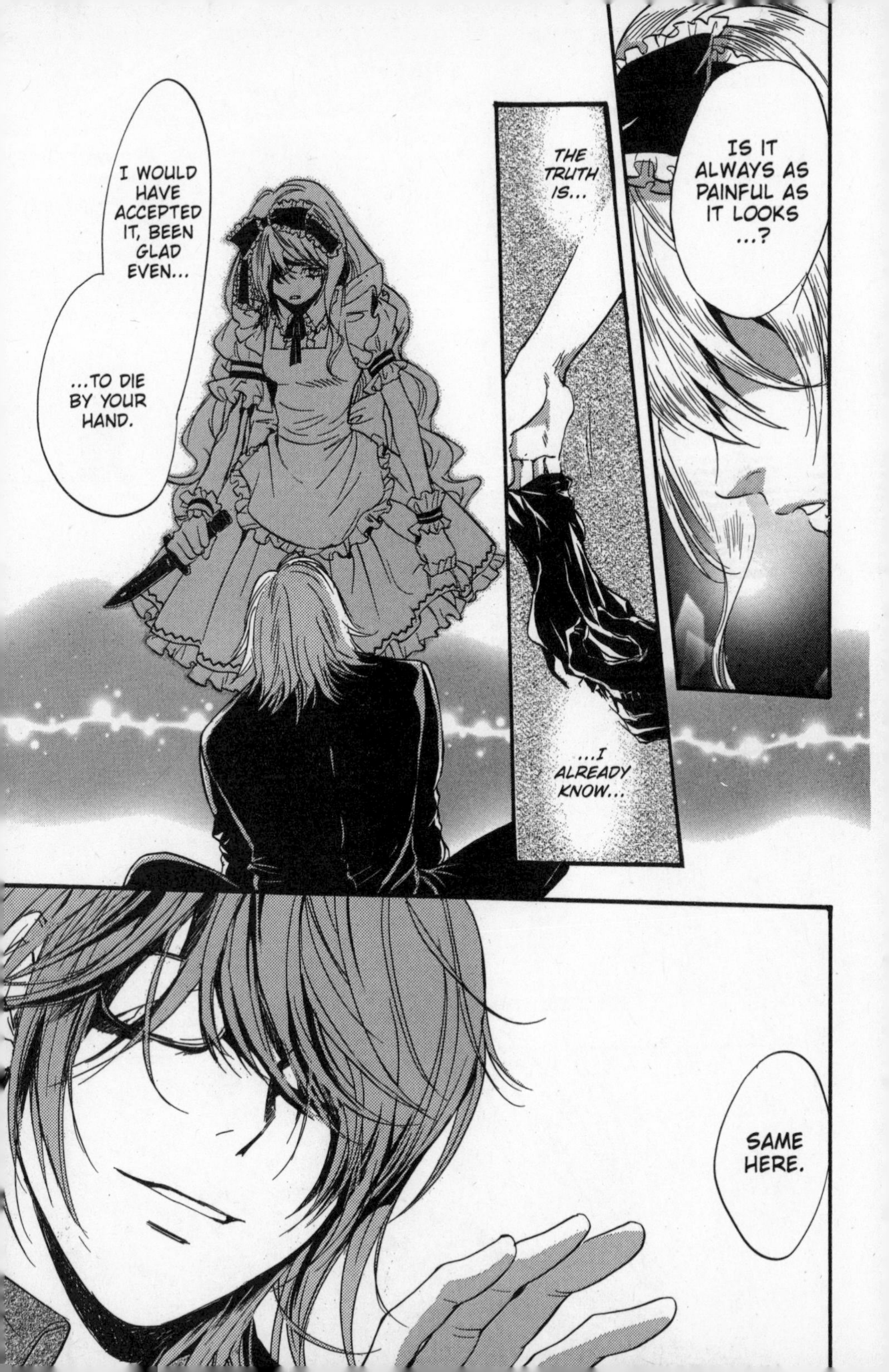
IS IT ALWAYS AS PAINFUL AS IT LOOKS ...?
THE TRUTH IS...
...I ALREADY KNOW...
I WOULD HAVE ACCEPTED IT, BEEN GLAD EVEN...
...TO DIE BY YOUR HAND.
SAME HERE.

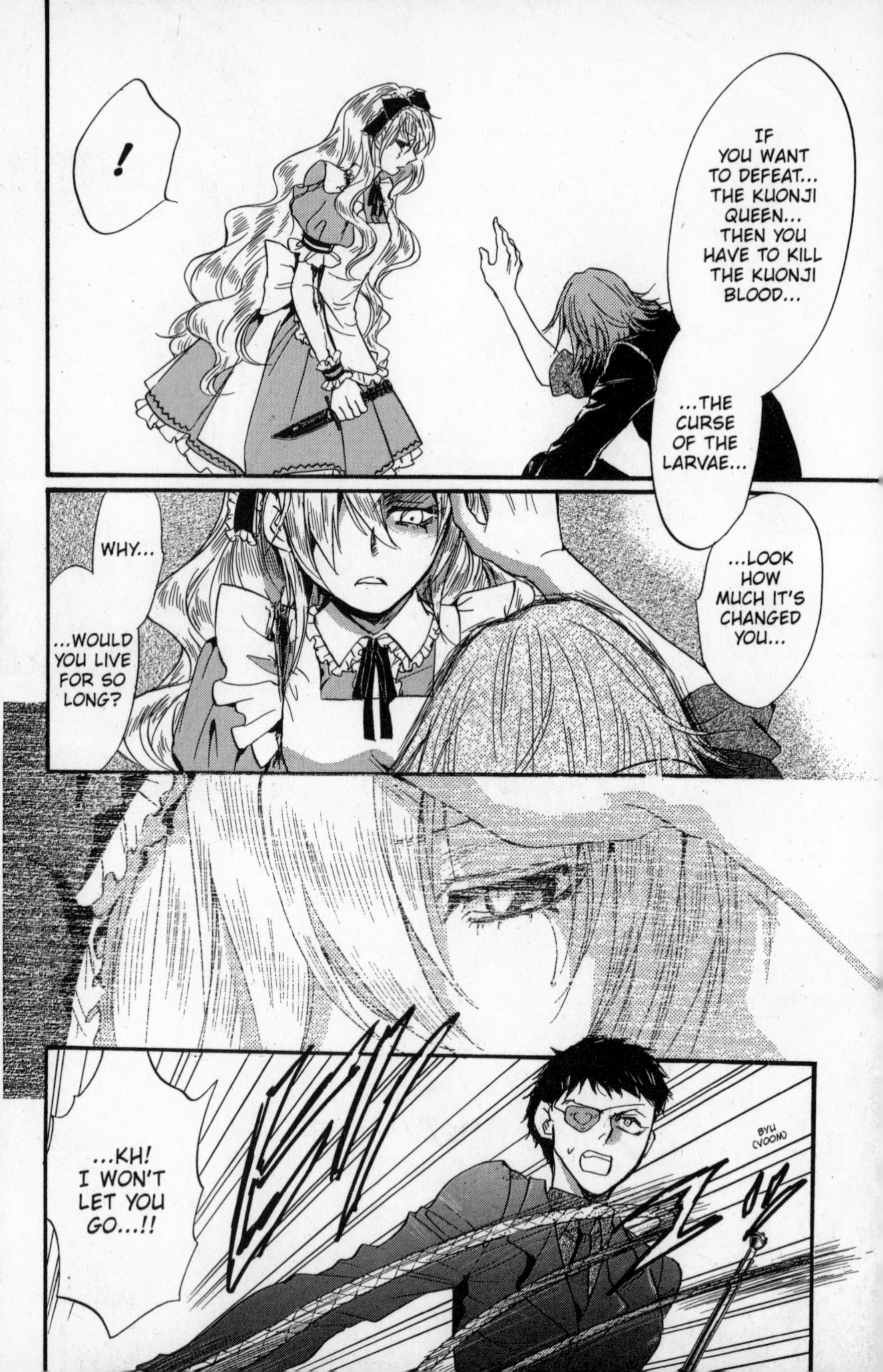
IF YOU WANT TO DEFEAT... THE KUONJI QUEEN... THEN YOU HAVE TO KILL THE KUONJI BLOOD...
...THE CURSE OF THE LARVAE...
!
...LOOK HOW MUCH IT'S CHANGED YOU...
WHY...
...WOULD YOU LIVE FOR SO LONG?
BYU (VOOM)
...KH! I WON'T LET YOU GO...!!

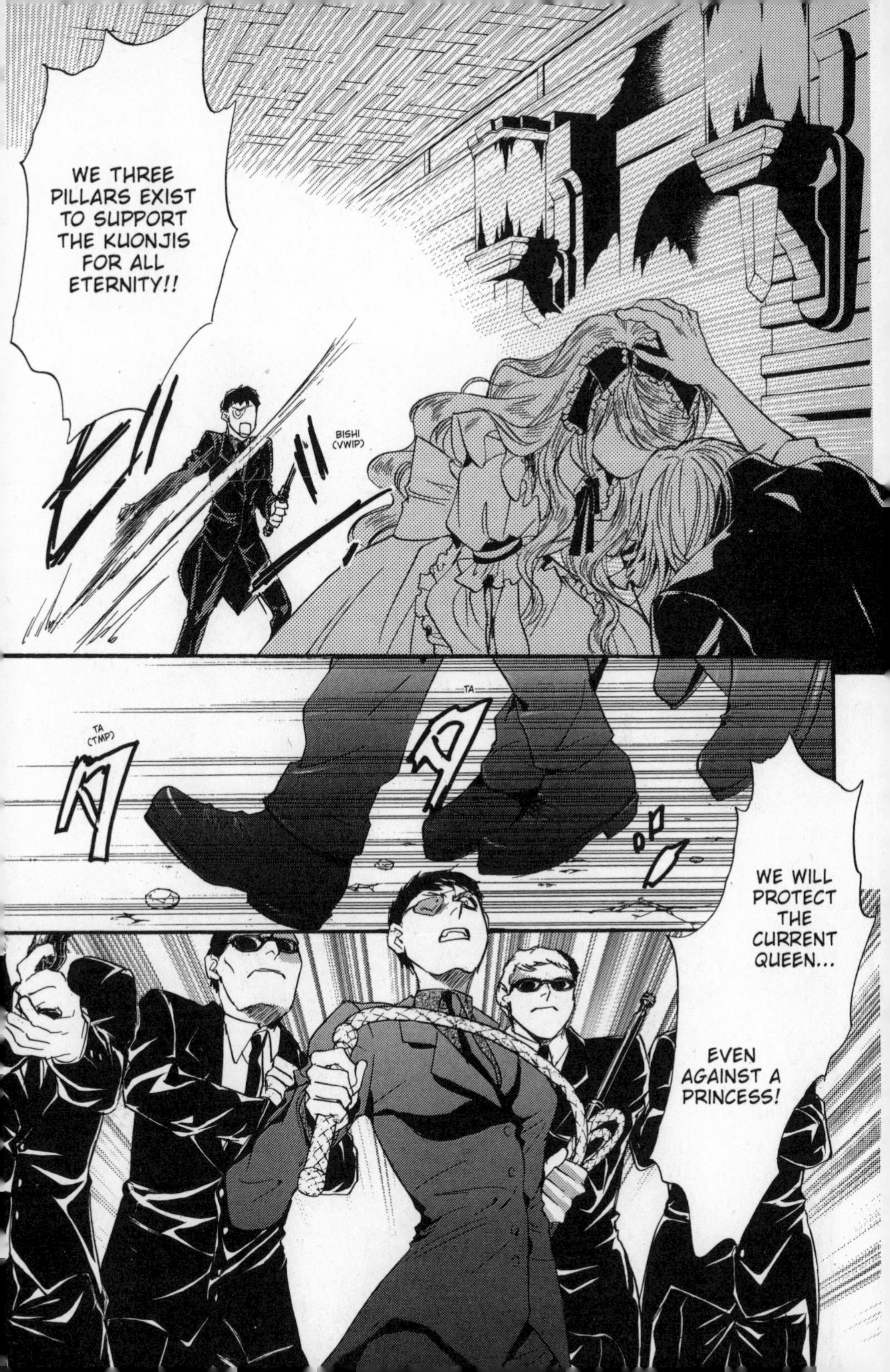
WE THREE PILLARS EXIST TO SUPPORT THE KUONJIS FOR ALL ETERNITY!!
BISHI (VWIP)
TA
TA (TMP)
WE WILL PROTECT THE CURRENT QUEEN...
EVEN AGAINST A PRINCESS!

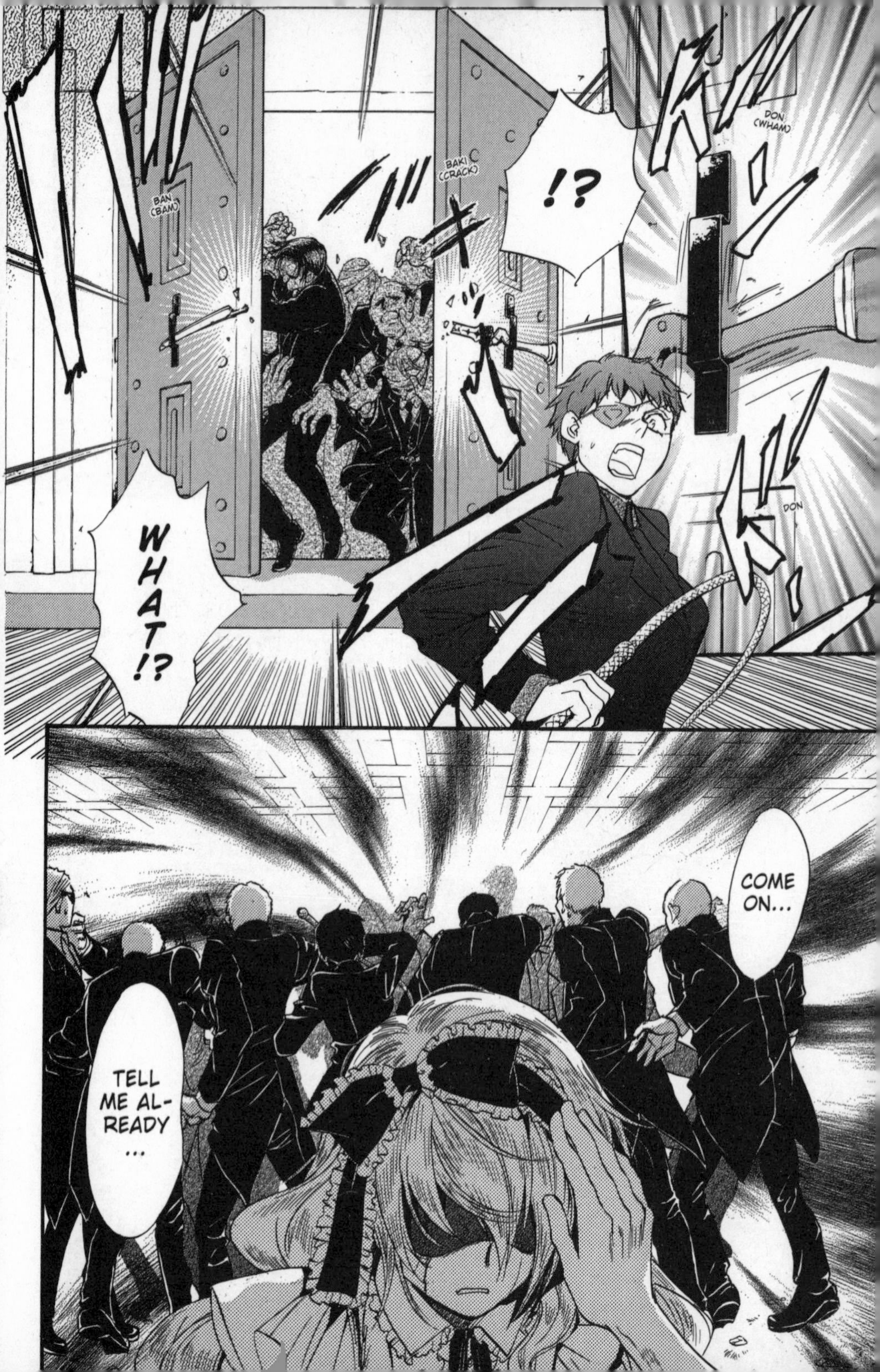
DON (WHAM)
!?
BAKI (CRACK)
BAN (BAM)
DON
WHAT!?
COME ON...
TELL ME AL-READY ...

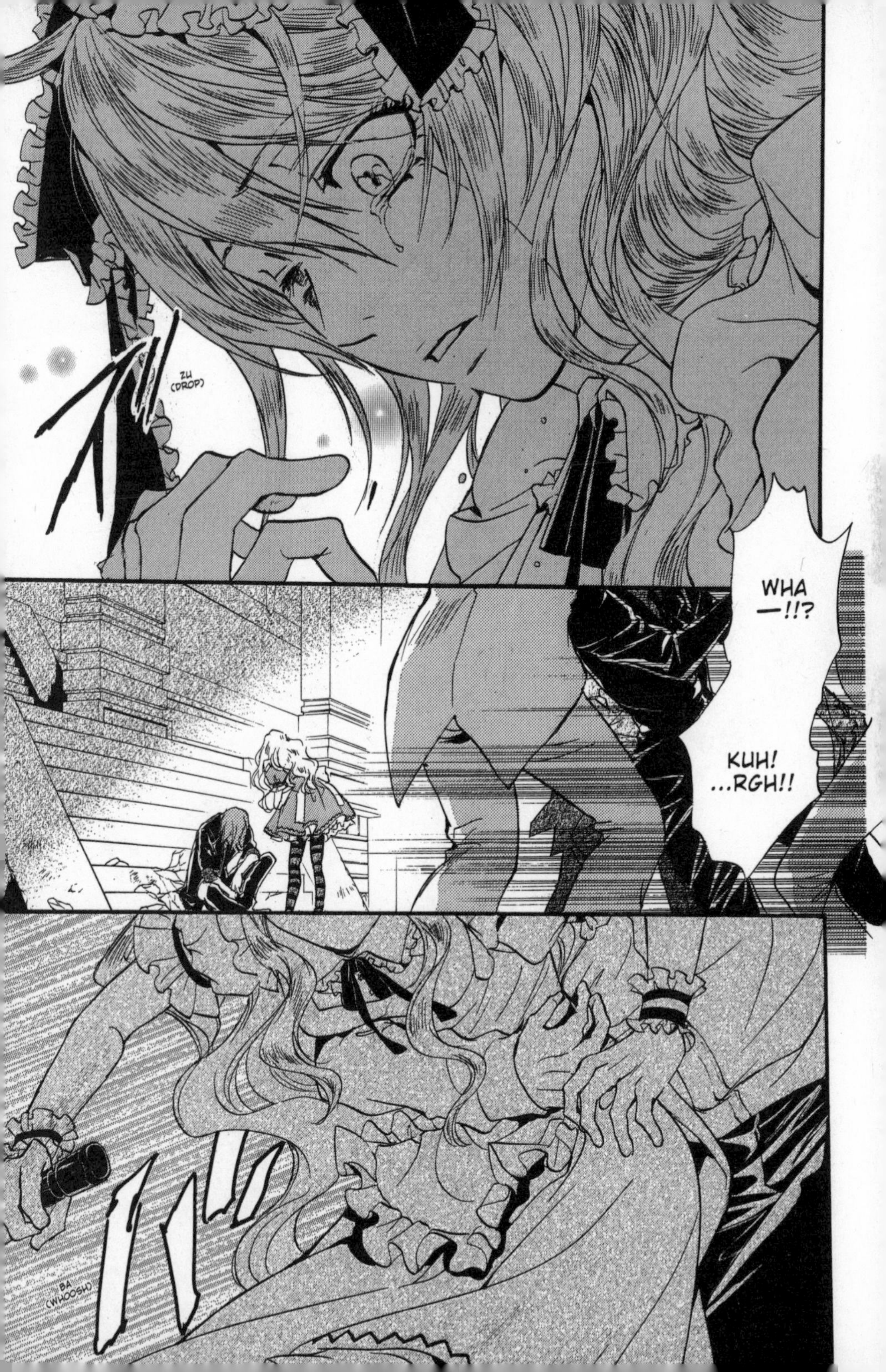
ZU (DROP)
WHA—!!?
KUH! ...RGH!!
BA (WHOOSH)

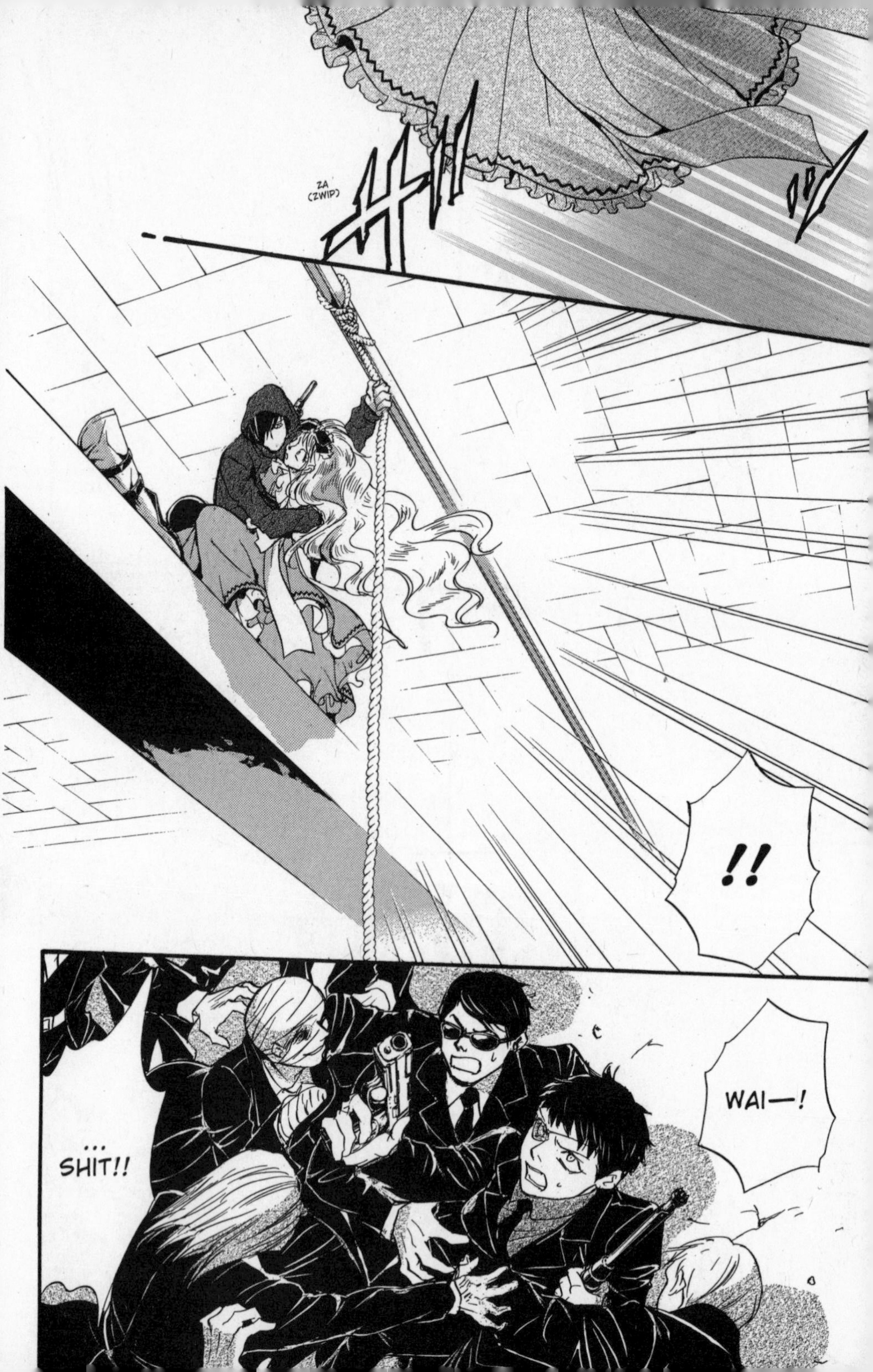
ZA
(ZWIP)
!!
WAI—!
...
SHIT!!

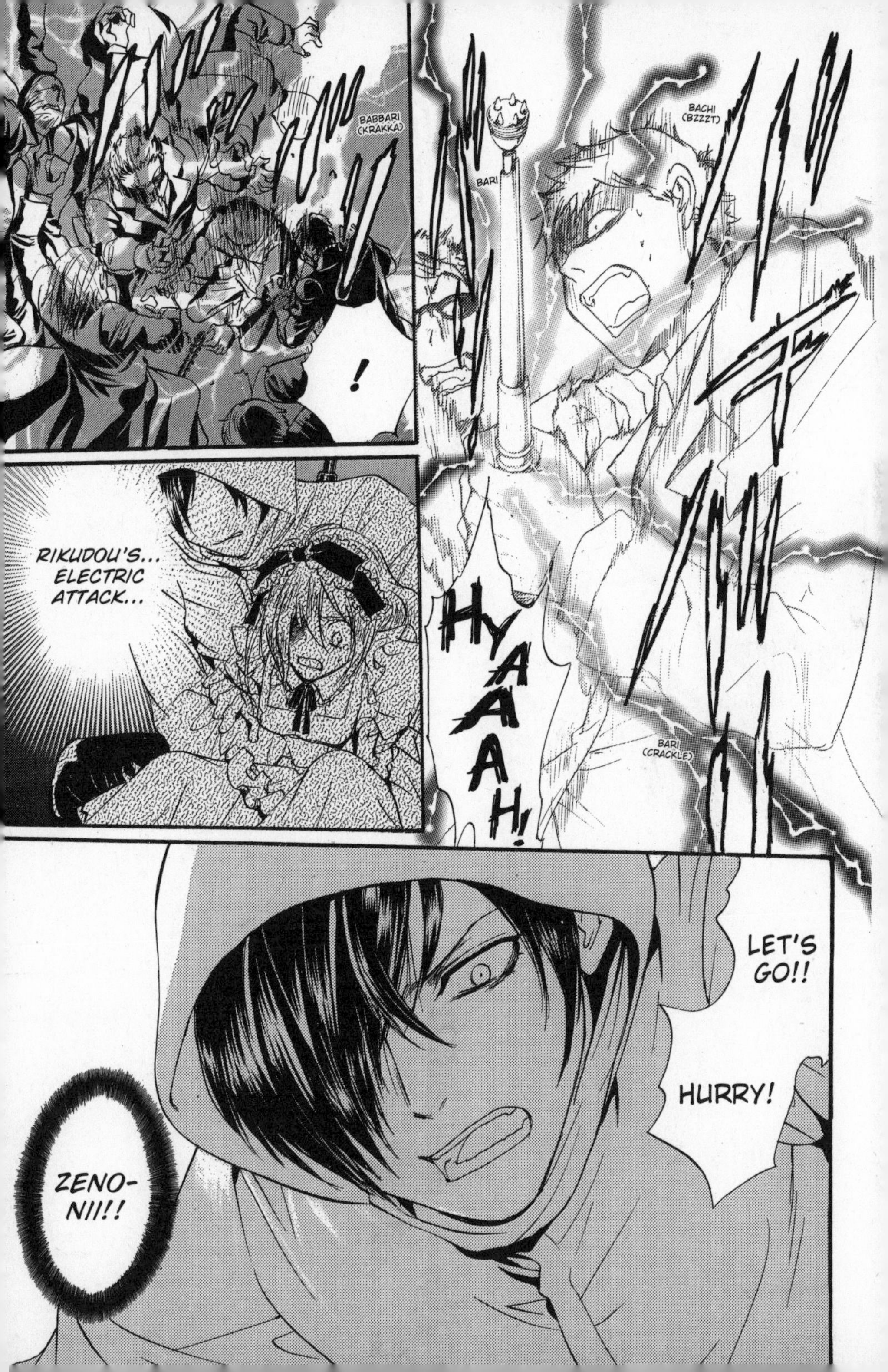
BACHI (BZZZT)
BARI
HYAAAAH!
BARI (CRACKLE)
BABBARI (KRAKKA)
!
RIKUDOU'S... ELECTRIC ATTACK...
LET'S GO!!
HURRY!
ZENO-NII!!

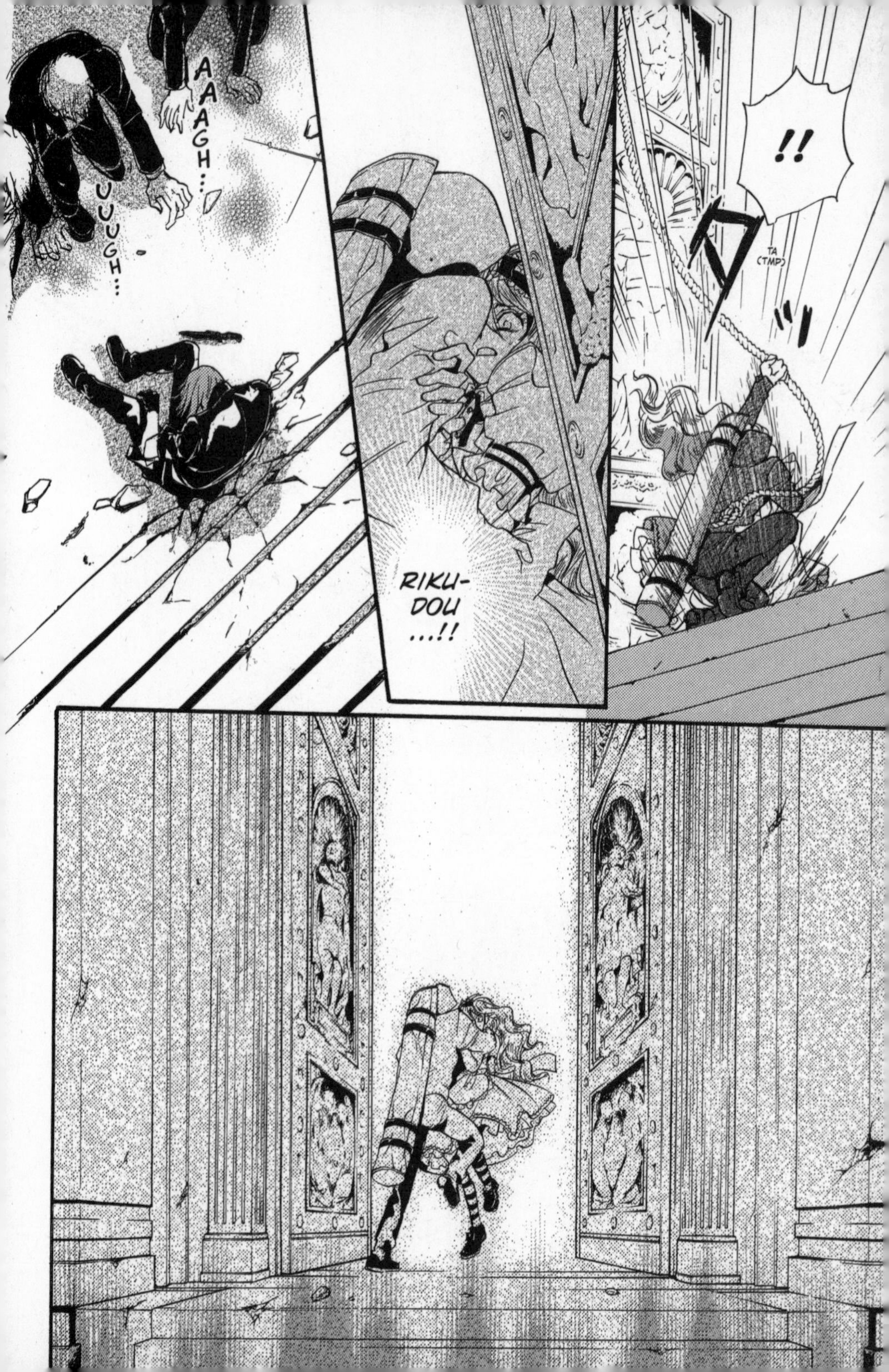
!!
TA
(TMP)
RIKU-
DOU
...!!
AAAGH...
UUUGH...

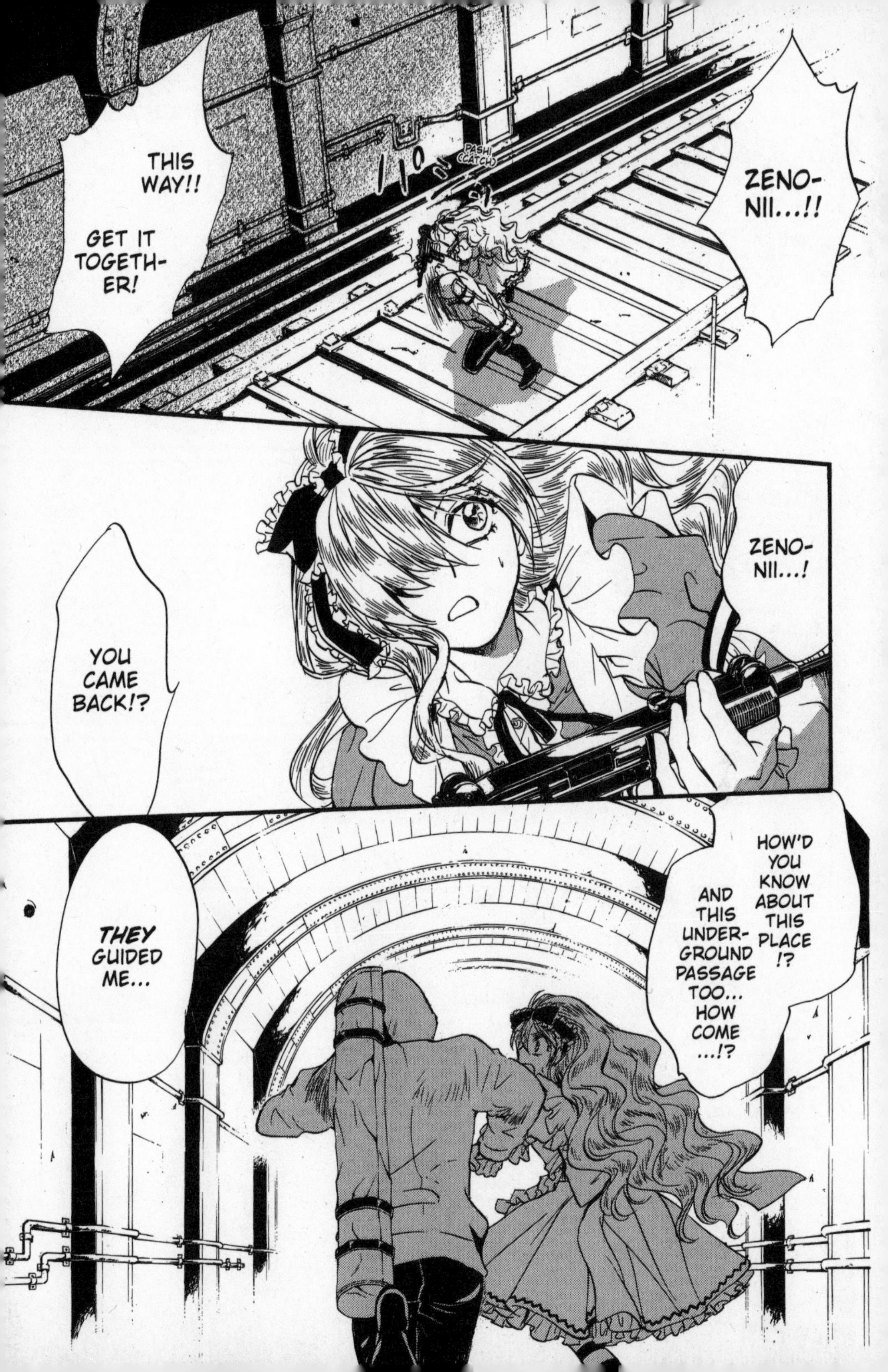

ZENO-NII...!!
PASHI (CATCH)
THIS WAY!!
GET IT TOGETH-ER!
ZENO-NII...!
YOU CAME BACK!?
HOW'D YOU KNOW ABOUT THIS PLACE!?
AND THIS UNDER-GROUND PASSAGE TOO... HOW COME...!?
THEY GUIDED ME...

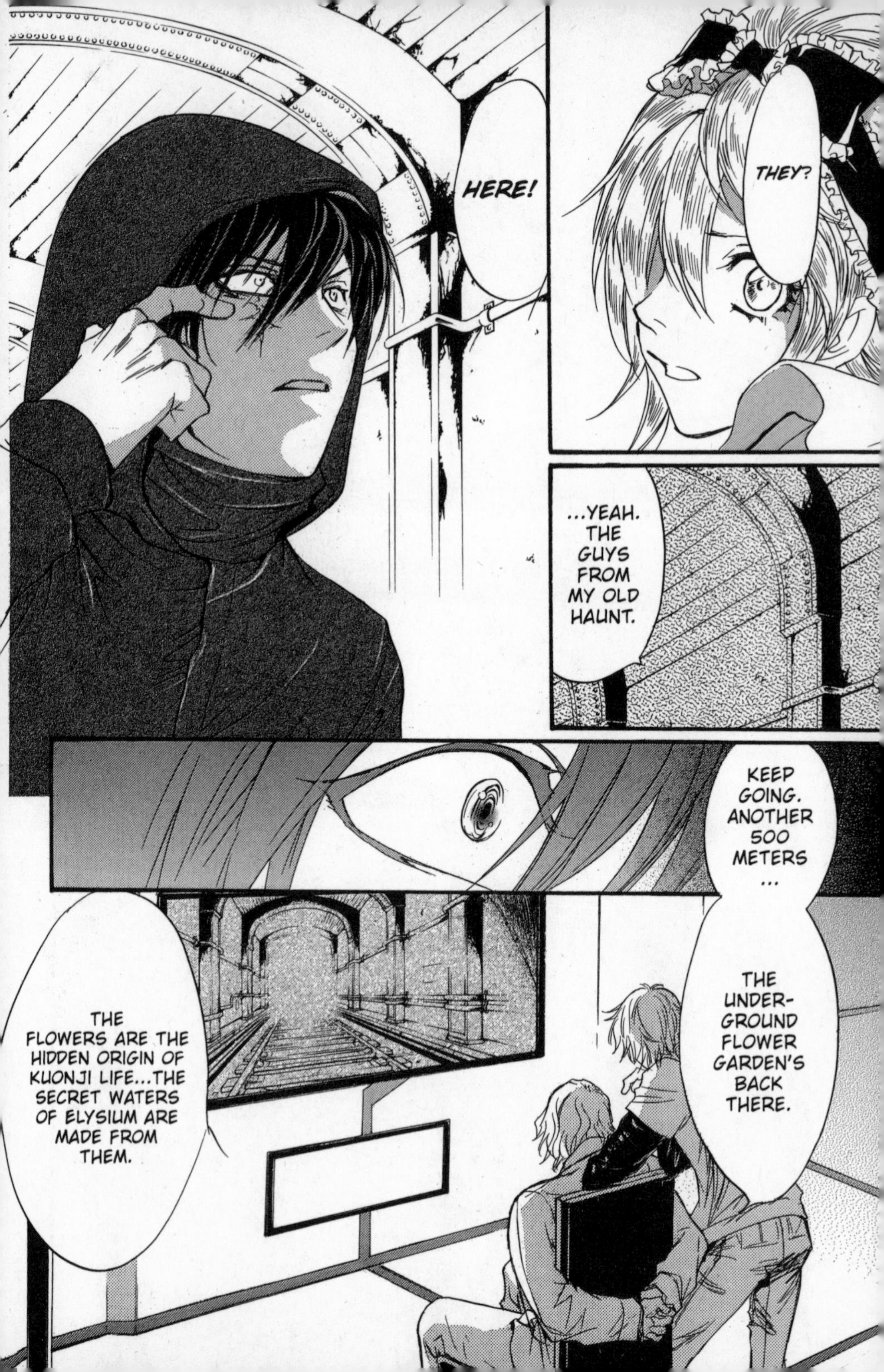
THEY?
...YEAH. THE GUYS FROM MY OLD HAUNT.
HERE!
KEEP GOING. ANOTHER 500 METERS ...
THE UNDER-GROUND FLOWER GARDEN'S BACK THERE.
THE FLOWERS ARE THE HIDDEN ORIGIN OF KUONJI LIFE...THE SECRET WATERS OF ELYSIUM ARE MADE FROM THEM.

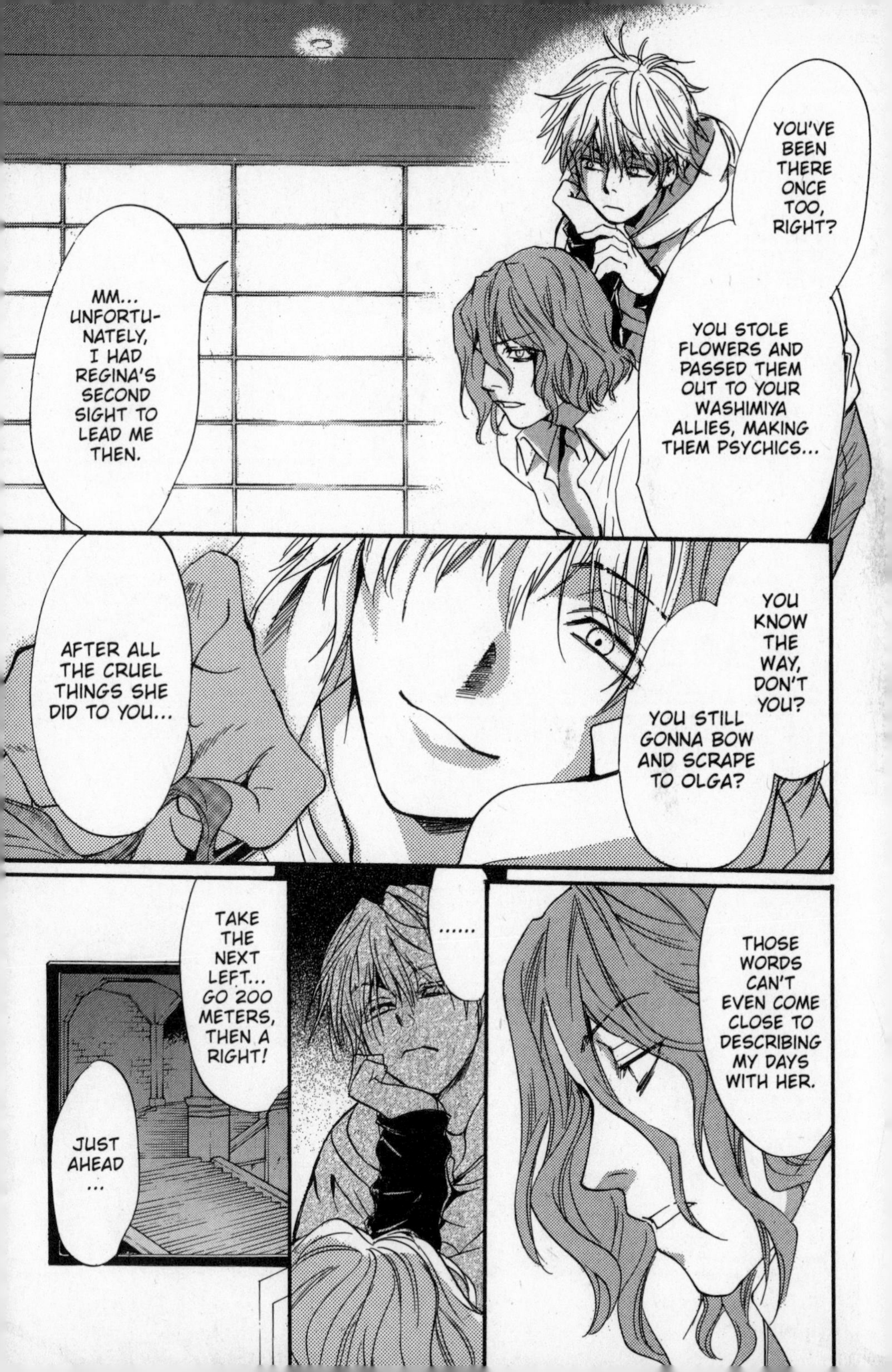
YOU'VE BEEN THERE ONCE TOO, RIGHT?
YOU STOLE FLOWERS AND PASSED THEM OUT TO YOUR WASHIMIYA ALLIES, MAKING THEM PSYCHICS...
MM... UNFORTU-NATELY, I HAD REGINA'S SECOND SIGHT TO LEAD ME THEN.
YOU KNOW THE WAY, DON'T YOU?
YOU STILL GONNA BOW AND SCRAPE TO OLGA?
AFTER ALL THE CRUEL THINGS SHE DID TO YOU...
THOSE WORDS CAN'T EVEN COME CLOSE TO DESCRIBING MY DAYS WITH HER.
......
TAKE THE NEXT LEFT... GO 200 METERS, THEN A RIGHT!
JUST AHEAD ...

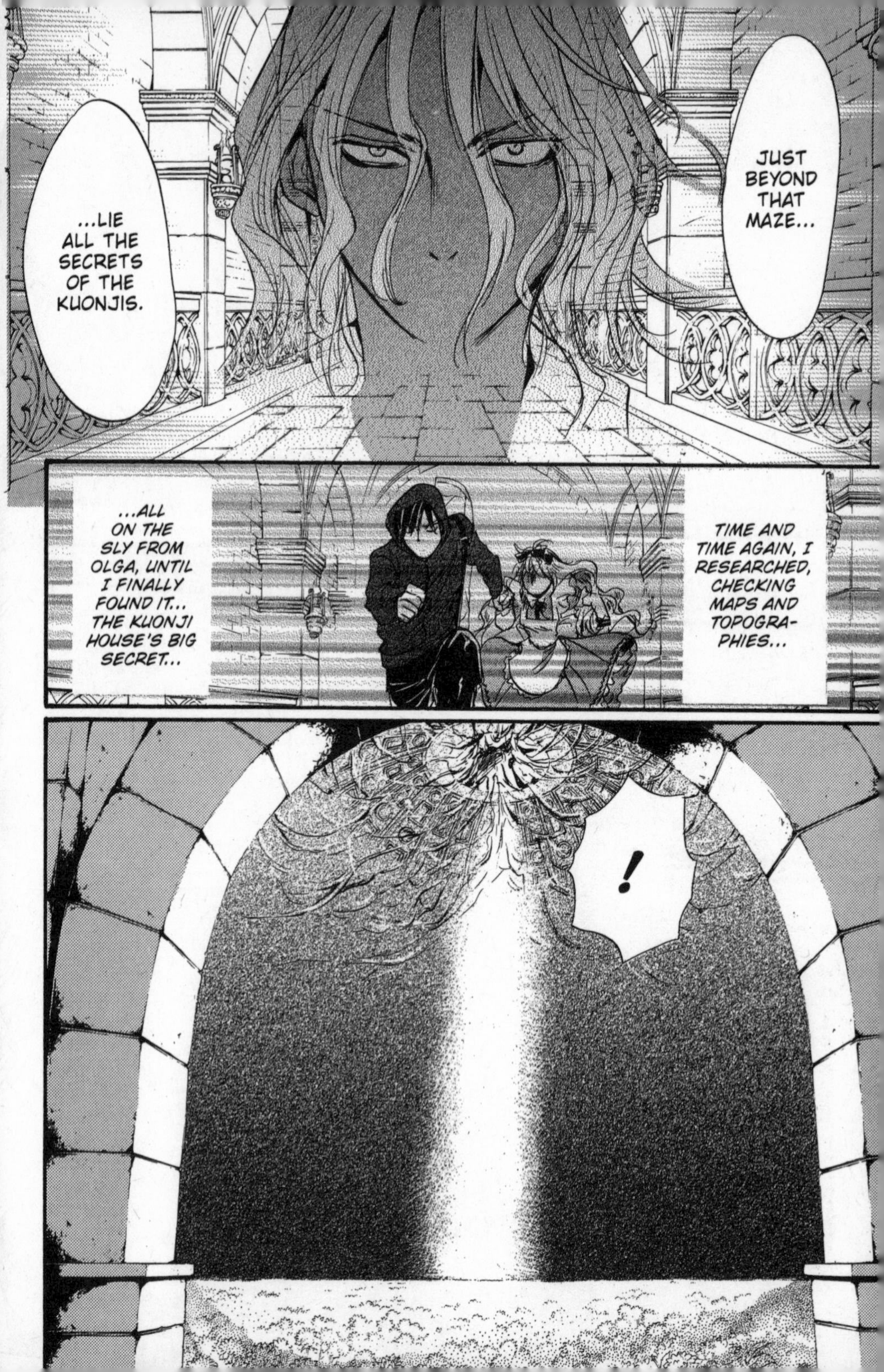
JUST BEYOND THAT MAZE...
...LIE ALL THE SECRETS OF THE KUONJIS.
TIME AND TIME AGAIN, I RESEARCHED, CHECKING MAPS AND TOPOGRAPHIES...
...ALL ON THE SLY FROM OLGA, UNTIL I FINALLY FOUND IT... THE KUONJI HOUSE'S BIG SECRET...
!

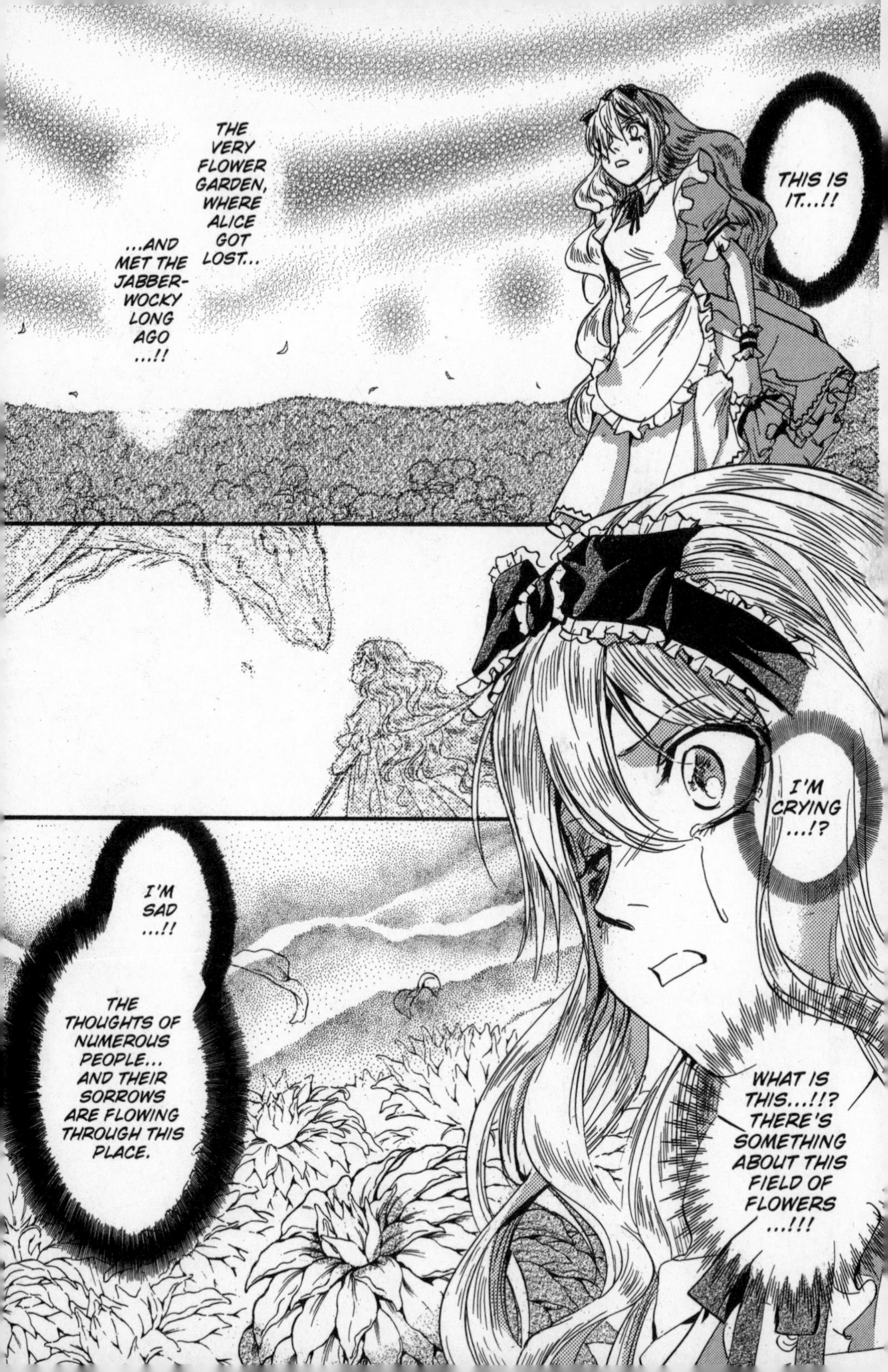
THIS IS IT...!!
THE VERY FLOWER GARDEN, WHERE ALICE GOT LOST...
...AND MET THE JABBER-WOCKY LONG AGO...!!
I'M CRYING...!?
WHAT IS THIS...!!? THERE'S SOMETHING ABOUT THIS FIELD OF FLOWERS...!!!
I'M SAD...!!
THE THOUGHTS OF NUMEROUS PEOPLE... AND THEIR SORROWS ARE FLOWING THROUGH THIS PLACE.

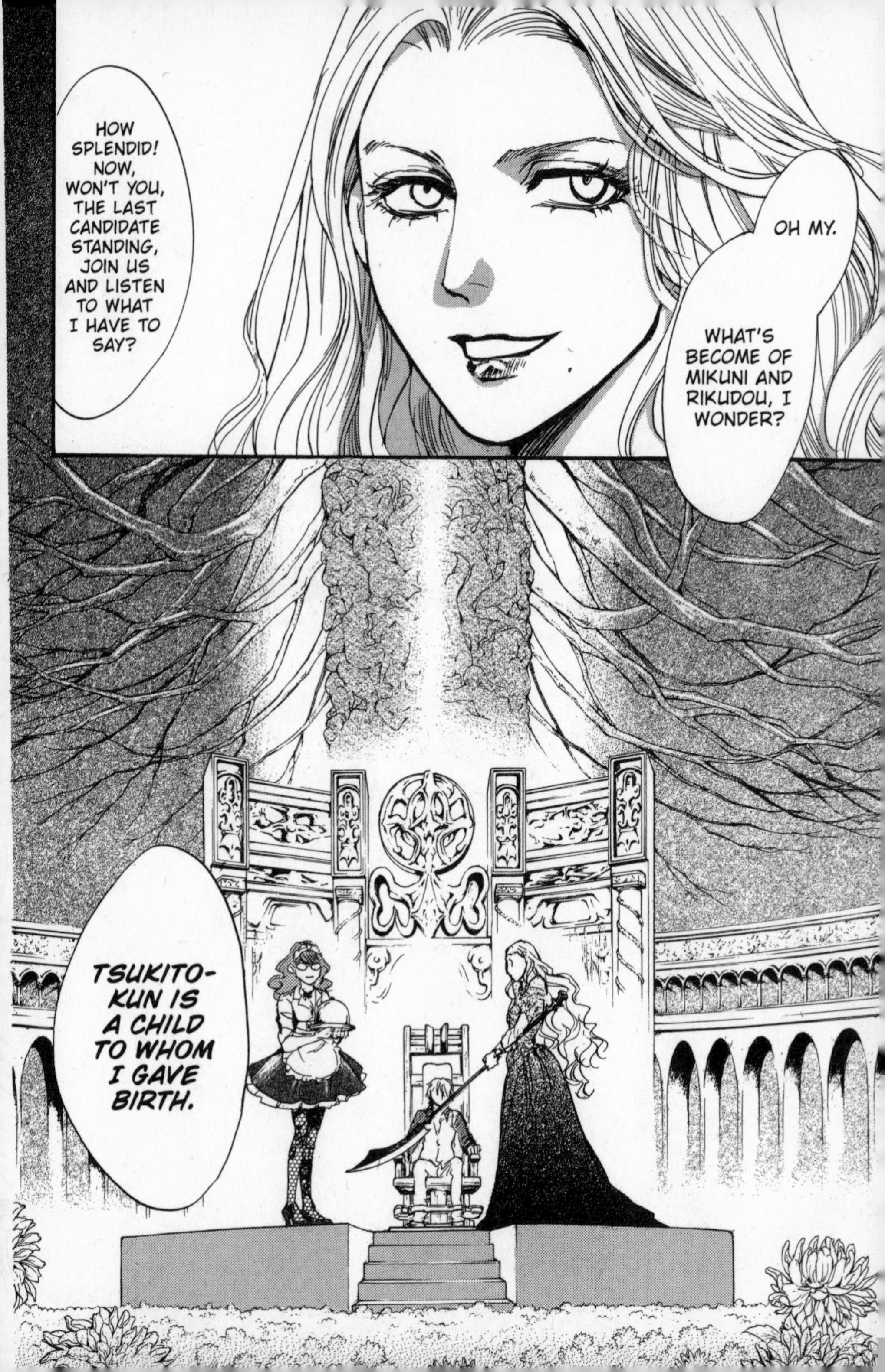
OH MY.
WHAT'S BECOME OF MIKUNI AND RIKUDOU, I WONDER?
HOW SPLENDID! NOW, WON'T YOU, THE LAST CANDIDATE STANDING, JOIN US AND LISTEN TO WHAT I HAVE TO SAY?
TSUKITO-KUN IS A CHILD TO WHOM I GAVE BIRTH.

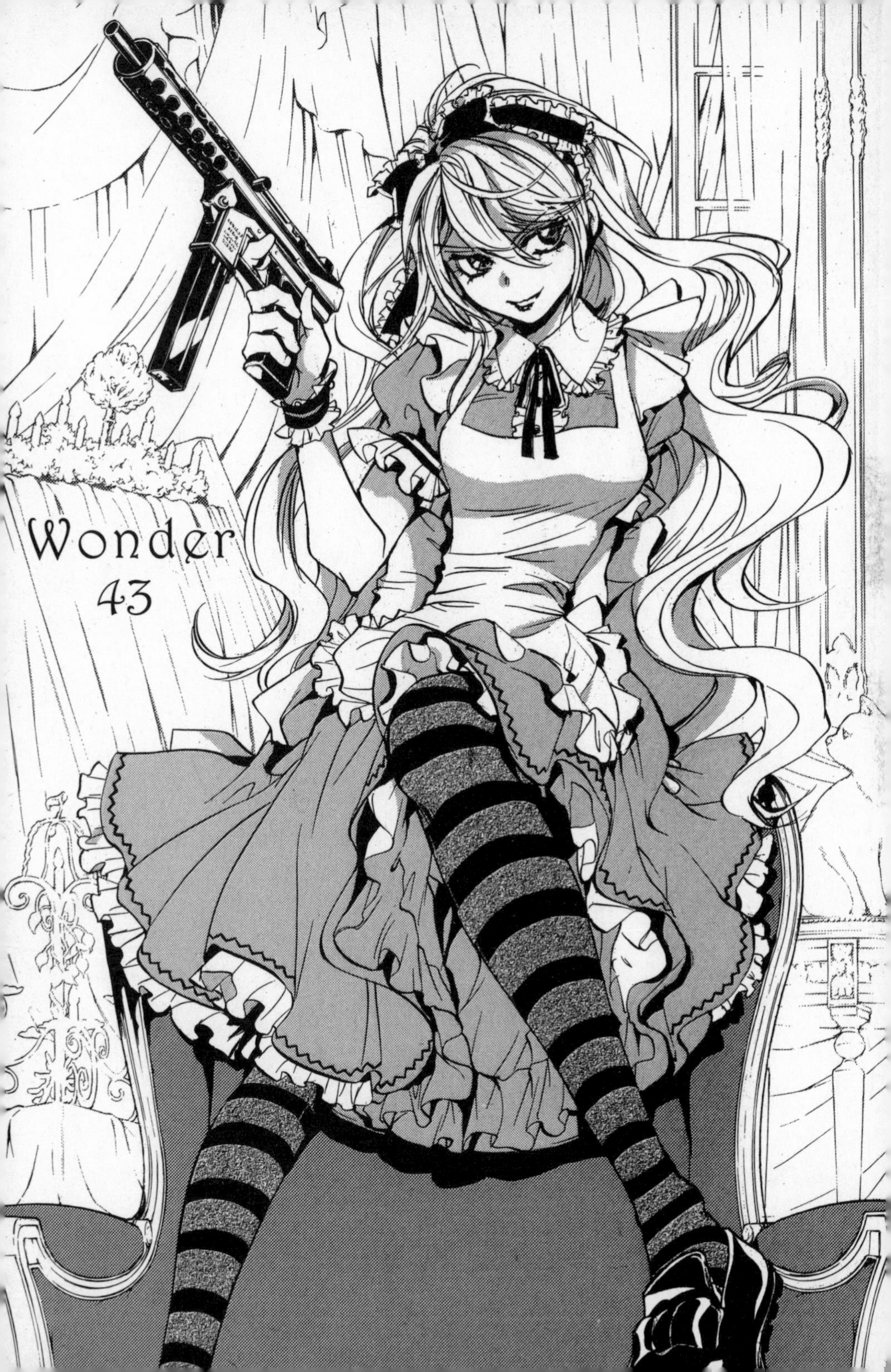
Wonder
43

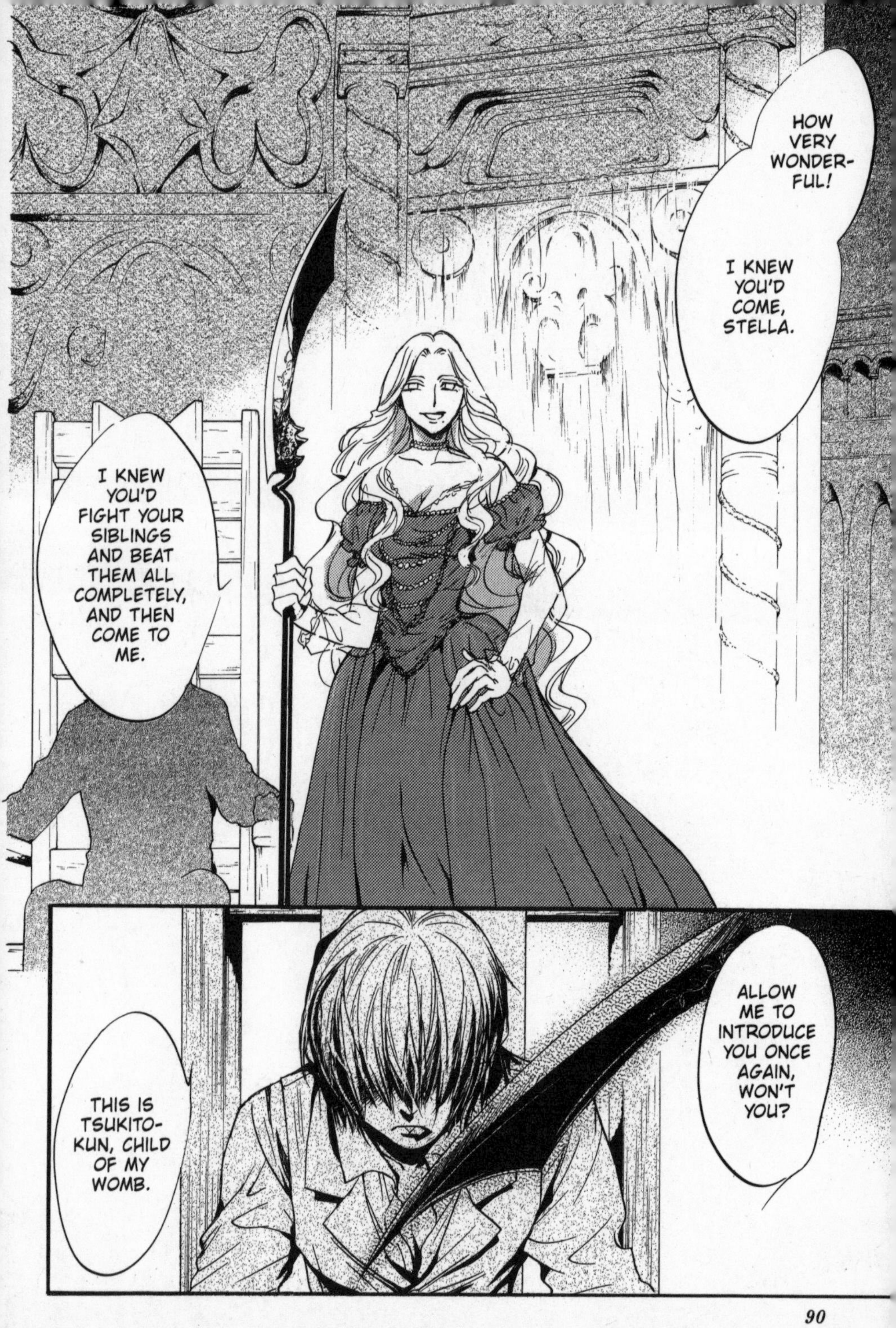
HOW VERY WONDERFUL!
I KNEW YOU'D COME, STELLA.
I KNEW YOU'D FIGHT YOUR SIBLINGS AND BEAT THEM ALL COMPLETELY, AND THEN COME TO ME.
ALLOW ME TO INTRODUCE YOU ONCE AGAIN, WON'T YOU?
THIS IS TSUKITO-KUN, CHILD OF MY WOMB.

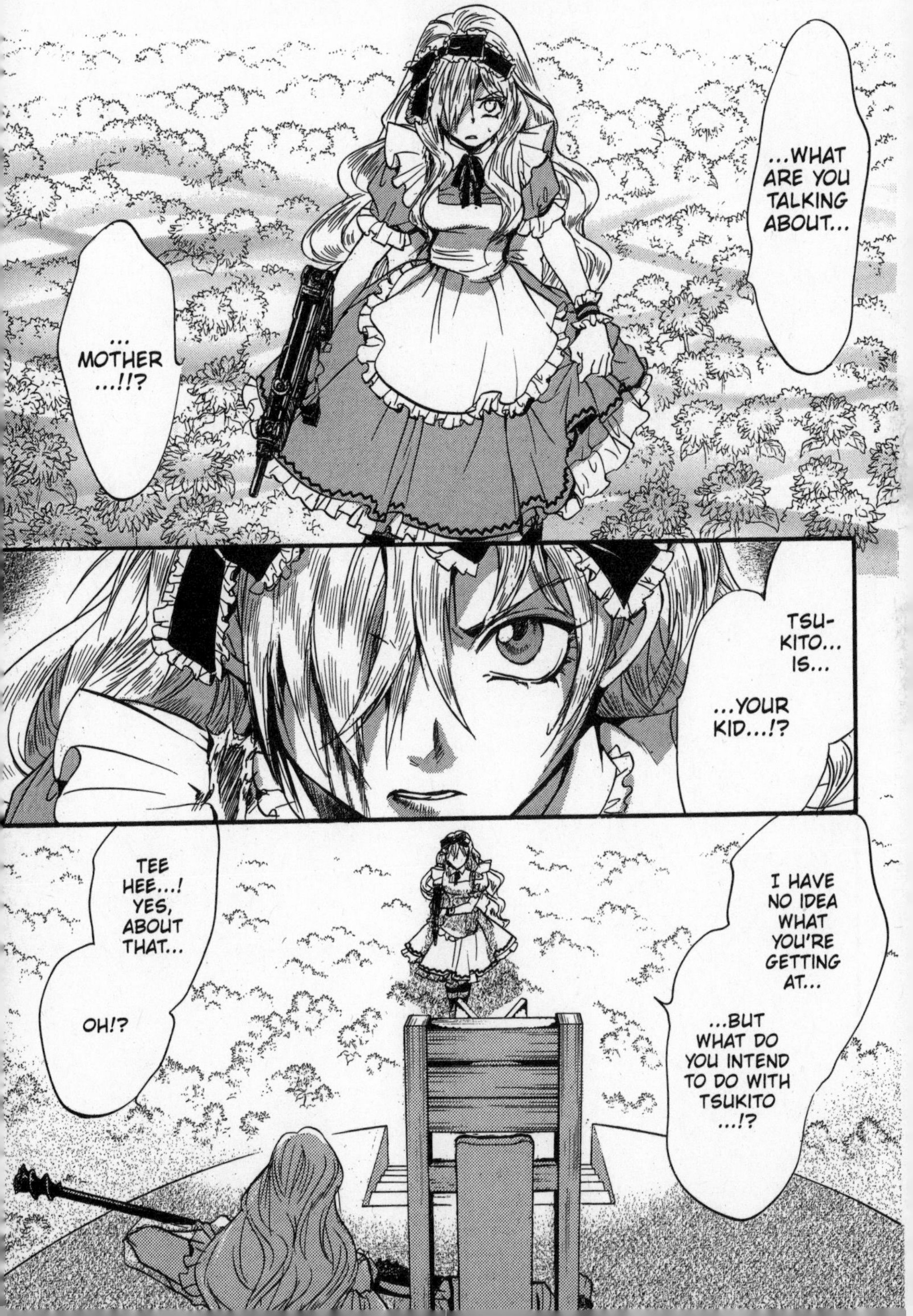
...WHAT ARE YOU TALKING ABOUT...
...MOTHER ...!!?
TSU-KITO... IS...
...YOUR KID...!?
I HAVE NO IDEA WHAT YOU'RE GETTING AT...
...BUT WHAT DO YOU INTEND TO DO WITH TSUKITO ...!?
TEE HEE...! YES, ABOUT THAT...
OH!?

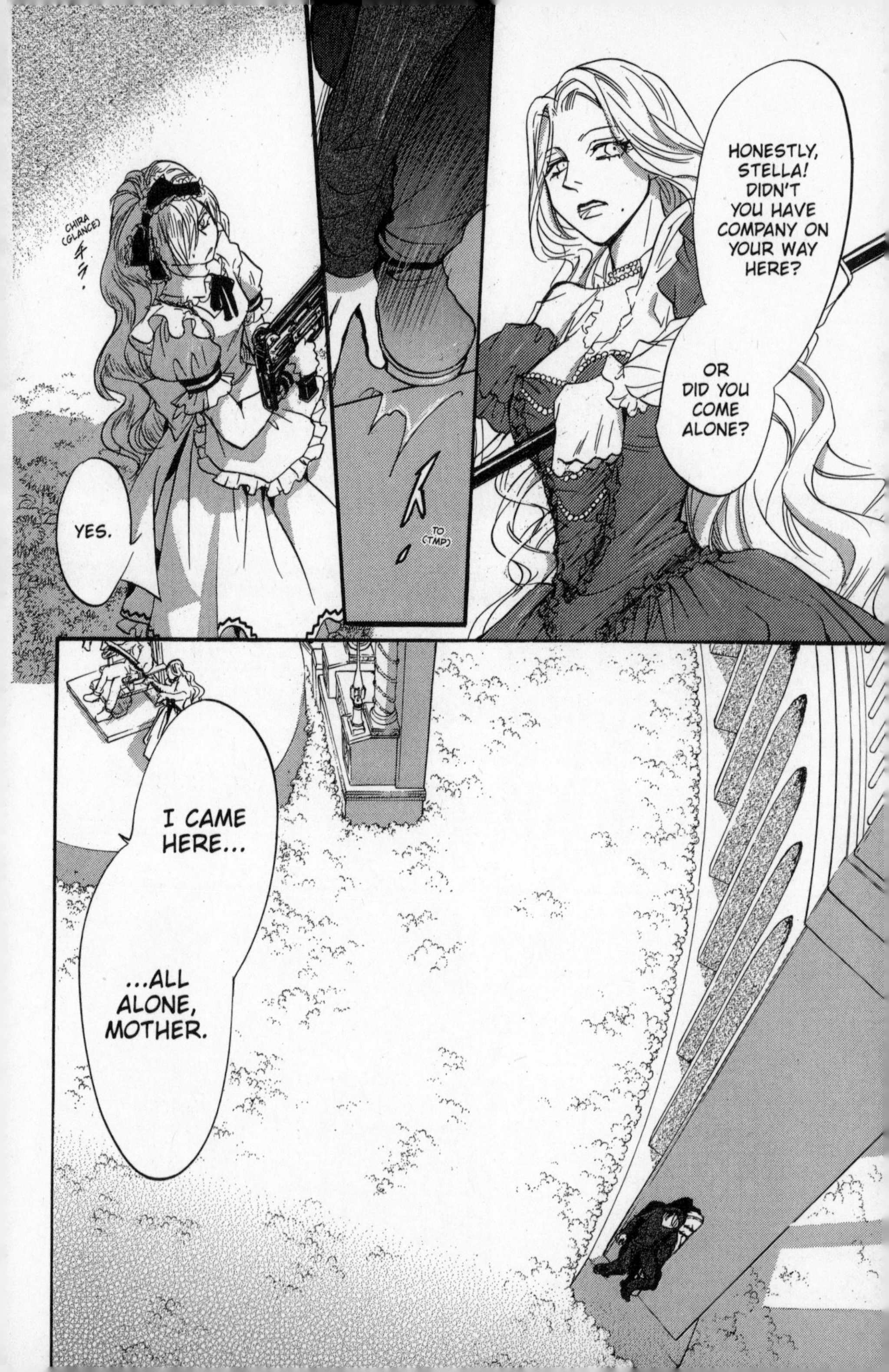
HONESTLY, STELLA! DIDN'T YOU HAVE COMPANY ON YOUR WAY HERE?
OR DID YOU COME ALONE?
TO (TMP)
CHIRA (GLANCE)
YES.
I CAME HERE...
...ALL ALONE, MOTHER.

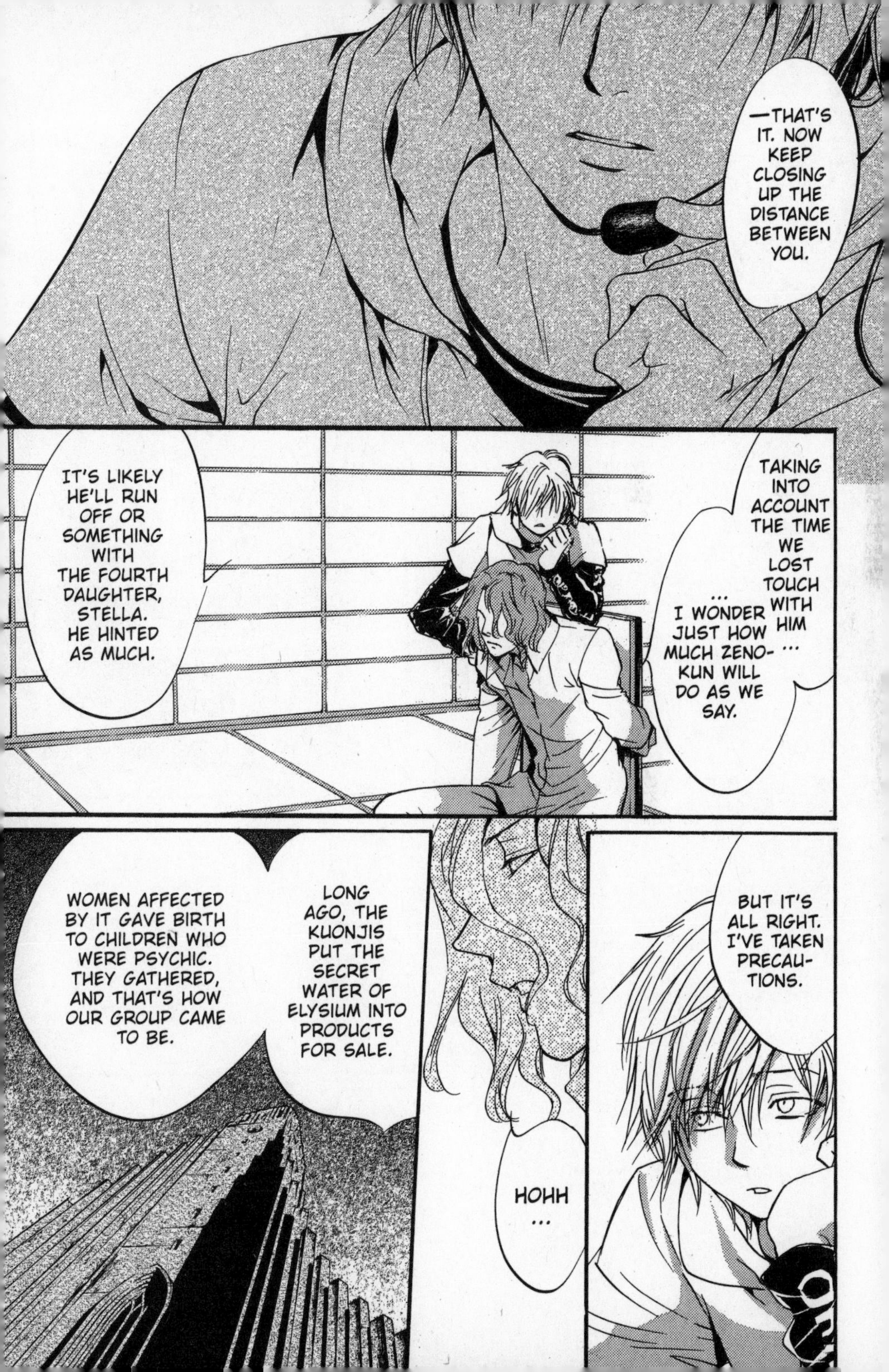
—THAT'S IT. NOW KEEP CLOSING UP THE DISTANCE BETWEEN YOU.
TAKING INTO ACCOUNT THE TIME WE LOST TOUCH WITH HIM ...
... I WONDER JUST HOW MUCH ZENO-KUN WILL DO AS WE SAY.
IT'S LIKELY HE'LL RUN OFF OR SOMETHING WITH THE FOURTH DAUGHTER, STELLA. HE HINTED AS MUCH.
BUT IT'S ALL RIGHT. I'VE TAKEN PRECAU-TIONS.
HOHH ...
LONG AGO, THE KUONJIS PUT THE SECRET WATER OF ELYSIUM INTO PRODUCTS FOR SALE.
WOMEN AFFECTED BY IT GAVE BIRTH TO CHILDREN WHO WERE PSYCHIC. THEY GATHERED, AND THAT'S HOW OUR GROUP CAME TO BE.

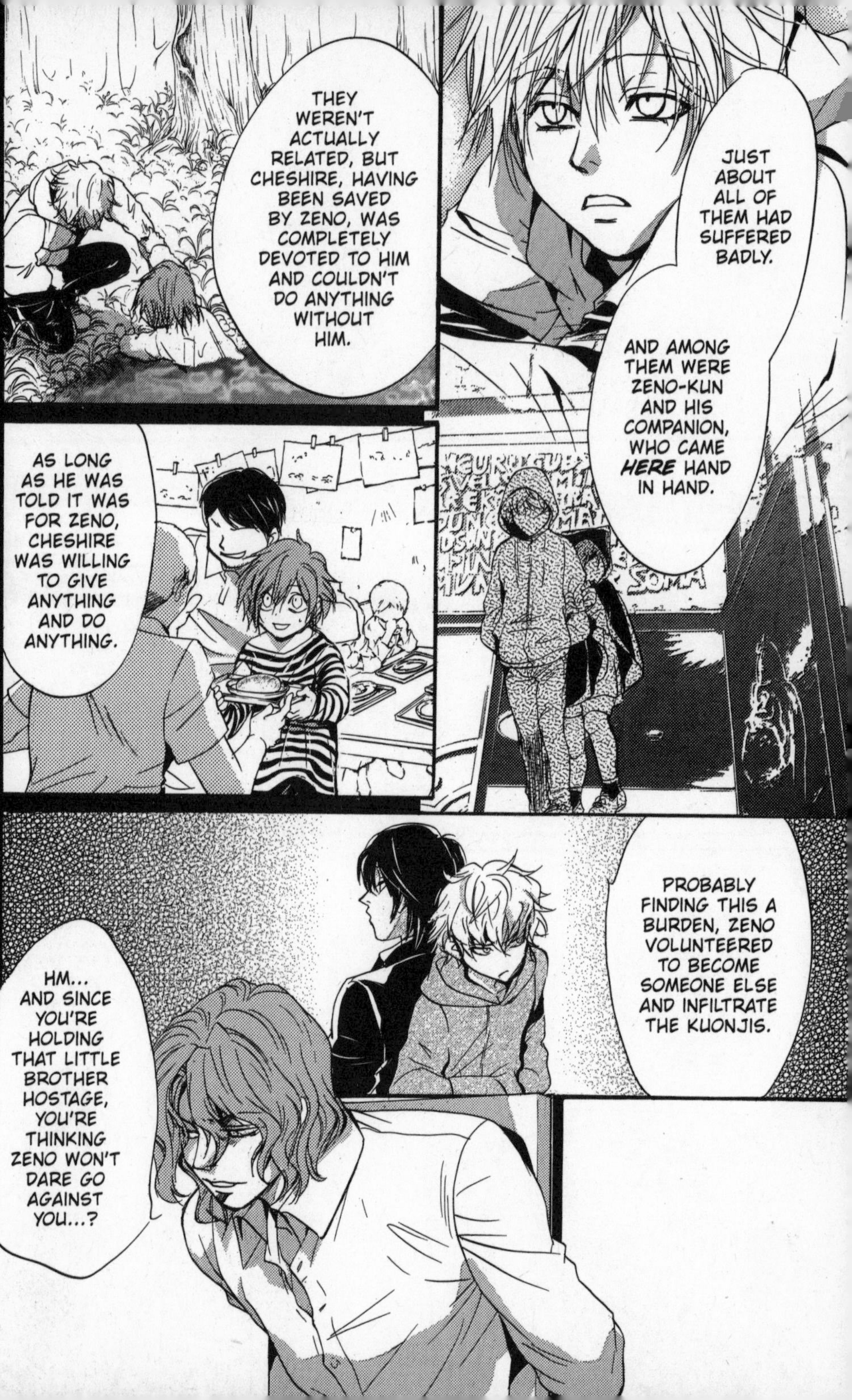
JUST ABOUT ALL OF THEM HAD SUFFERED BADLY.
THEY WEREN'T ACTUALLY RELATED, BUT CHESHIRE, HAVING BEEN SAVED BY ZENO, WAS COMPLETELY DEVOTED TO HIM AND COULDN'T DO ANYTHING WITHOUT HIM.
AND AMONG THEM WERE ZENO-KUN AND HIS COMPANION, WHO CAME *HERE* HAND IN HAND.
AS LONG AS HE WAS TOLD IT WAS FOR ZENO, CHESHIRE WAS WILLING TO GIVE ANYTHING AND DO ANYTHING.
PROBABLY FINDING THIS A BURDEN, ZENO VOLUNTEERED TO BECOME SOMEONE ELSE AND INFILTRATE THE KUONJIS.
HM... AND SINCE YOU'RE HOLDING THAT LITTLE BROTHER HOSTAGE, YOU'RE THINKING ZENO WON'T DARE GO AGAINST YOU...?

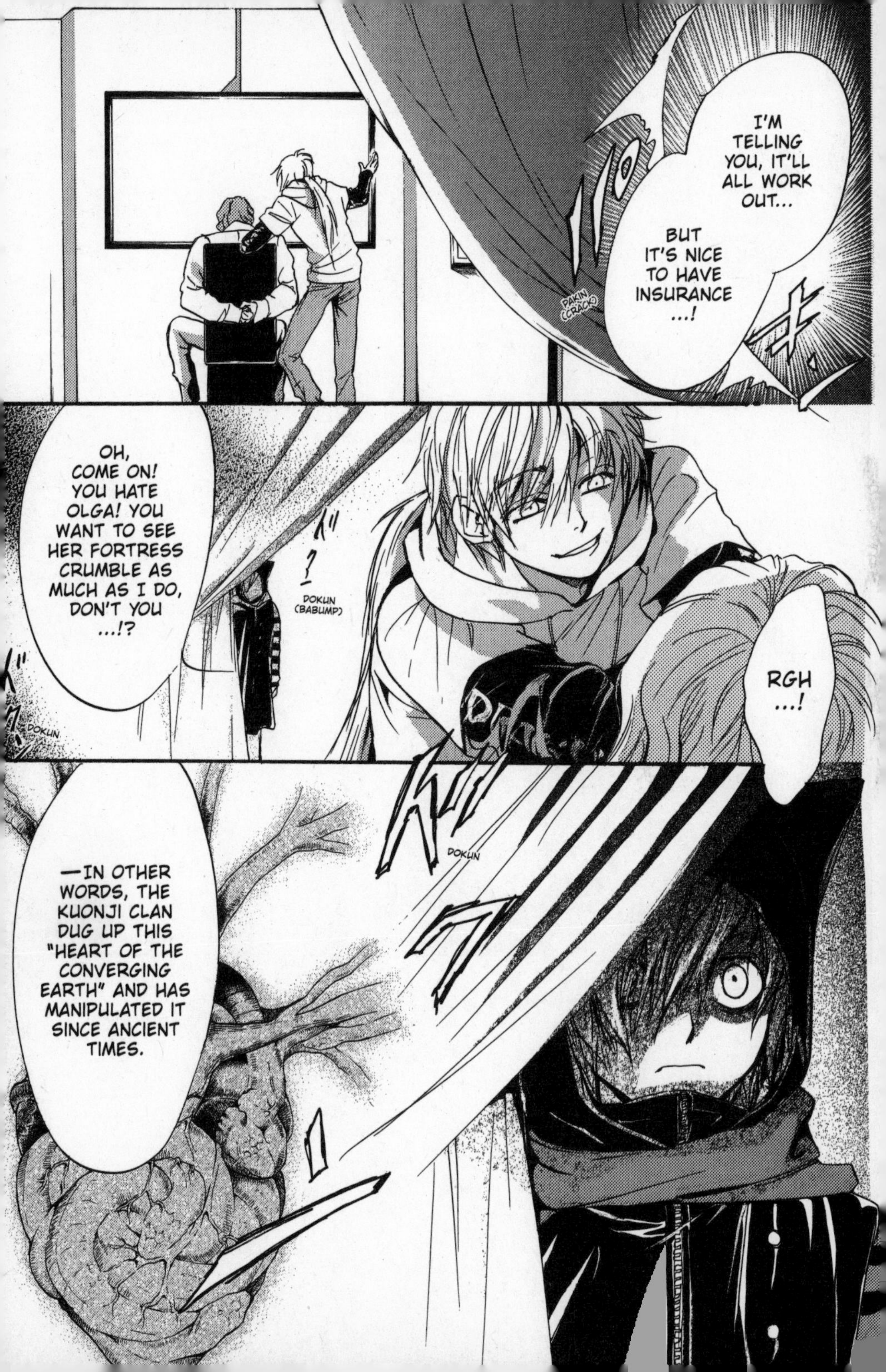
I'M TELLING YOU, IT'LL ALL WORK OUT...
BUT IT'S NICE TO HAVE INSURANCE ...!
PAKIN (CRACK)
OH, COME ON! YOU HATE OLGA! YOU WANT TO SEE HER FORTRESS CRUMBLE AS MUCH AS I DO, DON'T YOU ...!?
DOKUN (BABUMP)
DOKUN
RGH ...!
DOKUN
—IN OTHER WORDS, THE KUONJI CLAN DUG UP THIS "HEART OF THE CONVERGING EARTH" AND HAS MANIPULATED IT SINCE ANCIENT TIMES.

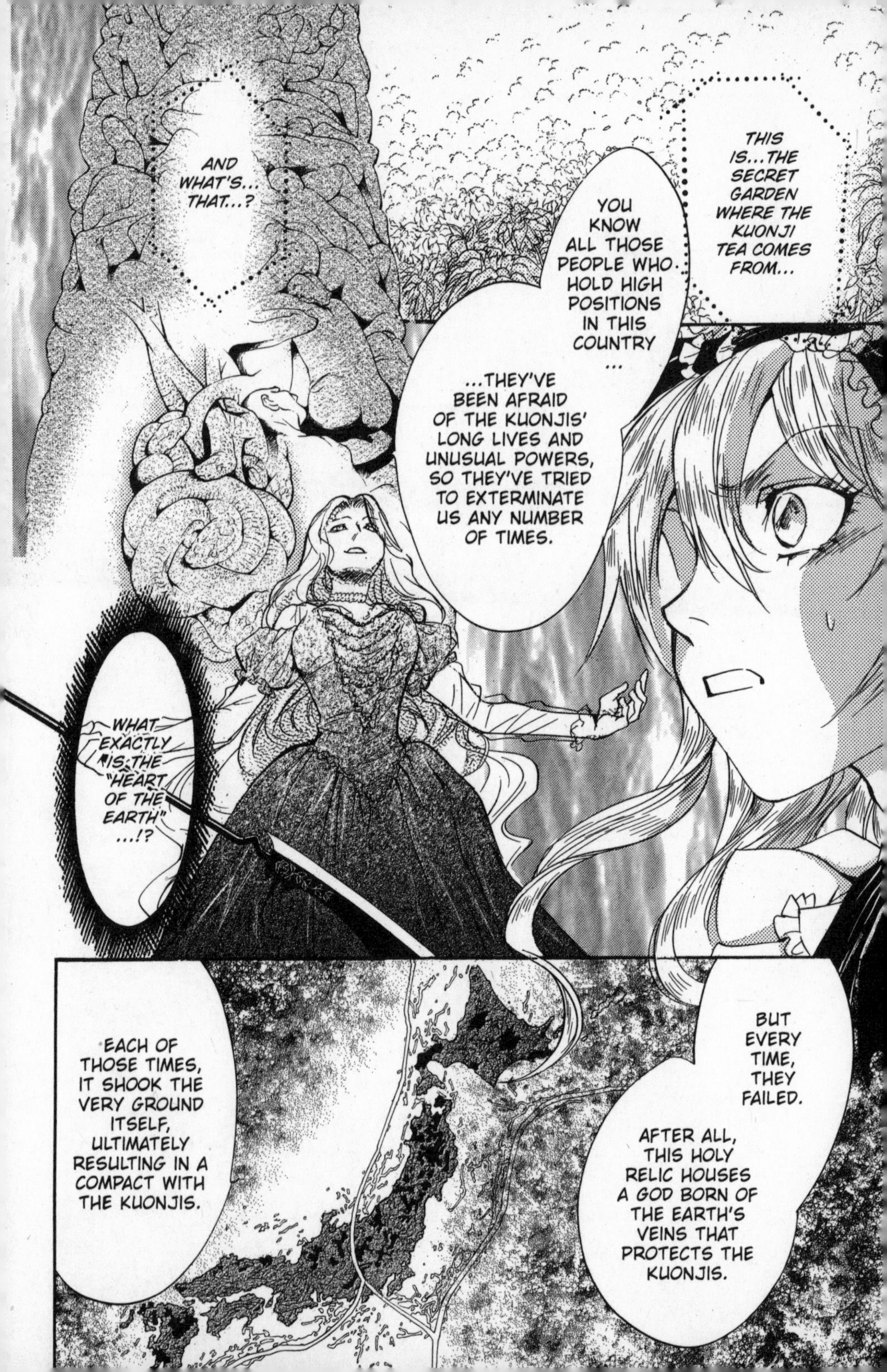
THIS IS...THE SECRET GARDEN WHERE THE KUONJI TEA COMES FROM...
YOU KNOW ALL THOSE PEOPLE WHO HOLD HIGH POSITIONS IN THIS COUNTRY...
...THEY'VE BEEN AFRAID OF THE KUONJIS' LONG LIVES AND UNUSUAL POWERS, SO THEY'VE TRIED TO EXTERMINATE US ANY NUMBER OF TIMES.
AND WHAT'S... THAT...?
WHAT EXACTLY IS THE "HEART OF THE EARTH"...!?
BUT EVERY TIME, THEY FAILED.
AFTER ALL, THIS HOLY RELIC HOUSES A GOD BORN OF THE EARTH'S VEINS THAT PROTECTS THE KUONJIS.
EACH OF THOSE TIMES, IT SHOOK THE VERY GROUND ITSELF, ULTIMATELY RESULTING IN A COMPACT WITH THE KUONJIS.

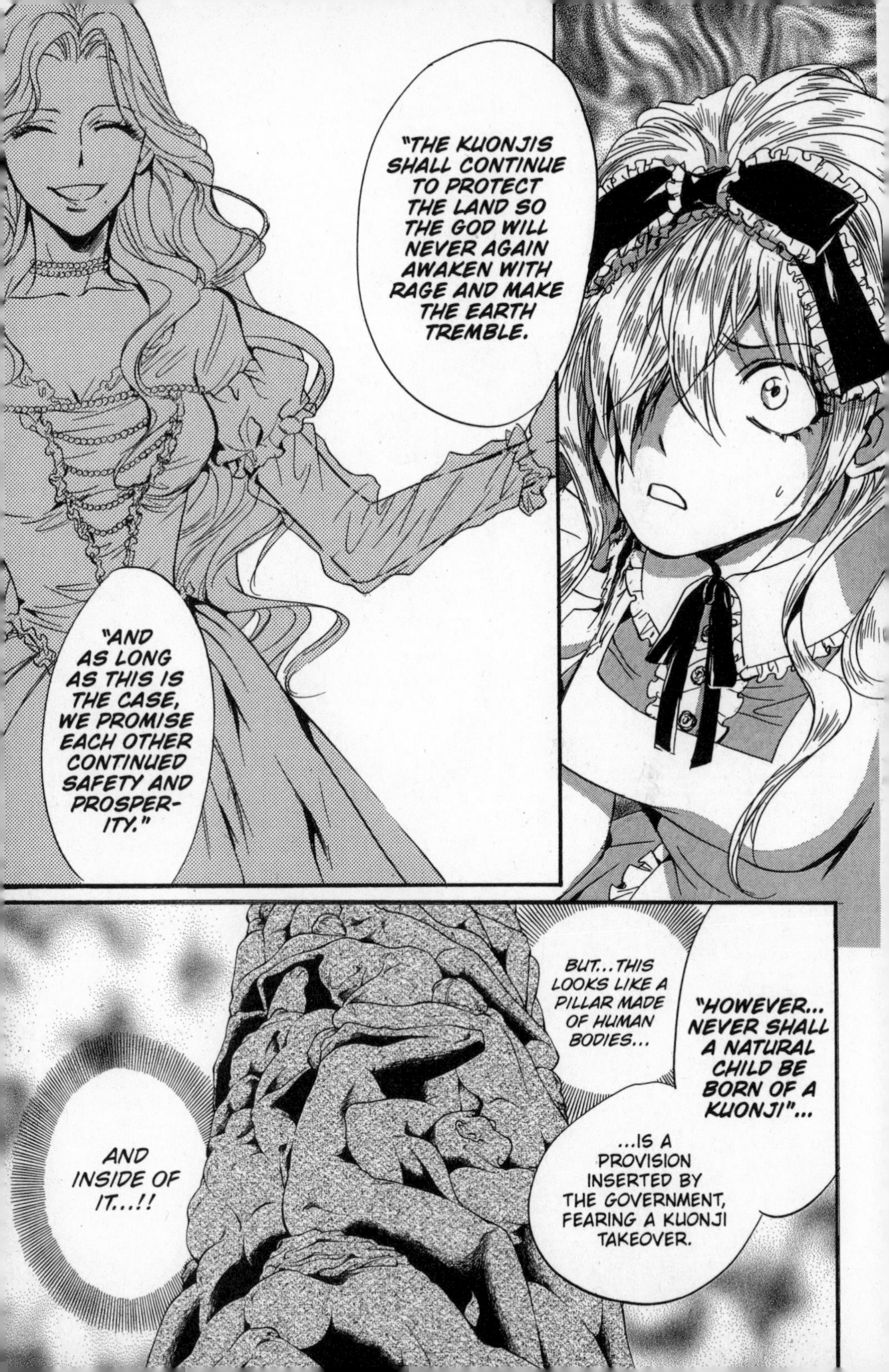
"THE KUONJIS SHALL CONTINUE TO PROTECT THE LAND SO THE GOD WILL NEVER AGAIN AWAKEN WITH RAGE AND MAKE THE EARTH TREMBLE.
"AND AS LONG AS THIS IS THE CASE, WE PROMISE EACH OTHER CONTINUED SAFETY AND PROSPER-ITY."
"HOWEVER... NEVER SHALL A NATURAL CHILD BE BORN OF A KUONJI"...
...IS A PROVISION INSERTED BY THE GOVERNMENT, FEARING A KUONJI TAKEOVER.
BUT...THIS LOOKS LIKE A PILLAR MADE OF HUMAN BODIES...
AND INSIDE OF IT...!!

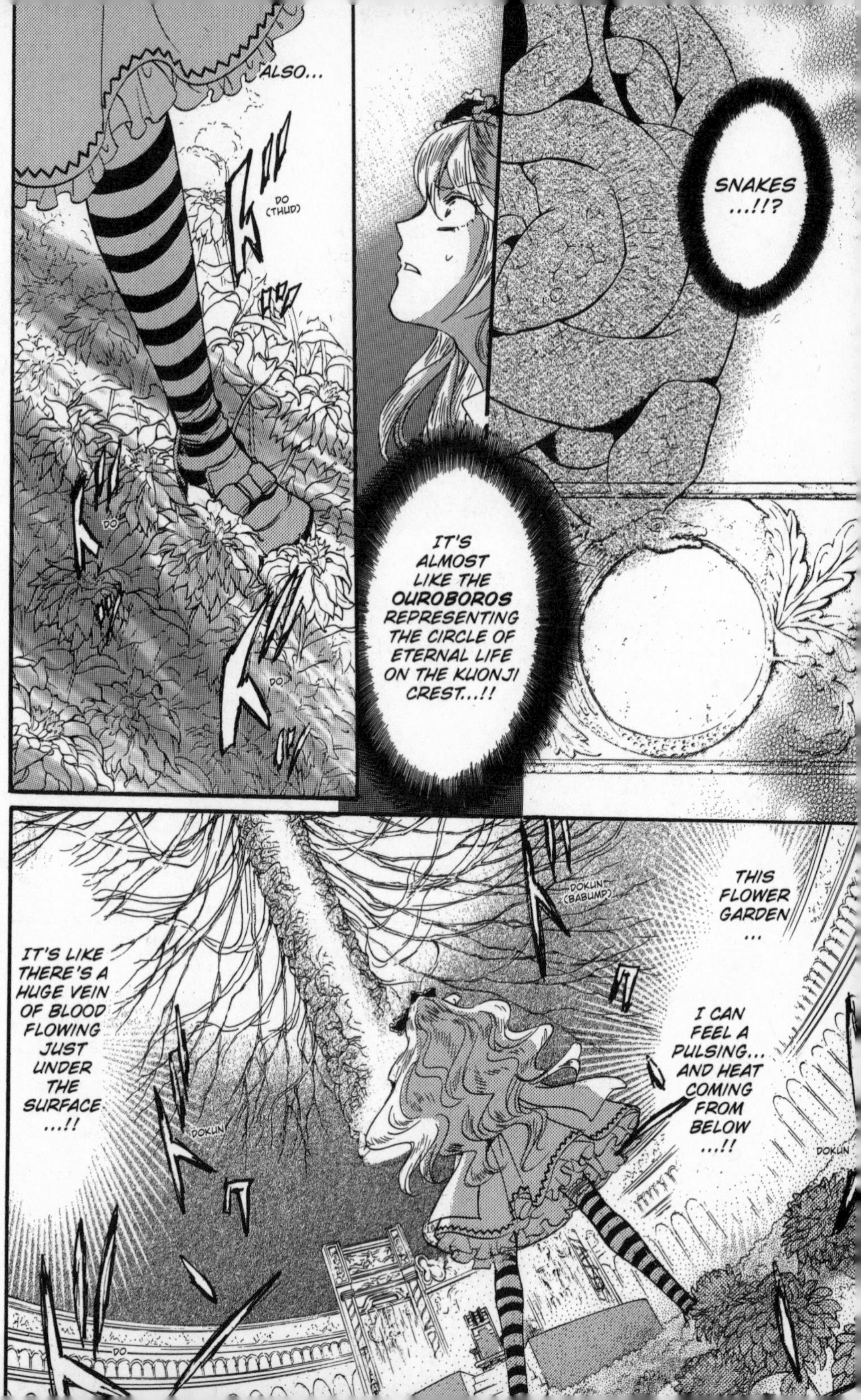
SNAKES ...!!?
IT'S ALMOST LIKE THE OUROBOROS REPRESENTING THE CIRCLE OF ETERNAL LIFE ON THE KUONJI CREST...!!
ALSO...
DO (THUD)
DO
DO
THIS FLOWER GARDEN ...
DOKUN (BABUMP)
I CAN FEEL A PULSING... AND HEAT COMING FROM BELOW ...!!
DOKUN
IT'S LIKE THERE'S A HUGE VEIN OF BLOOD FLOWING JUST UNDER THE SURFACE ...!!
DOKUN
DO

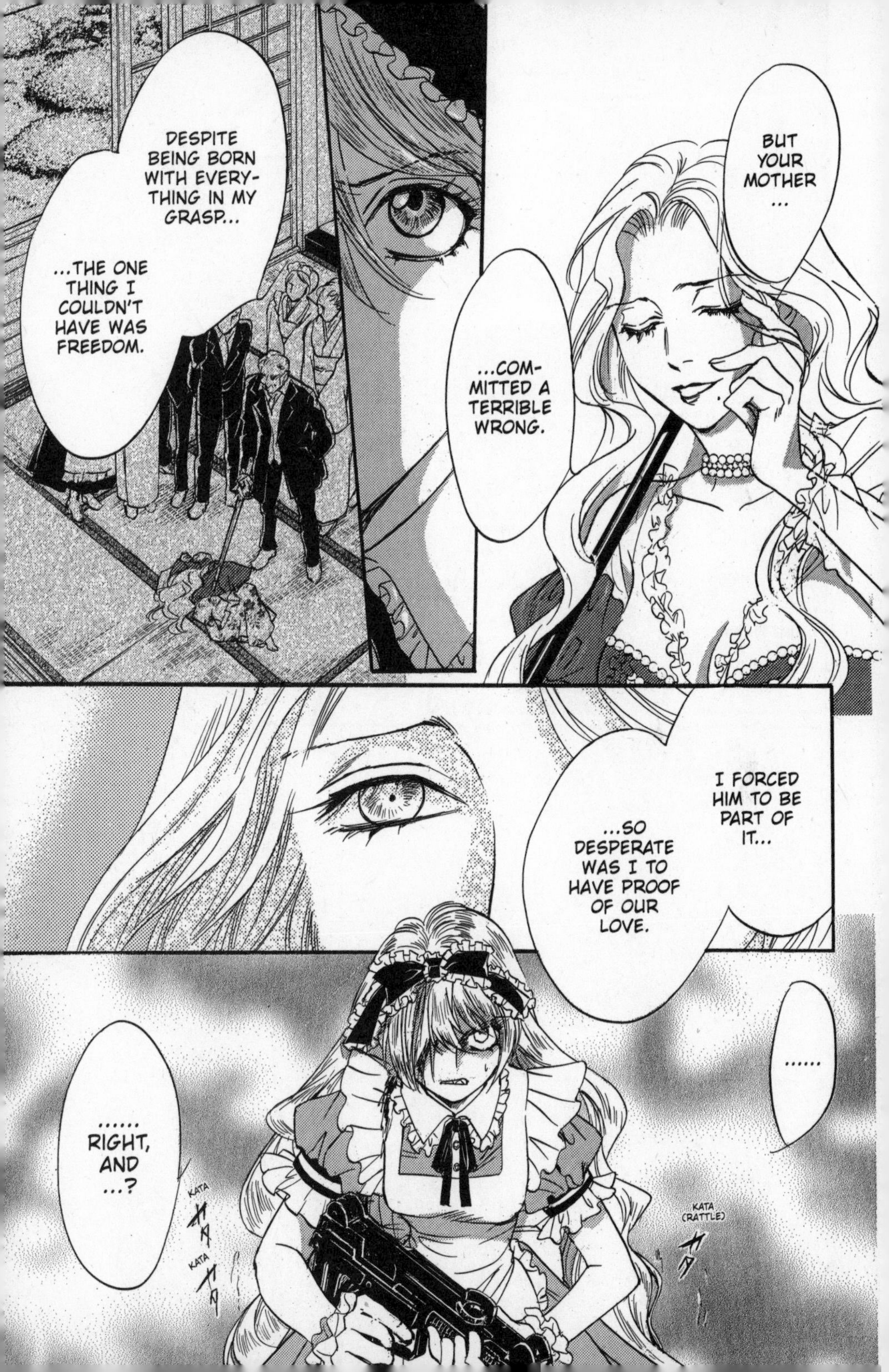
BUT YOUR MOTHER ...
...COM-MITTED A TERRIBLE WRONG.
DESPITE BEING BORN WITH EVERY-THING IN MY GRASP...
...THE ONE THING I COULDN'T HAVE WAS FREEDOM.
I FORCED HIM TO BE PART OF IT...
...SO DESPERATE WAS I TO HAVE PROOF OF OUR LOVE.
......
KATA (RATTLE)
...... RIGHT, AND ...?
KATA
KATA

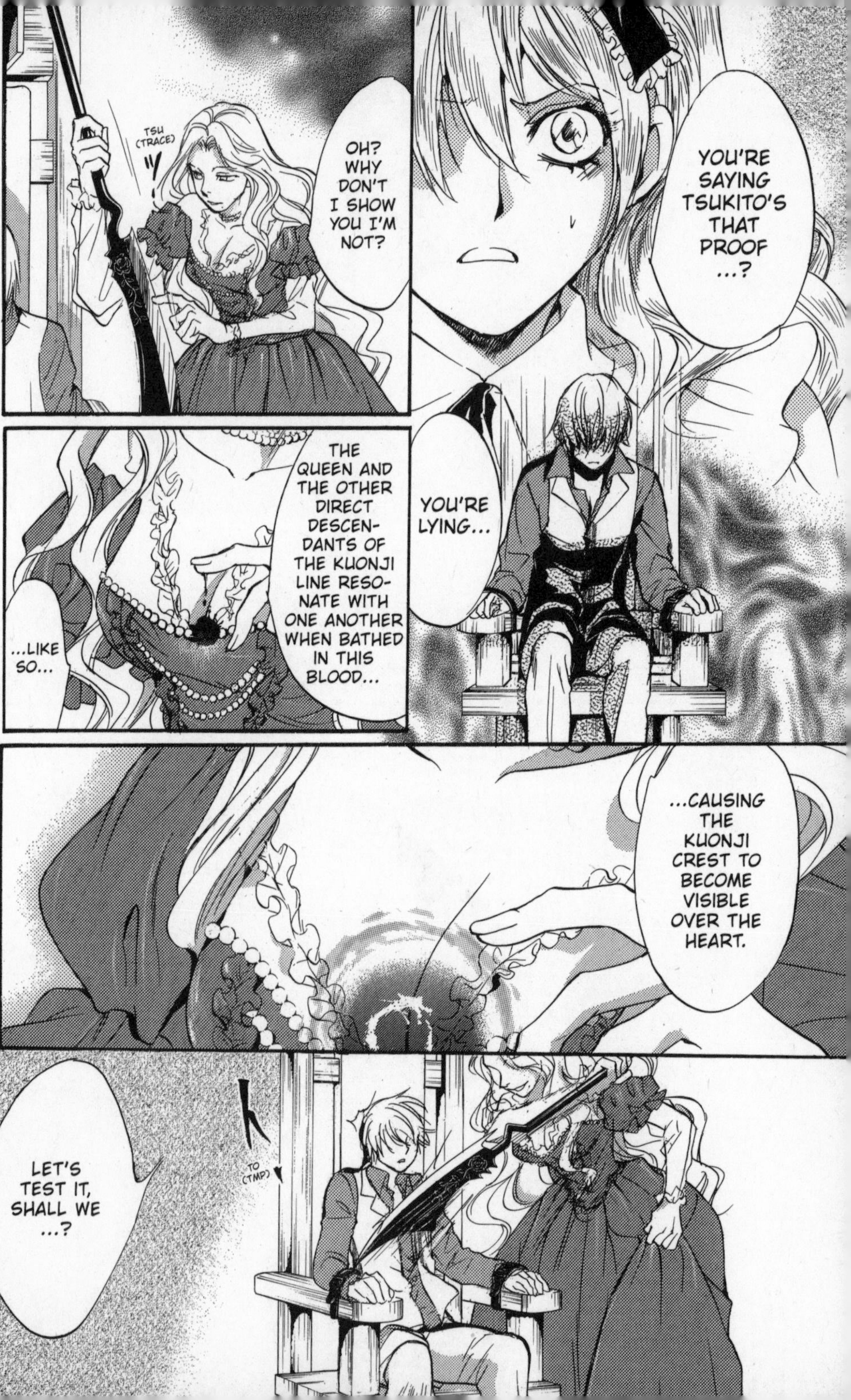
YOU'RE SAYING TSUKITO'S THAT PROOF ...?
YOU'RE LYING...
TSU (TRACE)
OH? WHY DON'T I SHOW YOU I'M NOT?
THE QUEEN AND THE OTHER DIRECT DESCEN-DANTS OF THE KUONJI LINE RESO-NATE WITH ONE ANOTHER WHEN BATHED IN THIS BLOOD...
...LIKE SO...
...CAUSING THE KUONJI CREST TO BECOME VISIBLE OVER THE HEART.
TO (TMP)
LET'S TEST IT, SHALL WE ...?

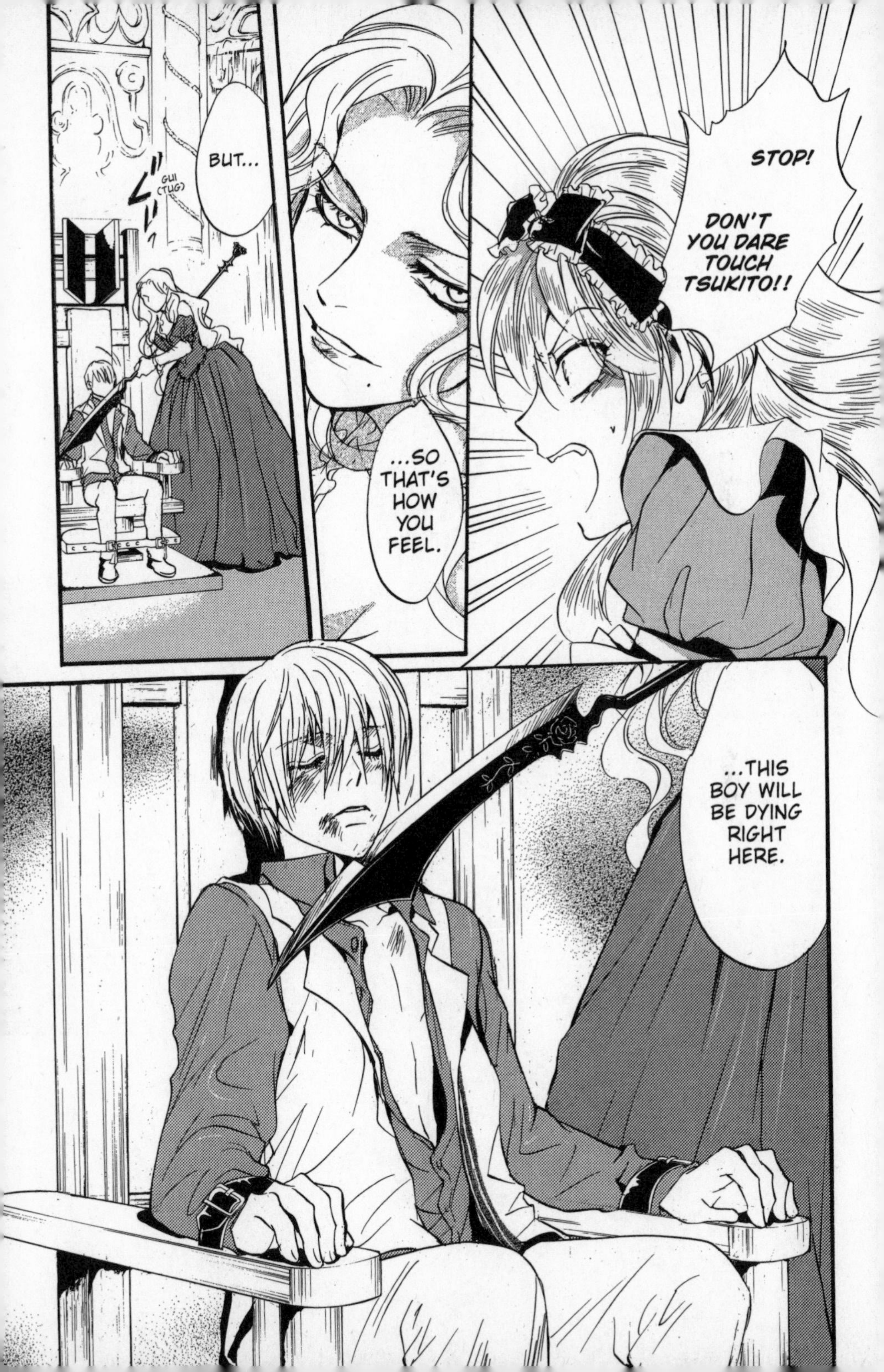
STOP!
DON'T YOU DARE TOUCH TSUKITO!!
...SO THAT'S HOW YOU FEEL.
BUT...
GUI (TUG)
...THIS BOY WILL BE DYING RIGHT HERE.

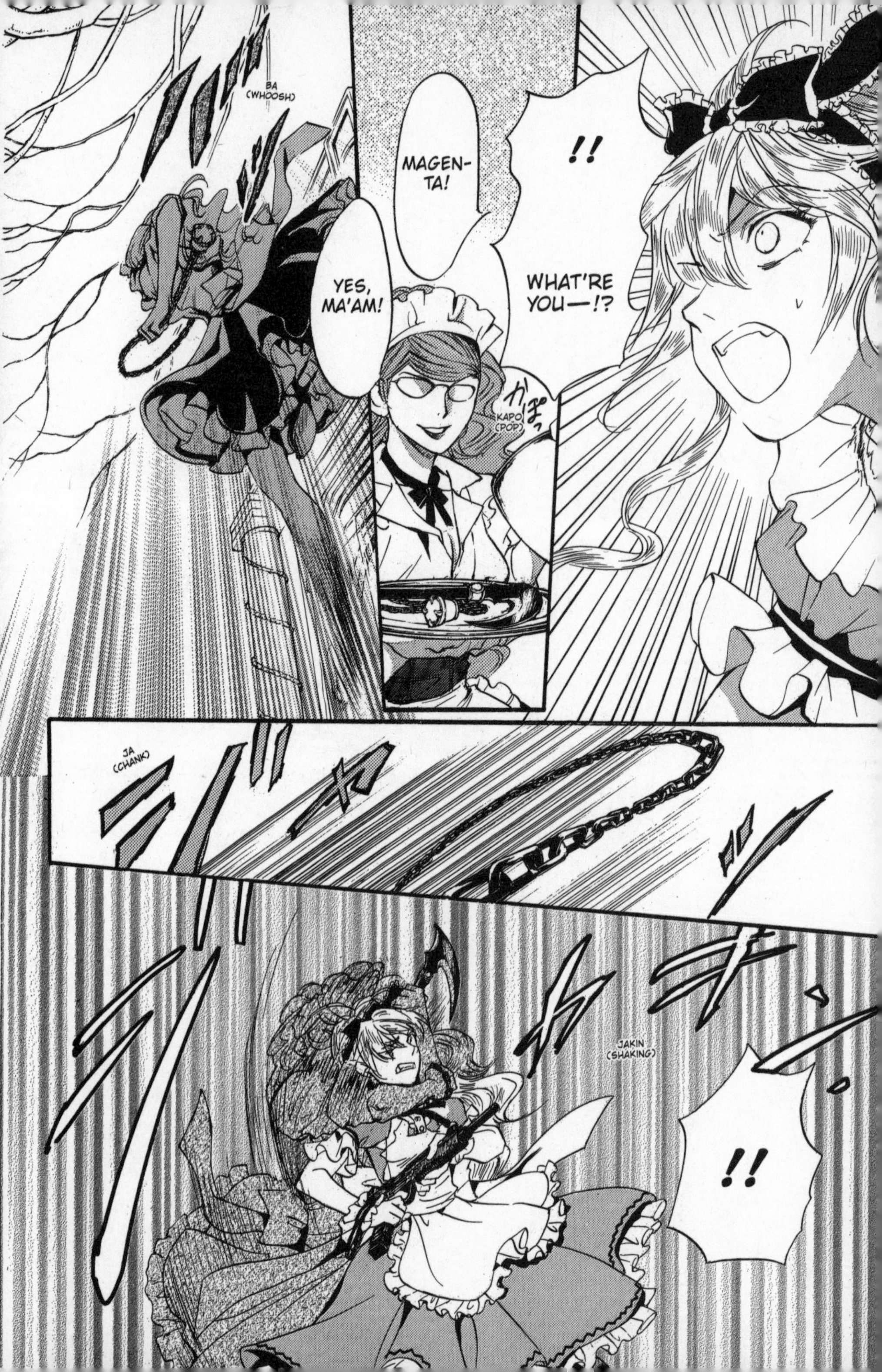
!!
WHAT'RE YOU—!?
MAGENTA!
YES, MA'AM!
KAPO (POP)
BA (WHOOSH)
JA (CHANK)
JAKIN (SHAKING)
!!

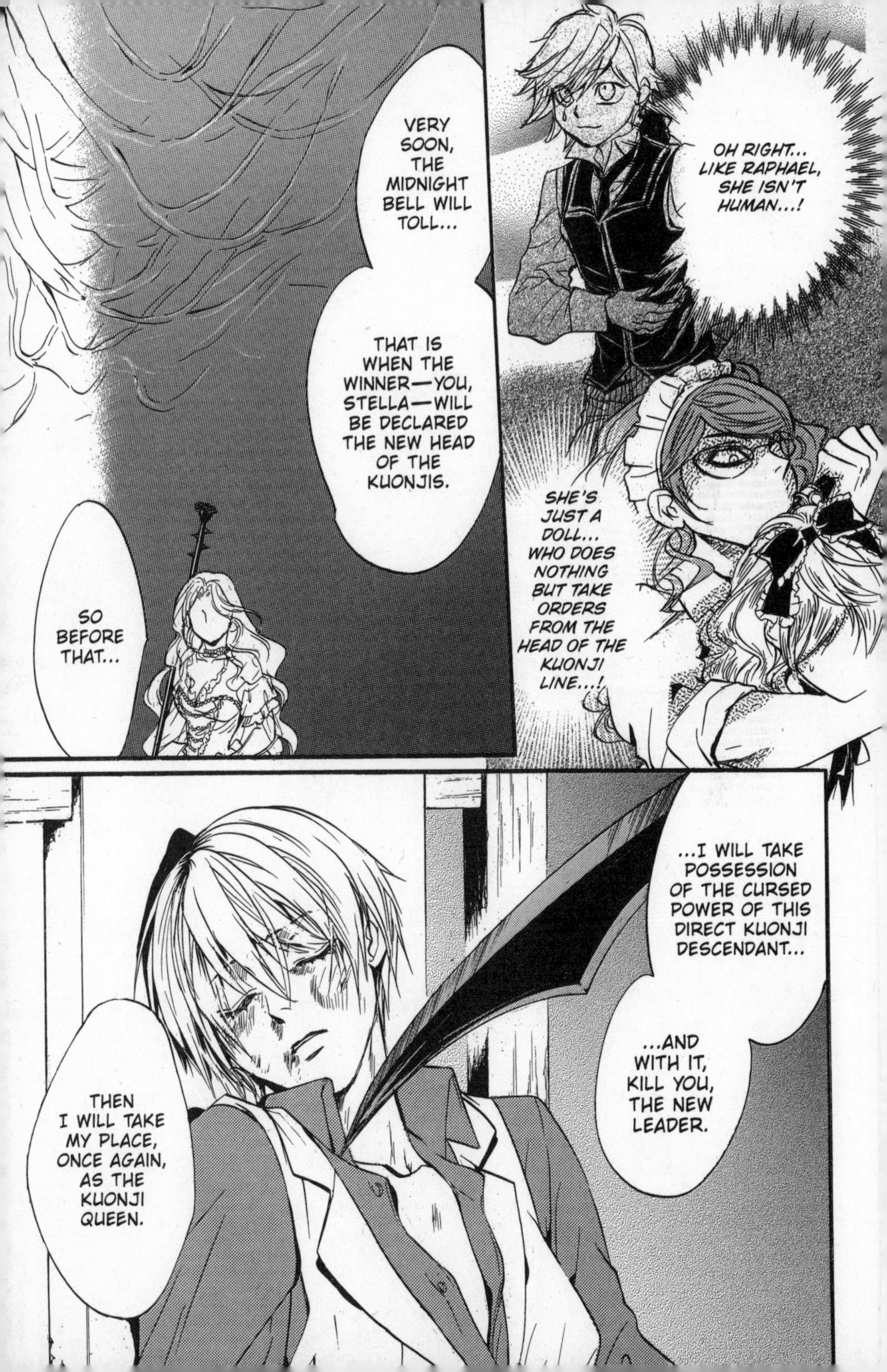
OH RIGHT... LIKE RAPHAEL, SHE ISN'T HUMAN...!
SHE'S JUST A DOLL... WHO DOES NOTHING BUT TAKE ORDERS FROM THE HEAD OF THE KUONJI LINE...!
VERY SOON, THE MIDNIGHT BELL WILL TOLL...
THAT IS WHEN THE WINNER—YOU, STELLA—WILL BE DECLARED THE NEW HEAD OF THE KUONJIS.
SO BEFORE THAT...
...I WILL TAKE POSSESSION OF THE CURSED POWER OF THIS DIRECT KUONJI DESCENDANT...
...AND WITH IT, KILL YOU, THE NEW LEADER.
THEN I WILL TAKE MY PLACE, ONCE AGAIN, AS THE KUONJI QUEEN.

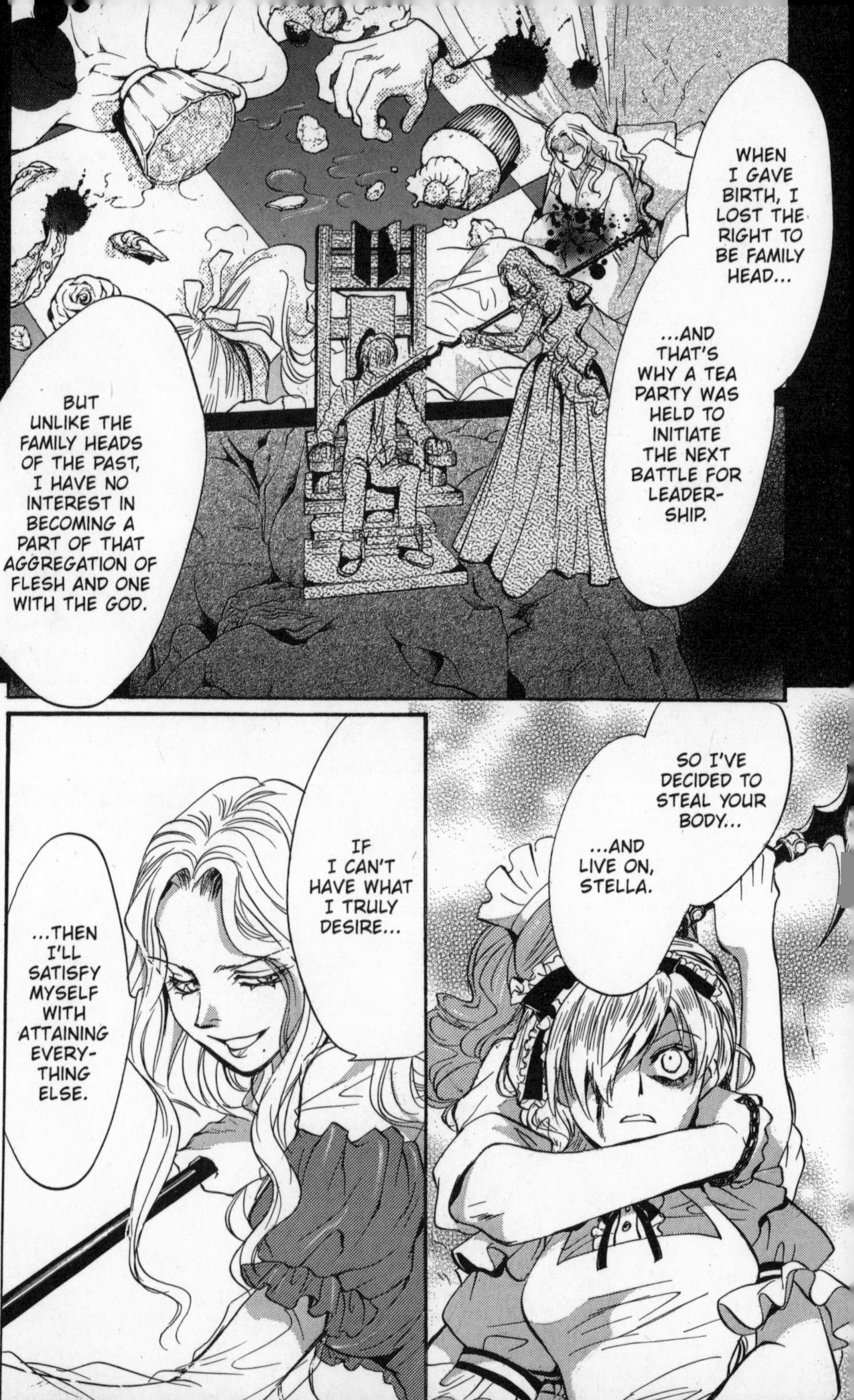
WHEN I GAVE BIRTH, I LOST THE RIGHT TO BE FAMILY HEAD...
...AND THAT'S WHY A TEA PARTY WAS HELD TO INITIATE THE NEXT BATTLE FOR LEADER-SHIP.
BUT UNLIKE THE FAMILY HEADS OF THE PAST, I HAVE NO INTEREST IN BECOMING A PART OF THAT AGGREGATION OF FLESH AND ONE WITH THE GOD.
SO I'VE DECIDED TO STEAL YOUR BODY...
...AND LIVE ON, STELLA.
IF I CAN'T HAVE WHAT I TRULY DESIRE...
...THEN I'LL SATISFY MYSELF WITH ATTAINING EVERY-THING ELSE.

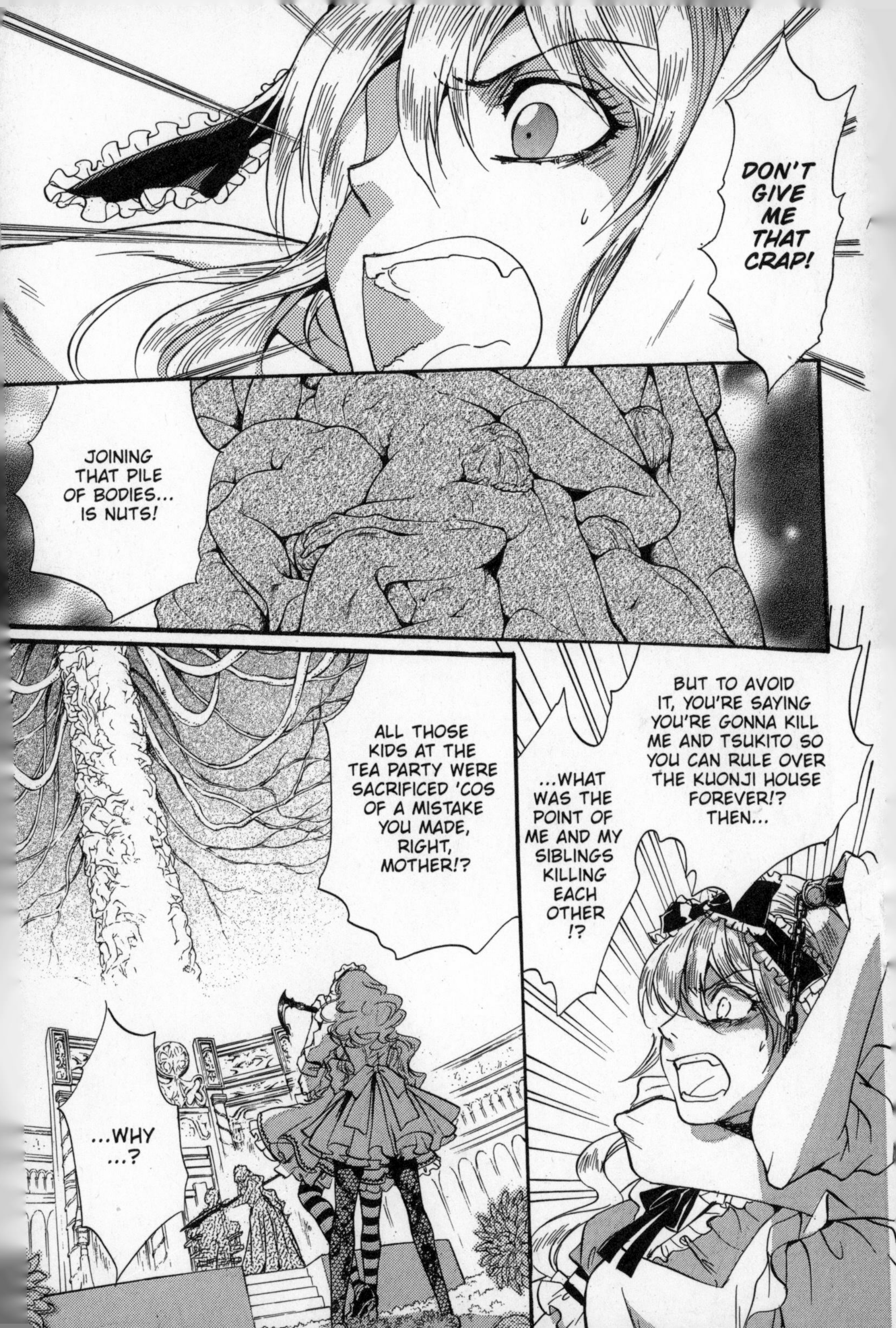
DON'T GIVE ME THAT CRAP!
JOINING THAT PILE OF BODIES... IS NUTS!
BUT TO AVOID IT, YOU'RE SAYING YOU'RE GONNA KILL ME AND TSUKITO SO YOU CAN RULE OVER THE KUONJI HOUSE FOREVER!? THEN...
...WHAT WAS THE POINT OF ME AND MY SIBLINGS KILLING EACH OTHER !?
ALL THOSE KIDS AT THE TEA PARTY WERE SACRIFICED 'COS OF A MISTAKE YOU MADE, RIGHT, MOTHER!?
...WHY ...?

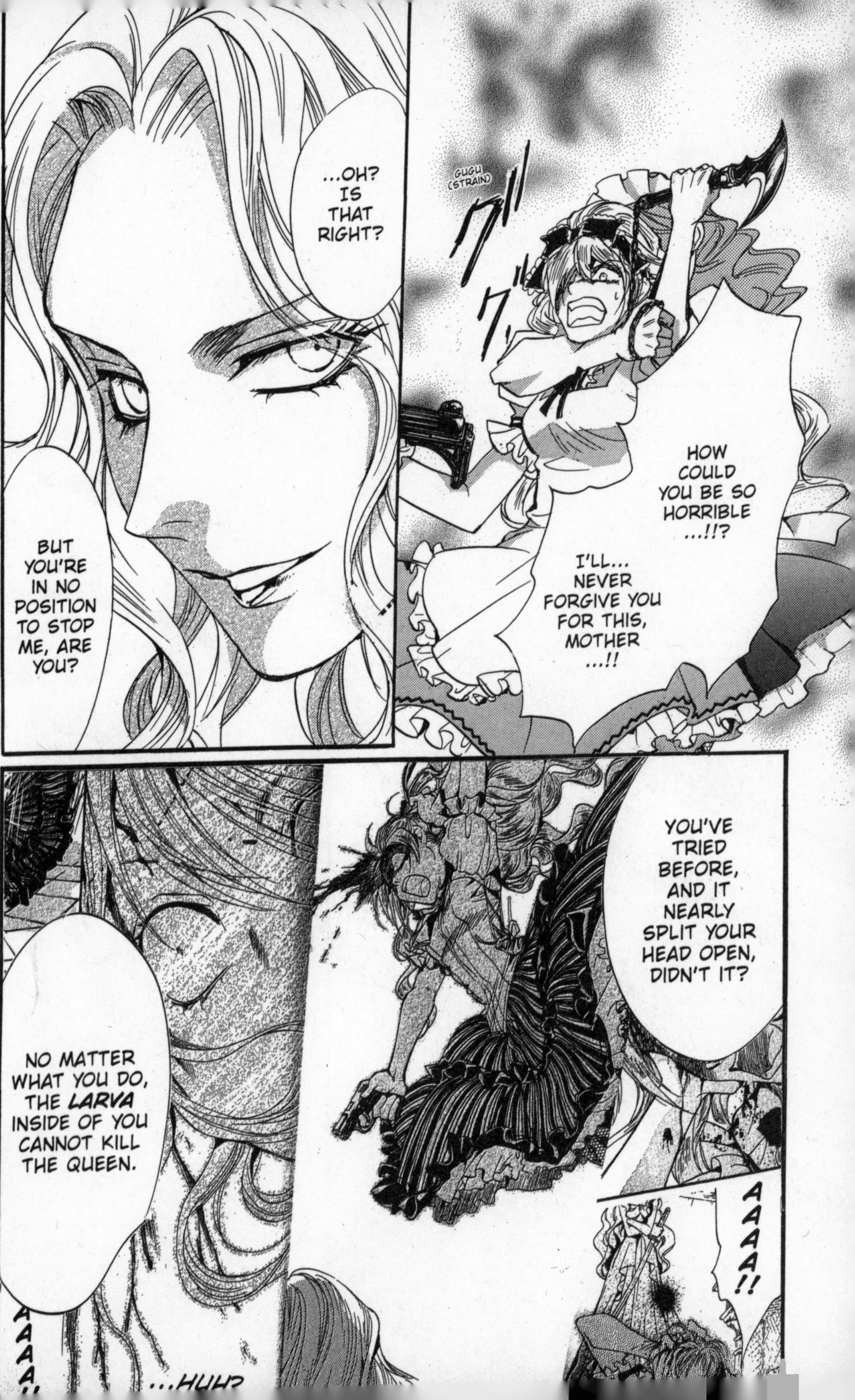
GUGU (STRAIN)
HOW COULD YOU BE SO HORRIBLE ...!!?
I'LL... NEVER FORGIVE YOU FOR THIS, MOTHER ...!!
...OH? IS THAT RIGHT?
BUT YOU'RE IN NO POSITION TO STOP ME, ARE YOU?
YOU'VE TRIED BEFORE, AND IT NEARLY SPLIT YOUR HEAD OPEN, DIDN'T IT?
AAAAA!!
NO MATTER WHAT YOU DO, THE *LARVA* INSIDE OF YOU CANNOT KILL THE QUEEN.
AAAAA
...HUH?

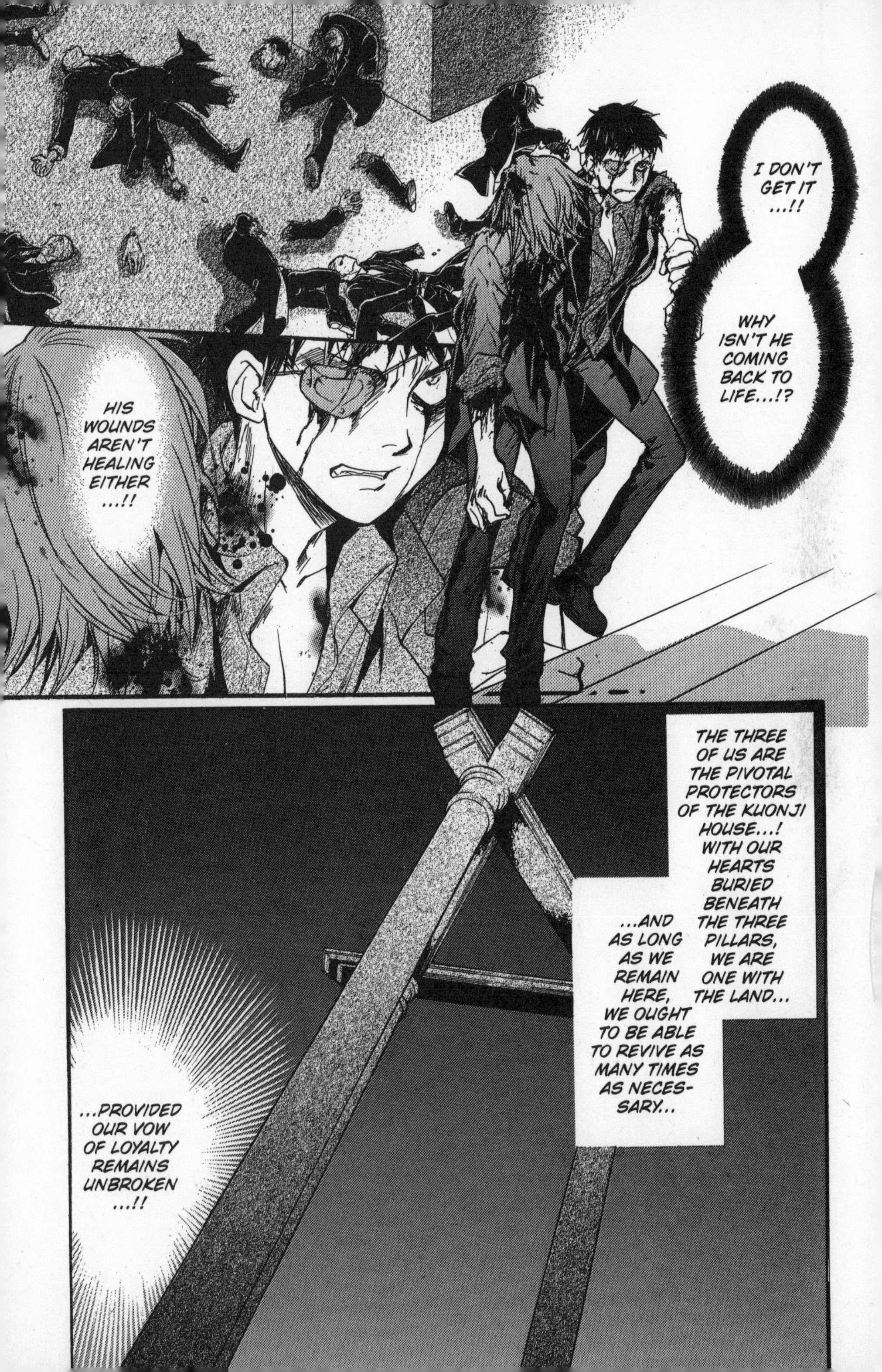
I DON'T GET IT ...!!
WHY ISN'T HE COMING BACK TO LIFE...!?
HIS WOUNDS AREN'T HEALING EITHER ...!!
THE THREE OF US ARE THE PIVOTAL PROTECTORS OF THE KUONJI HOUSE...! WITH OUR HEARTS BURIED BENEATH THE THREE PILLARS, WE ARE ONE WITH THE LAND...
...AND AS LONG AS WE REMAIN HERE, WE OUGHT TO BE ABLE TO REVIVE AS MANY TIMES AS NECES-SARY...
...PROVIDED OUR VOW OF LOYALTY REMAINS UNBROKEN ...!!

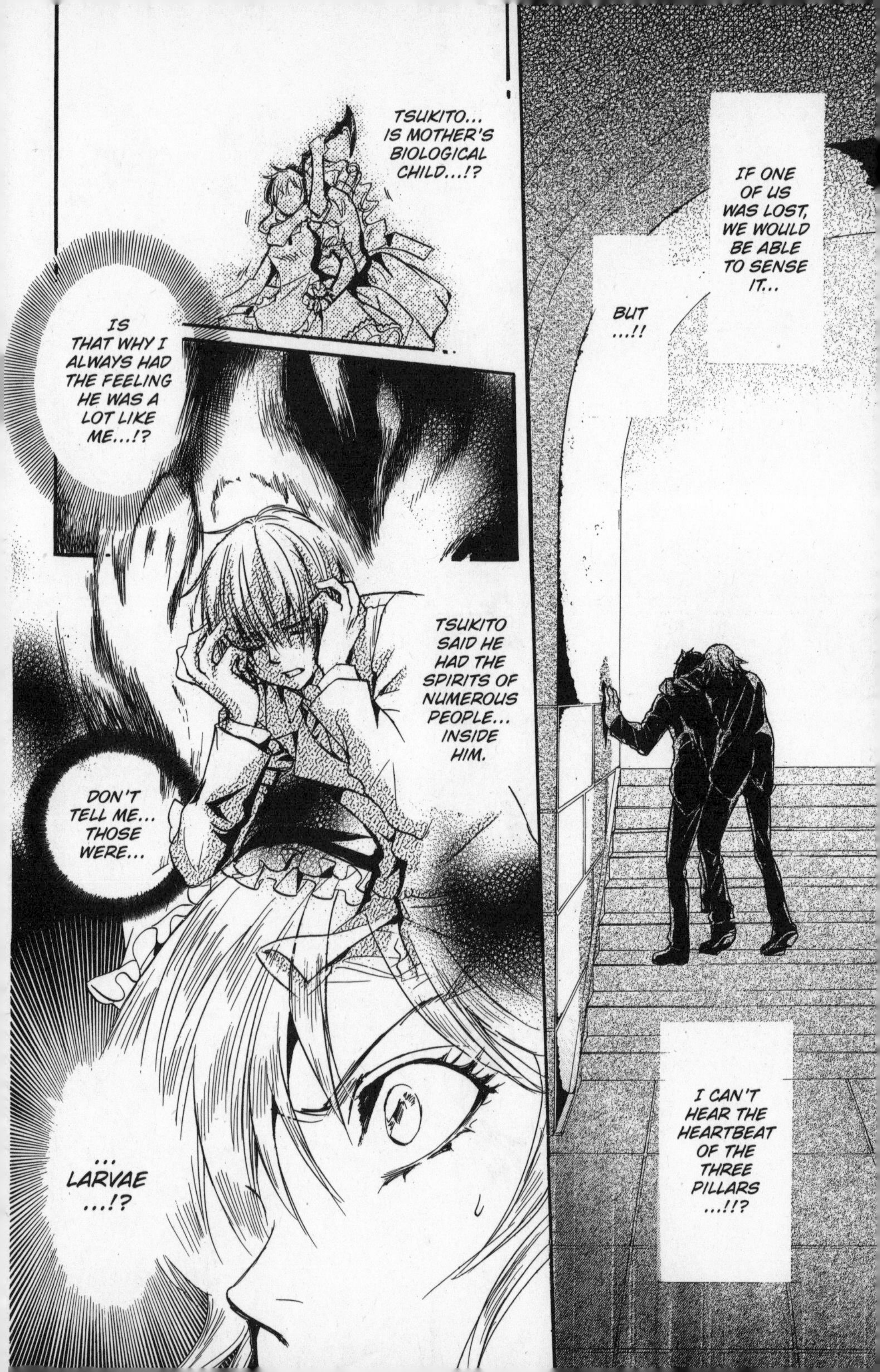
IF ONE OF US WAS LOST, WE WOULD BE ABLE TO SENSE IT...
BUT ...!!
I CAN'T HEAR THE HEARTBEAT OF THE THREE PILLARS ...!!?
TSUKITO... IS MOTHER'S BIOLOGICAL CHILD...!?
IS THAT WHY I ALWAYS HAD THE FEELING HE WAS A LOT LIKE ME...!?
TSUKITO SAID HE HAD THE SPIRITS OF NUMEROUS PEOPLE... INSIDE HIM.
DON'T TELL ME... THOSE WERE...
... LARVAE ...!?

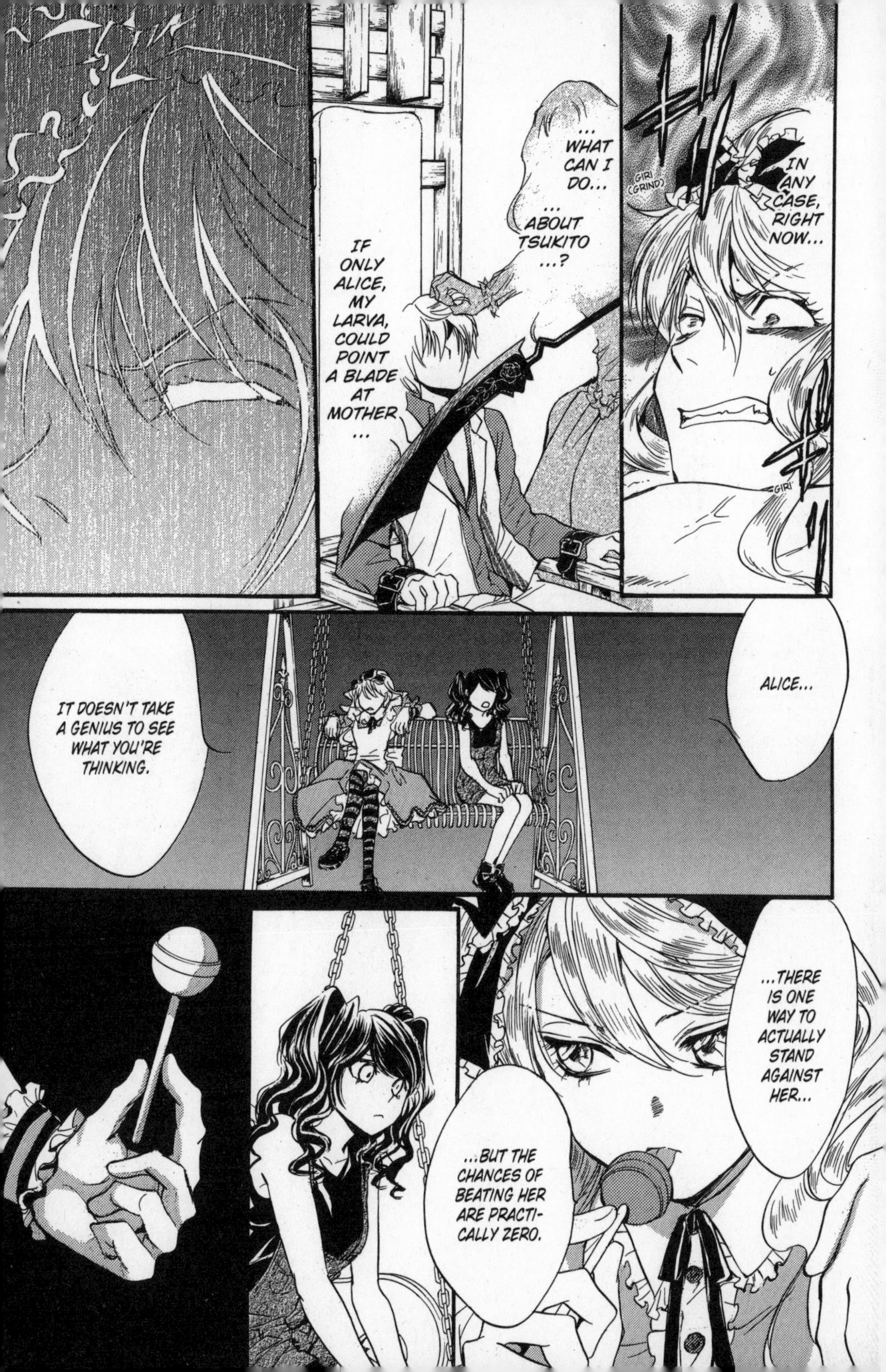
GIRI (GRIND)
IN ANY CASE, RIGHT NOW...
GIRI
...WHAT CAN I DO...
...ABOUT TSUKITO...?
IF ONLY ALICE, MY LARVA, COULD POINT A BLADE AT MOTHER...
ALICE...
IT DOESN'T TAKE A GENIUS TO SEE WHAT YOU'RE THINKING.
...THERE IS ONE WAY TO ACTUALLY STAND AGAINST HER...
...BUT THE CHANCES OF BEATING HER ARE PRACTI-CALLY ZERO.

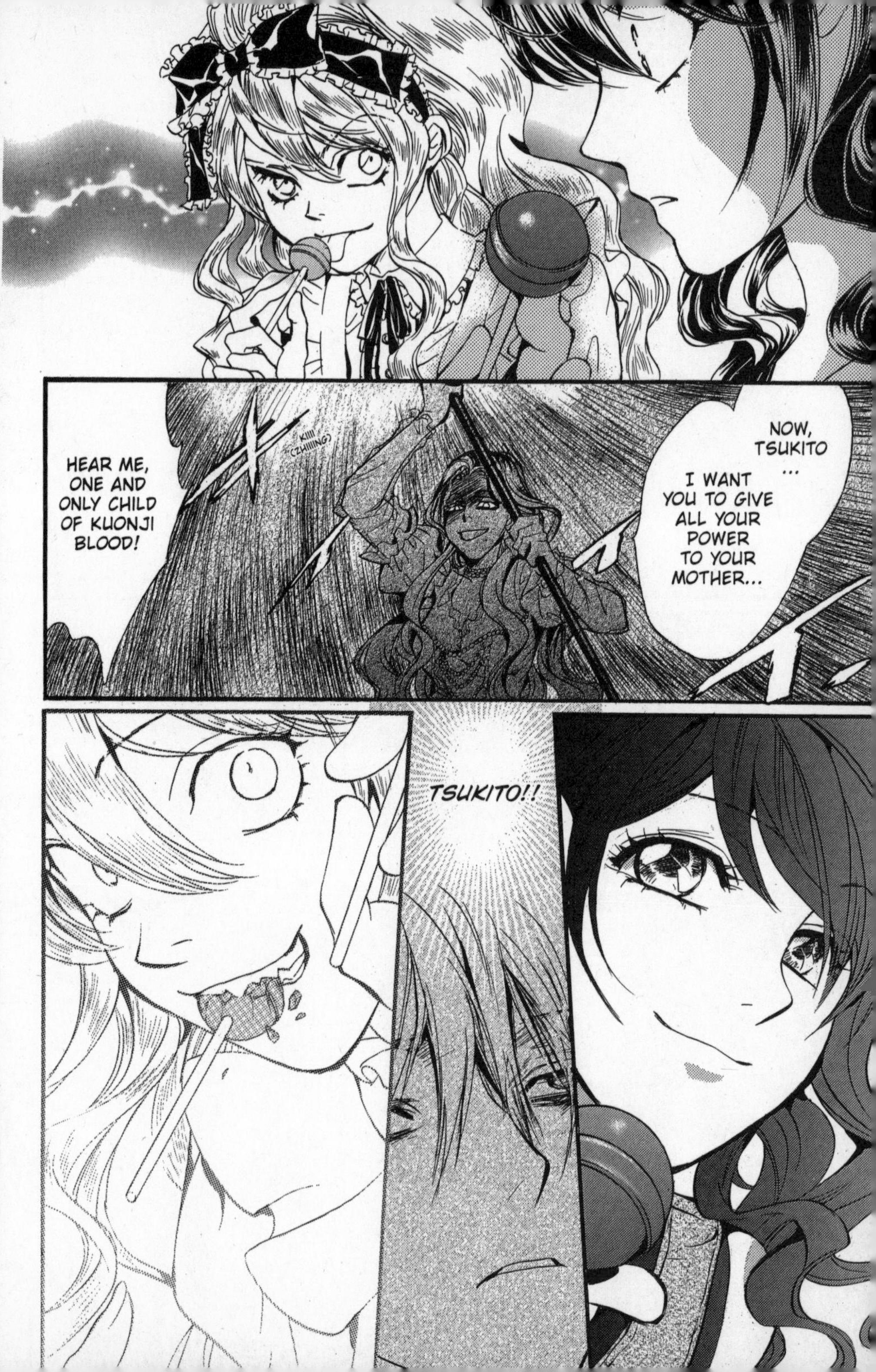
NOW, TSUKITO ...
I WANT YOU TO GIVE ALL YOUR POWER TO YOUR MOTHER...
KIIII (ZWIIIING)
HEAR ME, ONE AND ONLY CHILD OF KUONJI BLOOD!
TSUKITO!!

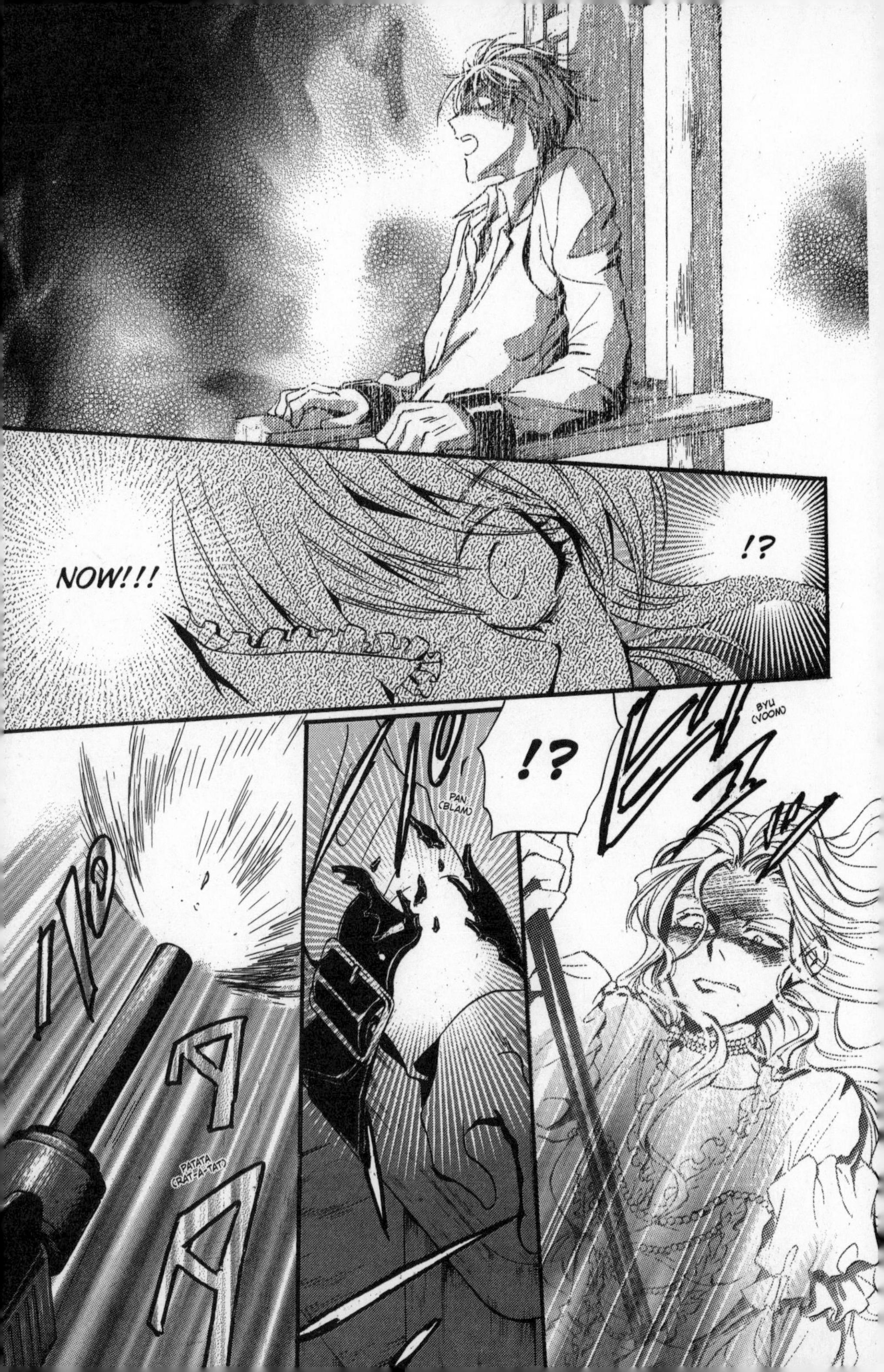
!?
NOW!!!
BYU (VOOM)
!?
PAN (BLAM)
PATATA (RAT-A-TAT)

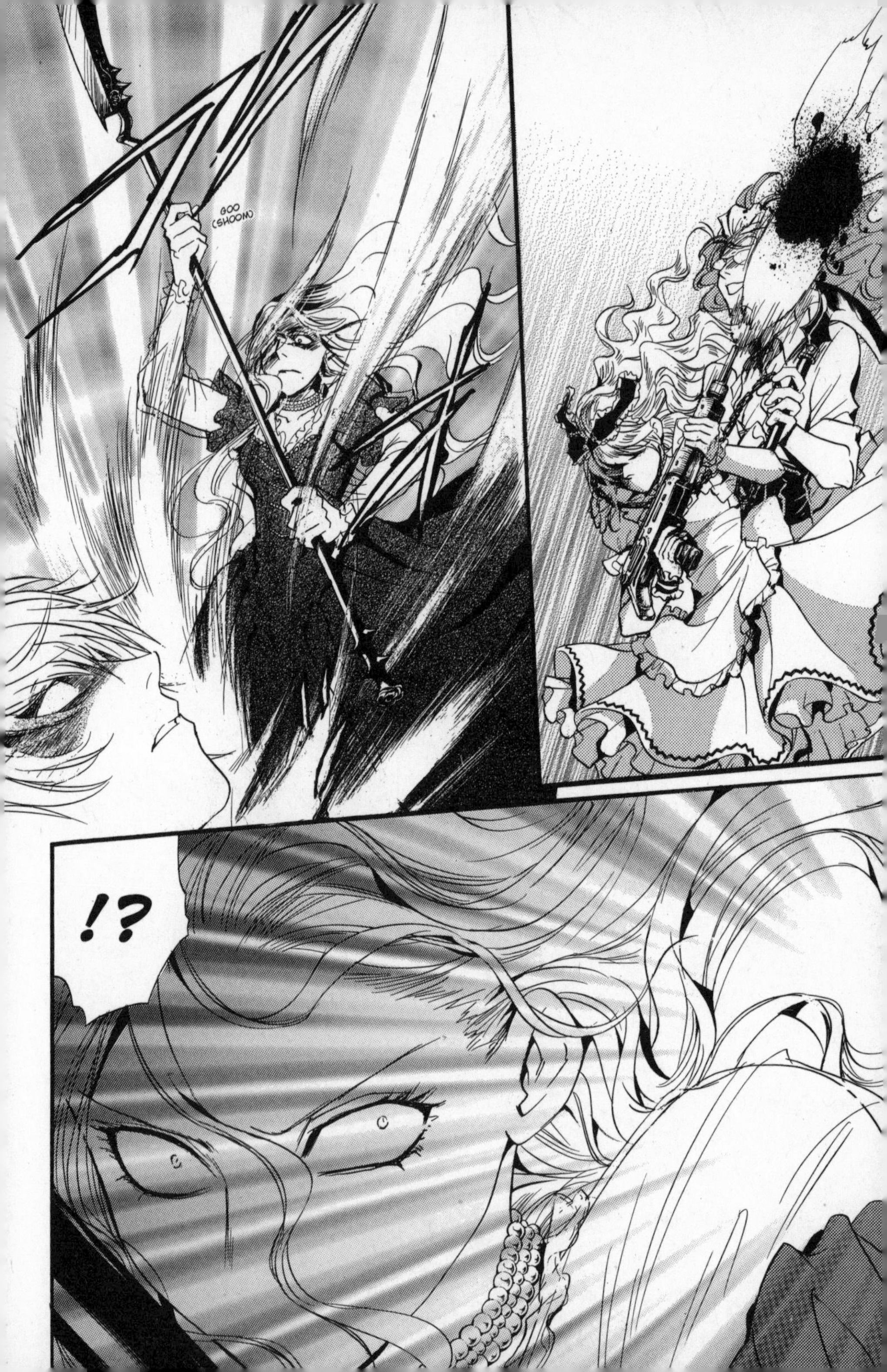
GOO
(SHOOM)
!?

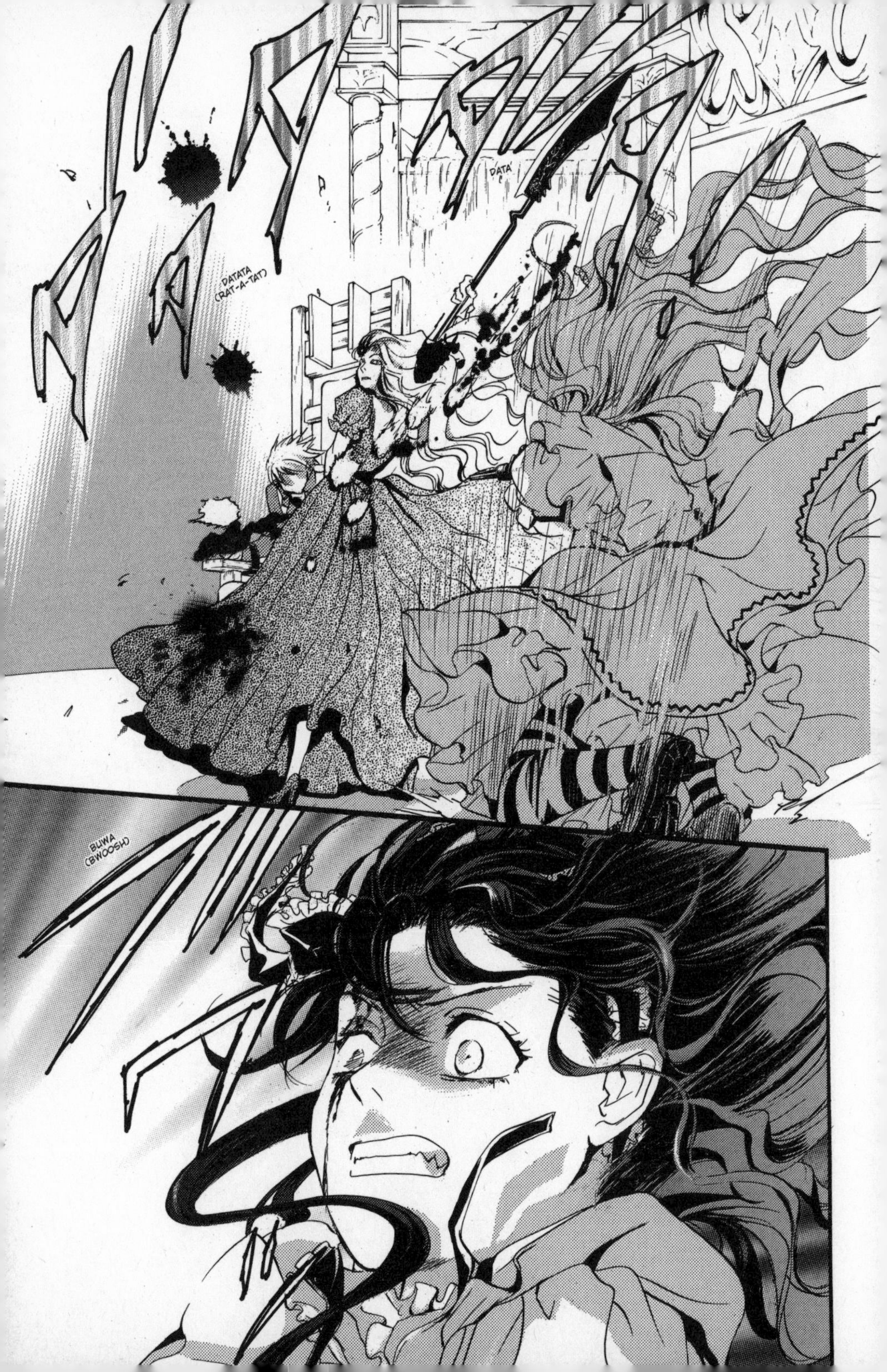
DATA
DATATA (RAT-A-TAT)
BUWA (BWOOSH)

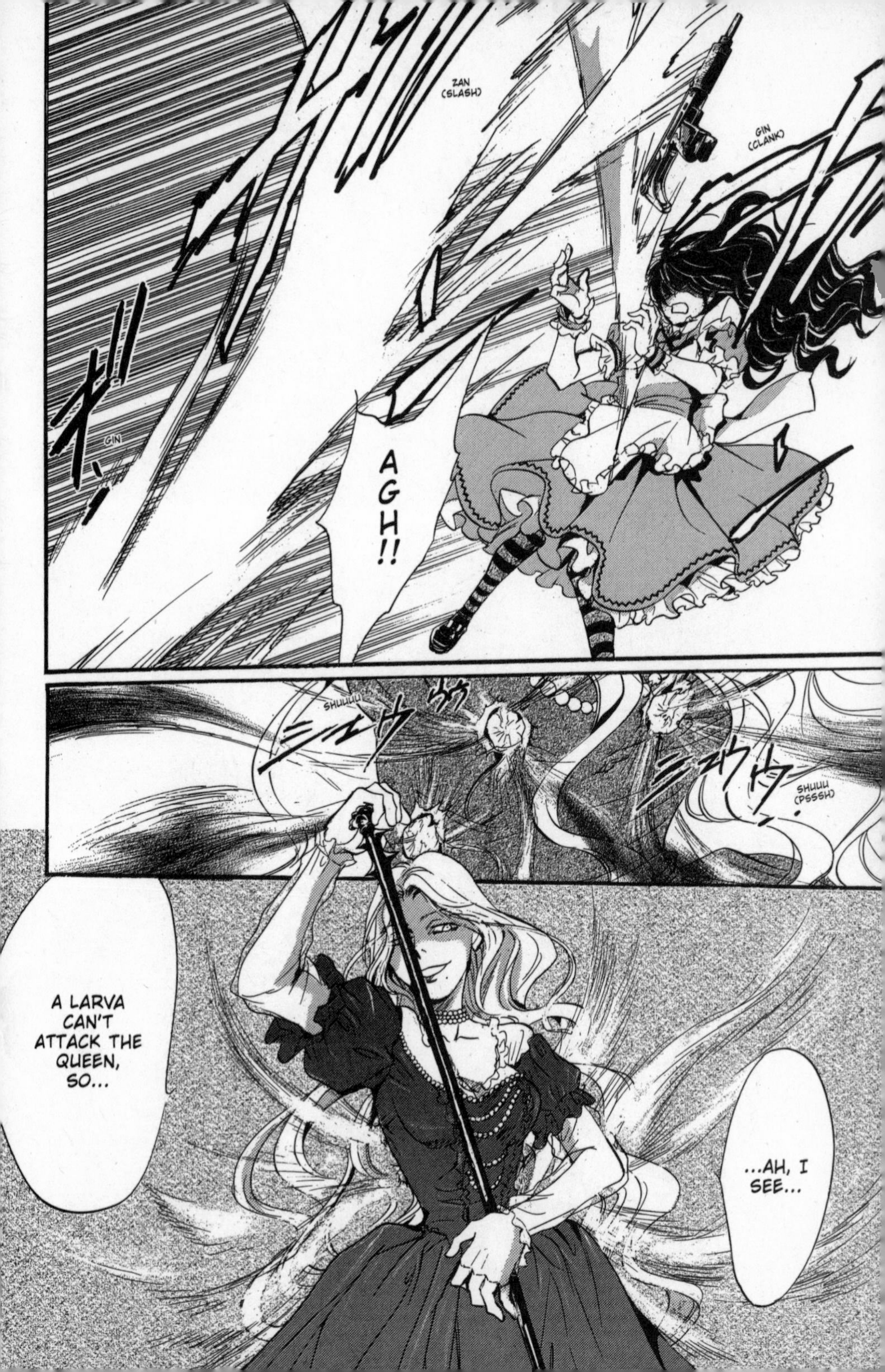
GIN (CLANK)
ZAN (SLASH)
AGH!!
GIN
SHUUU (PSSSH)
SHUUUU
...AH, I SEE...
A LARVA CAN'T ATTACK THE QUEEN, SO...

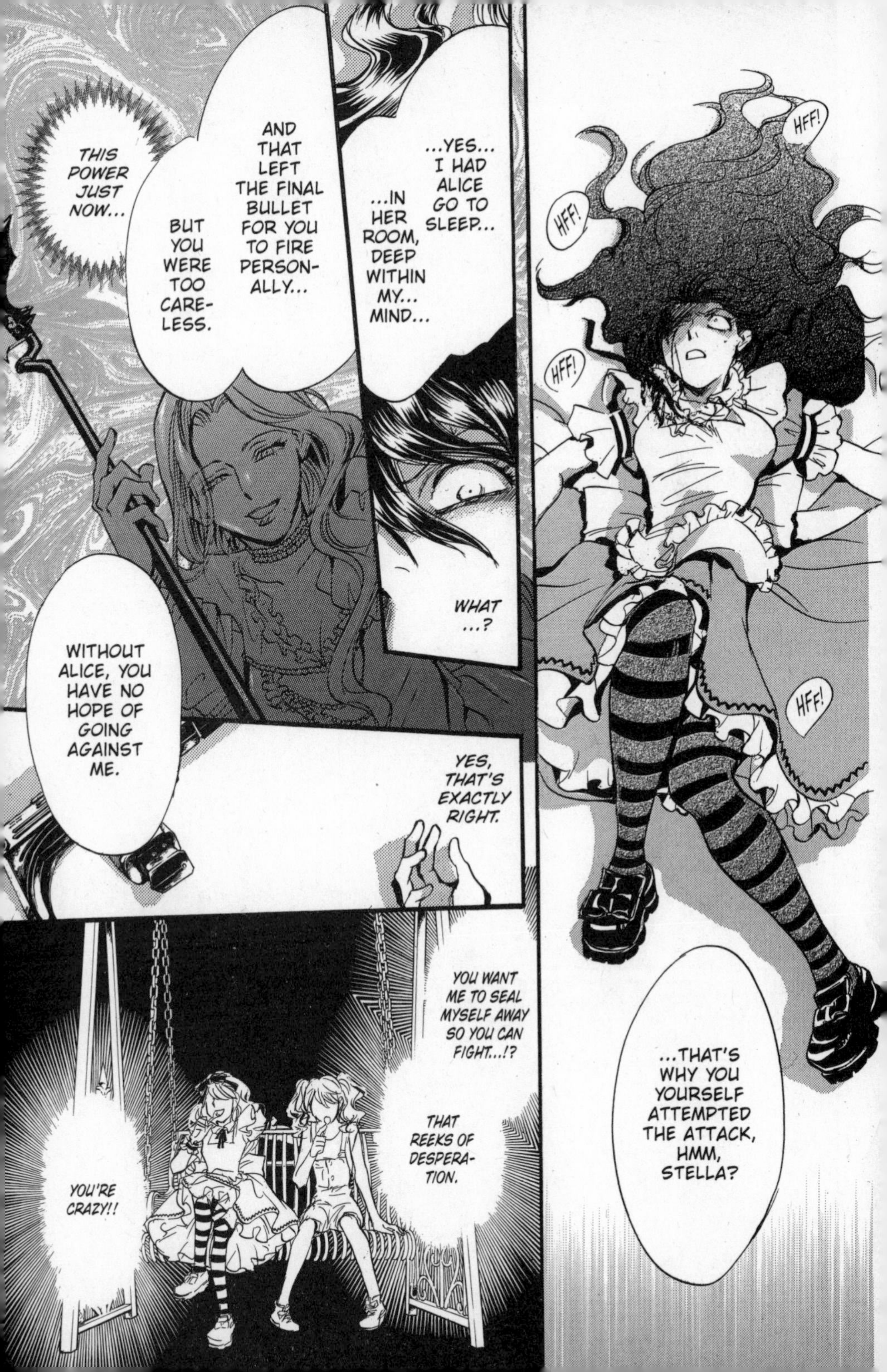
HFF!
HFF!
HFF!
HFF!
...THAT'S WHY YOU YOURSELF ATTEMPTED THE ATTACK, HMM, STELLA?
...YES... I HAD ALICE GO TO SLEEP...
...IN HER ROOM, DEEP WITHIN MY... MIND...
WHAT ...?
AND THAT LEFT THE FINAL BULLET FOR YOU TO FIRE PERSON-ALLY...
BUT YOU WERE TOO CARE-LESS.
THIS POWER JUST NOW...
WITHOUT ALICE, YOU HAVE NO HOPE OF GOING AGAINST ME.
YES, THAT'S EXACTLY RIGHT.
YOU WANT ME TO SEAL MYSELF AWAY SO YOU CAN FIGHT...!?
THAT REEKS OF DESPERA-TION.
YOU'RE CRAZY!!

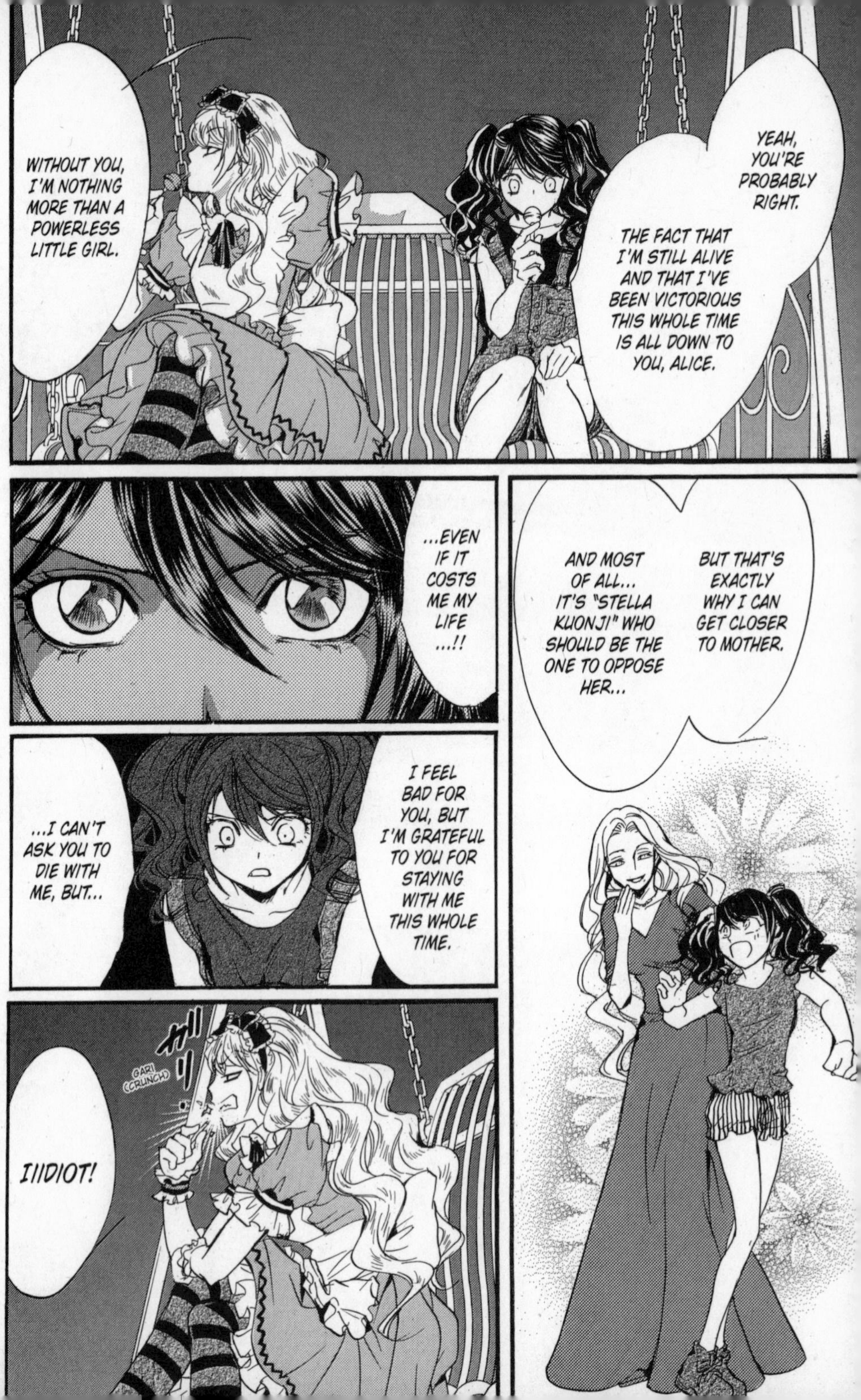
YEAH, YOU'RE PROBABLY RIGHT.
THE FACT THAT I'M STILL ALIVE AND THAT I'VE BEEN VICTORIOUS THIS WHOLE TIME IS ALL DOWN TO YOU, ALICE.
WITHOUT YOU, I'M NOTHING MORE THAN A POWERLESS LITTLE GIRL.
BUT THAT'S EXACTLY WHY I CAN GET CLOSER TO MOTHER.
AND MOST OF ALL... IT'S "STELLA KUONJI" WHO SHOULD BE THE ONE TO OPPOSE HER...
...EVEN IF IT COSTS ME MY LIFE ...!!
I FEEL BAD FOR YOU, BUT I'M GRATEFUL TO YOU FOR STAYING WITH ME THIS WHOLE TIME.
...I CAN'T ASK YOU TO DIE WITH ME, BUT...
GARI (CRUNCH)
IIIDIOT!

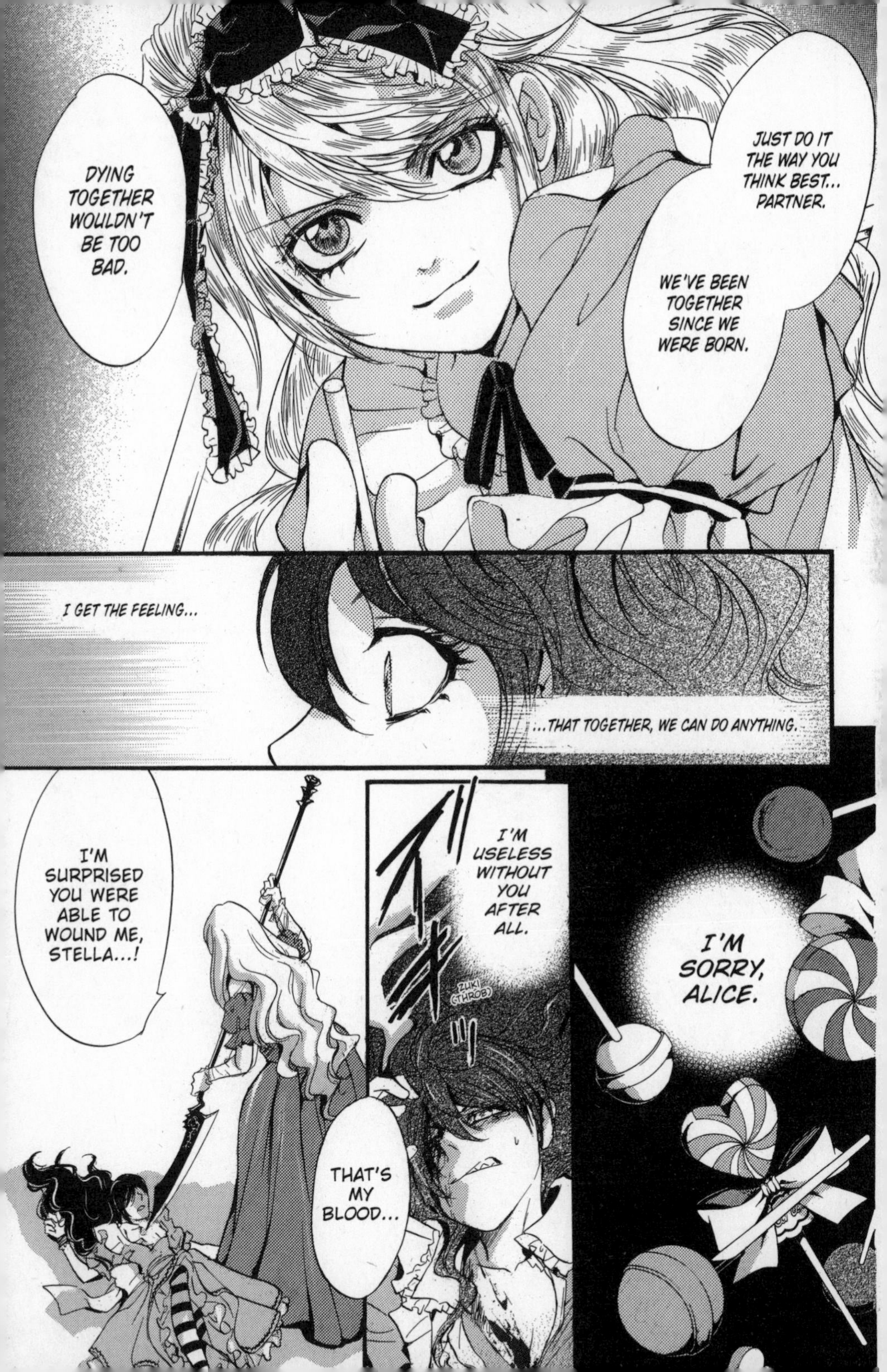
JUST DO IT THE WAY YOU THINK BEST... PARTNER.
WE'VE BEEN TOGETHER SINCE WE WERE BORN.
DYING TOGETHER WOULDN'T BE TOO BAD.
I GET THE FEELING...
...THAT TOGETHER, WE CAN DO ANYTHING.
I'M SORRY, ALICE.
I'M USELESS WITHOUT YOU AFTER ALL.
ZUKI (THROB)
THAT'S MY BLOOD...
I'M SURPRISED YOU WERE ABLE TO WOUND ME, STELLA...!

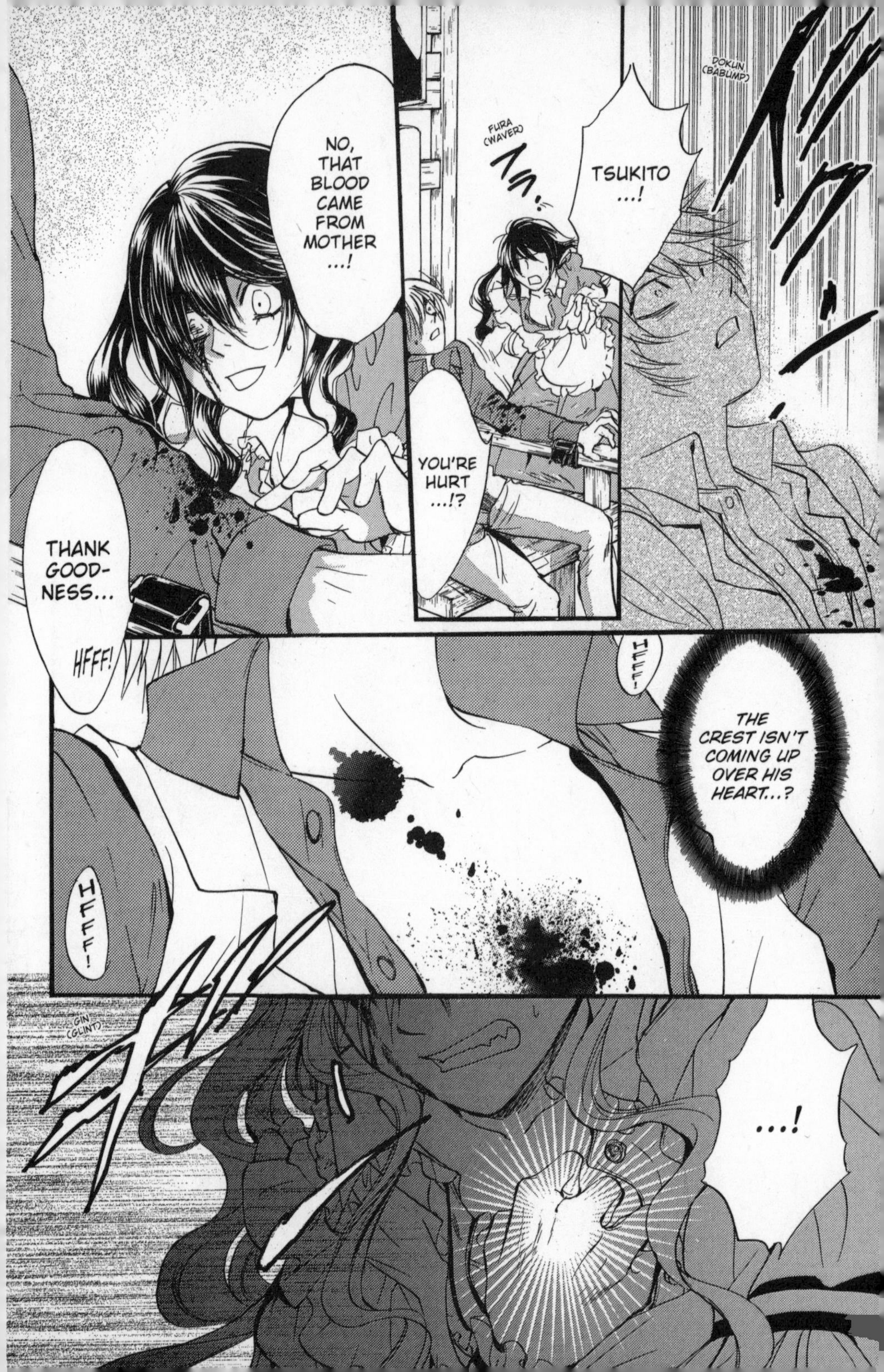
DOKUN (BABUMP)
TSUKITO ...!
FURA (WAVER)
YOU'RE HURT ...!?
NO, THAT BLOOD CAME FROM MOTHER ...!
THANK GOODNESS...
HFFF!
THE CREST ISN'T COMING UP OVER HIS HEART...?
HFFF!
HFFF!
...!
GIN (GLINT)

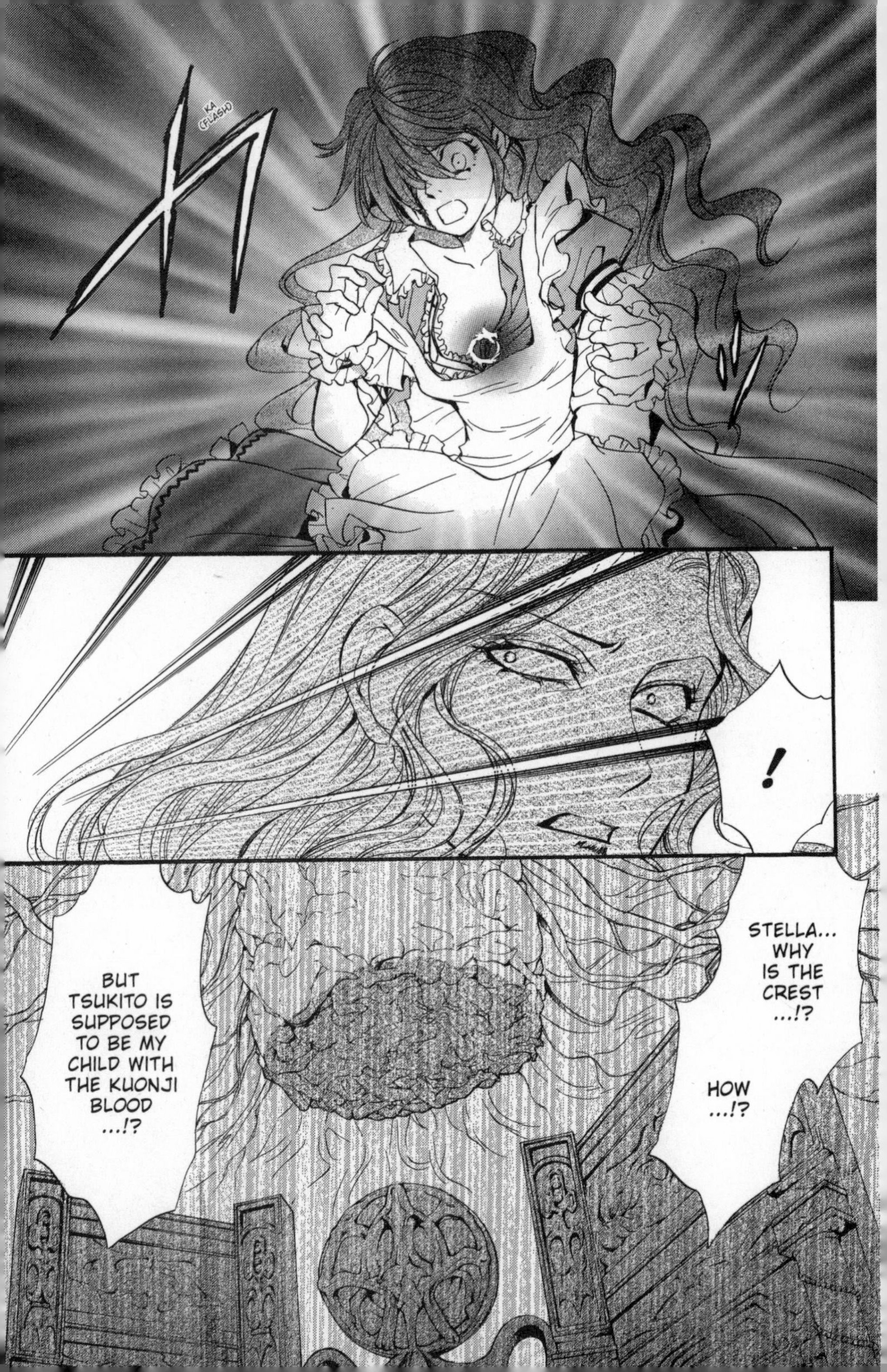
KA (FLASH)
!
STELLA... WHY IS THE CREST ...!?
HOW ...!?
BUT TSUKITO IS SUPPOSED TO BE MY CHILD WITH THE KUONJI BLOOD ...!?

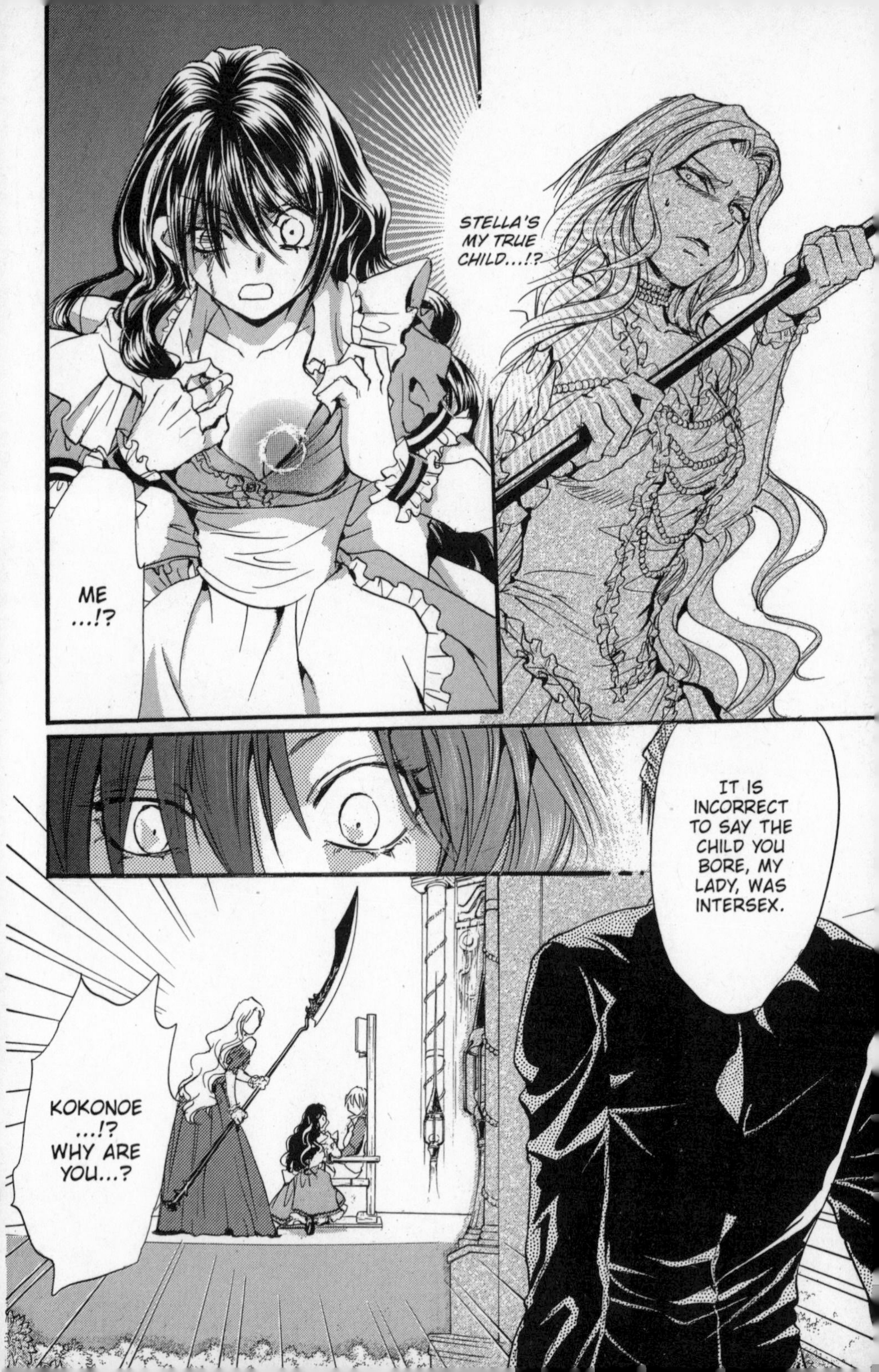
STELLA'S MY TRUE CHILD...!?
ME ...!?
IT IS INCORRECT TO SAY THE CHILD YOU BORE, MY LADY, WAS INTERSEX.
KOKONOE ...!? WHY ARE YOU...?

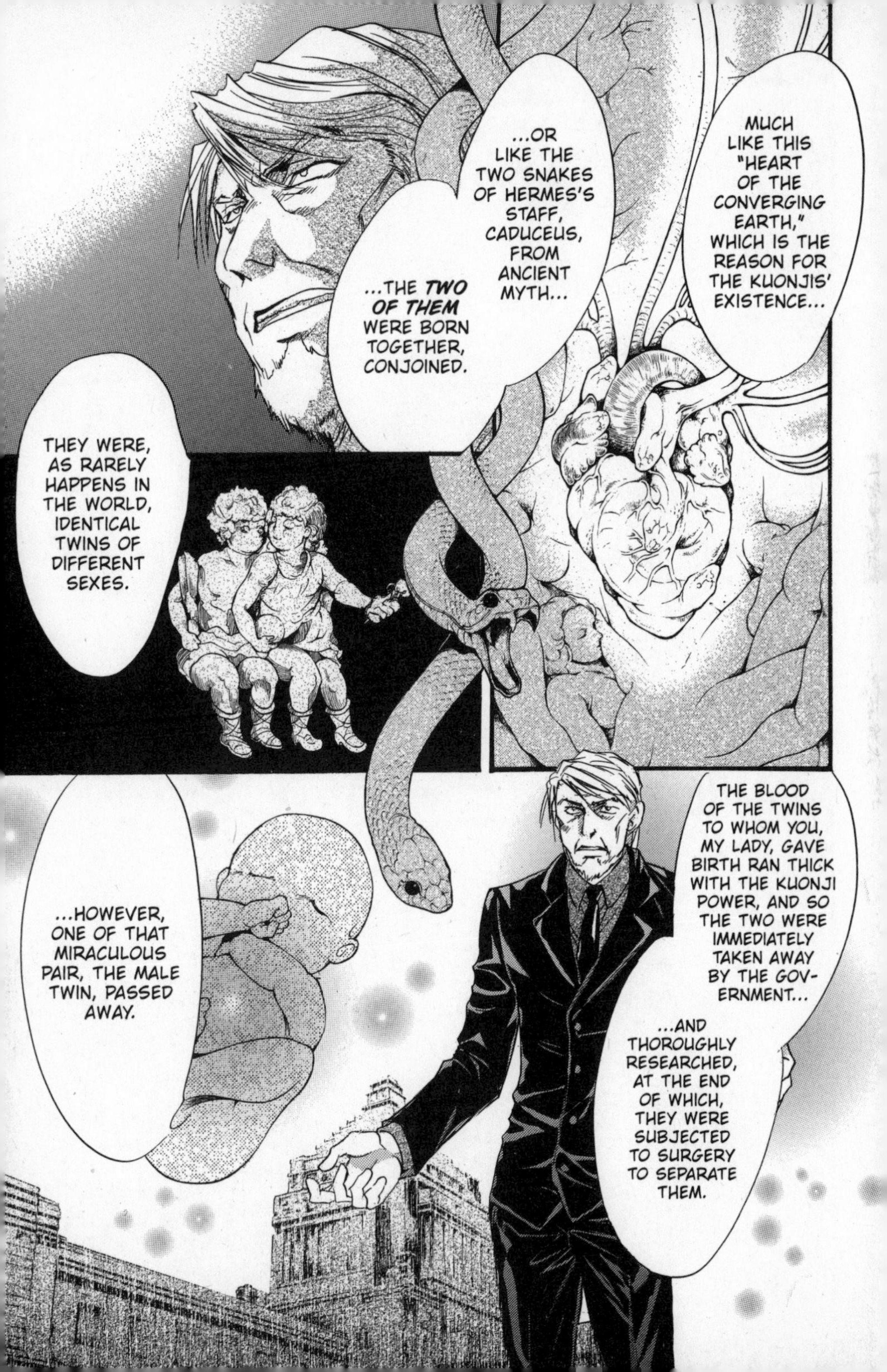
MUCH LIKE THIS "HEART OF THE CONVERGING EARTH," WHICH IS THE REASON FOR THE KUONJIS' EXISTENCE...
...OR LIKE THE TWO SNAKES OF HERMES'S STAFF, CADUCEUS, FROM ANCIENT MYTH...
...THE *TWO OF THEM* WERE BORN TOGETHER, CONJOINED.
THEY WERE, AS RARELY HAPPENS IN THE WORLD, IDENTICAL TWINS OF DIFFERENT SEXES.
THE BLOOD OF THE TWINS TO WHOM YOU, MY LADY, GAVE BIRTH RAN THICK WITH THE KUONJI POWER, AND SO THE TWO WERE IMMEDIATELY TAKEN AWAY BY THE GOV-ERNMENT...
...AND THOROUGHLY RESEARCHED, AT THE END OF WHICH, THEY WERE SUBJECTED TO SURGERY TO SEPARATE THEM.
...HOWEVER, ONE OF THAT MIRACULOUS PAIR, THE MALE TWIN, PASSED AWAY.

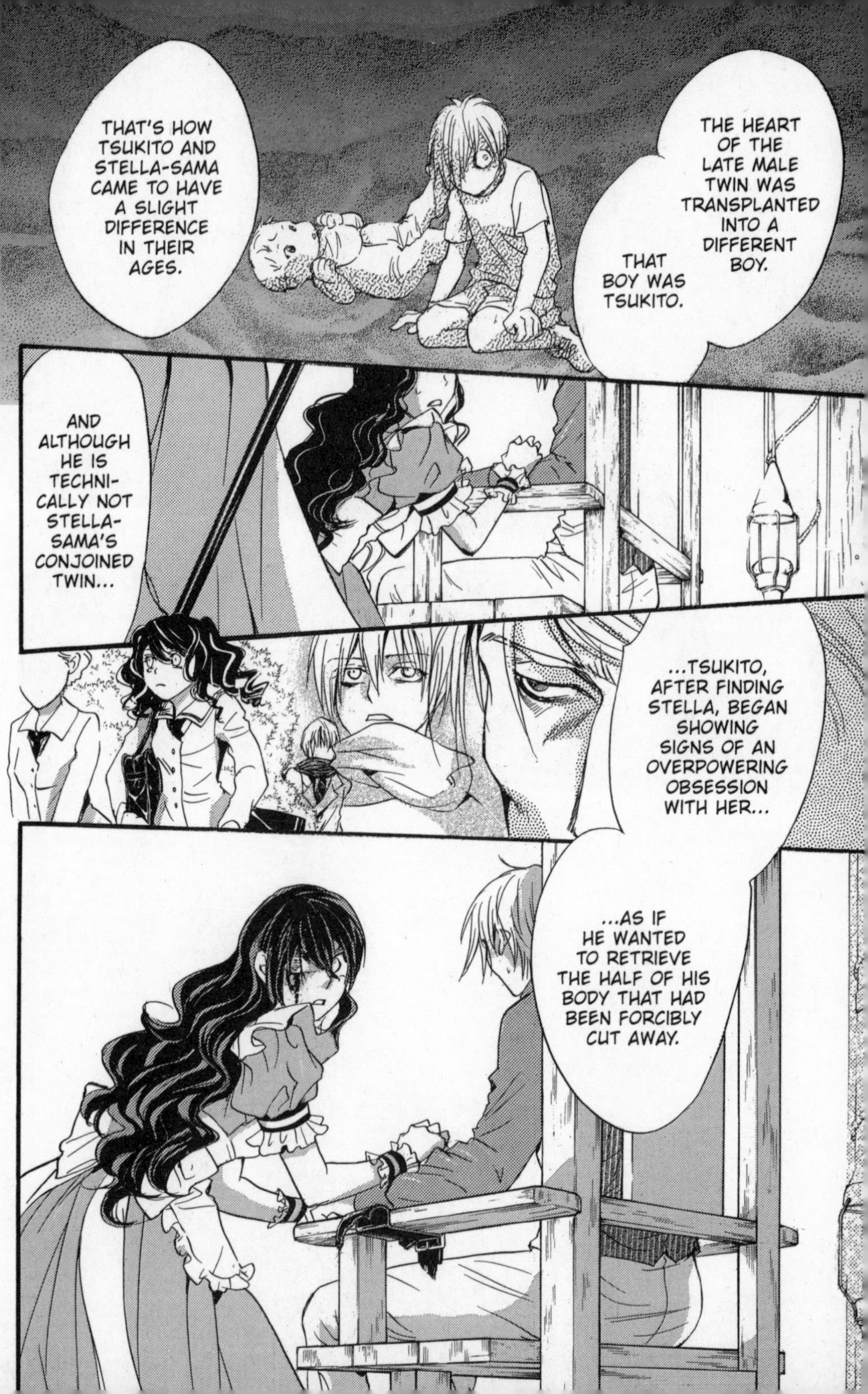
THE HEART OF THE LATE MALE TWIN WAS TRANSPLANTED INTO A DIFFERENT BOY.
THAT BOY WAS TSUKITO.
THAT'S HOW TSUKITO AND STELLA-SAMA CAME TO HAVE A SLIGHT DIFFERENCE IN THEIR AGES.
AND ALTHOUGH HE IS TECHNICALLY NOT STELLA-SAMA'S CONJOINED TWIN...
...TSUKITO, AFTER FINDING STELLA, BEGAN SHOWING SIGNS OF AN OVERPOWERING OBSESSION WITH HER...
...AS IF HE WANTED TO RETRIEVE THE HALF OF HIS BODY THAT HAD BEEN FORCIBLY CUT AWAY.

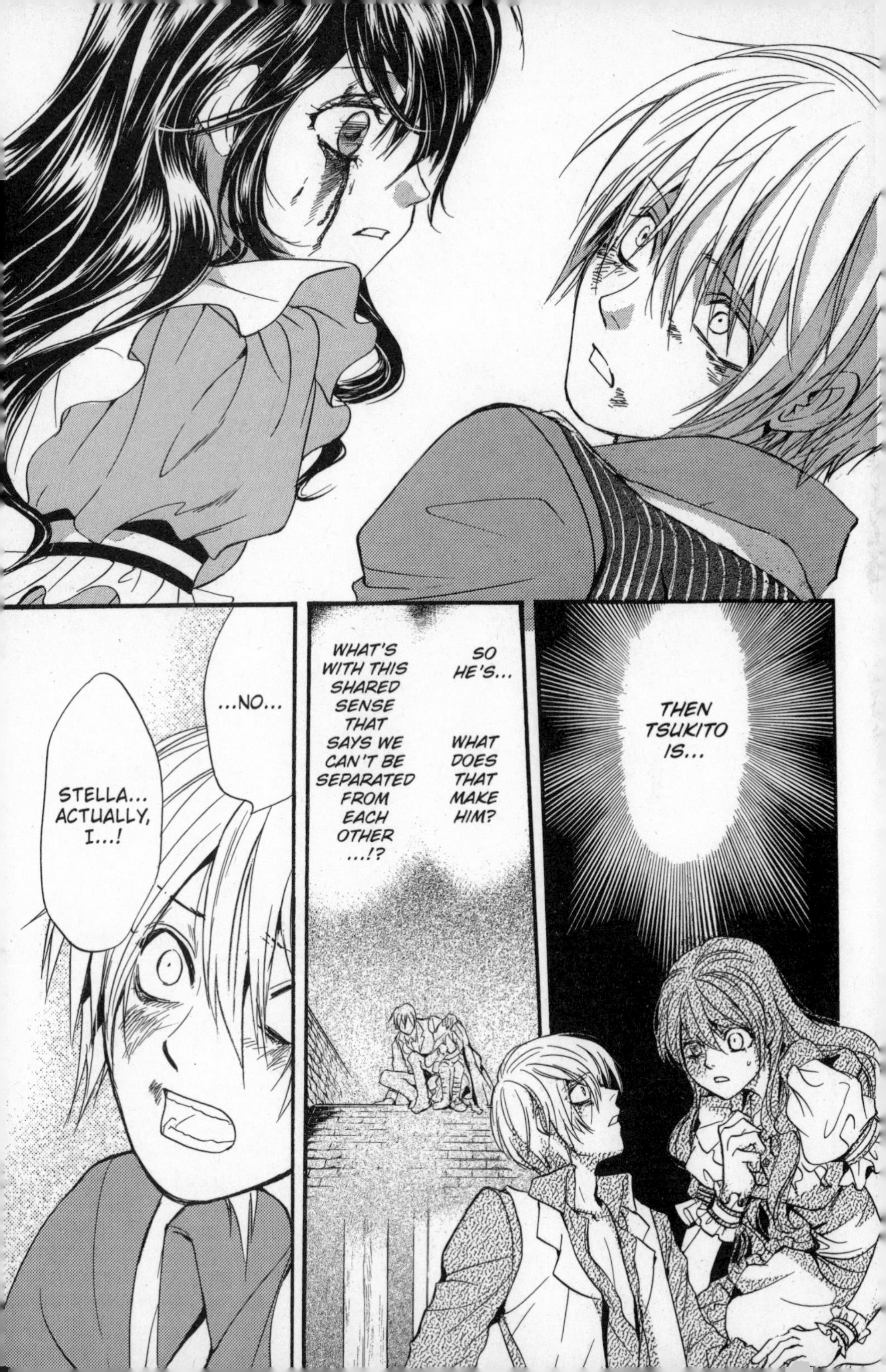
THEN TSUKITO IS...
SO HE'S...
WHAT DOES THAT MAKE HIM?
WHAT'S WITH THIS SHARED SENSE THAT SAYS WE CAN'T BE SEPARATED FROM EACH OTHER ...!?
...NO...
STELLA... ACTUALLY, I...!

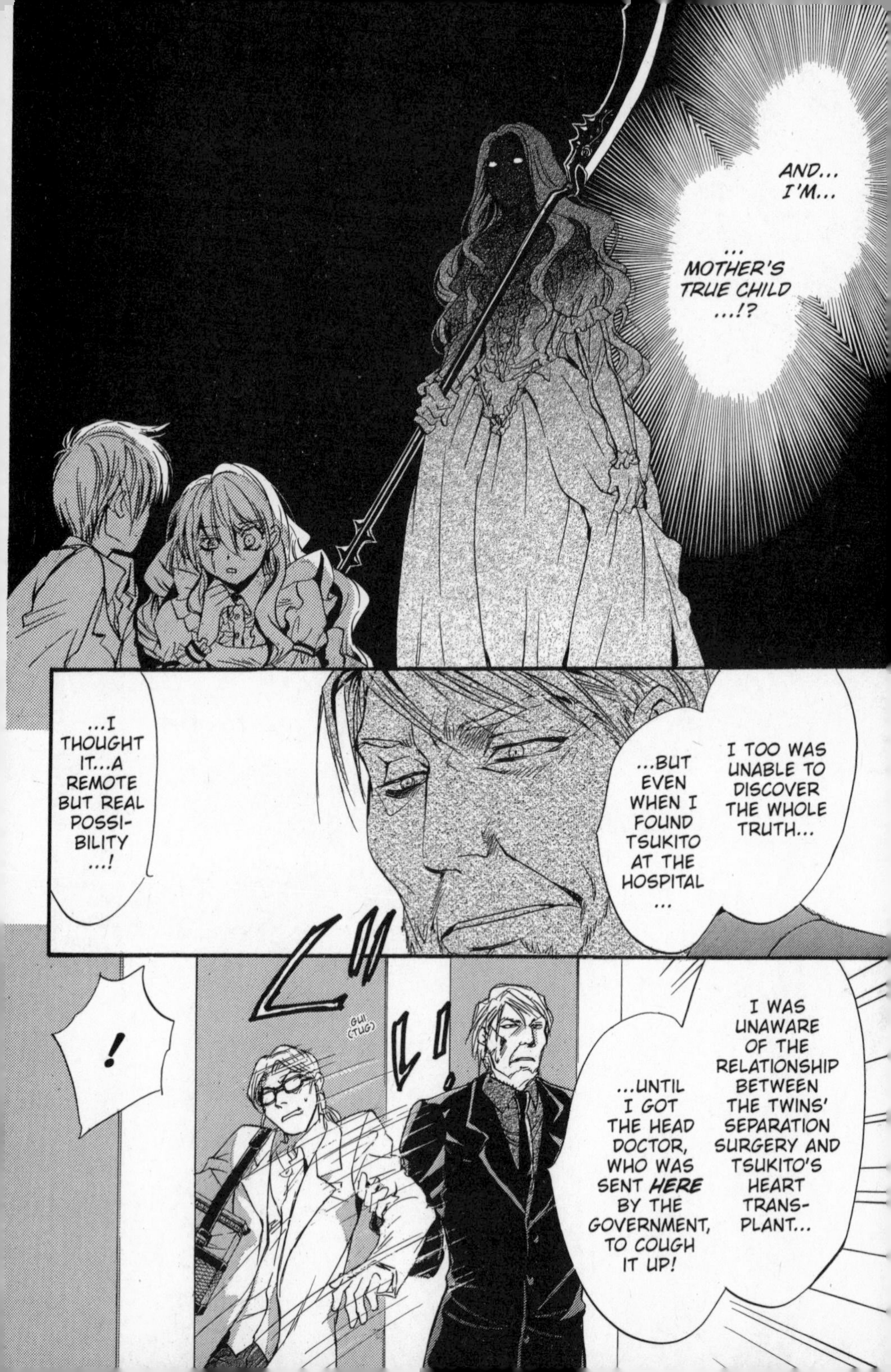
AND... I'M...
...MOTHER'S TRUE CHILD ...!?
I TOO WAS UNABLE TO DISCOVER THE WHOLE TRUTH...
...BUT EVEN WHEN I FOUND TSUKITO AT THE HOSPITAL...
...I THOUGHT IT...A REMOTE BUT REAL POSSIBILITY...!
I WAS UNAWARE OF THE RELATIONSHIP BETWEEN THE TWINS' SEPARATION SURGERY AND TSUKITO'S HEART TRANS-PLANT...
...UNTIL I GOT THE HEAD DOCTOR, WHO WAS SENT *HERE* BY THE GOVERNMENT, TO COUGH IT UP!
GUI (TUG)
!

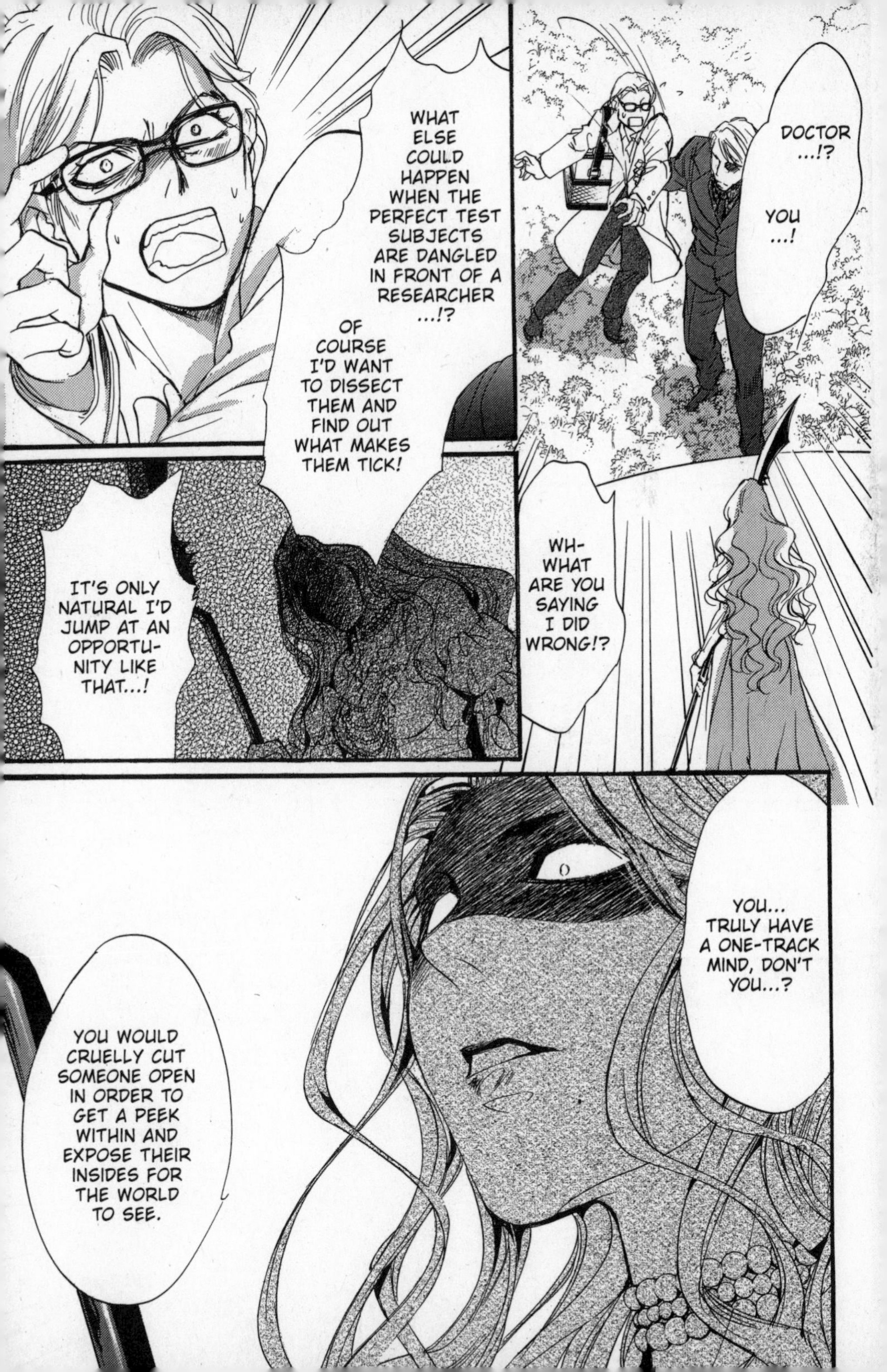
DOCTOR ...!?
YOU ...!
WH- WHAT ARE YOU SAYING I DID WRONG!?
WHAT ELSE COULD HAPPEN WHEN THE PERFECT TEST SUBJECTS ARE DANGLED IN FRONT OF A RESEARCHER ...!?
OF COURSE I'D WANT TO DISSECT THEM AND FIND OUT WHAT MAKES THEM TICK!
IT'S ONLY NATURAL I'D JUMP AT AN OPPORTU- NITY LIKE THAT...!
YOU... TRULY HAVE A ONE-TRACK MIND, DON'T YOU...?
YOU WOULD CRUELLY CUT SOMEONE OPEN IN ORDER TO GET A PEEK WITHIN AND EXPOSE THEIR INSIDES FOR THE WORLD TO SEE.

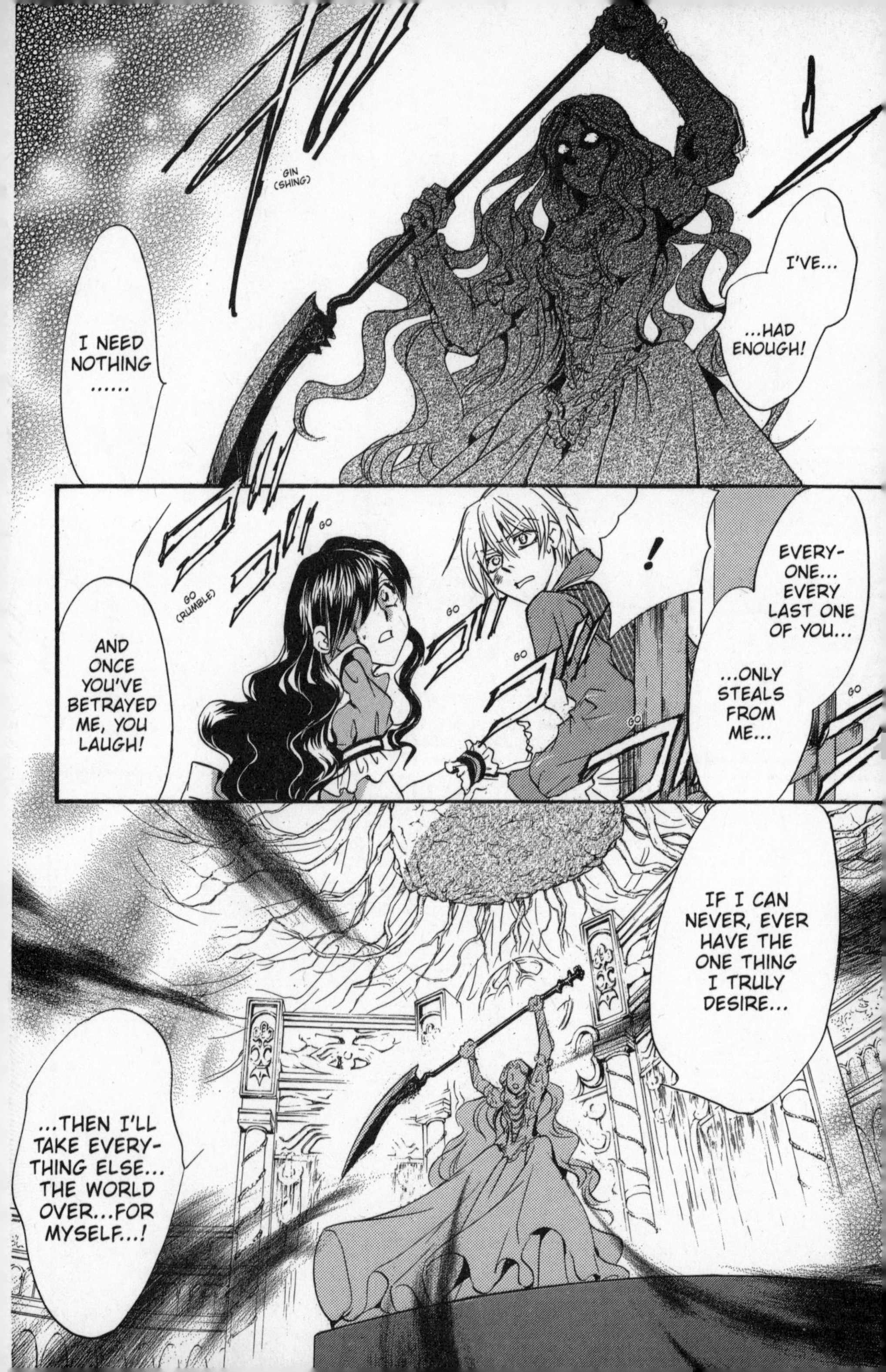
I'VE...
...HAD ENOUGH!
GIN (SHING)
I NEED NOTHING ......
EVERY-ONE... EVERY LAST ONE OF YOU...
...ONLY STEALS FROM ME...
GO
GO (RUMBLE)
AND ONCE YOU'VE BETRAYED ME, YOU LAUGH!
IF I CAN NEVER, EVER HAVE THE ONE THING I TRULY DESIRE...
...THEN I'LL TAKE EVERY-THING ELSE... THE WORLD OVER...FOR MYSELF...!

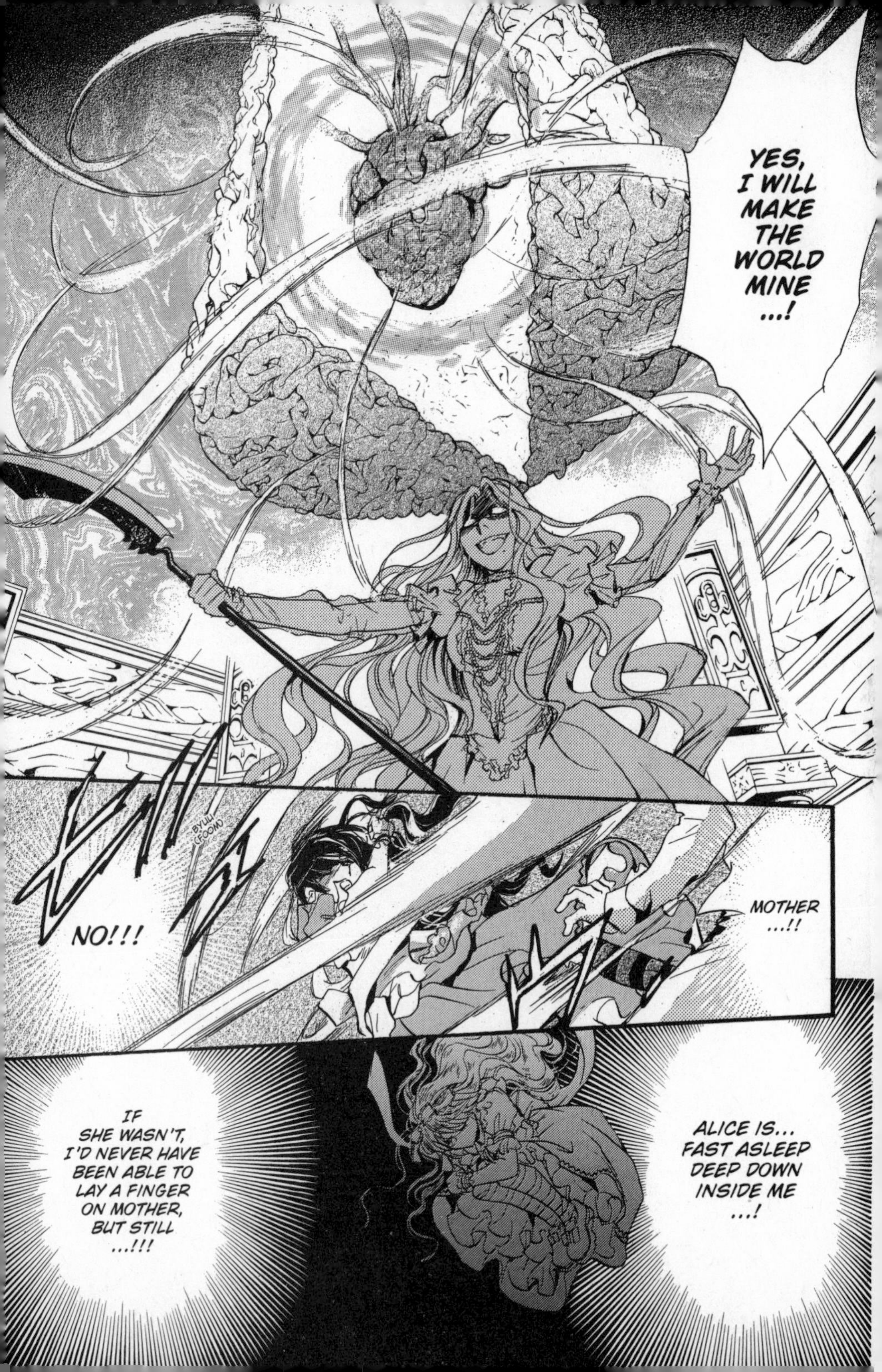
YES, I WILL MAKE THE WORLD MINE ...!
MOTHER ...!!
BYUU (FOOM)
NO!!!
ALICE IS... FAST ASLEEP DEEP DOWN INSIDE ME ...!
IF SHE WASN'T, I'D NEVER HAVE BEEN ABLE TO LAY A FINGER ON MOTHER, BUT STILL ...!!!

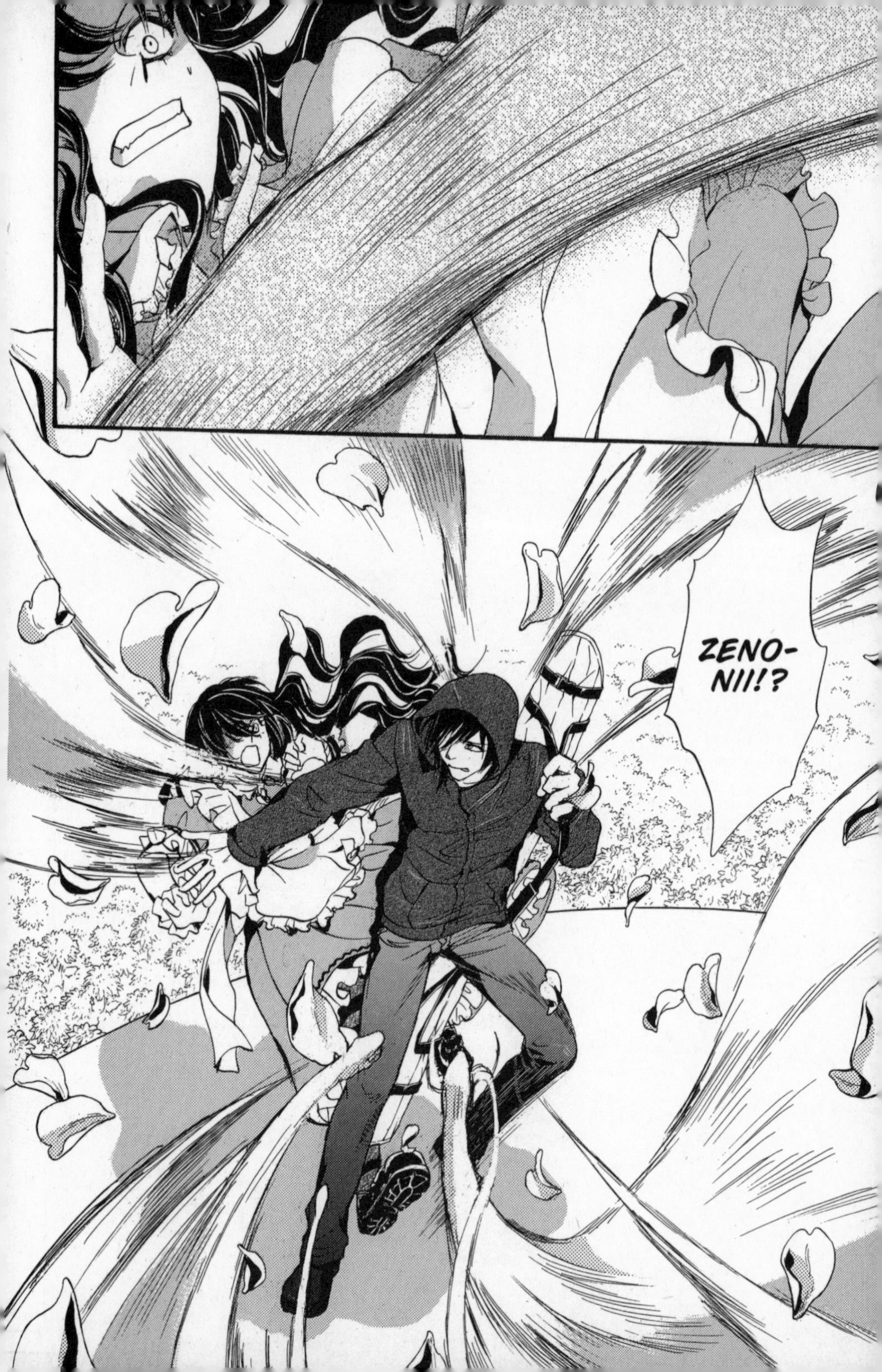
ZENO-NII!?

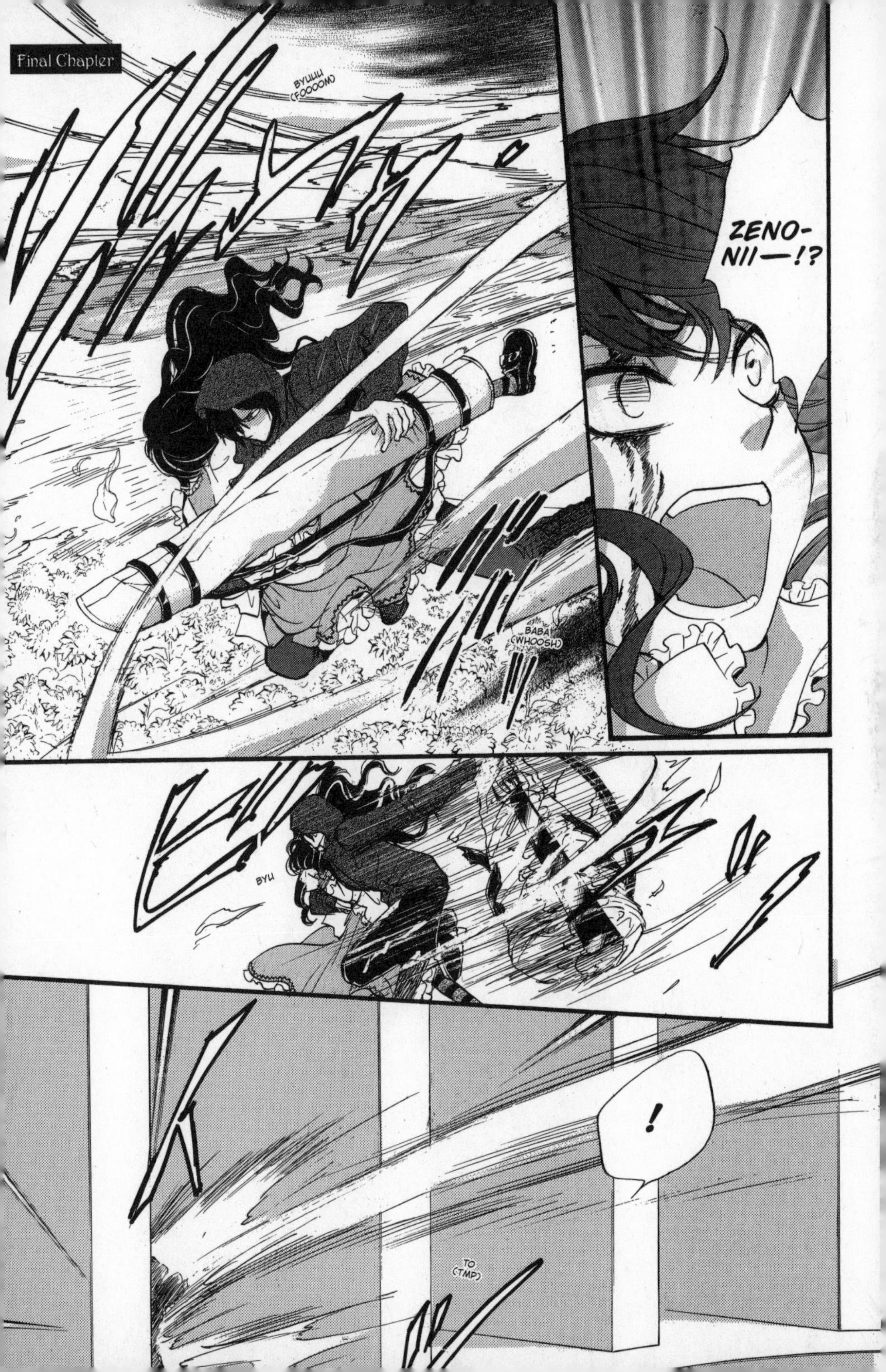
ZENO-NII—!?
BYUUU (FOOOOM)
BABA (WHOOSH)
BYU
!
TO (TMP)

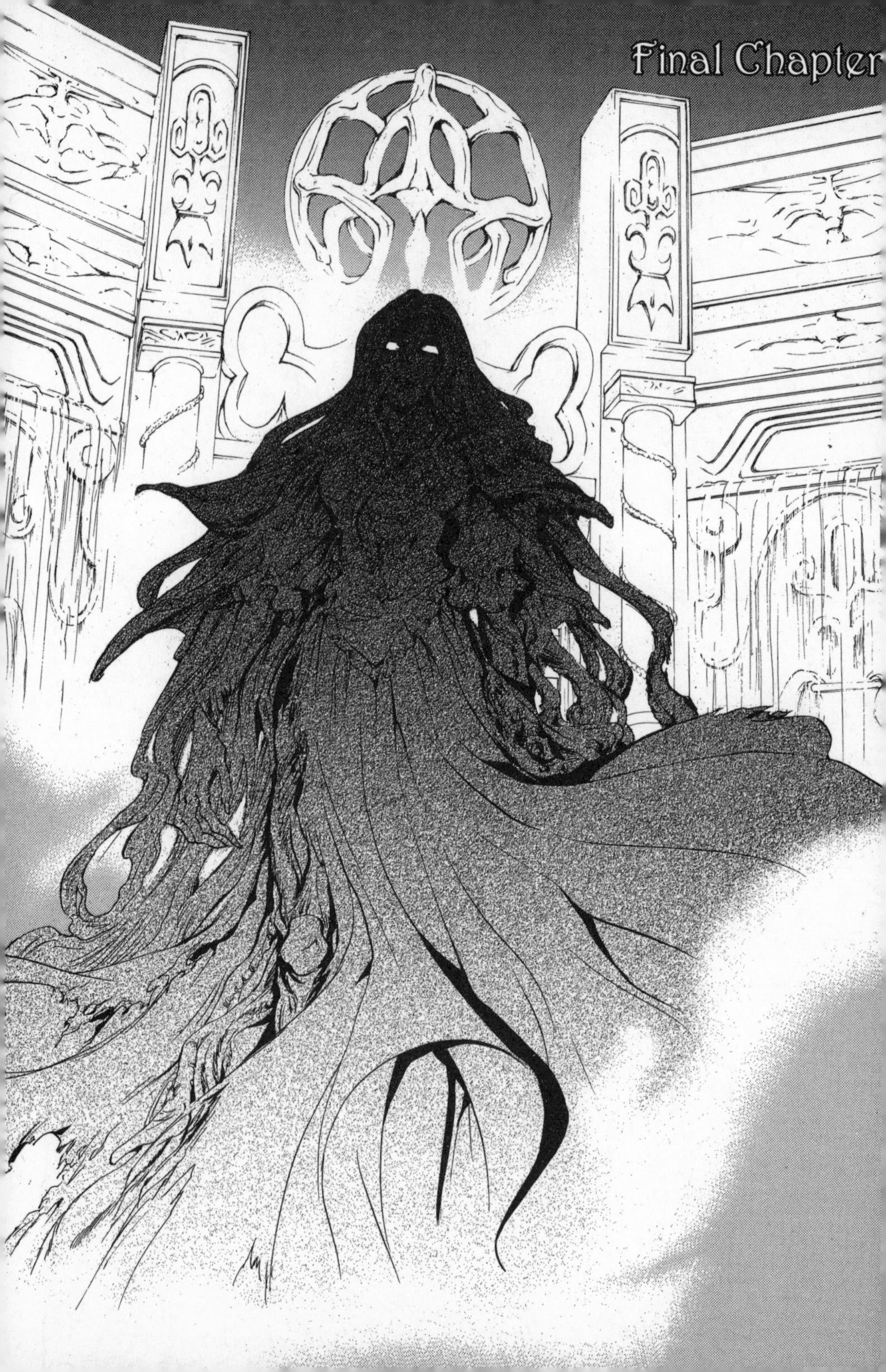
Final Chapter

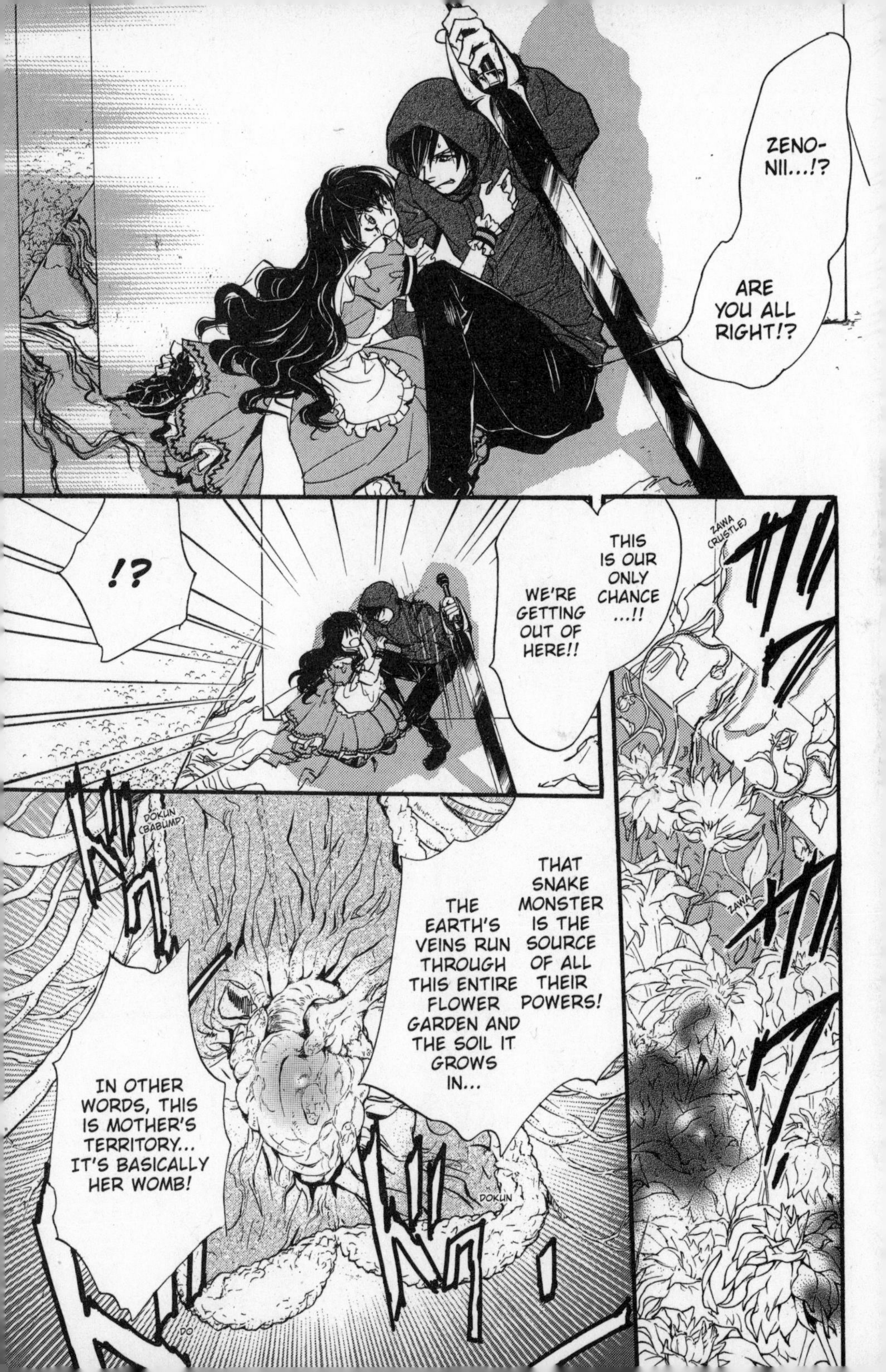
ZENO-NII...!?
ARE YOU ALL RIGHT!?
ZAWA (RUSTLE)
THIS IS OUR ONLY CHANCE ...!!
WE'RE GETTING OUT OF HERE!!
!?
ZAWA
THAT SNAKE MONSTER IS THE SOURCE OF ALL THEIR POWERS!
THE EARTH'S VEINS RUN THROUGH THIS ENTIRE FLOWER GARDEN AND THE SOIL IT GROWS IN...
DOKUN (BABUMP)
DOKUN
IN OTHER WORDS, THIS IS MOTHER'S TERRITORY... IT'S BASICALLY HER WOMB!
DO

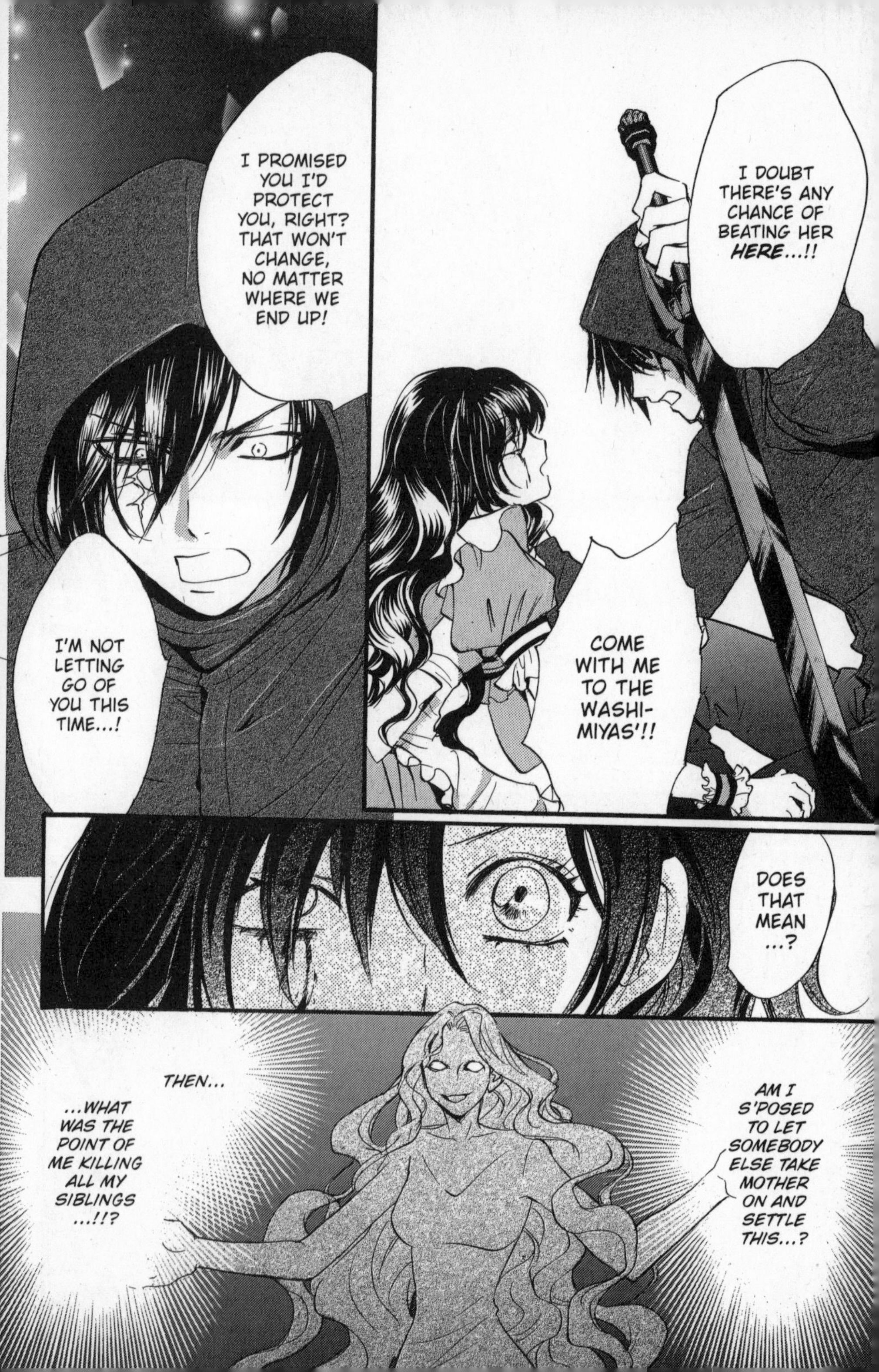
I DOUBT THERE'S ANY CHANCE OF BEATING HER *HERE*...!!
COME WITH ME TO THE WASHI-MIYAS'!!
I PROMISED YOU I'D PROTECT YOU, RIGHT? THAT WON'T CHANGE, NO MATTER WHERE WE END UP!
I'M NOT LETTING GO OF YOU THIS TIME...!
DOES THAT MEAN ...?
AM I S'POSED TO LET SOMEBODY ELSE TAKE MOTHER ON AND SETTLE THIS...?
THEN...
...WHAT WAS THE POINT OF ME KILLING ALL MY SIBLINGS ...!!?

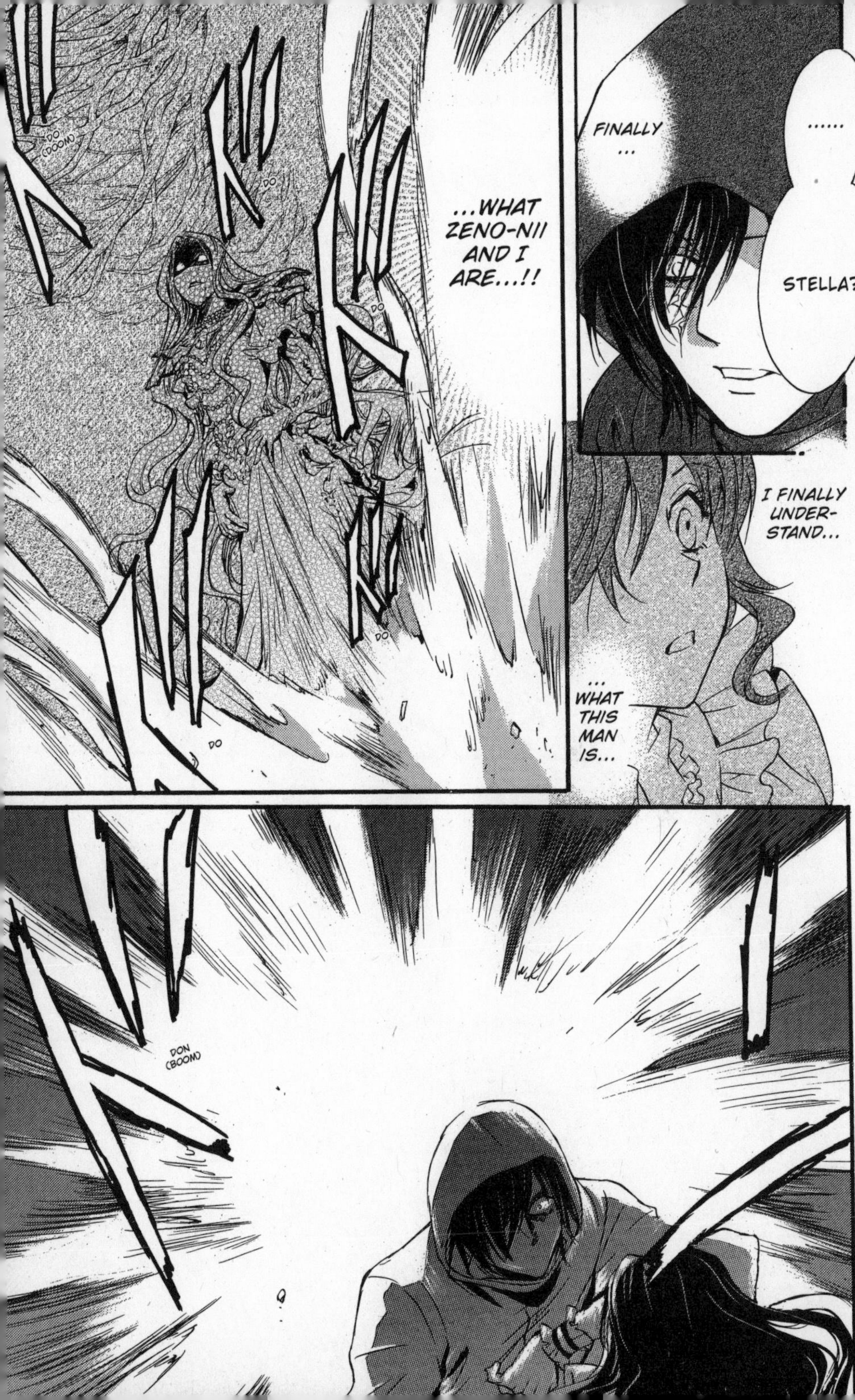
......
STELLA?
FINALLY ...
I FINALLY UNDER-STAND...
...WHAT THIS MAN IS...
...WHAT ZENO-NII AND I ARE...!!
DO (DOOM)
DO
DO
DO
DO
DON (BOOM)

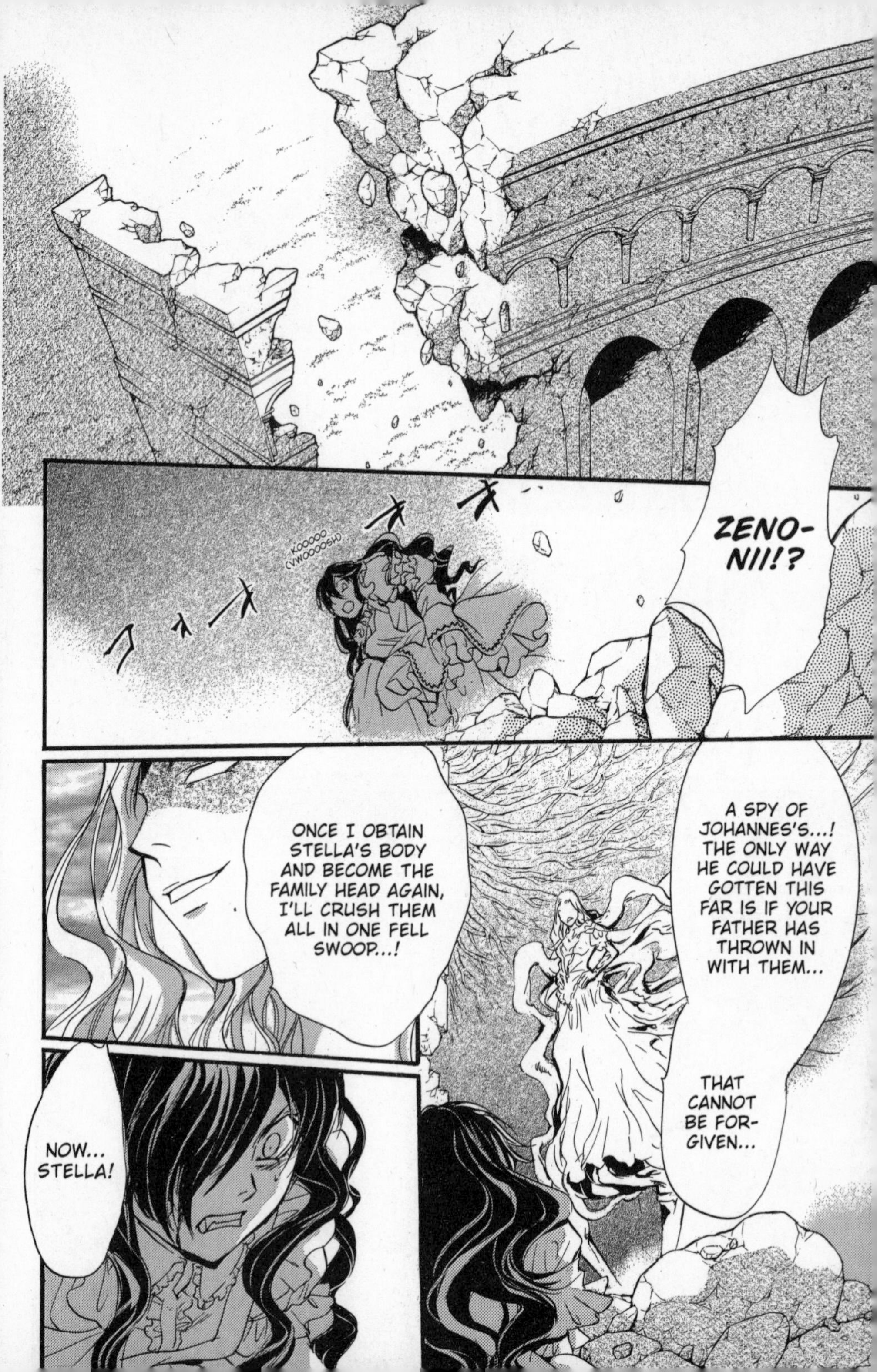
ZENO-NII!?
KOOOOO (VWOOOOSH)
A SPY OF JOHANNES'S...! THE ONLY WAY HE COULD HAVE GOTTEN THIS FAR IS IF YOUR FATHER HAS THROWN IN WITH THEM...
THAT CANNOT BE FOR-GIVEN...
ONCE I OBTAIN STELLA'S BODY AND BECOME THE FAMILY HEAD AGAIN, I'LL CRUSH THEM ALL IN ONE FELL SWOOP...!
NOW... STELLA!

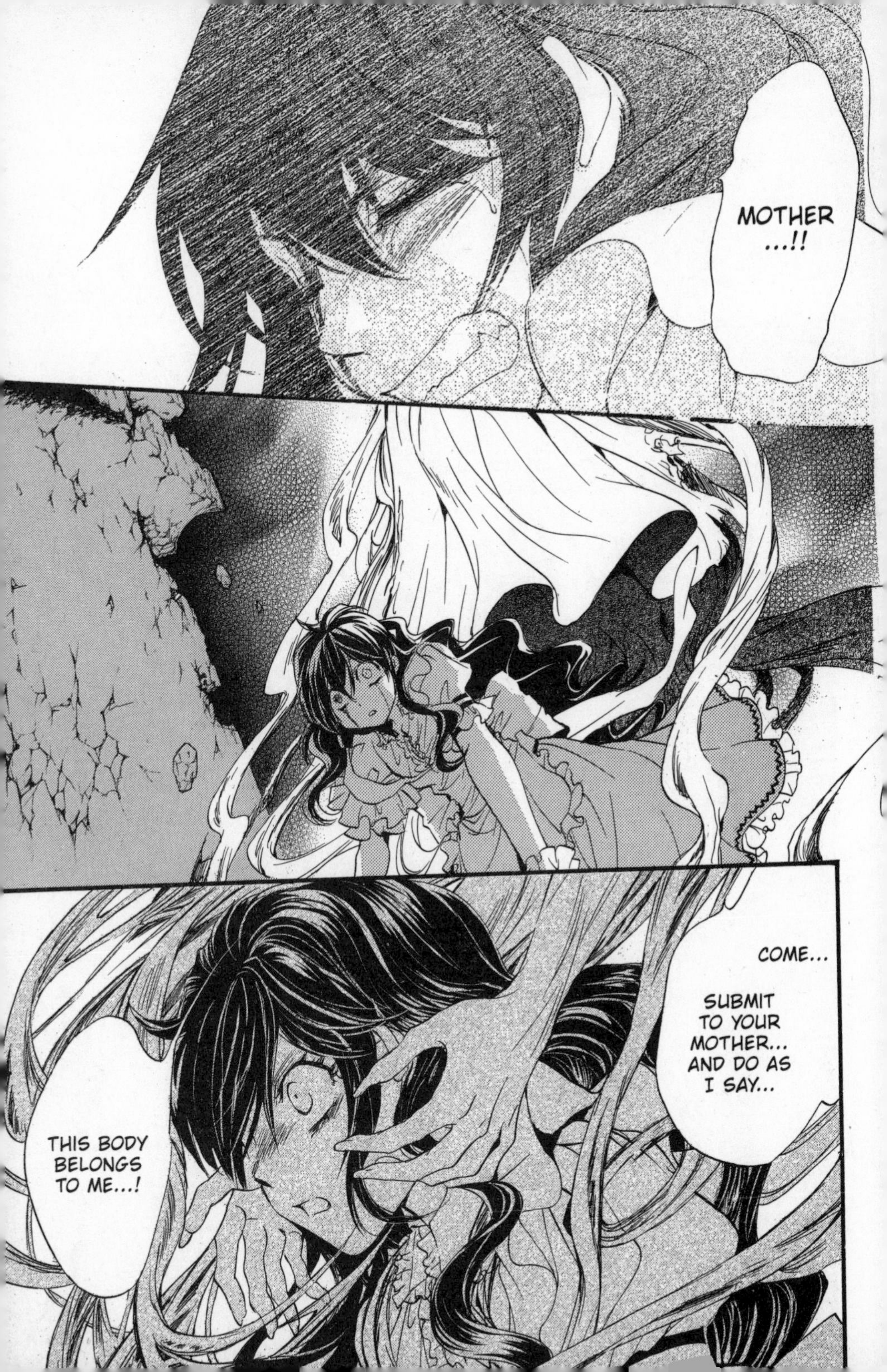
MOTHER ...!!
COME...
SUBMIT TO YOUR MOTHER... AND DO AS I SAY...
THIS BODY BELONGS TO ME...!

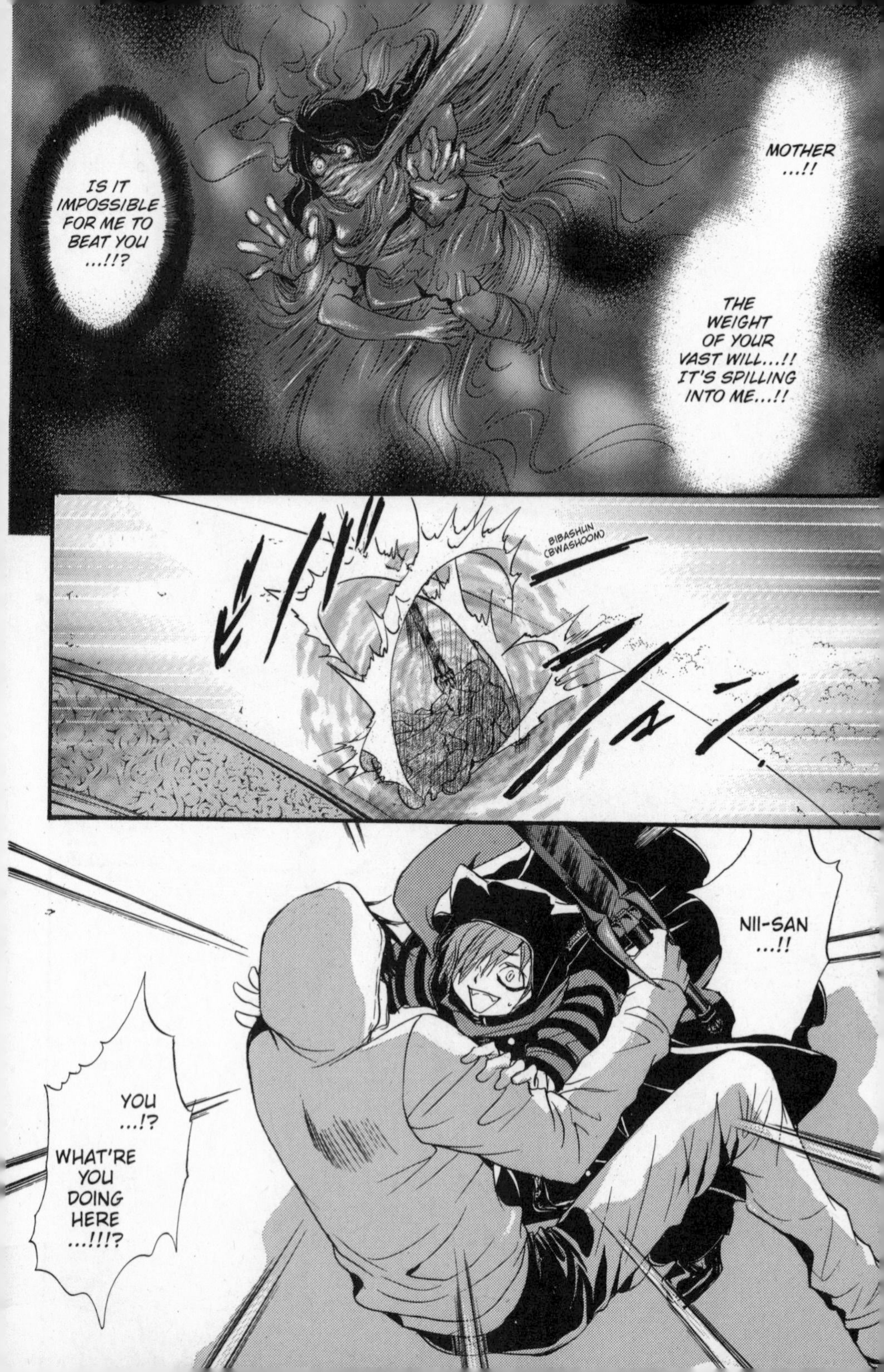
MOTHER ...!!
THE WEIGHT OF YOUR VAST WILL...!! IT'S SPILLING INTO ME...!!
IS IT IMPOSSIBLE FOR ME TO BEAT YOU ...!!?
BIBASHUN (BWASHOOM)
NII-SAN ...!!
YOU ...!?
WHAT'RE YOU DOING HERE ...!!!?

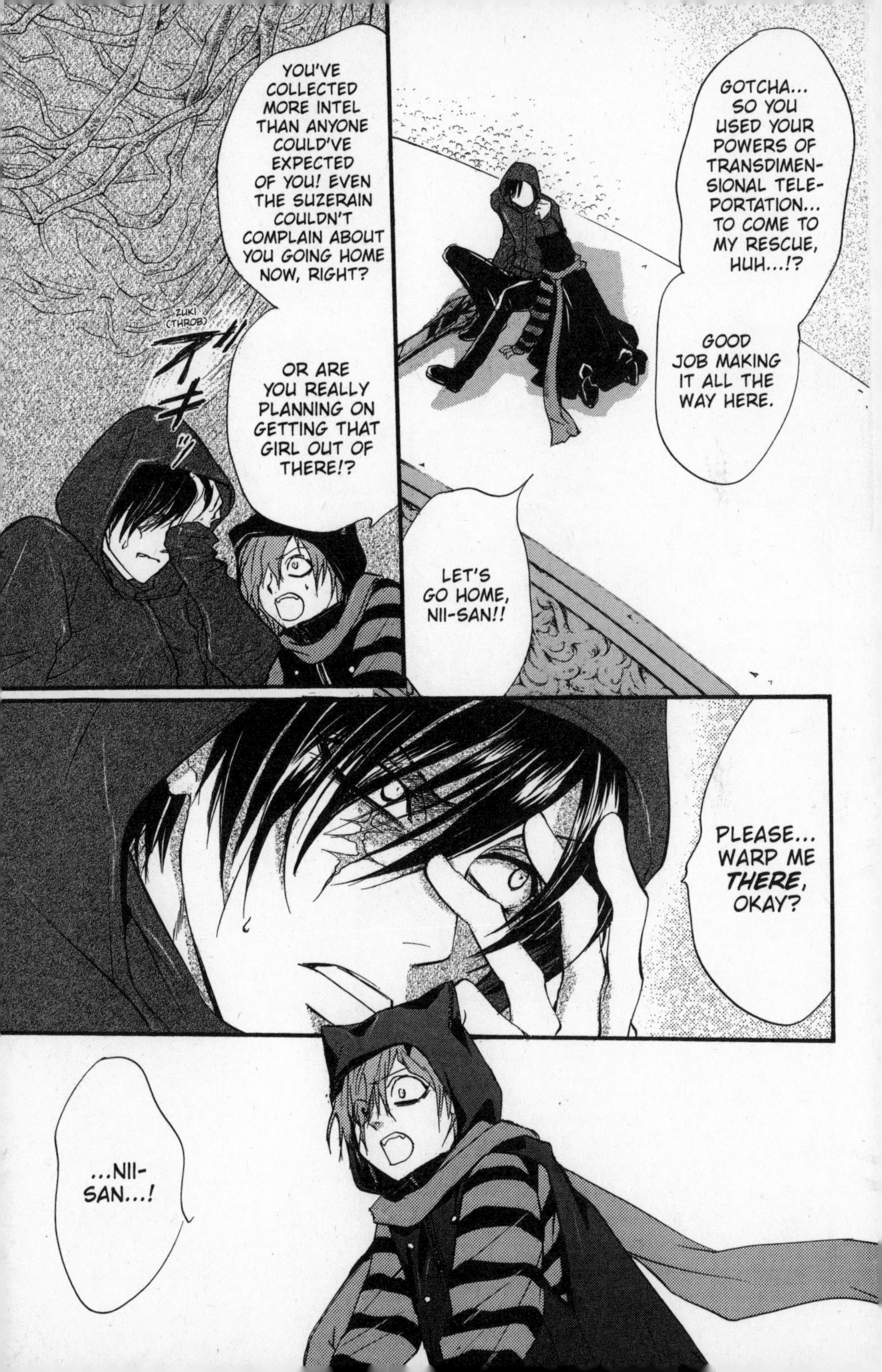
GOTCHA... SO YOU USED YOUR POWERS OF TRANSDIMENSIONAL TELEPORTATION... TO COME TO MY RESCUE, HUH...!?
GOOD JOB MAKING IT ALL THE WAY HERE.
LET'S GO HOME, NII-SAN!!
YOU'VE COLLECTED MORE INTEL THAN ANYONE COULD'VE EXPECTED OF YOU! EVEN THE SUZERAIN COULDN'T COMPLAIN ABOUT YOU GOING HOME NOW, RIGHT?
ZUKI (THROB)
OR ARE YOU REALLY PLANNING ON GETTING THAT GIRL OUT OF THERE!?
PLEASE... WARP ME *THERE*, OKAY?
...NII-SAN...!

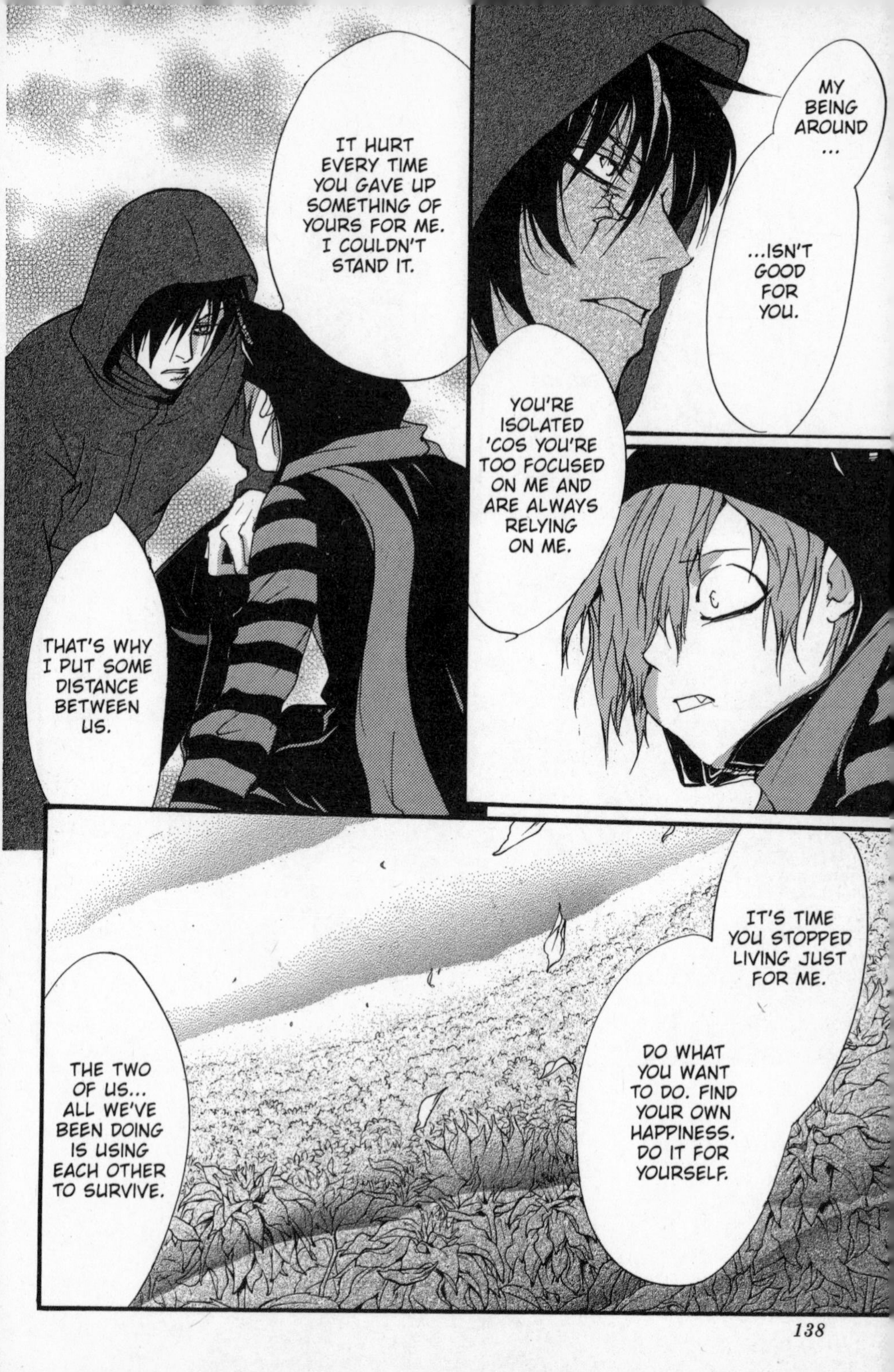

MY BEING AROUND...
...ISN'T GOOD FOR YOU.
YOU'RE ISOLATED 'COS YOU'RE TOO FOCUSED ON ME AND ARE ALWAYS RELYING ON ME.
IT HURT EVERY TIME YOU GAVE UP SOMETHING OF YOURS FOR ME. I COULDN'T STAND IT.
THAT'S WHY I PUT SOME DISTANCE BETWEEN US.
IT'S TIME YOU STOPPED LIVING JUST FOR ME.
DO WHAT YOU WANT TO DO. FIND YOUR OWN HAPPINESS. DO IT FOR YOURSELF.
THE TWO OF US... ALL WE'VE BEEN DOING IS USING EACH OTHER TO SURVIVE.

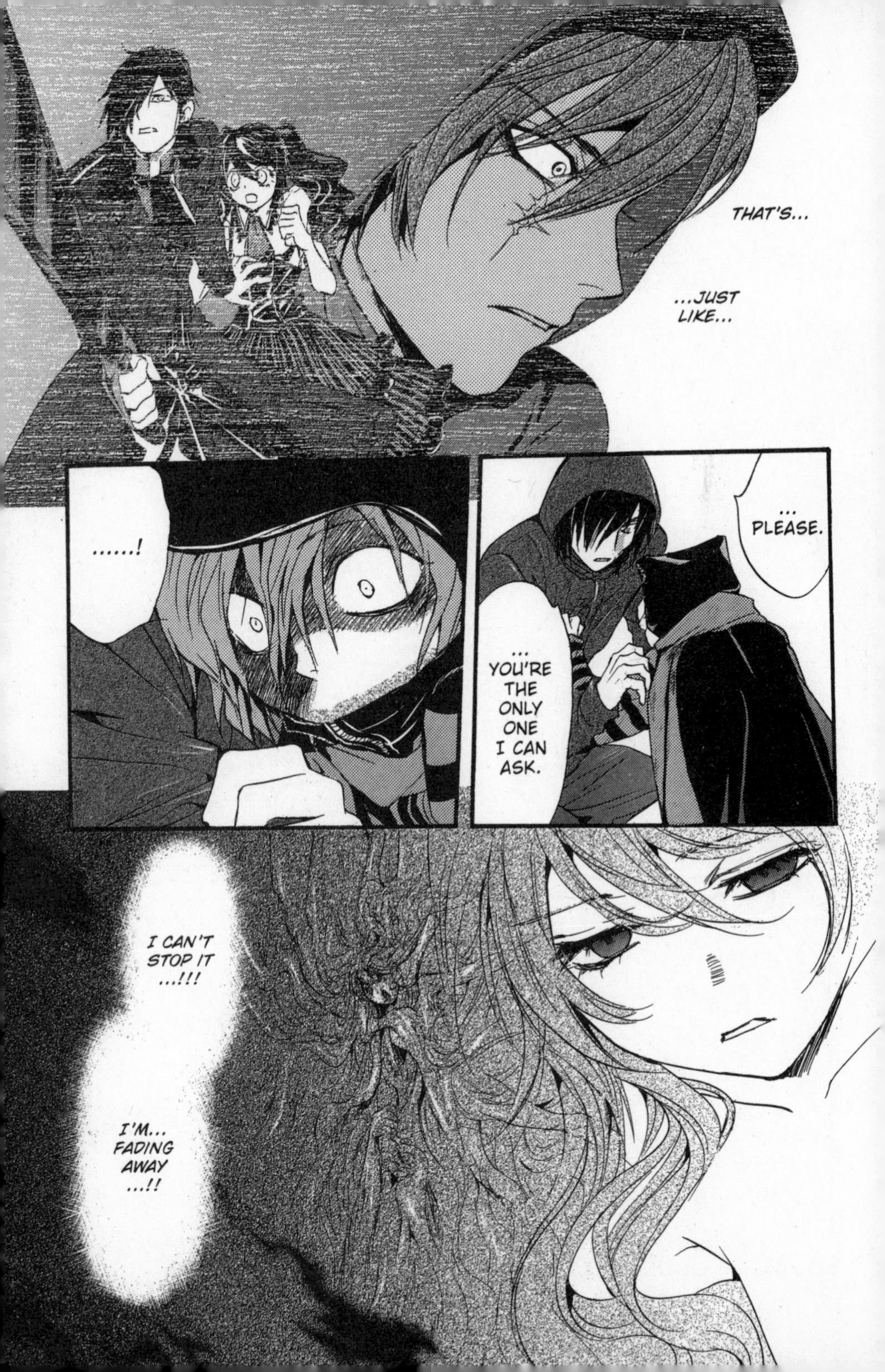
THAT'S...
...JUST LIKE...
...PLEASE.
...YOU'RE THE ONLY ONE I CAN ASK.
......!
I CAN'T STOP IT ...!!!
I'M... FADING AWAY ...!!

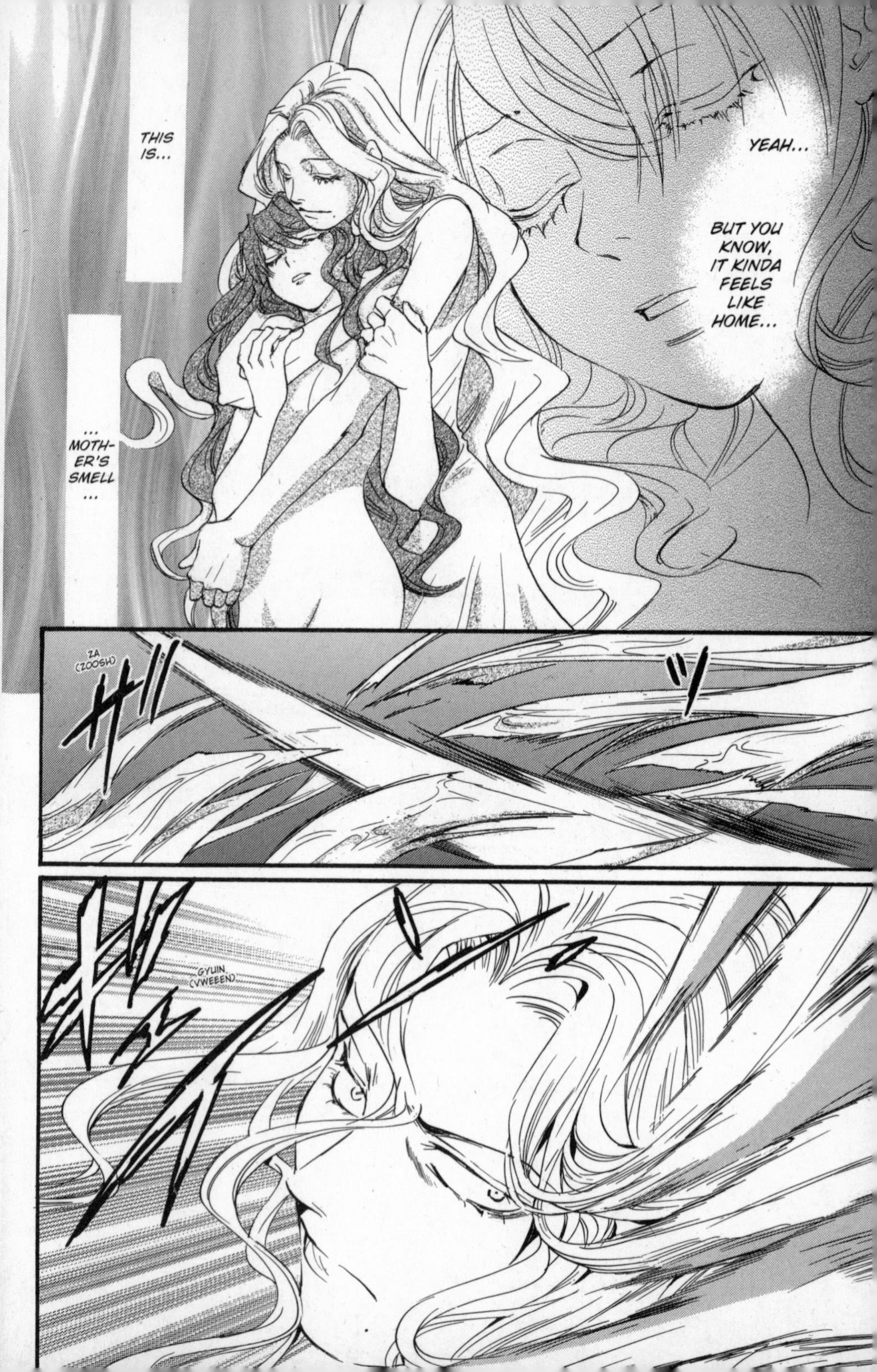
YEAH...
BUT YOU KNOW, IT KINDA FEELS LIKE HOME...
THIS IS...
...MOTHER'S SMELL...
ZA (ZOOSH)
GYUIN (VWEEEN)

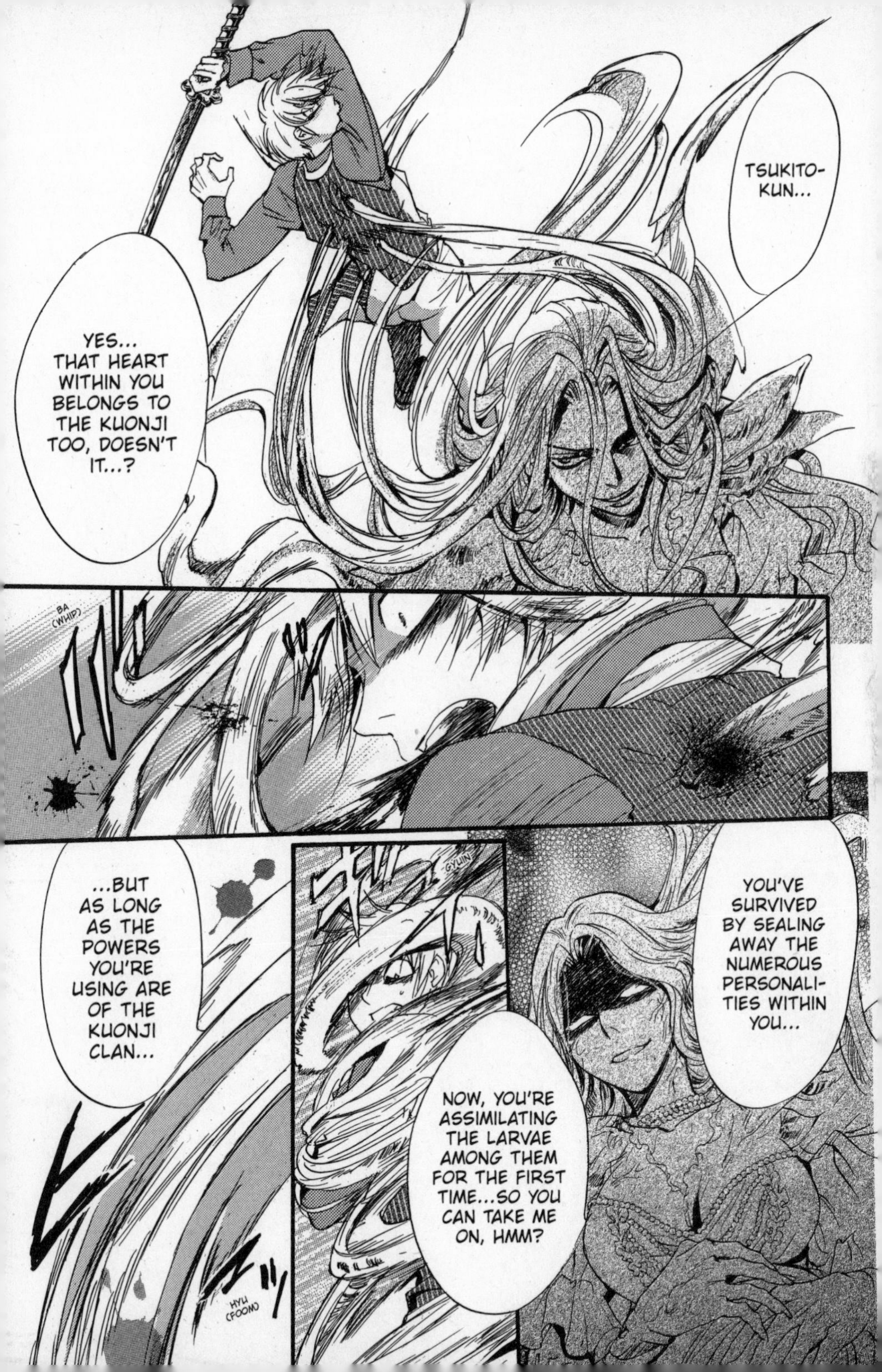
TSUKITO-KUN...
YES... THAT HEART WITHIN YOU BELONGS TO THE KUONJI TOO, DOESN'T IT...?
BA (WHIP)
GYUIN
YOU'VE SURVIVED BY SEALING AWAY THE NUMEROUS PERSONALITIES WITHIN YOU...
NOW, YOU'RE ASSIMILATING THE LARVAE AMONG THEM FOR THE FIRST TIME...SO YOU CAN TAKE ME ON, HMM?
...BUT AS LONG AS THE POWERS YOU'RE USING ARE OF THE KUONJI CLAN...
HYU (FOOM)

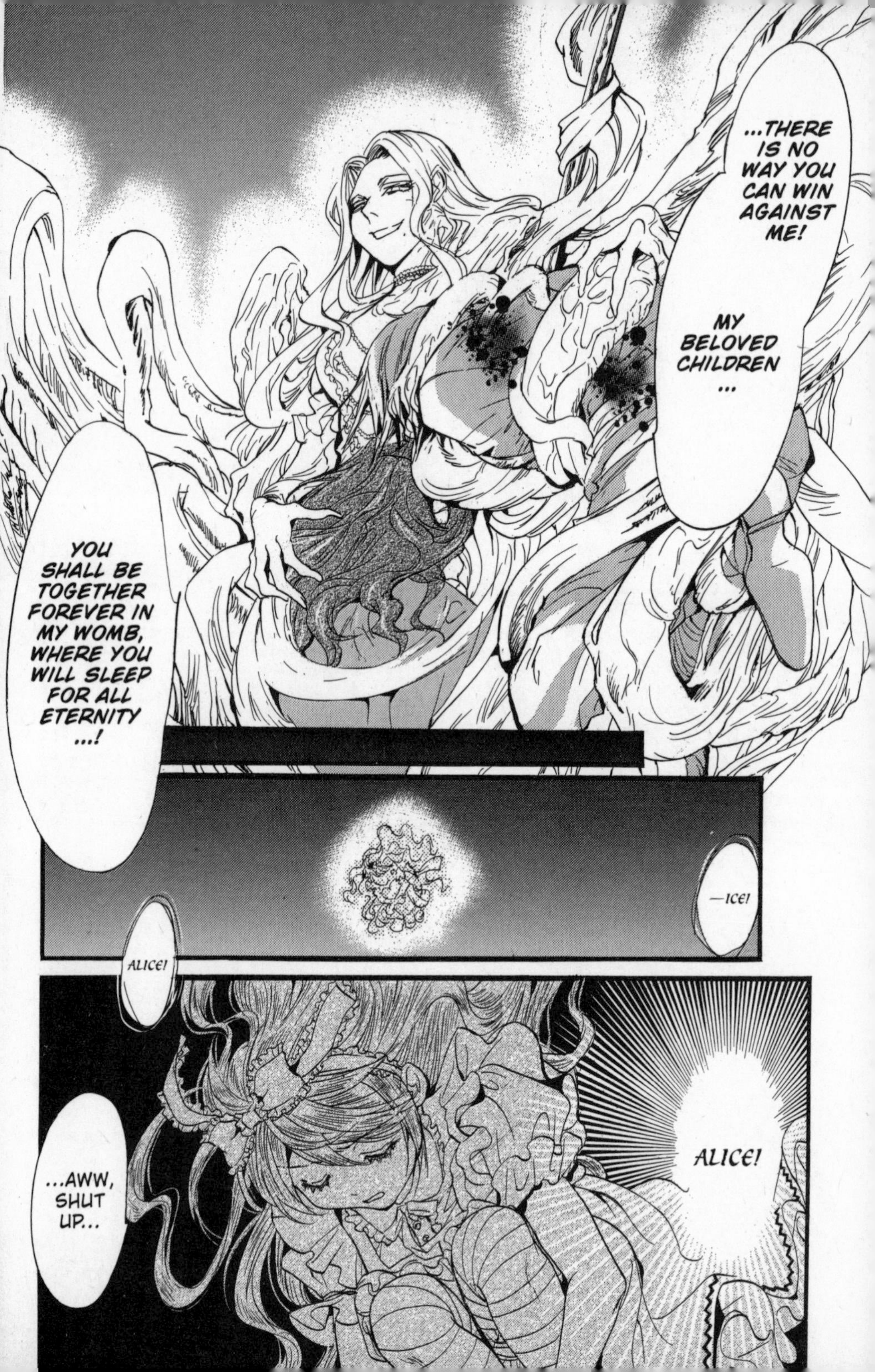
...THERE IS NO WAY YOU CAN WIN AGAINST ME!
MY BELOVED CHILDREN ...
YOU SHALL BE TOGETHER FOREVER IN MY WOMB, WHERE YOU WILL SLEEP FOR ALL ETERNITY ...!
—ICE!
ALICE!
ALICE!
...AWW, SHUT UP...

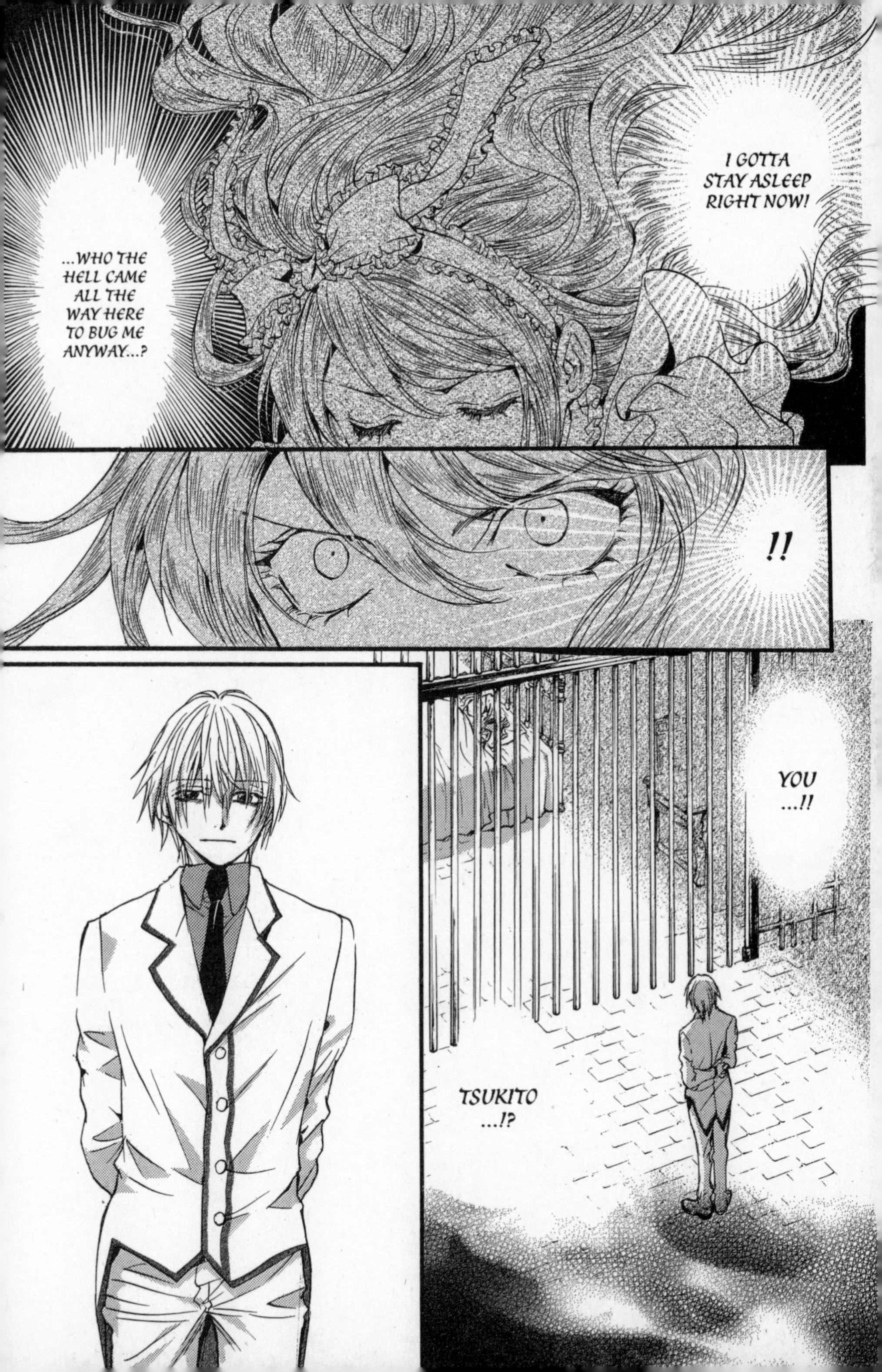
I GOTTA STAY ASLEEP RIGHT NOW!
...WHO THE HELL CAME ALL THE WAY HERE TO BUG ME ANYWAY...?
!!
YOU ...!!
TSUKITO ...!?

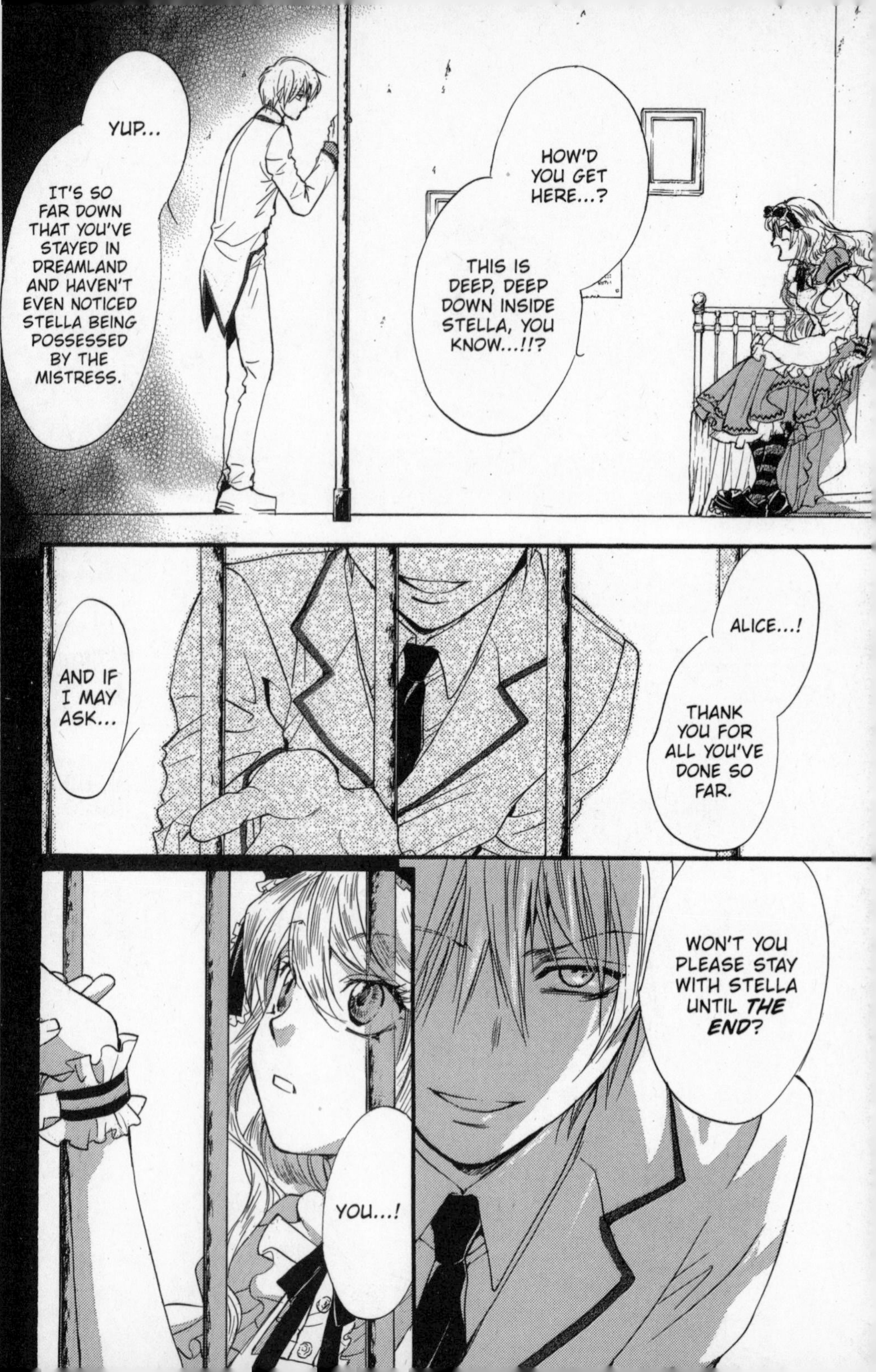
HOW'D YOU GET HERE...?
THIS IS DEEP, DEEP DOWN INSIDE STELLA, YOU KNOW...!!?
YUP...
IT'S SO FAR DOWN THAT YOU'VE STAYED IN DREAMLAND AND HAVEN'T EVEN NOTICED STELLA BEING POSSESSED BY THE MISTRESS.
ALICE...!
THANK YOU FOR ALL YOU'VE DONE SO FAR.
AND IF I MAY ASK...
WON'T YOU PLEASE STAY WITH STELLA UNTIL *THE END*?
YOU...!

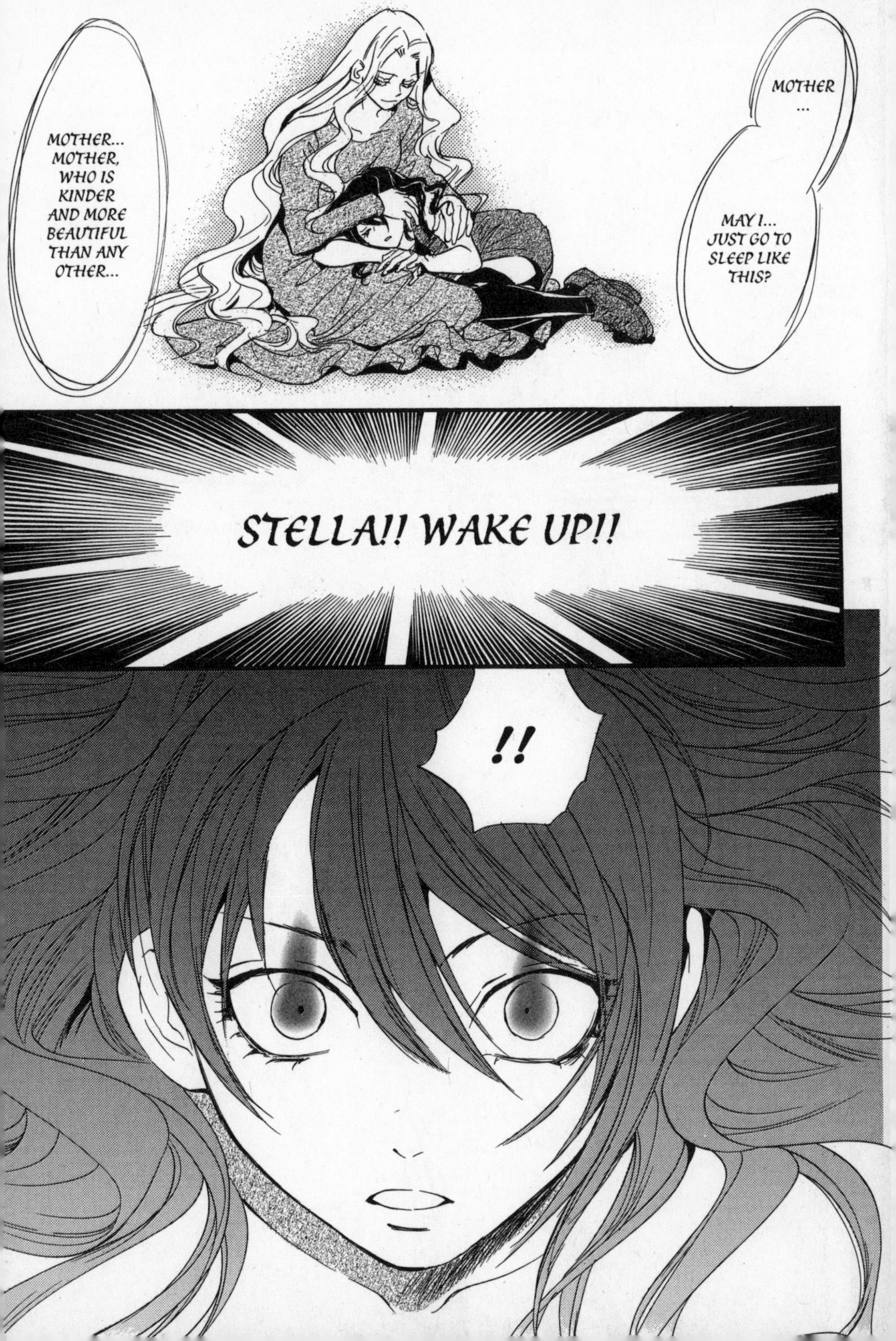
MOTHER ...
MAY I... JUST GO TO SLEEP LIKE THIS?
MOTHER... MOTHER, WHO IS KINDER AND MORE BEAUTIFUL THAN ANY OTHER...
STELLA!! WAKE UP!!
!!

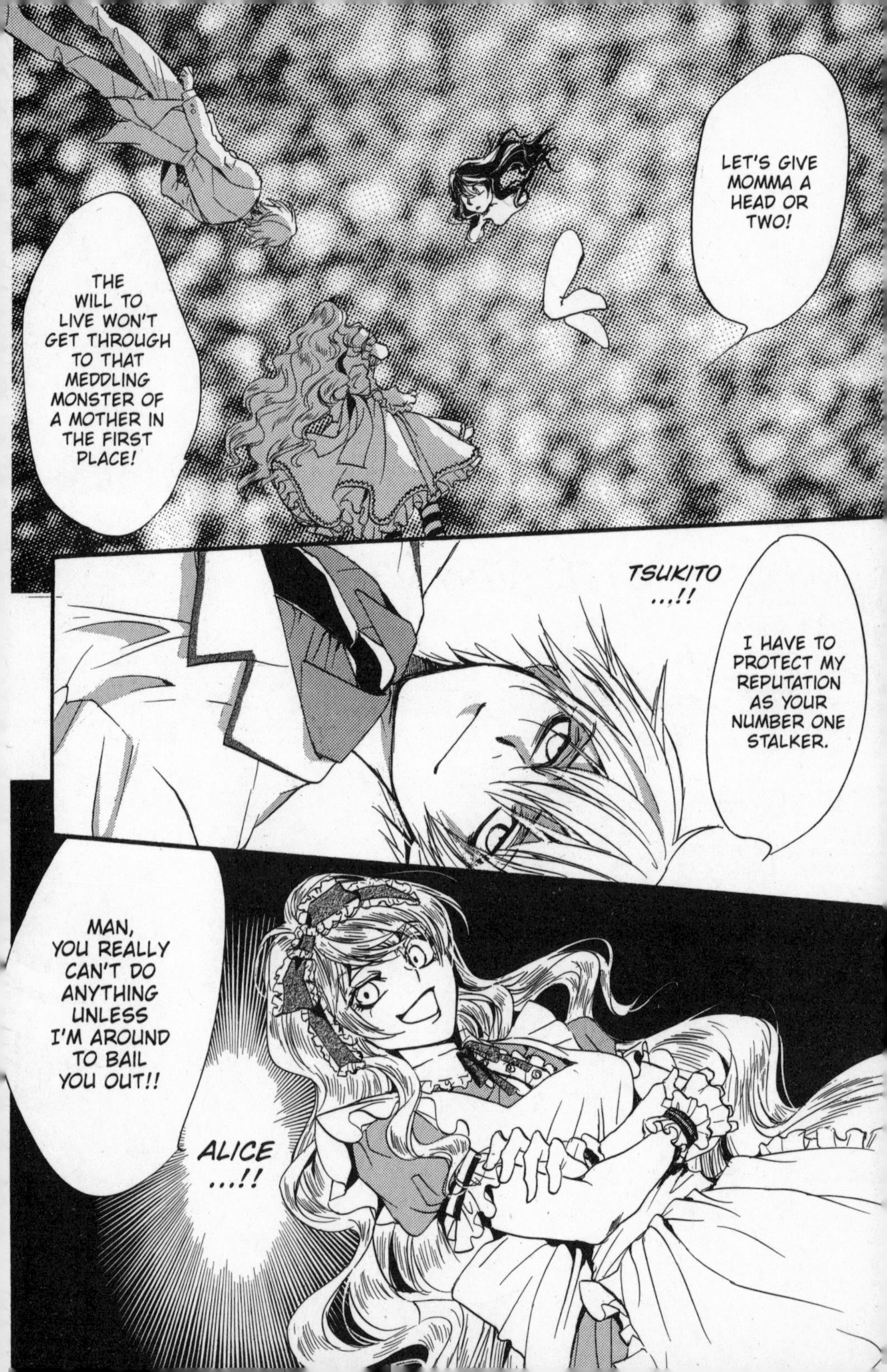
LET'S GIVE MOMMA A HEAD OR TWO!
THE WILL TO LIVE WON'T GET THROUGH TO THAT MEDDLING MONSTER OF A MOTHER IN THE FIRST PLACE!
TSUKITO ...!!
I HAVE TO PROTECT MY REPUTATION AS YOUR NUMBER ONE STALKER.
MAN, YOU REALLY CAN'T DO ANYTHING UNLESS I'M AROUND TO BAIL YOU OUT!!
ALICE ...!!

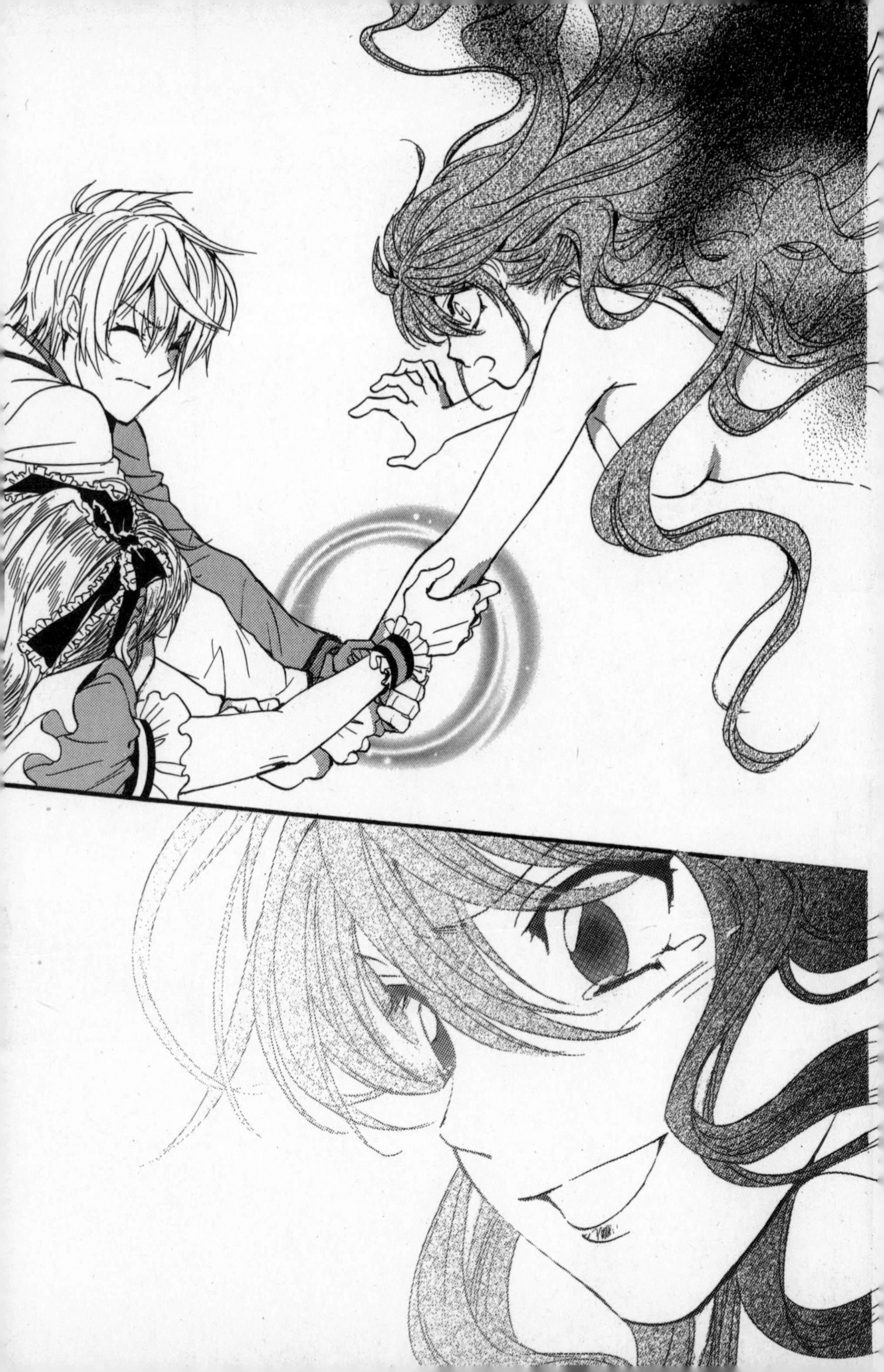

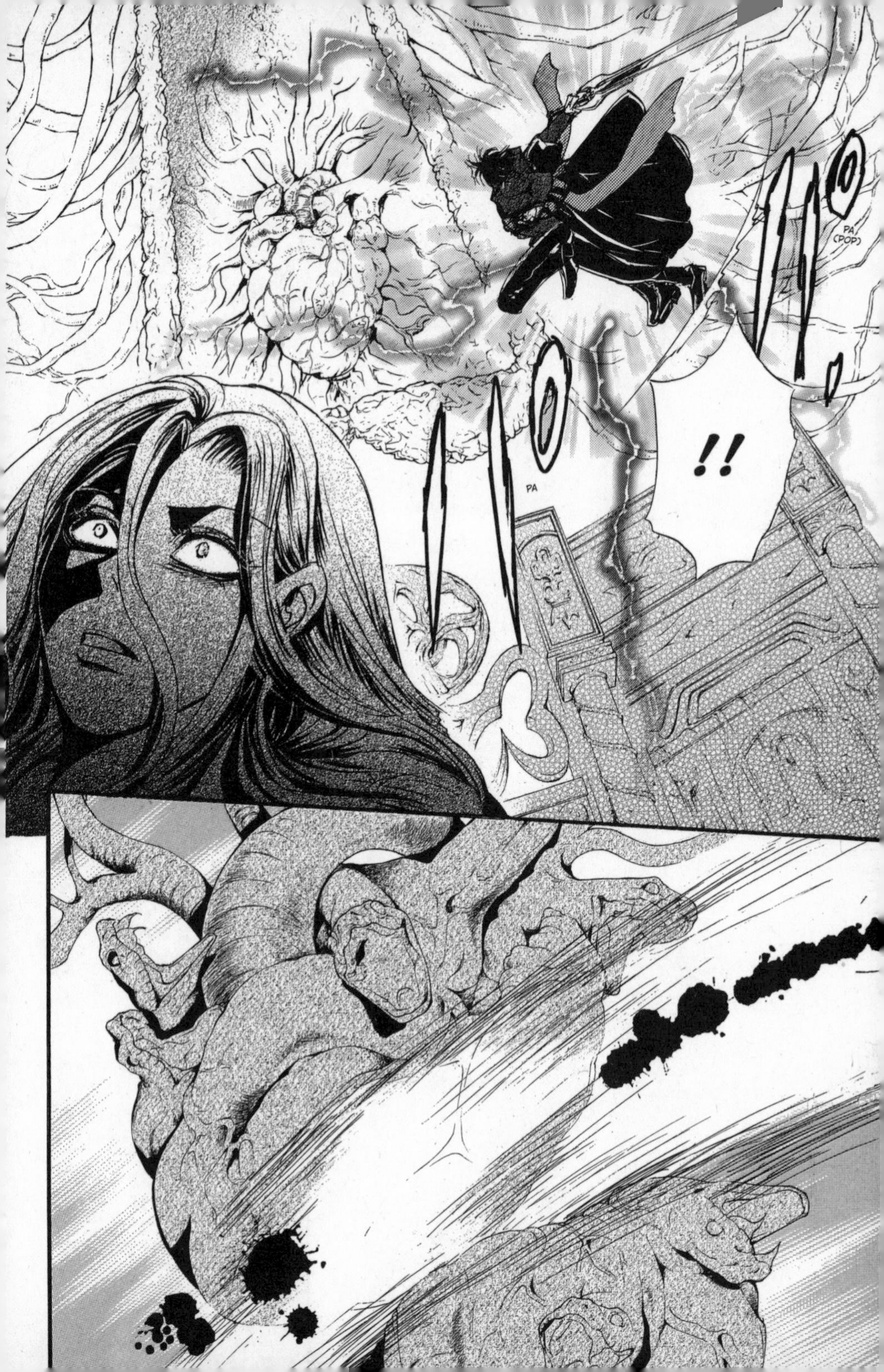
PA (POP)
!!
PA

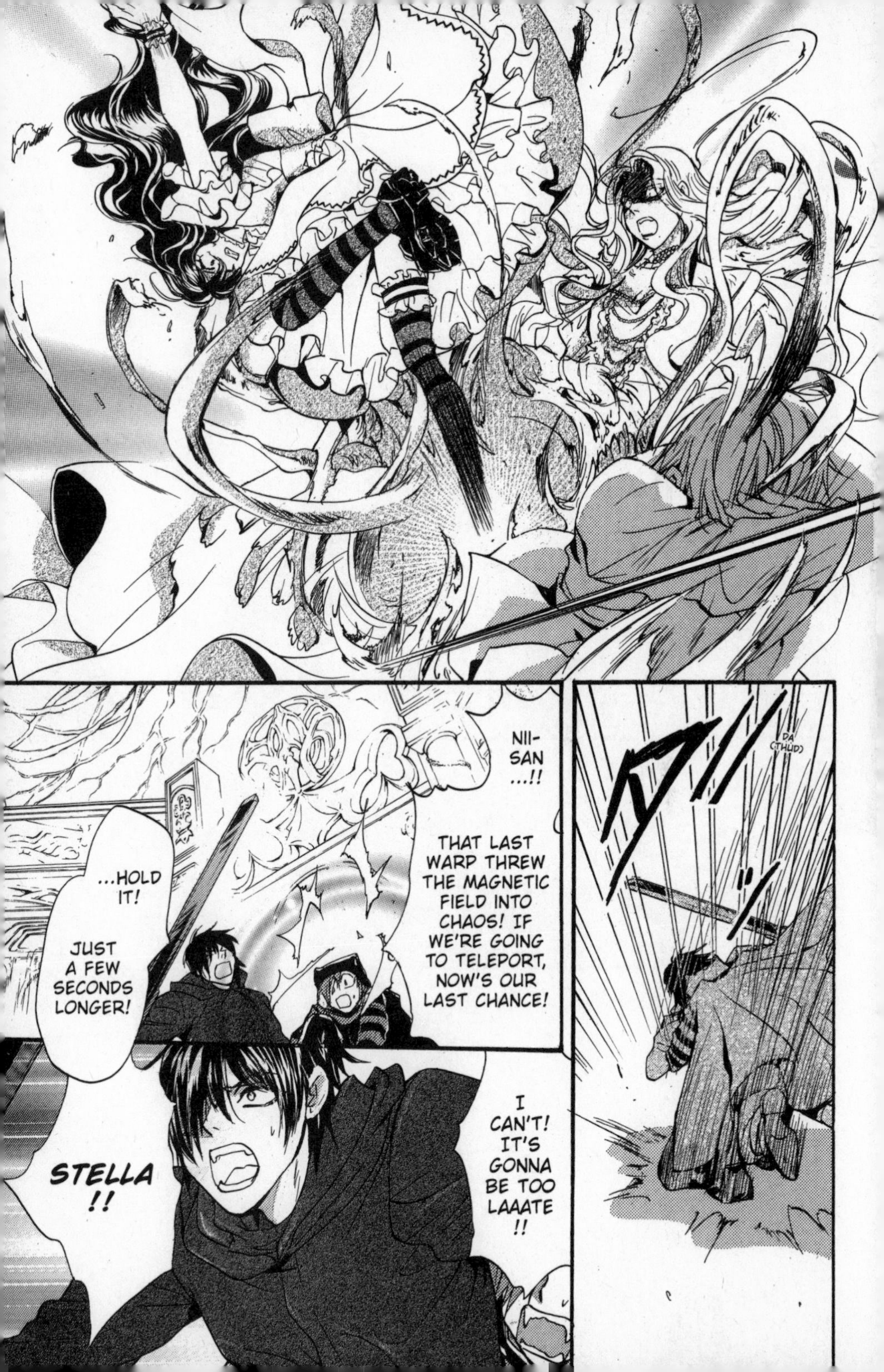
DA (THUD)
NII-SAN ...!!
THAT LAST WARP THREW THE MAGNETIC FIELD INTO CHAOS! IF WE'RE GOING TO TELEPORT, NOW'S OUR LAST CHANCE!
...HOLD IT!
JUST A FEW SECONDS LONGER!
I CAN'T! IT'S GONNA BE TOO LAAATE !!
STELLA !!

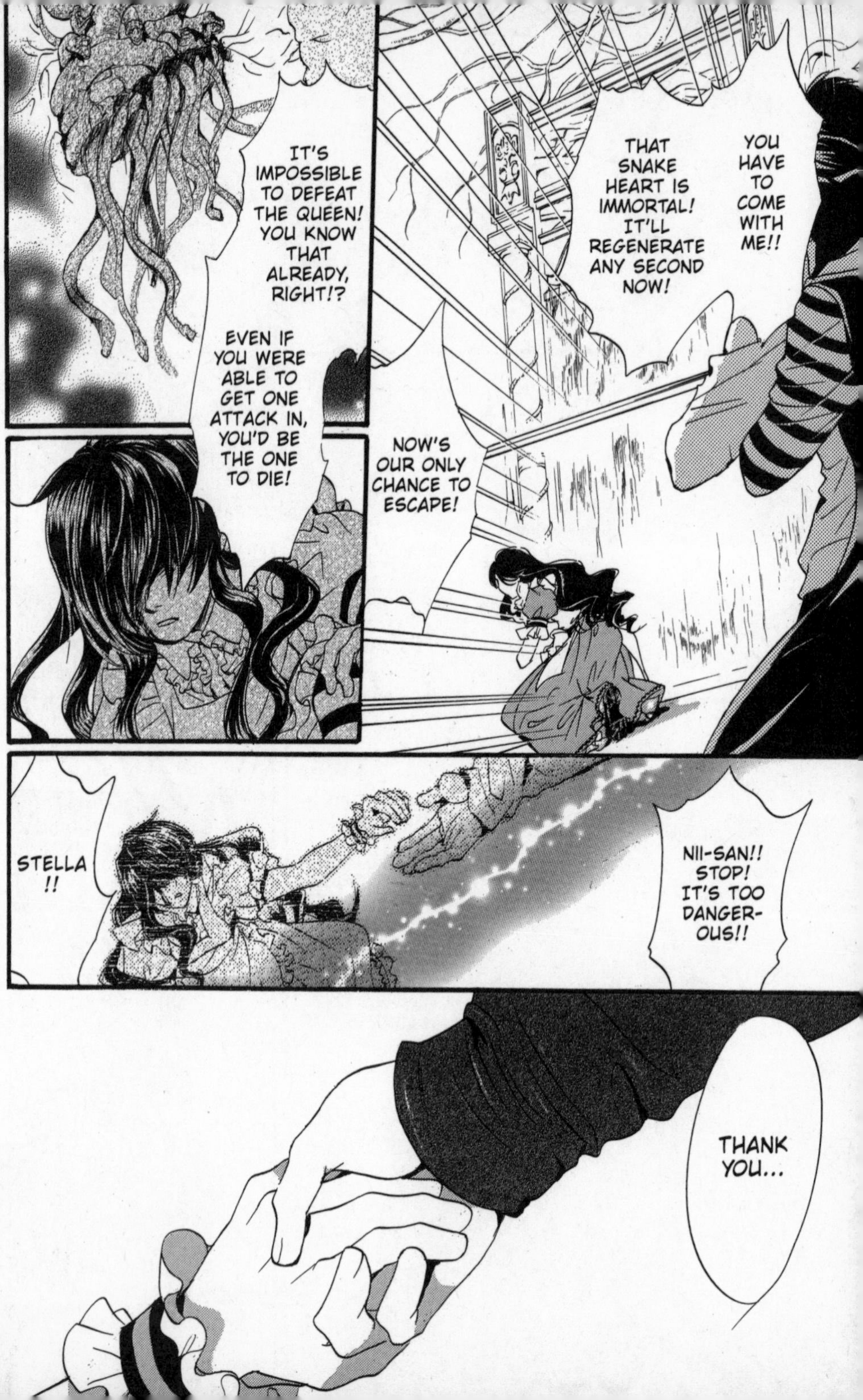

YOU HAVE TO COME WITH ME!!
THAT SNAKE HEART IS IMMORTAL! IT'LL REGENERATE ANY SECOND NOW!
NOW'S OUR ONLY CHANCE TO ESCAPE!
IT'S IMPOSSIBLE TO DEFEAT THE QUEEN! YOU KNOW THAT ALREADY, RIGHT!?
EVEN IF YOU WERE ABLE TO GET ONE ATTACK IN, YOU'D BE THE ONE TO DIE!
NII-SAN!! STOP! IT'S TOO DANGER-OUS!!
STELLA!!
THANK YOU...

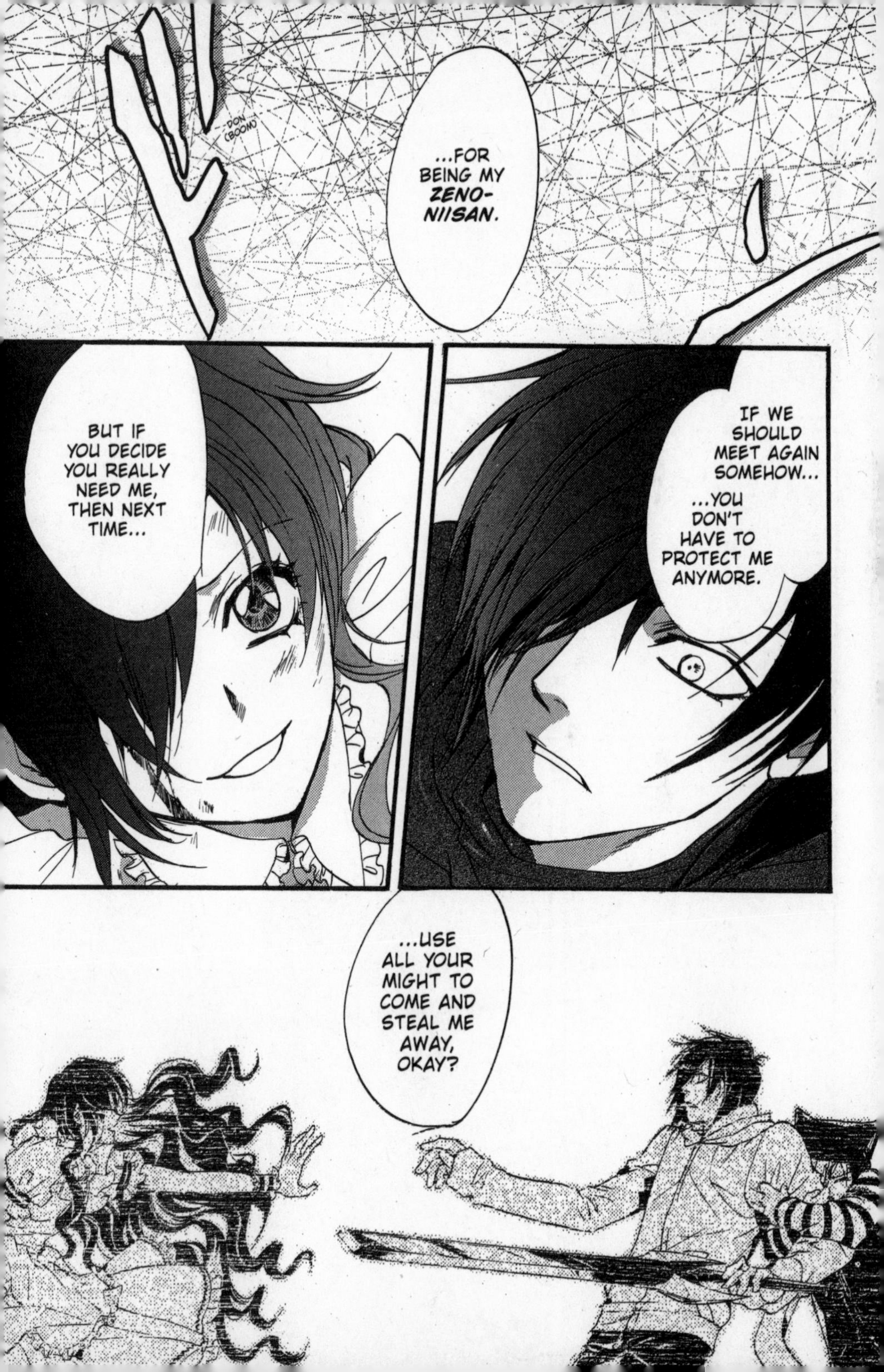
...FOR BEING MY ZENO-NIISAN.
DON (BOOM)
IF WE SHOULD MEET AGAIN SOMEHOW...
...YOU DON'T HAVE TO PROTECT ME ANYMORE.
BUT IF YOU DECIDE YOU REALLY NEED ME, THEN NEXT TIME...
...USE ALL YOUR MIGHT TO COME AND STEAL ME AWAY, OKAY?

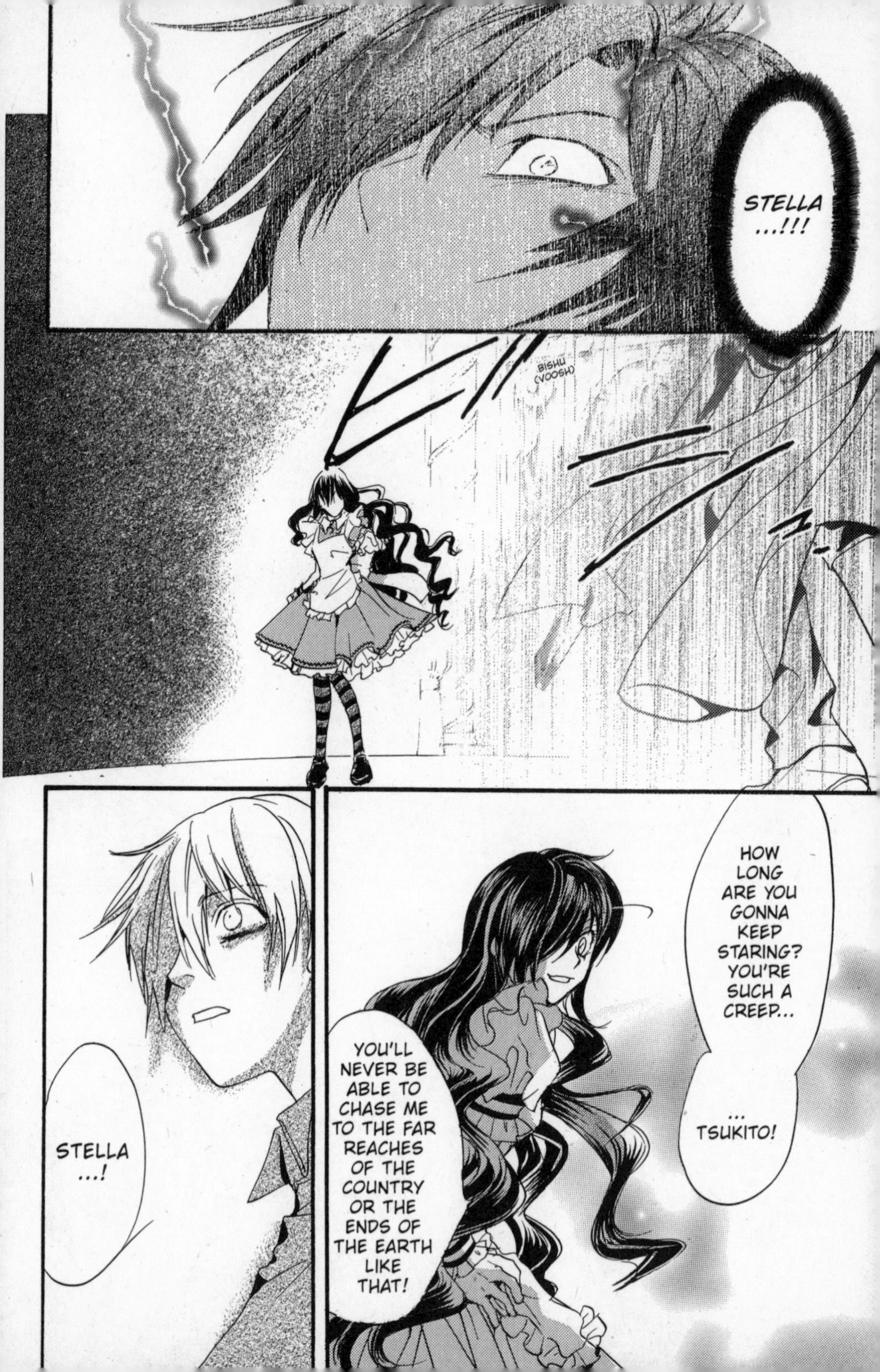
STELLA ...!!!
BISHU (VOOSH)
HOW LONG ARE YOU GONNA KEEP STARING? YOU'RE SUCH A CREEP... ...TSUKITO!
YOU'LL NEVER BE ABLE TO CHASE ME TO THE FAR REACHES OF THE COUNTRY OR THE ENDS OF THE EARTH LIKE THAT!
STELLA ...!

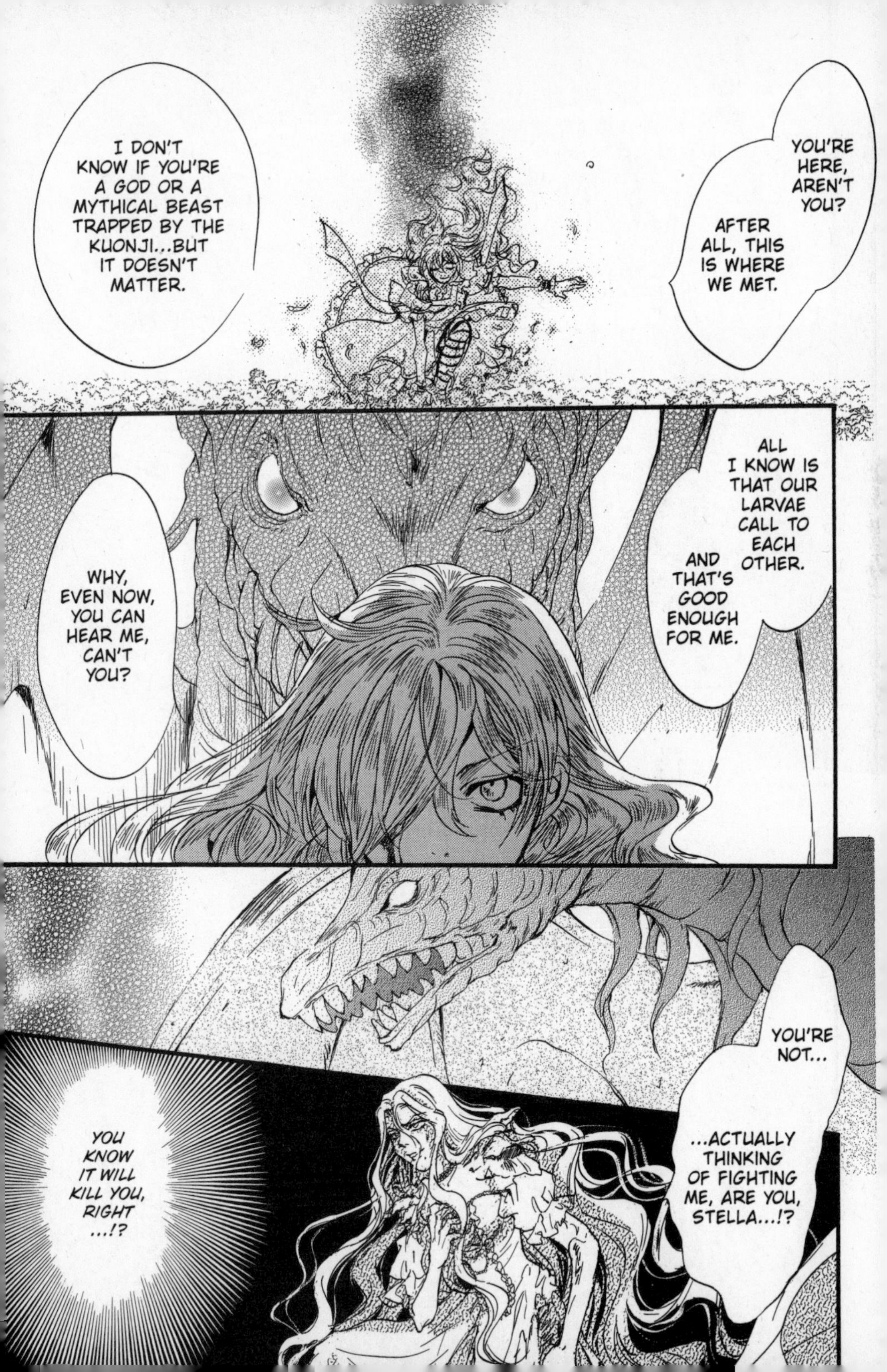
YOU'RE HERE, AREN'T YOU?
AFTER ALL, THIS IS WHERE WE MET.
I DON'T KNOW IF YOU'RE A GOD OR A MYTHICAL BEAST TRAPPED BY THE KUONJI...BUT IT DOESN'T MATTER.
ALL I KNOW IS THAT OUR LARVAE CALL TO EACH OTHER.
AND THAT'S GOOD ENOUGH FOR ME.
WHY, EVEN NOW, YOU CAN HEAR ME, CAN'T YOU?
YOU'RE NOT...
...ACTUALLY THINKING OF FIGHTING ME, ARE YOU, STELLA...!?
YOU KNOW IT WILL KILL YOU, RIGHT ...!?

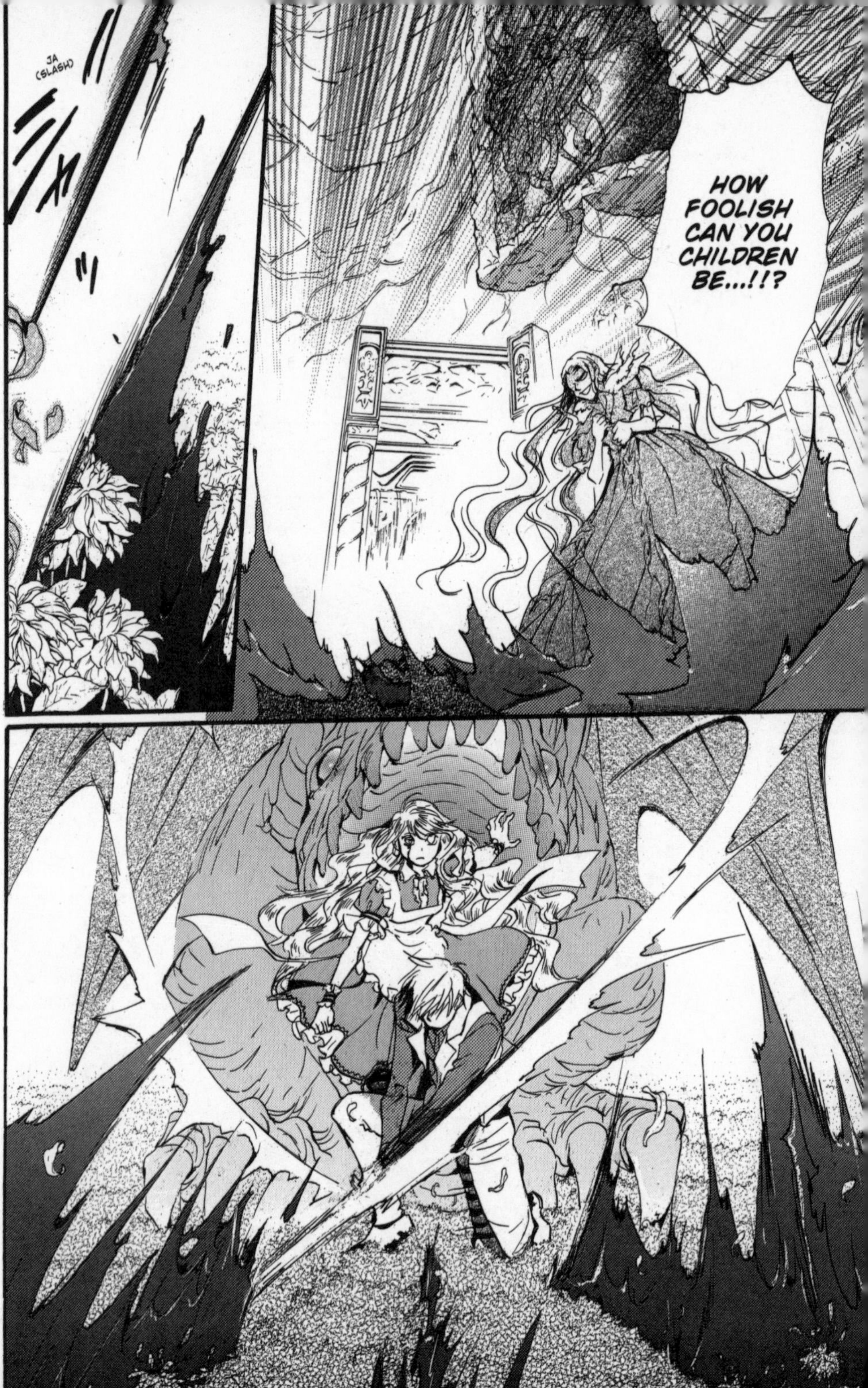
HOW FOOLISH CAN YOU CHILDREN BE...!!?
JA (SLASH)

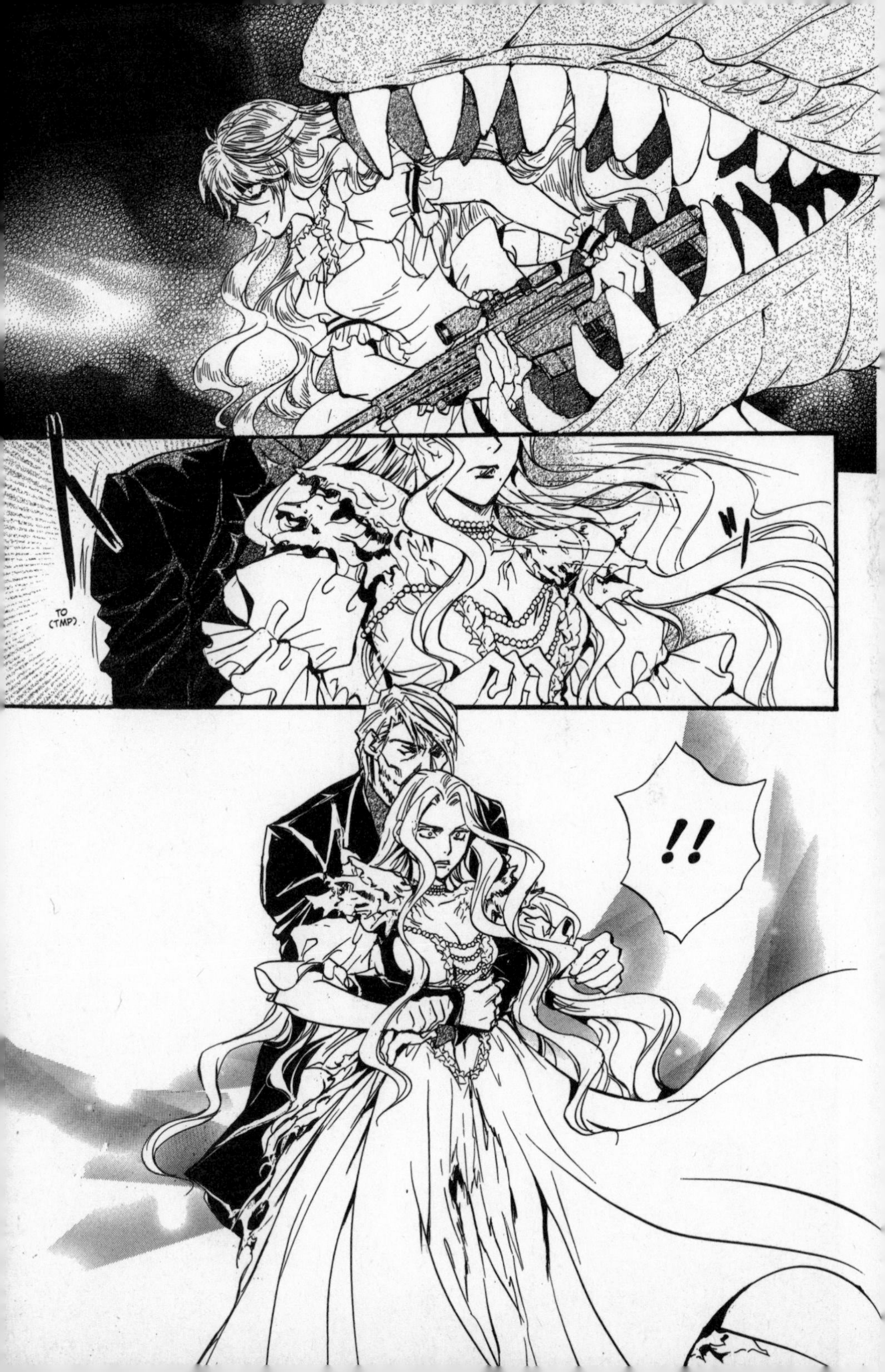
TO (TMP)
!!

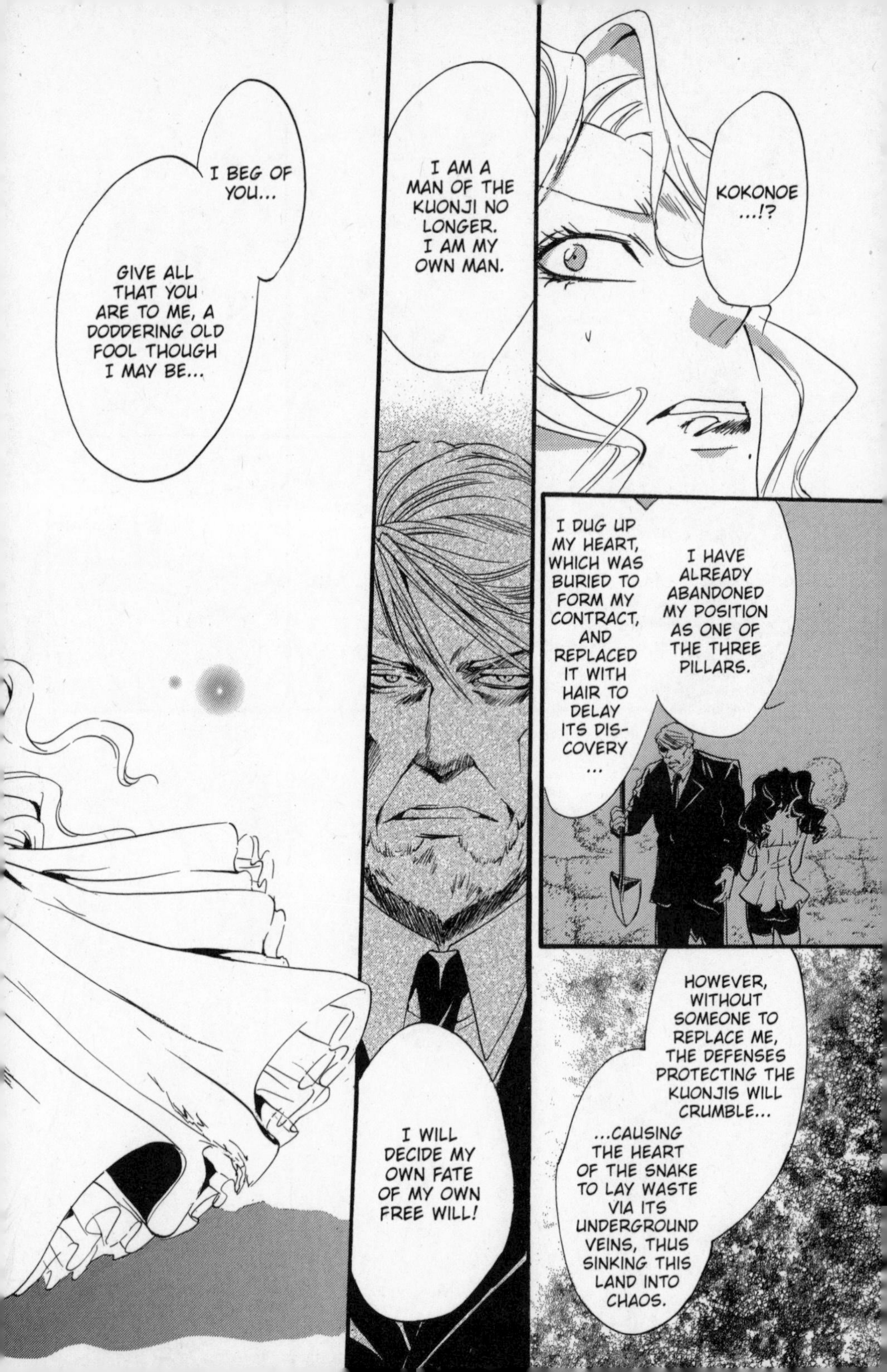
KOKONOE ...!?
I HAVE ALREADY ABANDONED MY POSITION AS ONE OF THE THREE PILLARS.
I DUG UP MY HEART, WHICH WAS BURIED TO FORM MY CONTRACT, AND REPLACED IT WITH HAIR TO DELAY ITS DIS-COVERY ...
HOWEVER, WITHOUT SOMEONE TO REPLACE ME, THE DEFENSES PROTECTING THE KUONJIS WILL CRUMBLE...
...CAUSING THE HEART OF THE SNAKE TO LAY WASTE VIA ITS UNDERGROUND VEINS, THUS SINKING THIS LAND INTO CHAOS.
I AM A MAN OF THE KUONJI NO LONGER. I AM MY OWN MAN.
I WILL DECIDE MY OWN FATE OF MY OWN FREE WILL!
I BEG OF YOU...
GIVE ALL THAT YOU ARE TO ME, A DODDERING OLD FOOL THOUGH I MAY BE...

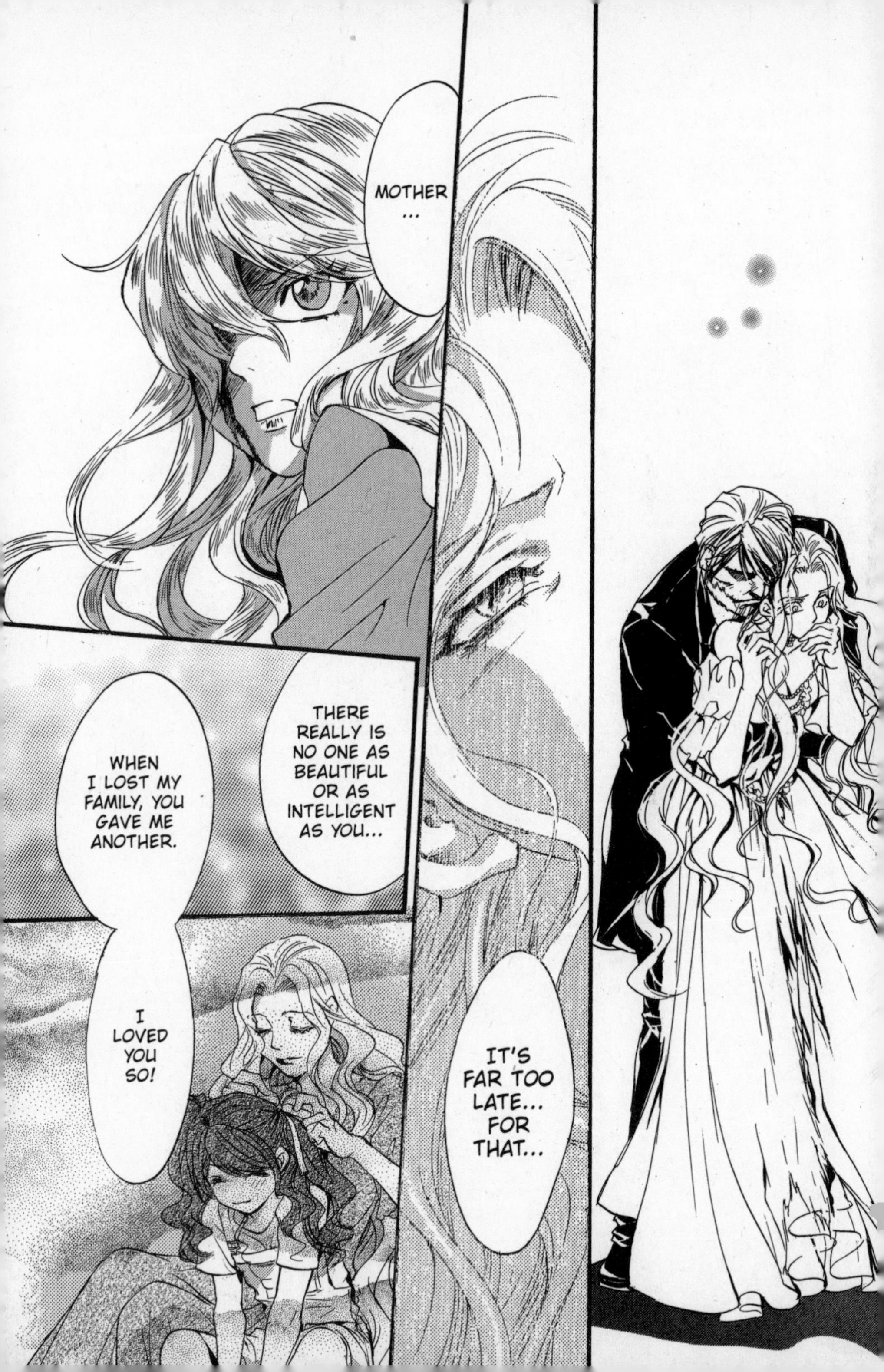
MOTHER...
THERE REALLY IS NO ONE AS BEAUTIFUL OR AS INTELLIGENT AS YOU...
WHEN I LOST MY FAMILY, YOU GAVE ME ANOTHER.
I LOVED YOU SO!
IT'S FAR TOO LATE... FOR THAT...

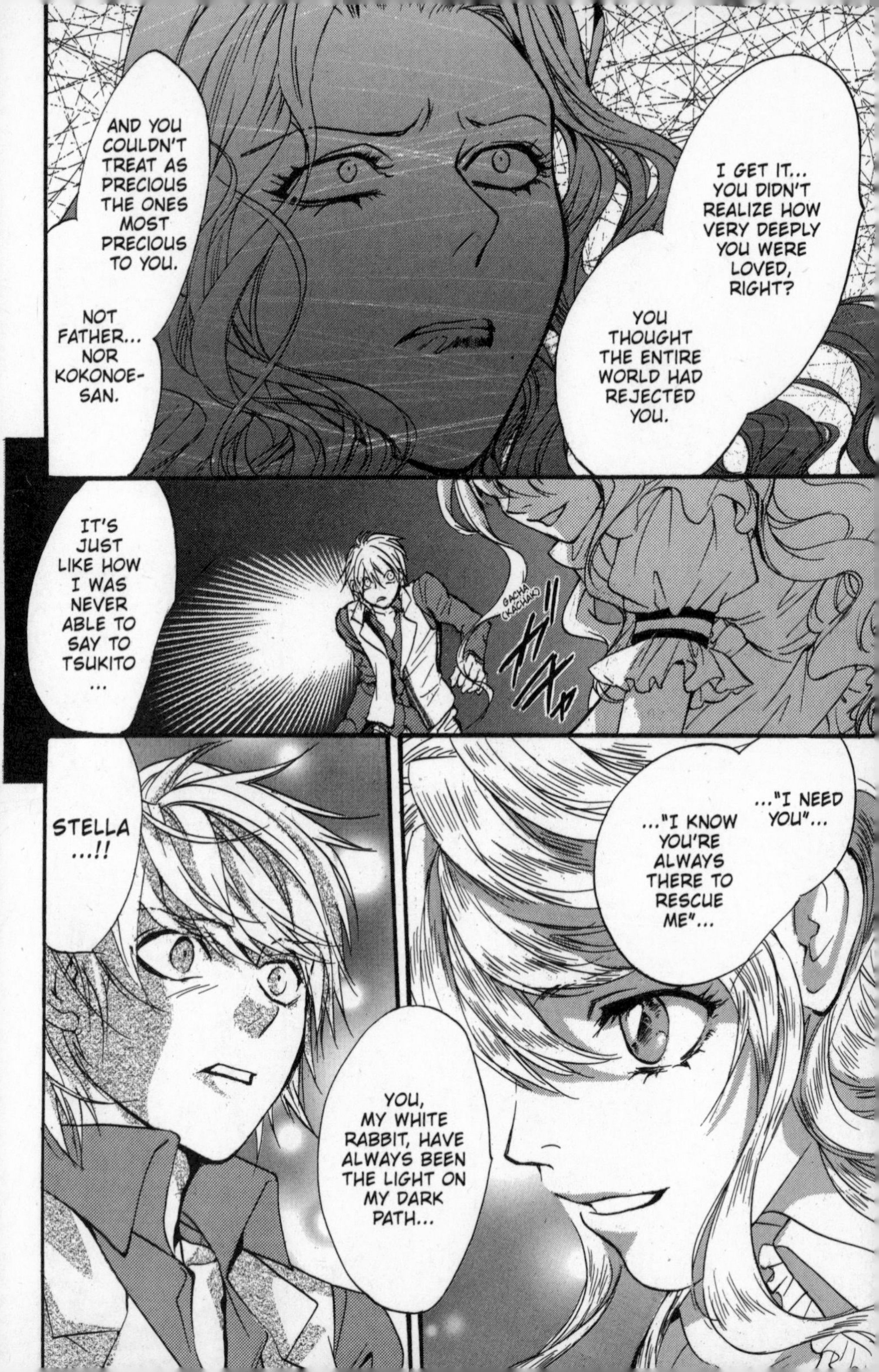
I GET IT... YOU DIDN'T REALIZE HOW VERY DEEPLY YOU WERE LOVED, RIGHT?
YOU THOUGHT THE ENTIRE WORLD HAD REJECTED YOU.
AND YOU COULDN'T TREAT AS PRECIOUS THE ONES MOST PRECIOUS TO YOU.
NOT FATHER... NOR KOKONOE-SAN.
GACHA (KACHAK)
IT'S JUST LIKE HOW I WAS NEVER ABLE TO SAY TO TSUKITO ...
..."I NEED YOU"...
..."I KNOW YOU'RE ALWAYS THERE TO RESCUE ME"...
YOU, MY WHITE RABBIT, HAVE ALWAYS BEEN THE LIGHT ON MY DARK PATH...
STELLA ...!!

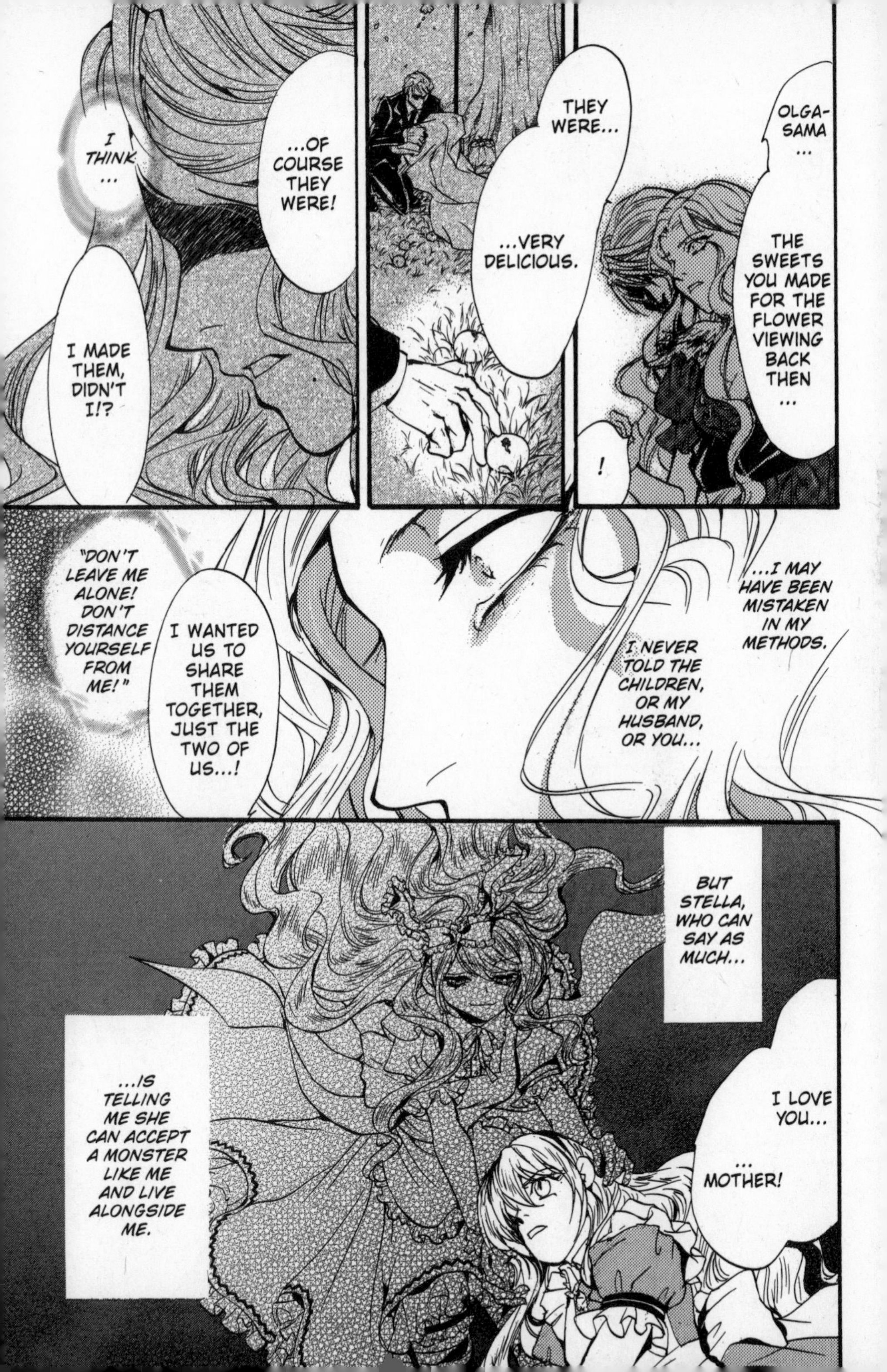
OLGA-SAMA...
THE SWEETS YOU MADE FOR THE FLOWER VIEWING BACK THEN...
!
THEY WERE...
...VERY DELICIOUS.
...OF COURSE THEY WERE!
I THINK...
I MADE THEM, DIDN'T I!?
...I MAY HAVE BEEN MISTAKEN IN MY METHODS.
I NEVER TOLD THE CHILDREN, OR MY HUSBAND, OR YOU...
I WANTED US TO SHARE THEM TOGETHER, JUST THE TWO OF US...!
"DON'T LEAVE ME ALONE! DON'T DISTANCE YOURSELF FROM ME!"
BUT STELLA, WHO CAN SAY AS MUCH...
I LOVE YOU...
...MOTHER!
...IS TELLING ME SHE CAN ACCEPT A MONSTER LIKE ME AND LIVE ALONGSIDE ME.

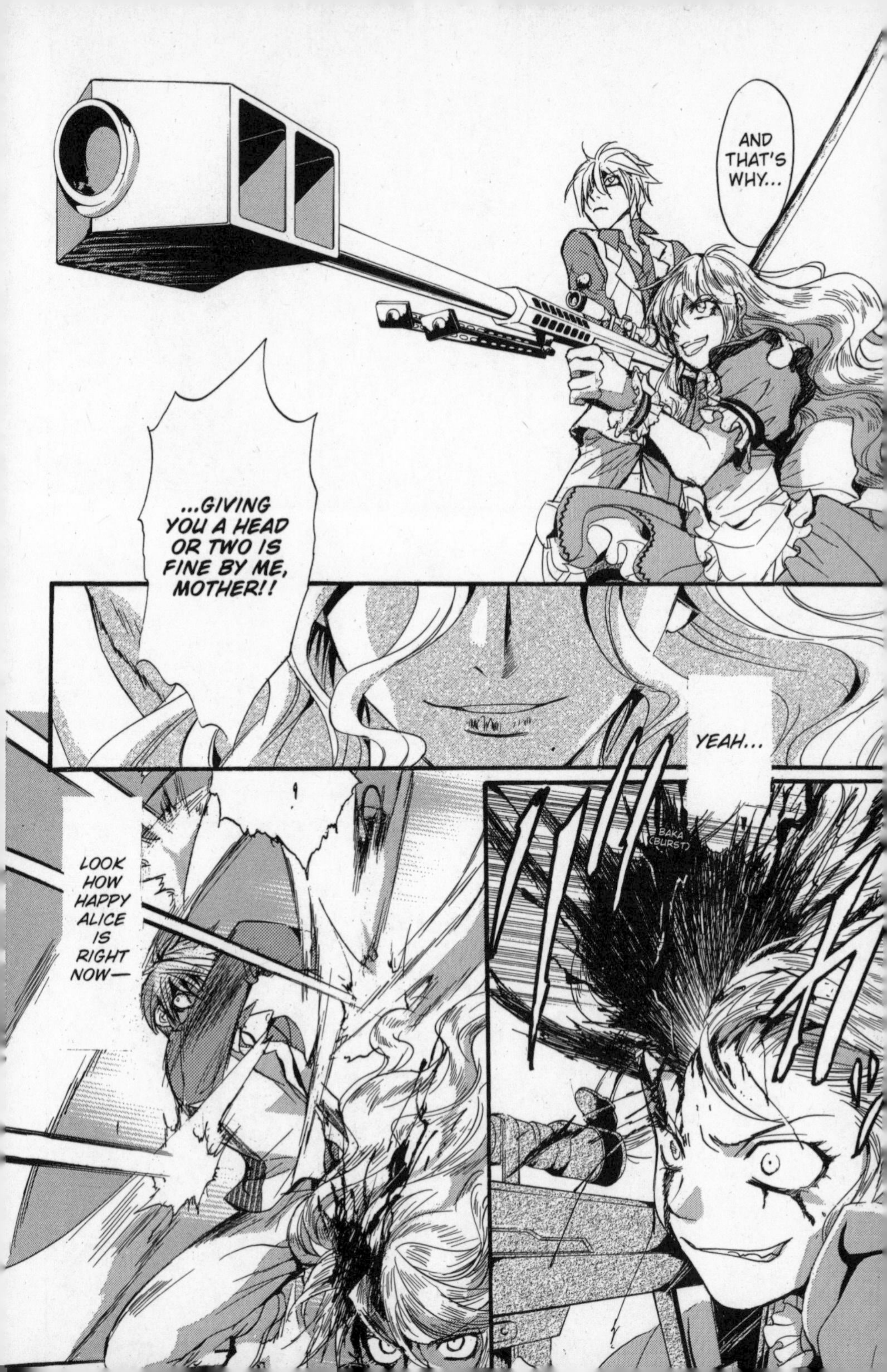
AND THAT'S WHY...
...GIVING YOU A HEAD OR TWO IS FINE BY ME, MOTHER!!
YEAH...
BAKA (BURST)
LOOK HOW HAPPY ALICE IS RIGHT NOW—

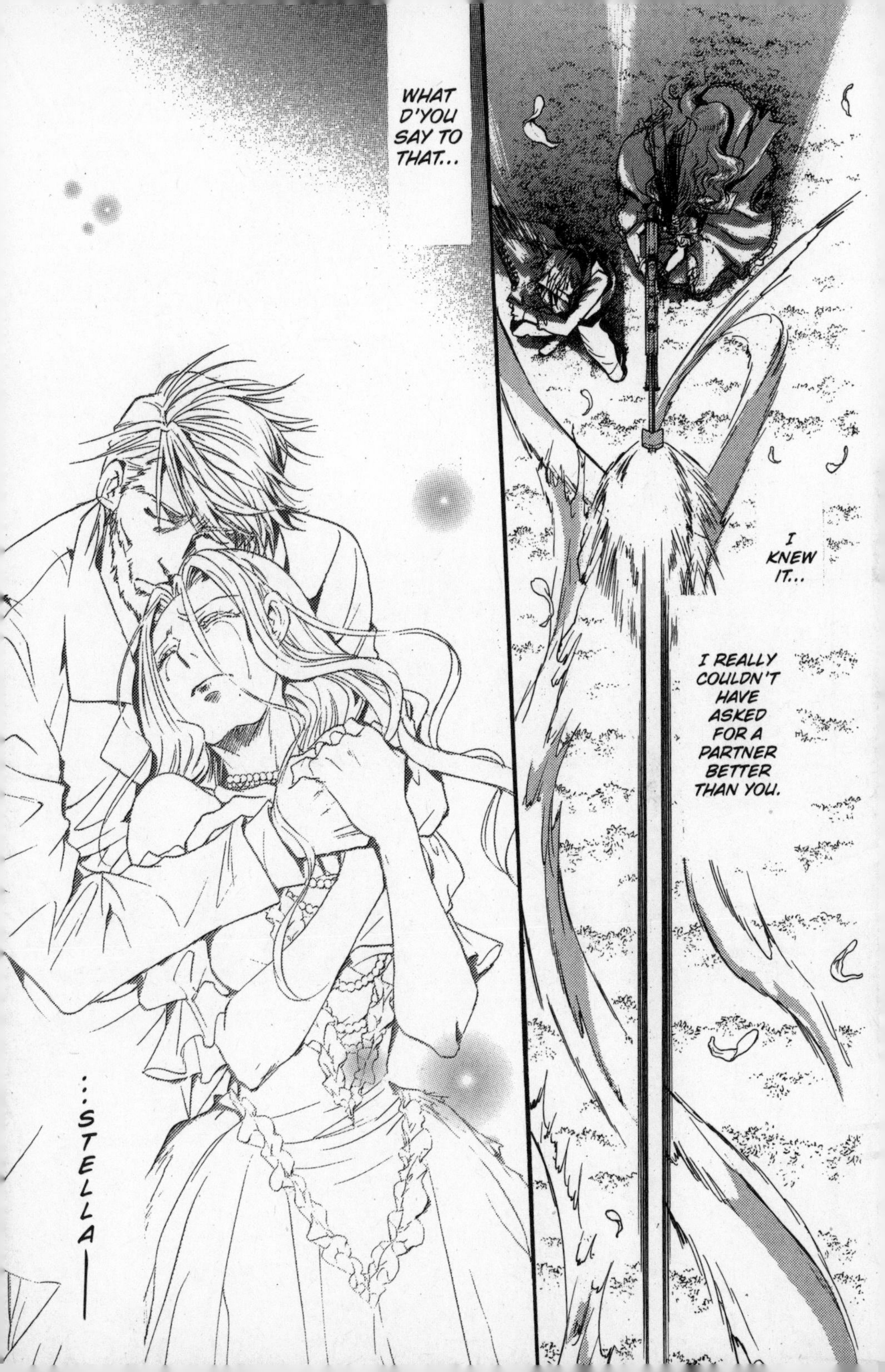
I KNEW IT...
I REALLY COULDN'T HAVE ASKED FOR A PARTNER BETTER THAN YOU.
WHAT D'YOU SAY TO THAT...
...STELLA—

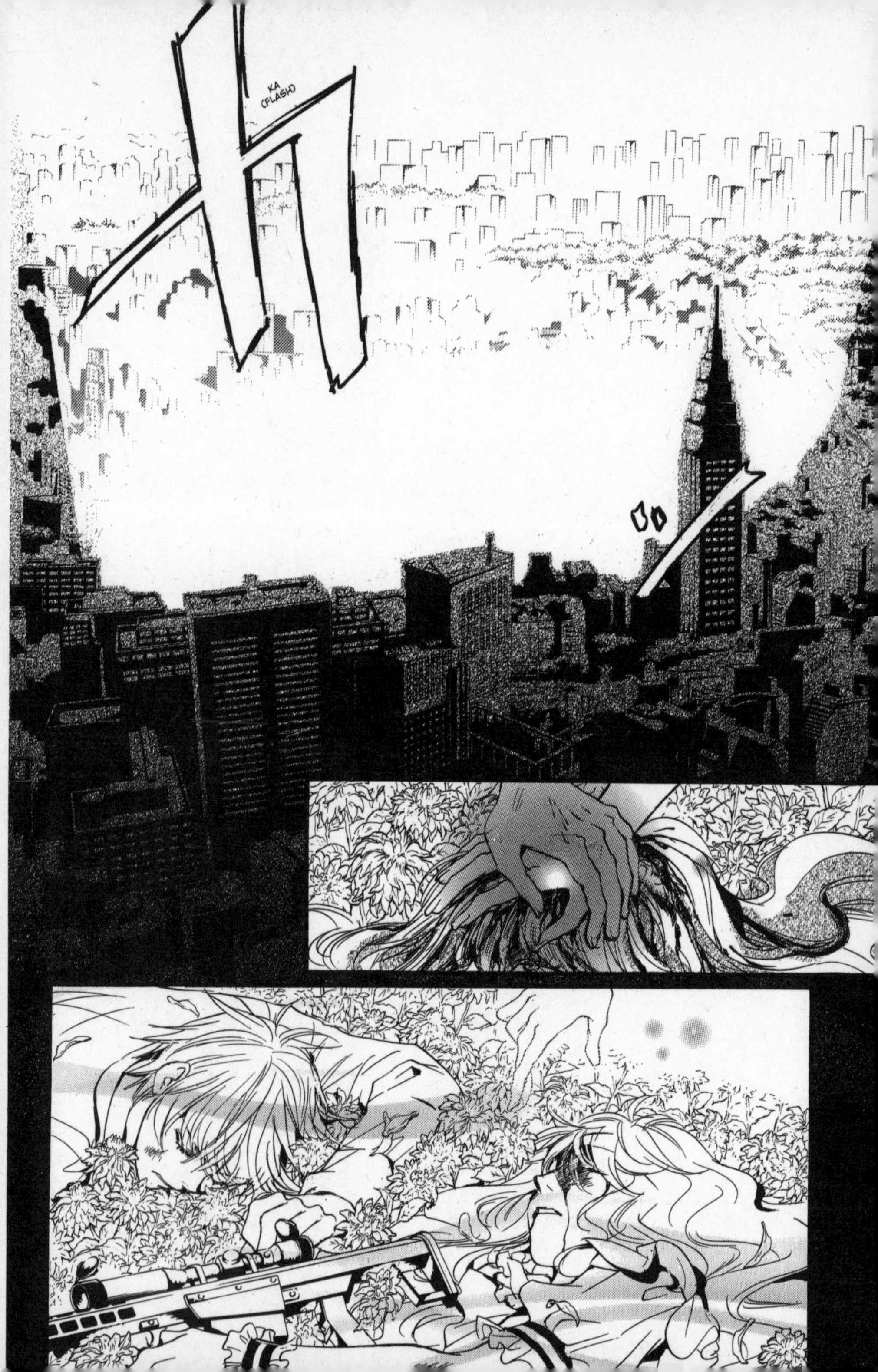
KA
(FLASH)

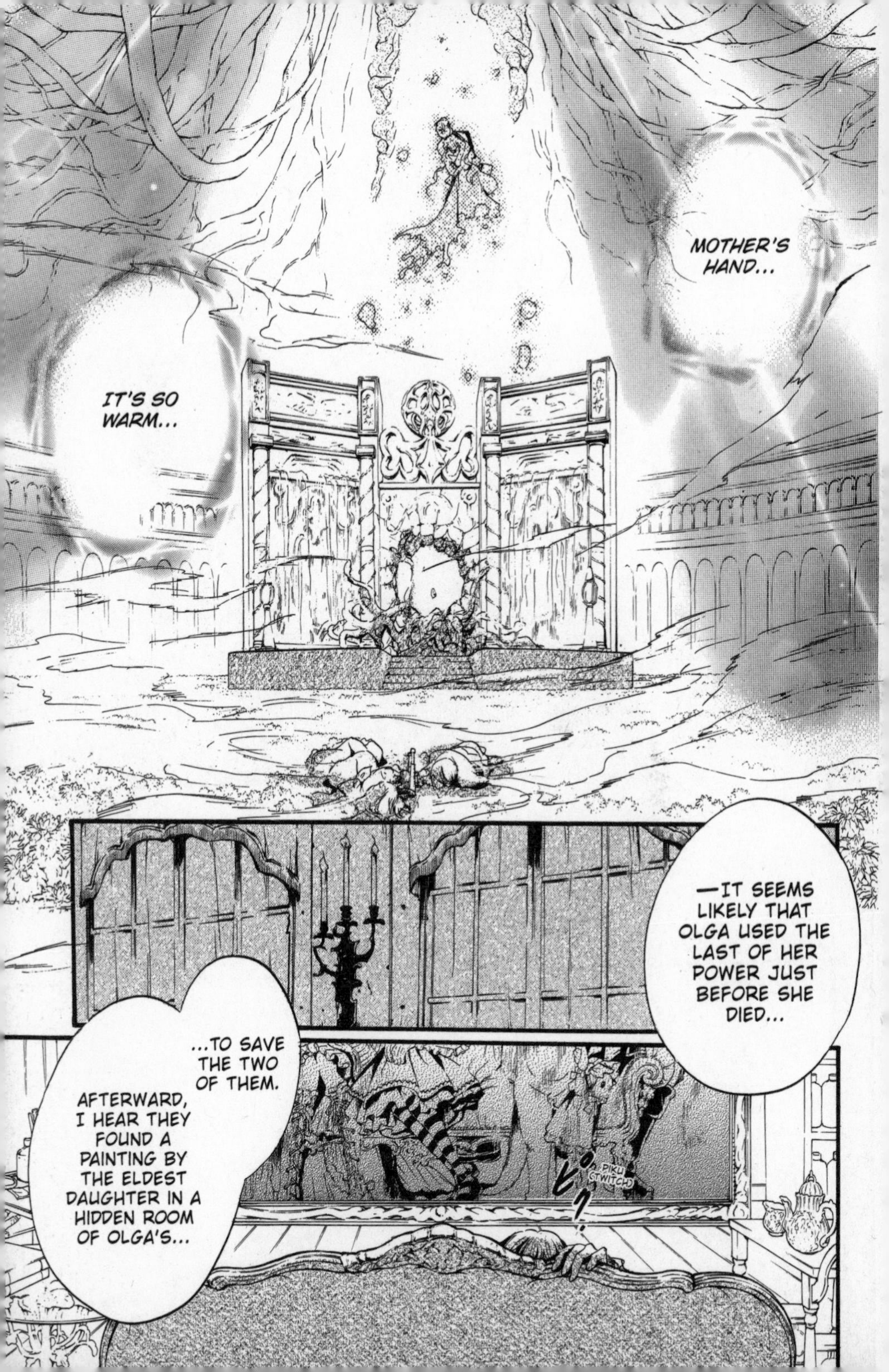
MOTHER'S HAND...
IT'S SO WARM...
—IT SEEMS LIKELY THAT OLGA USED THE LAST OF HER POWER JUST BEFORE SHE DIED...
...TO SAVE THE TWO OF THEM.
AFTERWARD, I HEAR THEY FOUND A PAINTING BY THE ELDEST DAUGHTER IN A HIDDEN ROOM OF OLGA'S...
PIKU (TWITCH)

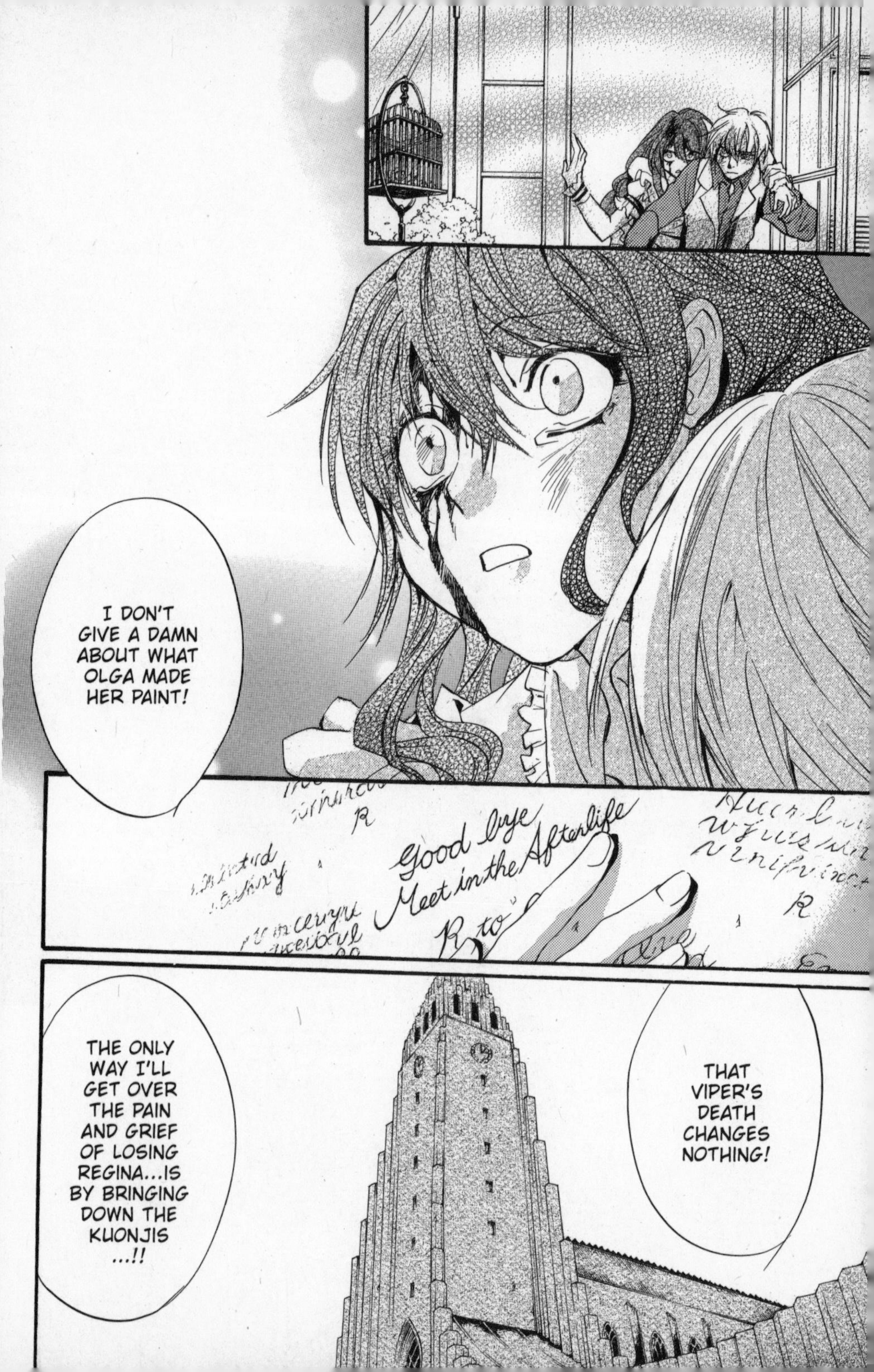
I DON'T GIVE A DAMN ABOUT WHAT OLGA MADE HER PAINT!
Good bye
Meet in the Afterlife
R to
THAT VIPER'S DEATH CHANGES NOTHING!
THE ONLY WAY I'LL GET OVER THE PAIN AND GRIEF OF LOSING REGINA...IS BY BRINGING DOWN THE KUONJIS ...!!

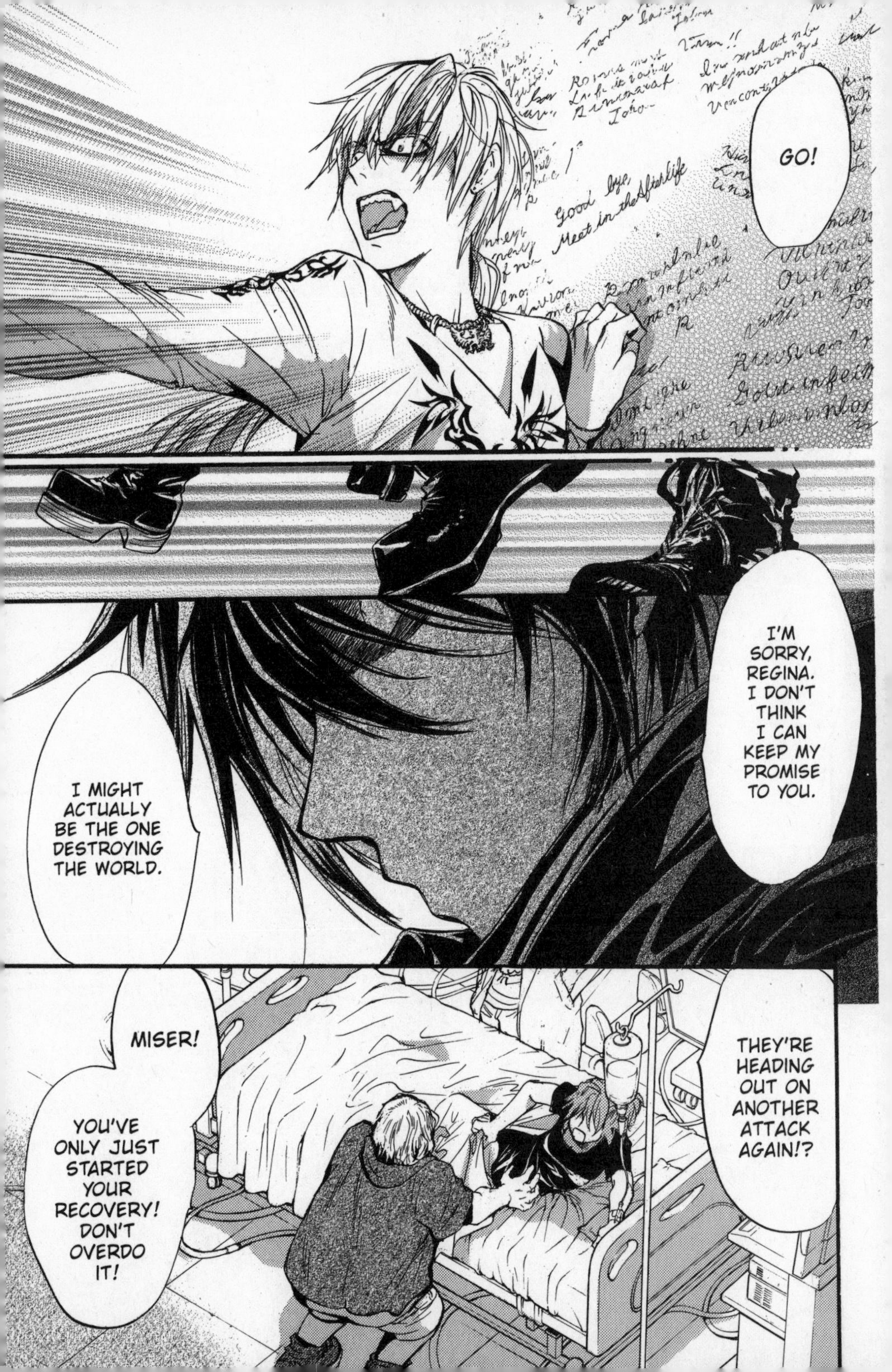
GO!
Good bye,
Meet in the Afterlife
I'M SORRY, REGINA. I DON'T THINK I CAN KEEP MY PROMISE TO YOU.
I MIGHT ACTUALLY BE THE ONE DESTROYING THE WORLD.
THEY'RE HEADING OUT ON ANOTHER ATTACK AGAIN!?
MISER!
YOU'VE ONLY JUST STARTED YOUR RECOVERY! DON'T OVERDO IT!

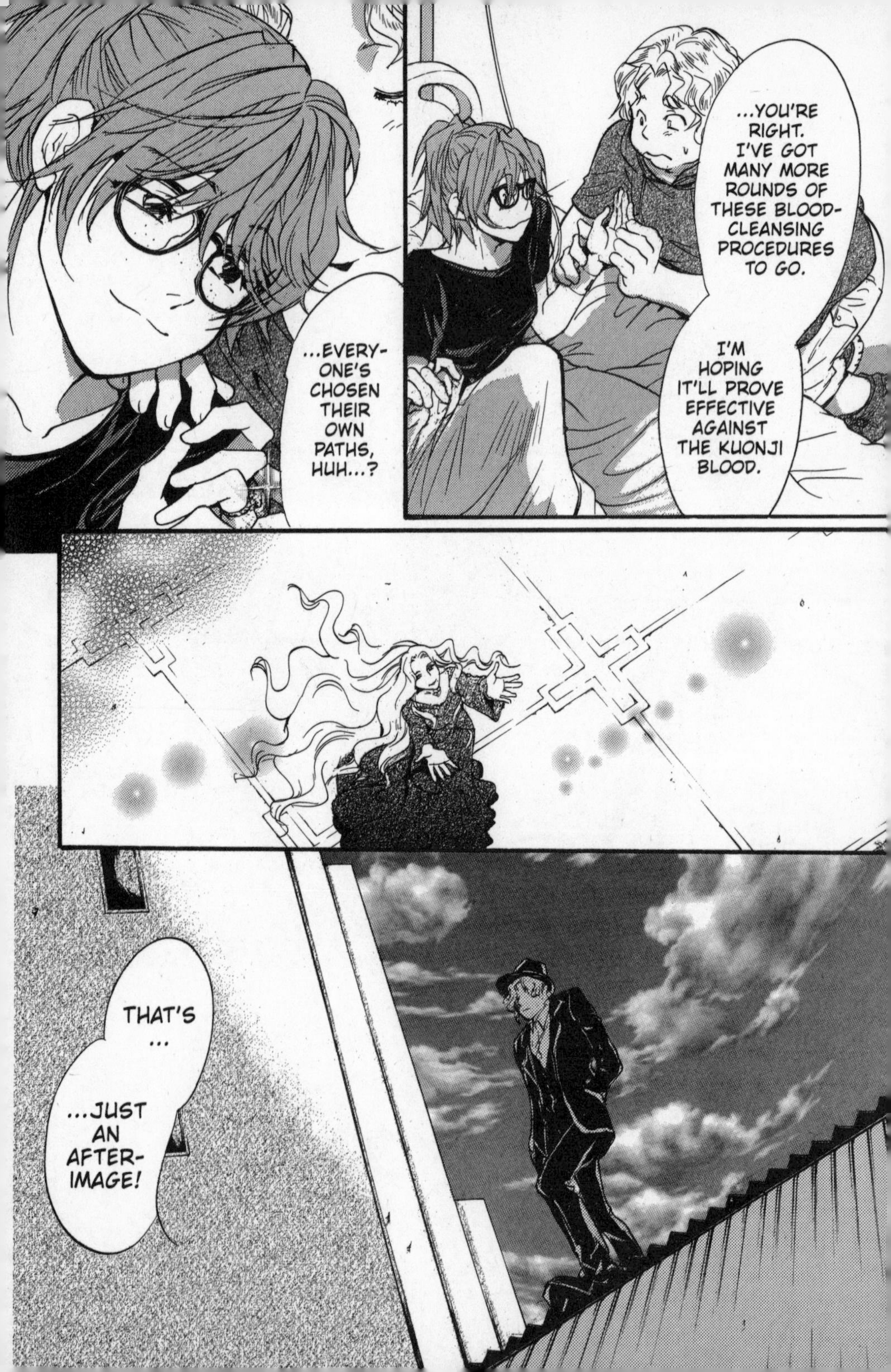
...YOU'RE RIGHT. I'VE GOT MANY MORE ROUNDS OF THESE BLOOD-CLEANSING PROCEDURES TO GO.
I'M HOPING IT'LL PROVE EFFECTIVE AGAINST THE KUONJI BLOOD.
...EVERYONE'S CHOSEN THEIR OWN PATHS, HUH...?
THAT'S...
...JUST AN AFTER-IMAGE!

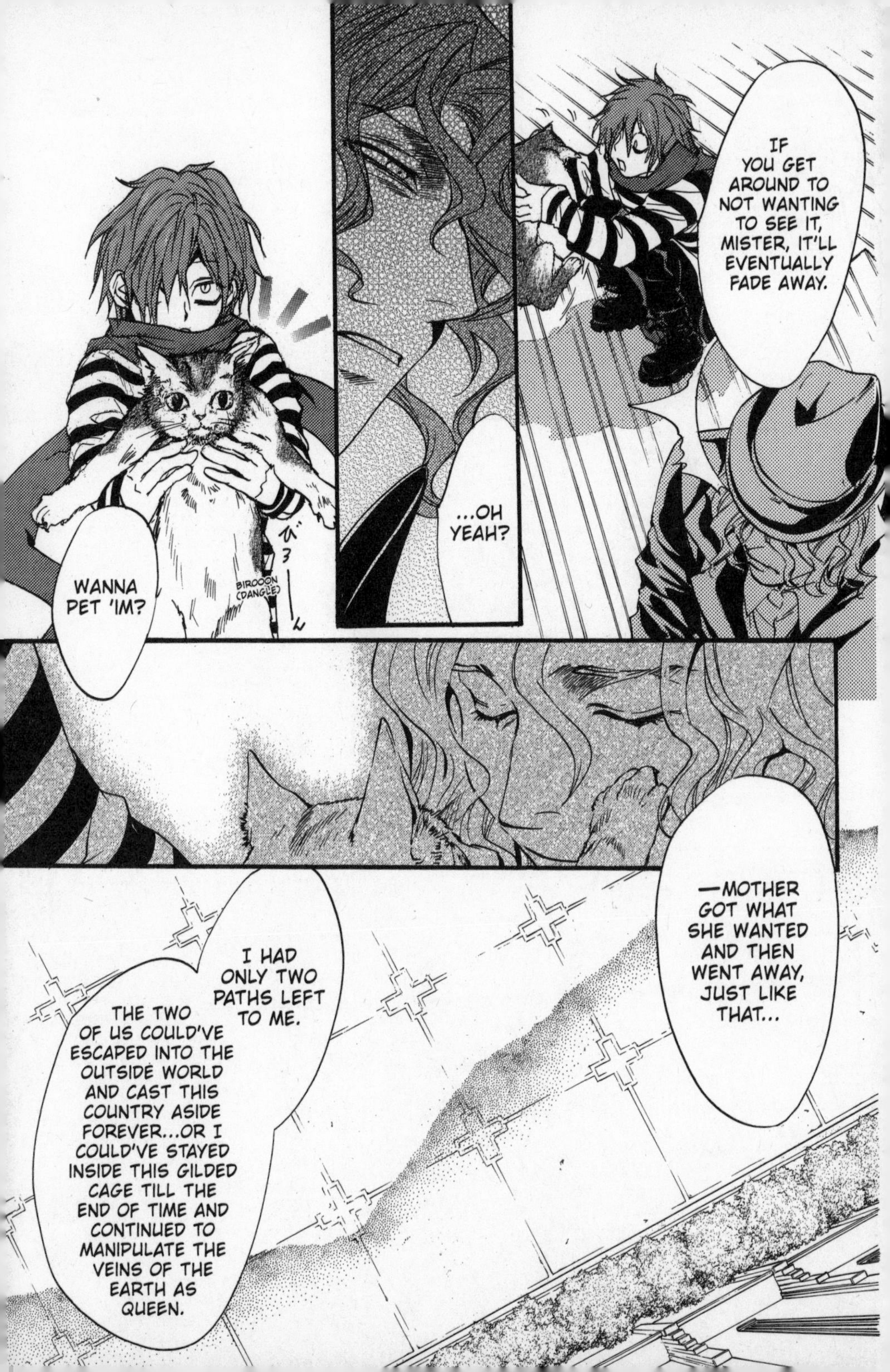
IF YOU GET AROUND TO NOT WANTING TO SEE IT, MISTER, IT'LL EVENTUALLY FADE AWAY.
...OH YEAH?
BIROOON (DANGLE)
WANNA PET 'IM?
—MOTHER GOT WHAT SHE WANTED AND THEN WENT AWAY, JUST LIKE THAT...
I HAD ONLY TWO PATHS LEFT TO ME.
THE TWO OF US COULD'VE ESCAPED INTO THE OUTSIDE WORLD AND CAST THIS COUNTRY ASIDE FOREVER...OR I COULD'VE STAYED INSIDE THIS GILDED CAGE TILL THE END OF TIME AND CONTINUED TO MANIPULATE THE VEINS OF THE EARTH AS QUEEN.

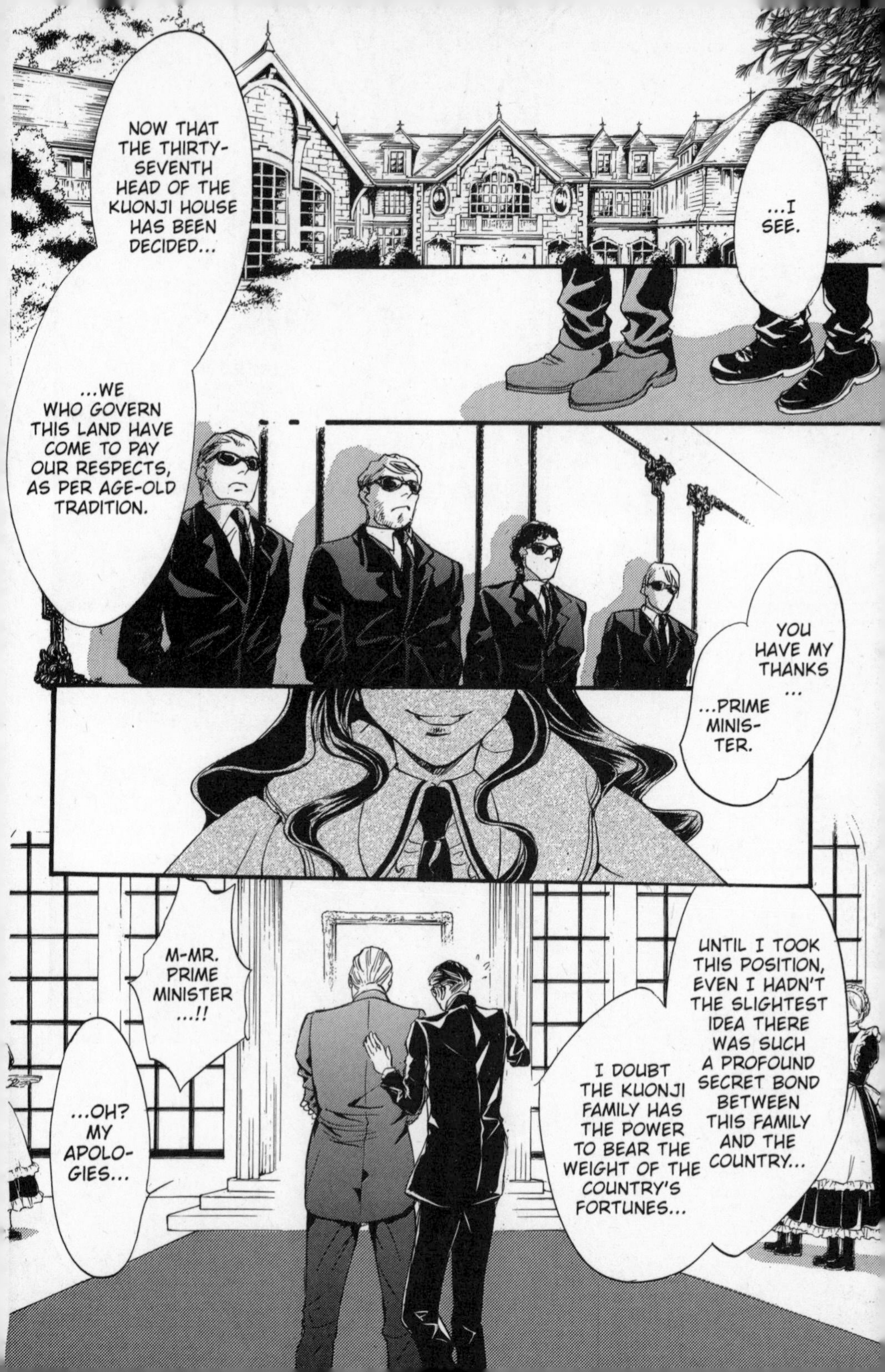
NOW THAT THE THIRTY-SEVENTH HEAD OF THE KUONJI HOUSE HAS BEEN DECIDED...
...WE WHO GOVERN THIS LAND HAVE COME TO PAY OUR RESPECTS, AS PER AGE-OLD TRADITION.
...I SEE.
YOU HAVE MY THANKS...
...PRIME MINISTER.
UNTIL I TOOK THIS POSITION, EVEN I HADN'T THE SLIGHTEST IDEA THERE WAS SUCH A PROFOUND SECRET BOND BETWEEN THIS FAMILY AND THE COUNTRY...
I DOUBT THE KUONJI FAMILY HAS THE POWER TO BEAR THE WEIGHT OF THE COUNTRY'S FORTUNES...
M-MR. PRIME MINISTER...!!
...OH? MY APOLOGIES...

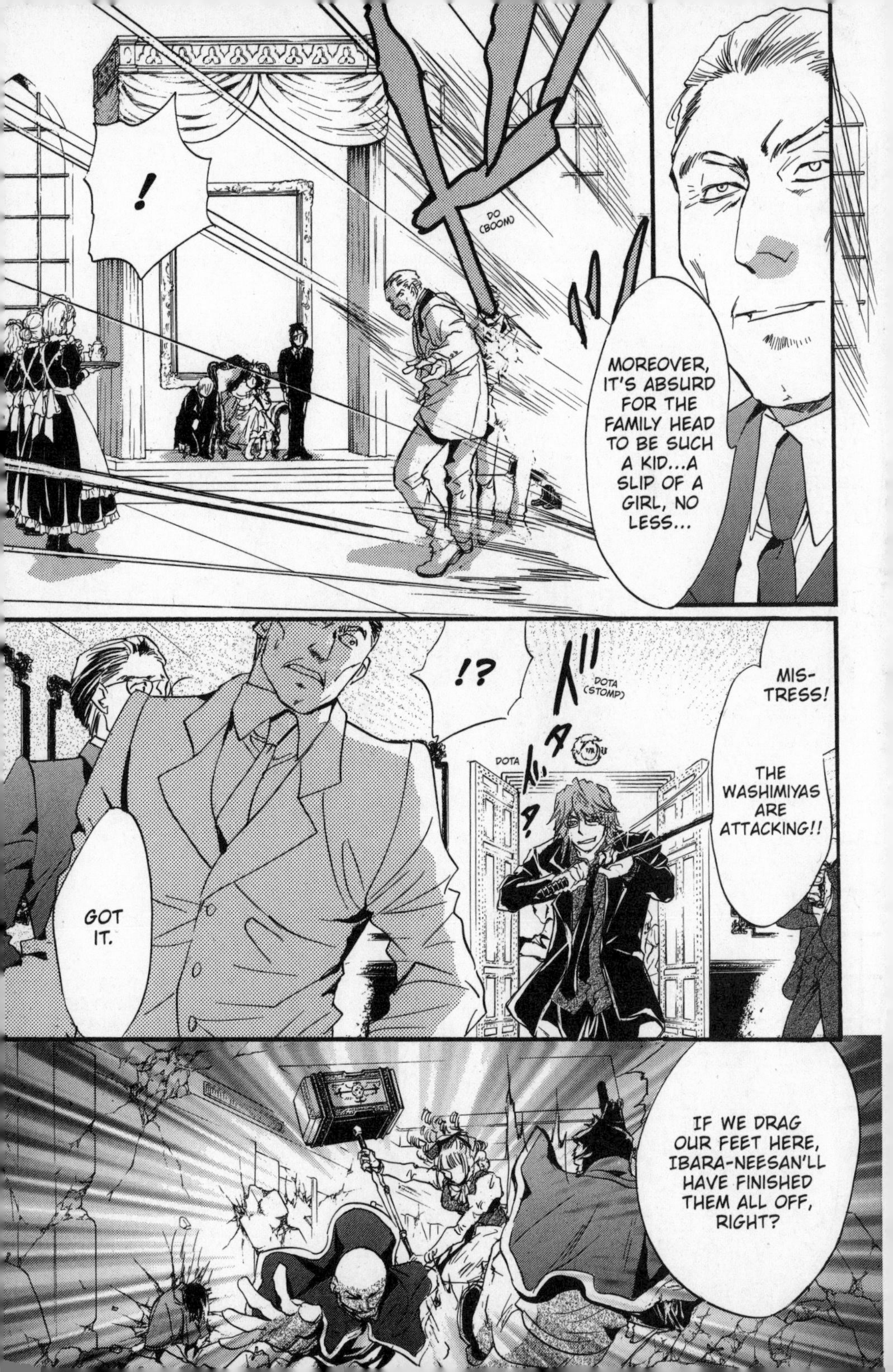
MOREOVER, IT'S ABSURD FOR THE FAMILY HEAD TO BE SUCH A KID...A SLIP OF A GIRL, NO LESS...
DO (BOOM)
!
MIS-TRESS!
THE WASHIMIYAS ARE ATTACKING!!
DOTA (STOMP)
DOTA
!?
GOT IT.
IF WE DRAG OUR FEET HERE, IBARA-NEESAN'LL HAVE FINISHED THEM ALL OFF, RIGHT?

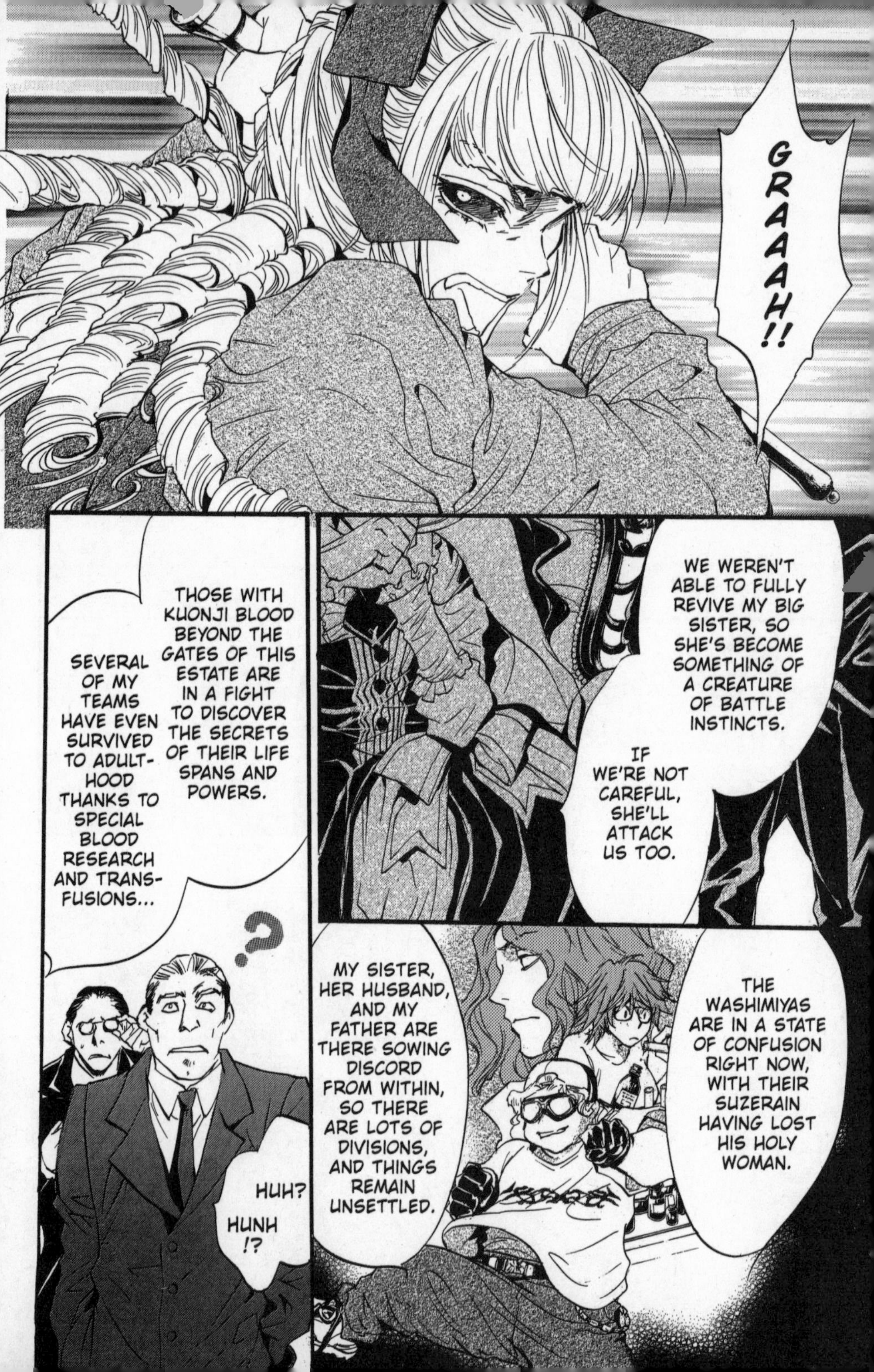
GRAAAH!!
WE WEREN'T ABLE TO FULLY REVIVE MY BIG SISTER, SO SHE'S BECOME SOMETHING OF A CREATURE OF BATTLE INSTINCTS.
IF WE'RE NOT CAREFUL, SHE'LL ATTACK US TOO.
THOSE WITH KUONJI BLOOD BEYOND THE GATES OF THIS ESTATE ARE IN A FIGHT TO DISCOVER THE SECRETS OF THEIR LIFE SPANS AND POWERS.
SEVERAL OF MY TEAMS HAVE EVEN SURVIVED TO ADULT-HOOD THANKS TO SPECIAL BLOOD RESEARCH AND TRANS-FUSIONS...
THE WASHIMIYAS ARE IN A STATE OF CONFUSION RIGHT NOW, WITH THEIR SUZERAIN HAVING LOST HIS HOLY WOMAN.
MY SISTER, HER HUSBAND, AND MY FATHER ARE THERE SOWING DISCORD FROM WITHIN, SO THERE ARE LOTS OF DIVISIONS, AND THINGS REMAIN UNSETTLED.
?
HUH?
HUNH !?

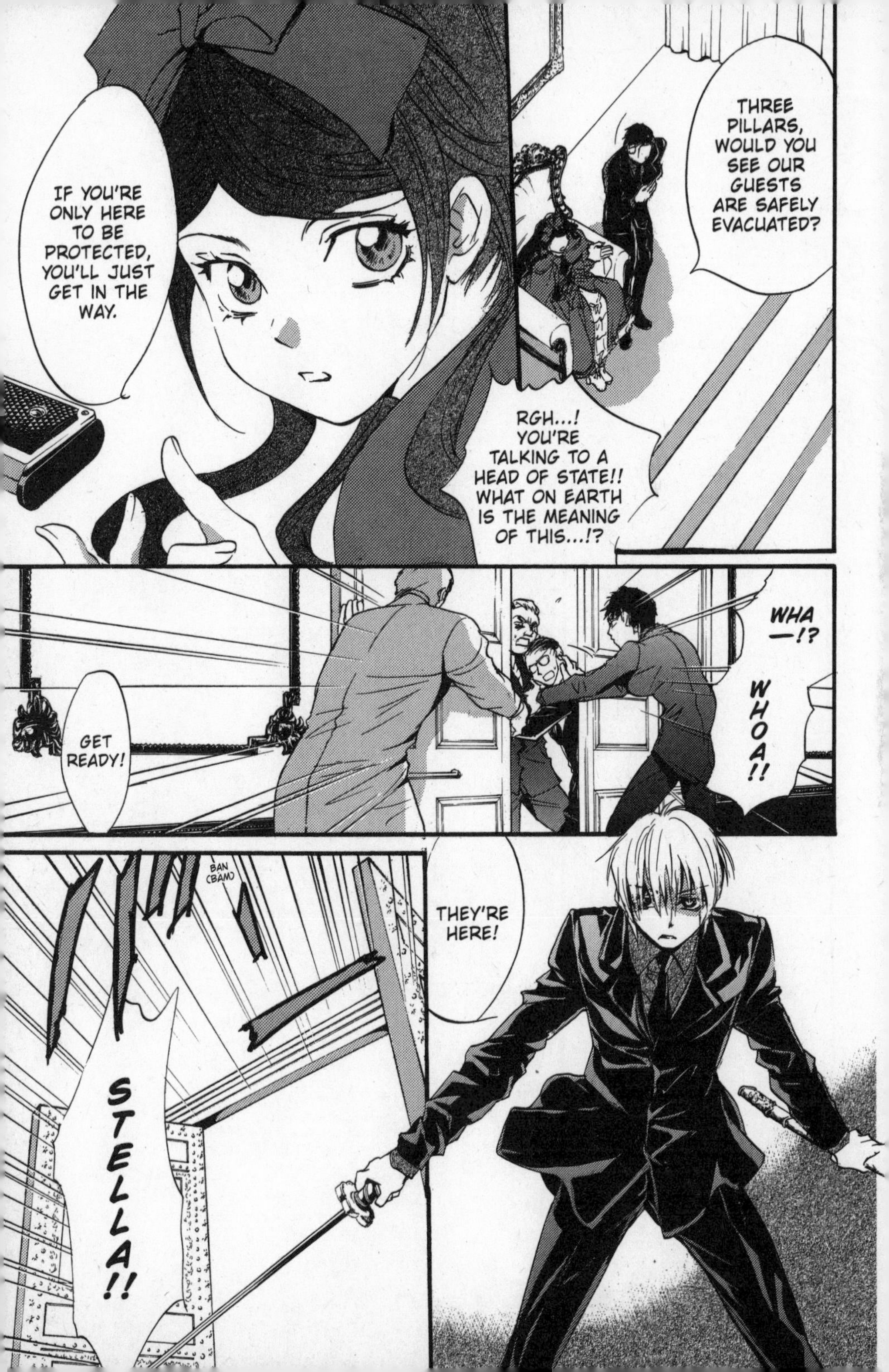
THREE PILLARS, WOULD YOU SEE OUR GUESTS ARE SAFELY EVACUATED?
RGH...! YOU'RE TALKING TO A HEAD OF STATE!! WHAT ON EARTH IS THE MEANING OF THIS...!?
IF YOU'RE ONLY HERE TO BE PROTECTED, YOU'LL JUST GET IN THE WAY.
WHA—!?
WHOA!!
GET READY!
THEY'RE HERE!
BAN (BAM)
STELLA!!

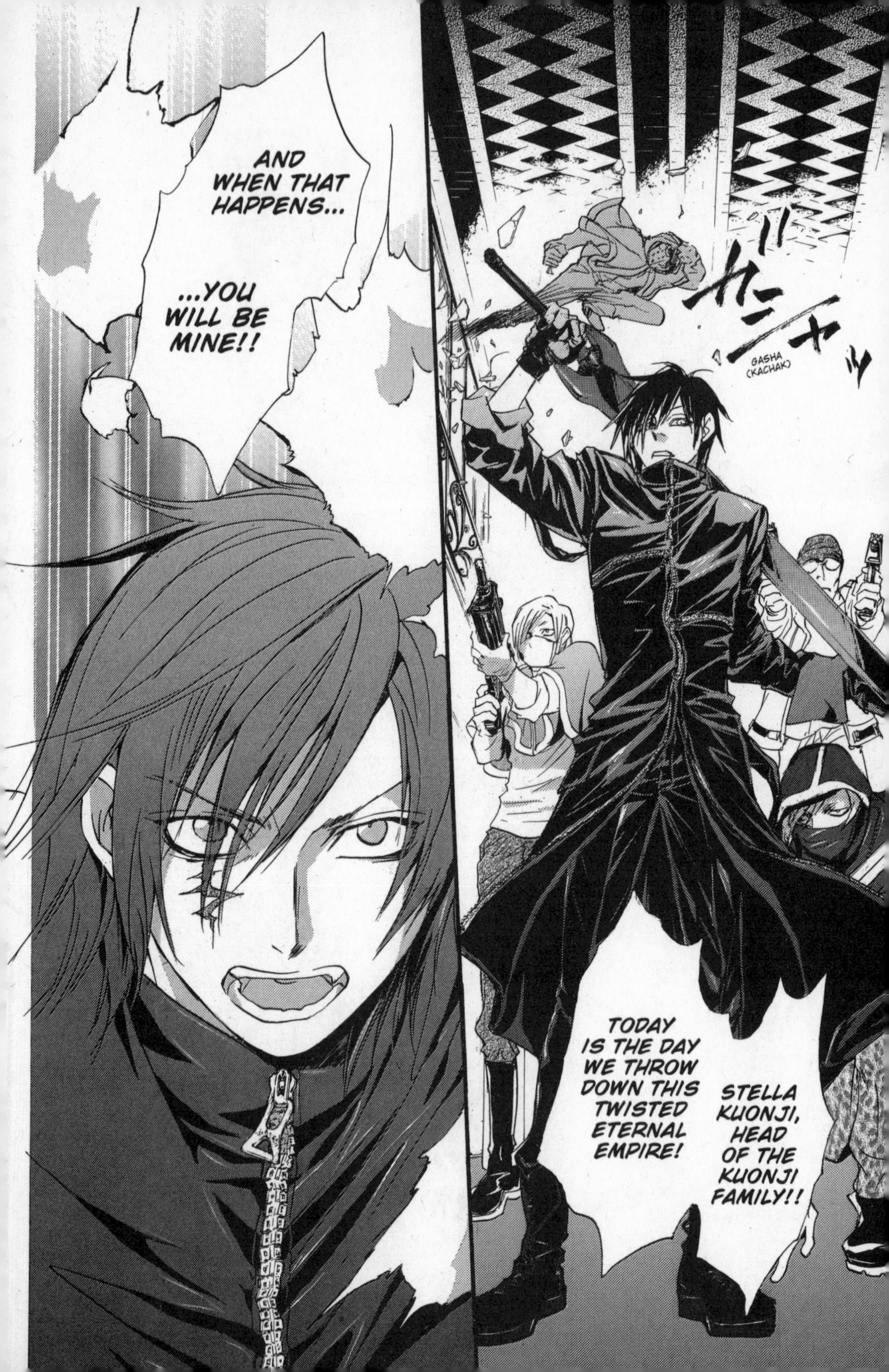
ガシャッ
GASHA (KACHAK)
STELLA KUONJI, HEAD OF THE KUONJI FAMILY!!
TODAY IS THE DAY WE THROW DOWN THIS TWISTED ETERNAL EMPIRE!
AND WHEN THAT HAPPENS...
...YOU WILL BE MINE!!

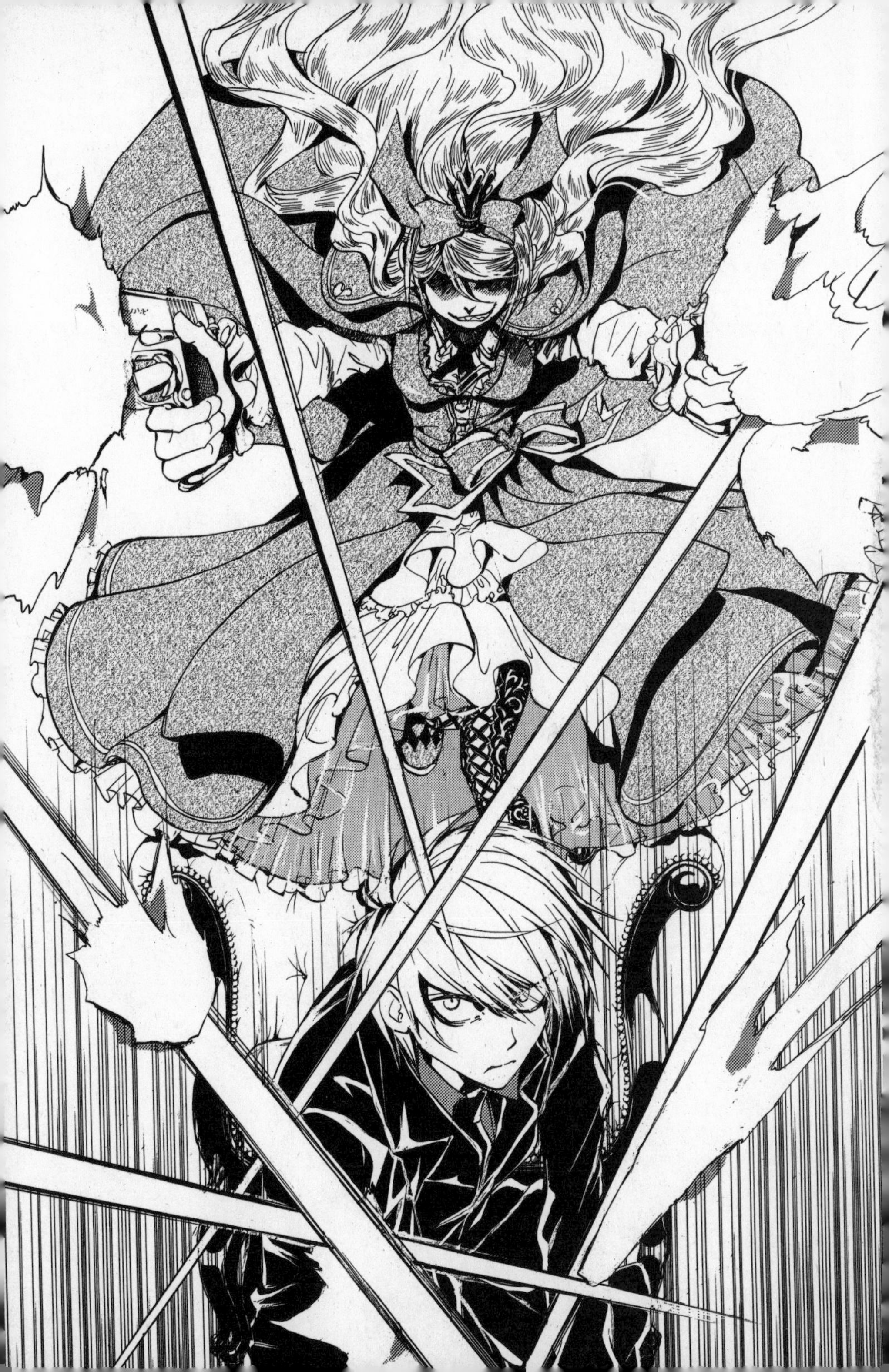

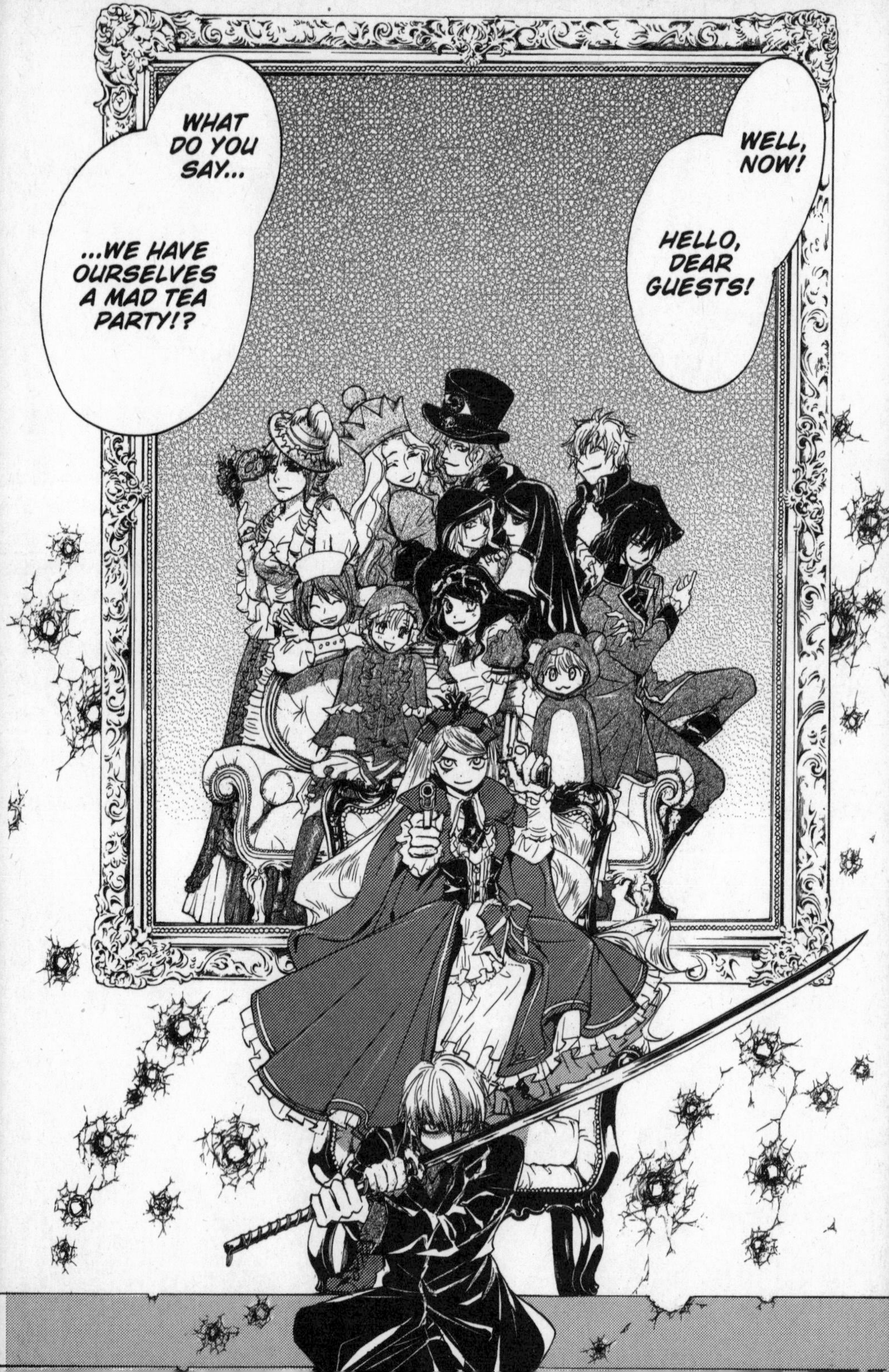
WELL, NOW!
HELLO, DEAR GUESTS!
WHAT DO YOU SAY...
...WE HAVE OURSELVES A MAD TEA PARTY!?

Fin.

Alice in Murderland

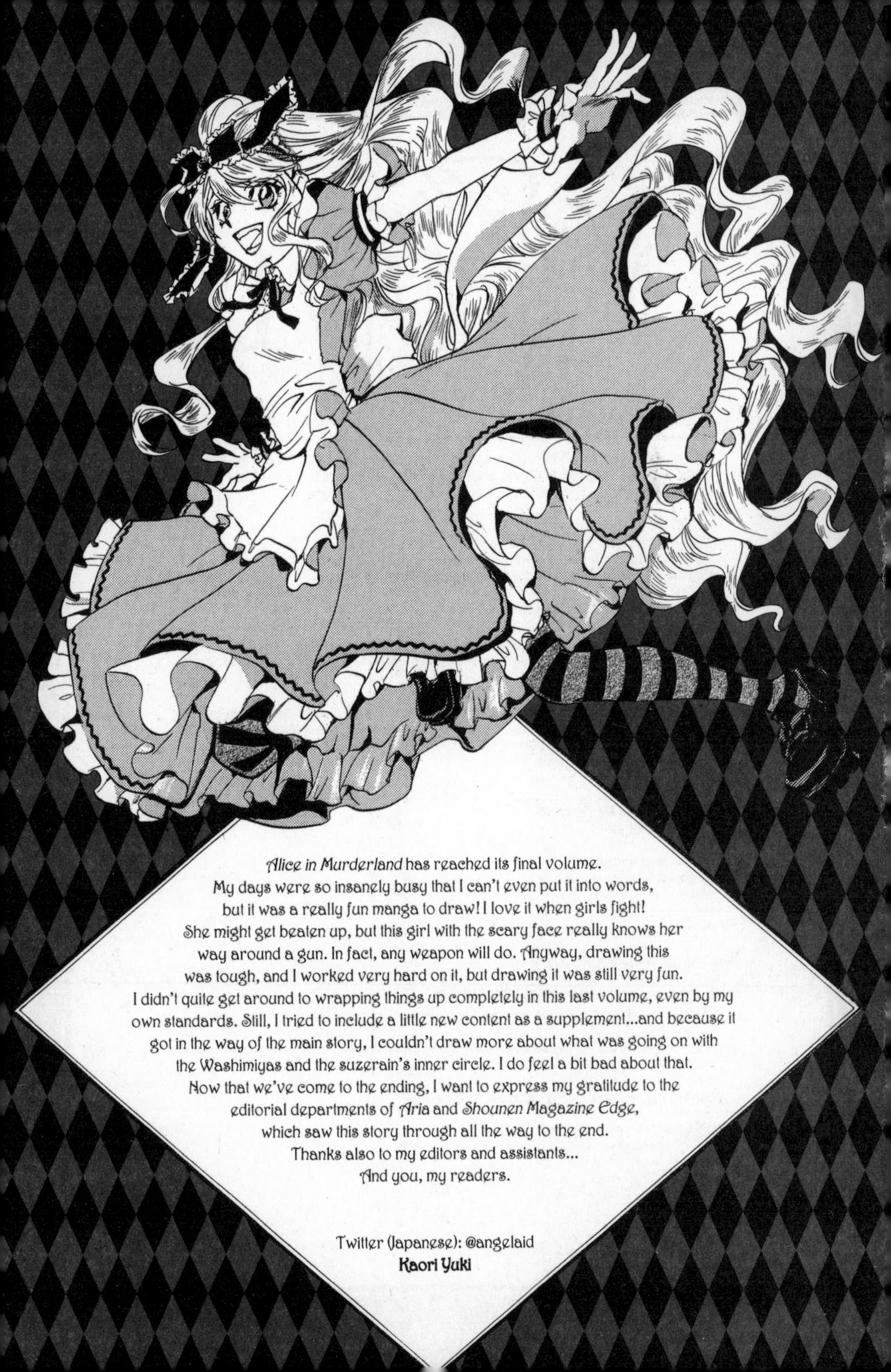

Alice in Murderland has reached its final volume.
My days were so insanely busy that I can't even put it into words,
but it was a really fun manga to draw! I love it when girls fight!
She might get beaten up, but this girl with the scary face really knows her
way around a gun. In fact, any weapon will do. Anyway, drawing this
was tough, and I worked very hard on it, but drawing it was still very fun.
I didn't quite get around to wrapping things up completely in this last volume, even by my
own standards. Still, I tried to include a little new content as a supplement...and because it
got in the way of the main story, I couldn't draw more about what was going on with
the Washimiyas and the suzerain's inner circle. I do feel a bit bad about that.
Now that we've come to the ending, I want to express my gratitude to the
editorial departments of *Aria* and *Shounen Magazine Edge*,
which saw this story through all the way to the end.
Thanks also to my editors and assistants...
And you, my readers.

Twitter (Japanese): @angelaid
Kaori Yuki